THE
HUNGRY
CYCLIST

THE HUNGRY CYCLIST

PEDALLING THE AMERICAS IN SEARCH OF THE PERFECT MEAL

TOM KEVILL-DAVIES

Collins

Collins
An imprint of
HarperCollins Publishers
77-85 Fulham Palace Road
London
W6 8JB

www.collins.co.uk

First published in 2009 by Collins

10 9 8 7 6 5 4 3 2 1

Text © Tom Kevill-Davies

A catalogue record for this book is available from the British Library

Isbn-13 978-0-00-727884-8

Design and typeset by seagulls.net
Printed and bound in Great Britain by Clays Ltd, St Ives plc

Mixed Sources
Product group from well-managed
forests and other controlled sources
www.fsc.org Cert no. SW-COC-1806
© 1996 Forest Stewardship Council
FSC

FSC is a non-profit international organisation established to promote the
responsible management of the world's forests. Products carrying the FSC
label are independently certified to assure consumers that they come
from forests that are managed to meet the social, economic and
ecological needs of present and future generations.

Find out more about HarperCollins and the environment at
www.harpercollins.co.uk/green

Tom Kevill-Davies grew up in East Anglia and having studied sculpture and product design, had a variety of different jobs, including working at Christie's, before becoming a creative in a small advertising agency. It was then that he decided to embark upon his gastronomic adventure, cycling from New York City to Rio de Janeiro in search of the perfect meal. Since embarking on the trip, Tom has made regular appearances on BBC Radio 4's *Excess Baggage* as well as being a feature writer for *The Rough Guide*. Tom currently lives in South London with his five bicycles.

CONTENTS

For my parents with love and thanks.

'Mamas, don't let your babies grow up to be cowboys...'

PROLOGUE

It seems only right that the seed of what was to become the Hungry Cyclist would be planted at the end of a fateful cycling holiday in France, a country the natives would argue, justifiably, is the centre of the gastronomic universe, and also the birthplace of the bicycle. But at the start of that journey, waiting in the darkness while the impatient growls of a hundred cars and trucks echoed off the metal walls of a cross-Channel ferry, I had no idea what lay ahead.

The air filled with the choking smell of diesel and combustion, and men in orange jumpsuits hurried to disconnect heavy chains. The jaws of the boat fell open, daylight cut through the darkness as if the stone had been rolled back on an ancient tomb, and our cycling holiday had begun. Squeezed into our finest Lycra, like a pair of badly stuffed sausages, we rolled our bicycles out of the fume-filled hulk of the ferry and into the fresh air of France's hottest summer on record. We squinted into the bright sunshine.

It was summer and an old friend, Charlie Pyper, and I would use eighteen of our cherished twenty-five days of annual leave to cycle down through France. For ten days we would pedal our way through the back roads of the French countryside, and when the job was done enjoy a week of relaxing and pleasurable wound-licking. It would be a holiday of a little exercise, country roads, superb restaurants, good wine and lashings of cheese. That was the plan.

As a fierce heat-wave gripped the continent, old ladies perished without air-conditioning in Paris apartments and nursing homes, forest fires swept through the hills of Provence and the world's media screamed headlines about global warming and climate change. Meanwhile, Charlie and I took to the hills and lanes that connected the small villages of Normandy. It quickly became clear that I was having a great time, but on each gentle incline I looked back at a wheezing, red-faced mess of a man, cursing, sweating and panting. An affable and chunky six-footer, Charlie dwarfed his slim racer like a cycling bear in a circus, and each slight hill was met with an onslaught of Essex's finest abuse.

'Bloody French hills. The fucking map said this bit was flat. I thought you said this was going to be a holiday.'

Exhausted at the end of a long first day, the small bed and breakfast we collapsed into could not have come soon enough for us both. But for Charlie it had come too late. He endured a sleepless night of cramps induced by dehydration, and nightmares about bicycles, derailleurs and hills. I woke from a good night's sleep to find him at breakfast in the garden, his concentration focused on our map.

'We can hire a car twenty kilometres from here,' he said glumly without bringing his eyes up from the map. A buttery piece of croissant hung in my mouth as my jaw momentarily unhinged itself from the top of my face.

'You what?'

Having endured his graphic complaints for most of the previous day, and been woken by his cramped agonies during the night, I knew he wasn't happy. But this was Charlie. The toughest guy I knew; the football legend; the hard-hitting, fast-bowling cricket star; my well-needed back-up in school punch-ups; a hero. And he wanted to quit. I couldn't understand it.

'Come on, mate. It'll get better today, I promise. We can stop for a long lunch. We can find a nice river for a swim.'

My optimistic words and false promises fell on deaf and sunburnt ears.

'Sorry, mate, it's just that I'm not really enjoying any of this. I guess I'm not a cyclist,' he offered remorsefully before painfully pulling himself out of his seat and waddling back to our room with all the appearance of a man who had been violated by a rugby team.

'Well, I'm going on!'

Back in our room, preparing to leave, I found Charlie awkwardly rubbing his undercarriage with a proprietary soothing cream, and we were soon both back in our unflattering Power Ranger costumes. We said our goodbyes, and arranged to meet for lunch. I headed south towards the Loire valley and the cathedral of Chartres. Charlie pedalled west in search of the nearest car rental office.

For the next week I spent each day cycling a hundred or so miles through the French countryside. Charlie spent his days driving the same distance, meeting me in the evenings and at pre-organised lunch stops.

'Right. This little town here has a nice-looking brasserie and a stunning medieval monastery,' Charlie would announce with all the authority of a general directing his troops, circling the relevant area of his map, laid out on the bonnet of his car, with a well-informed finger.

'Medieval monastery! You've never even been to church. Are you feeling all right?'

'It's culture. And if you can make another sixty kilometres after lunch, this little town has a very comfortable-looking hotel with a great set menu and two knives and forks in the Michelin guide.'

'Two knives and forks! I better get a move on.'

'Good. I'll see you for lunch in two hours.'

I had my orders, and I was on my own again and at my happiest. It wasn't that I didn't enjoy the company, but out there on the back roads of France life was so peaceful, so calm and so far away from the fast world of advertising I had briefly left behind in London. Moving silently, apart from the spinning of my wheels and creaking of my saddle, I passed through vineyards and fields, small villages and quiet towns. My nostrils filled with the scent of newly fallen rain or the yeasty aromas from a local boulangerie, and I peered over fences into tidy vegetable patches and spied through windows at old ladies preparing their lunch behind heavy machine-laced curtains. Chartres, Bourges, Sancerre, Le Puy. Following the slow-moving waters of the Loire, I gradually made my way south and it became clear I was falling in love with a country that had previously only existed as a blur through the window of a cramped car on family holidays.

Showing the utmost respect for France's sacred midday hour, when clanking metal shutters are pulled down over shop fronts, roundabouts become congested with hungry and impatient Frenchmen and the whole of France comes to a grinding halt for lunch, I did the same. Pulling into lively restaurants packed with feasting Frenchmen and bustling with the happy sounds of conversation and the clink of cutlery on china, I enjoyed plat du jour after plat du jour and formule after formule. Plates of hefty steak frites; fresh and gooey goat's cheese salads; golden, oozing croque-mesdame; flavoursome slabs of hearty pâté, all washed down with glasses of cool, crisp rosé. Crêpes suzette, doused in Cointreau, and a small cup of espresso would jump-start my afternoon's ride, and after working off my calorie-packed lunch I would cover enough miles to ensure that I arrived famished at my evening's destination, primed to demolish the five-course extravaganza that awaited me.

Peeling off my Lycra, enjoying a necessary shower and putting on some less disturbingly noisome clothes, I would wander with Charlie into town for dinner. Chilled crayfish and cucumber soup; crispy frog's legs; snails drowned in garlic butter; oak-smoked duck breast salad; rabbit in a mustard and white wine sauce; marbled tête de veau; garlic-infused pommes dauphinoise; lavender-scented crème brûlée, and cheese. Endless amounts of smoky, unctuous cheese that smelt of the farmyards of France.

Food had never tasted so good, and as my pedal-powered gastronomic holiday came to an end I realised I had cycled head-first into one of France's greatest secrets. Cycling and food are one of the great French double acts.

Like seared foie gras and a good Sauternes; chateaubriand and Château Lafite; Napoleon and Josephine; Asterix and Obelix, and

Sarko and Carla, food and cycling are the perfect partners. Because on a bicycle food is your fuel, your four-star, your *essence*, and if you don't fill up, you aren't going anywhere.

It is no coincidence that the most prestigious cycling race on earth, the Tour de France, originated in the land of gastronomy. In the early years of this great race, brave competitors' minds, and indeed other parts of their anatomy, were never far from food. Before the days of multi-million-Euro sponsorship and luxury padded Lycra, hard-up riders would protect their assets by placing a tender cut of beef inside their shorts and between their legs. By the end of the day these choice cuts of meat had been tenderised and marinated and would be cooked and enjoyed, providing those hungry cyclists with the ultimate comfort food.

I know there are deluded pedallers out there who, for reasons unknown to me, are happy to survive on factory-made energy bars when out on the road. But unless you are trailing Lance Armstrong over the Alps, it beats me why anyone would want to put them-selves through the jaw-aching misery of eating a synthetically flavoured hunk of Plasticine.

There is so much more to this magical marriage of gears and gastronomy than simply refuelling and it's not just your taste buds that are exposed to flavours. From the seat of a bicycle you pedal with every one of your five senses. You feel the sun that ripens the wheat that will make your bread. You hear the shrill morning call of the cockerel that will end up steeped in red wine as your *coq au vin*. You whiz past hypnotic lines of grape-laden vines that provide a relaxing glass of wine at the end of the day, and you can't escape the pungent whiff of contented cows, shel-tering at midday under a tree, who will give you a stinking Epoisses as runny and pungent as a ripe cowpat. On a bicycle you work for your food, you get fit and you build an appetite, and you are totally exposed to the terrain, climate and culture that results in what you are eating. Shielded behind the window of a car or a high-speed train or with your head squashed inside a motorcycle helmet, you miss out on these vital sensual experiences that quite simply make food taste better.

🚲

A career in advertising, a girlfriend, a car, a stack of bills, a mobile phone, weekend weddings, savings and foolish ideas about getting on the property ladder. There were more than enough reasons not to go, but I couldn't help giving it more thought. After my happy holiday in France I would come home from a hard day's work and stare at the large map of the world Blu-tacked to my bedroom wall. I wanted more. I was a food lover with a newfound passion for cycling, and all I wanted to do now was cycle and eat my way around the world.

Africa looked a bit hot for a bike ride and Russia a bit too cold; Europe was too expensive, Australia was too far away and, never a competent linguist, I was scared by the languages of Asia. I was left contemplating the Americas. Two great continents that would allow me to pedal from the United States and Canada all the way to Brazil and Argentina.

I did a little research into cycle touring, and soon found that the popular choice was the route along the Pacific coast from the wilds of Alaska to Terra del Fuego at the tip of Argentina. But call me a bluff old hedonist, if I was going to cycle the best part of 15,000 miles by myself, the last thing I wanted to do was start and finish my trip in two of the coldest and most desolate places on earth. I'm sure the thought of cycling from the northernmost point to the southernmost point of the Americas leaves many adventurers salivating with excitement, but, for me, being surrounded by rocks, penguins and little else, while surviving on porridge and Kendal mint cake, was not what I had in mind as the climax to my continent-crossing labour of love. I wanted to start in the culinary Mecca of America, in a city that didn't sleep, and I wanted to finish in the sunshine, surrounded by bronzed bottoms and bikinis, sipping caipirinhas on Ipanema beach. It was set. I would ride my bicycle from New York City to Rio de Janeiro in search of the perfect meal. Now all I needed was a bicycle.

🚲

'Good bike for long cycle tour.' Click!

God only knows how people prepared for a trip like this, or in fact did anything, before the advent of the internet. Comfortably ensconced at my computer I was able to live vicariously through the lives of other cycle tourists. I could read their websites, eye up their equipment lists and prepare my own, and it quickly became clear that neither of the two bicycles I owned would be coming with me to America. One was so old and weather-beaten it barely made it to the local pub, and the other, the beloved racer that had carried me through France, was too lightweight and flimsy to cope with heavy panniers and the rough terrain of the Americas.

It wasn't cheap, but eventually I settled on a chunky, British racing-green touring bicycle, with a very smart and traditional leather saddle. I was promised that if I looked after the bike, it would look after me, and for a completely inexperienced wannabe cycle tourist, this was all I wanted: to ride my bicycle and not have to worry about broken spokes, loose bottom brackets, a bent *derailleur* and other such dilemmas. After Christmas I set a departure date, handed in my notice at work, explained to my girlfriend that this was a journey I had to make, and woke every morning to be greeted by the violent pink Post-it note that clung to my bathroom door.

14 MAY - LEAVING

Front and rear panniers, rainproof map holder, cycling shoes, a camping stove, lightweight knives and forks, a torch you can wrap around your head like a Davey lamp, waterproof jacket, windproof trousers, camping soap, inflatable mattress, multi-season sleeping bag, a tent. The list of equipment I apparently needed was endless, but as my departure date shrunk from months to weeks to days away, I gradually accumulated all the gear. Buying a one-way ticket to New York, arranging travel insurance, selling my car, cancelling my mobile phone contract, vaccines, injections, visas and maps, were all on a lengthy 'to do' list, along with getting into some kind of physical shape. Loading my panniers with heavy cookbooks, to mimic my load when away, I set off on half-hearted weekend cycling trips into the English countryside. It got dark early, it was cold, it rained, it snowed and it was miserable, but naively I assumed that in America, the land of the free and the home of the brave, everything would be fine.

> The first step towards getting somewhere is to decide that you are not going to stay where you are.
>
> *John Pierpont Morgan*

CHAPTER 1

all the gear and no idea

LEAVING NEW YORK AND GOING THE WRONG WAY

> I have always struggled to achieve excellence. One thing that cycling has taught me is that if you can achieve something without a struggle, it's not going to be satisfying.
>
> *Greg Lemond*

'Yo, bike boy, why you so hungry?'

The deep and demanding New York accent rose above the aggressive throb of hip-hop beat that shook the otherwise peaceful Nyack Forest, some twenty kilometres north of Manhattan.

Just keep cycling, Tom – try not to attract any attention, I told myself, forgetting that I was sitting atop an overloaded touring bicycle, flying a Union Jack, with an audacious, fluorescent-yellow sign hanging from my rear, announcing that I was:

Eating my way from NYC to Rio.
www.thehungrycyclist.com

'Yeah, you! I don't see no other brothers riding a bike, get over here!' came another growl. Glancing over my shoulder through the leaves and branches, I was able to make out a gang of menacing Hispanics hidden in a clearing between the trees.

'Me? Really? Yes,' I muttered nervously, before dismounting my bicycle and pushing it awkwardly down the forest track towards this daunting group of bare-chested men.

In baggy trousers and with bulging muscles covered in the kind of tattoos that seemed to be inspired by particularly grue-some nightmares, this group of eight hoodlums stood before me, their silver chains, diamond-stud earrings, long knives and skew-ers glistening in the afternoon sunshine. My heart pounded and cold beads of sweat dribbled down my back.

I'm going to get gang-banged, I thought, and I haven't even made it out of New Jersey.

'So you gonna tell me about da Hungry Cyclist?' said the largest and most fearsome of the giants through his thick goatee beard, which more than compensated for the lack of hair on his shaven head.

'Yeah, well ... Um, I'm going to ride my bicycle from New York City to Rio de Janeiro, in search of the perfect meal.'

And it had all seemed like such a good idea back at home. A grand tour, an escape, a well-overdue adventure. But standing here now, on day one of my 'trip of a lifetime', in front of this line-up of professional wrestlers, hit men and gangsters, I began to wonder what the hell I was doing.

'Well, if yo' one of those TV chef people,' the leader scowled, 'you ain't leaving till you tasted my mama's Puerto Rican rice.'

'No, no, no ...' Before I could explain that I was anything but one of those TV chef people, and that in fact I was little more than an overexcited, underprepared, ex-advertising executive who liked food and riding his bike, the leading giant had uncrossed his thigh-sized arms, draped one of them over my shoulders and was leading me towards a little old lady sitting peacefully at a wooden picnic table, chopping away at a small pile of lipstick-red chillies.

The hulk of a man squatted before his mother and after exchanging a few quiet words, in what I assumed was Spanish, planted a tender kiss on her forehead and I was ordered to take a seat. A paper picnic plate was placed in front of me, I was armed with a plastic knife and fork (no good at all if I was going to have to fight my way out of this unnerving situation) and a piece of tinfoil covering a large dish was removed, revealing a mountain of spicy-looking rice that released a cloud of sweet-smelling steam into the afternoon.

'Ahh ... Puerto Rican rice, my favourite.' Whatever that is, I pondered, while one of the men shovelled a large portion on to my plate with the grace of a bulldozer. I loaded my fork and nervously, under the watchful eyes of all present, passed it to my mouth. Everything fell silent. I could no longer hear the menacing thud of hip-hop music or the wind playing in the leaves of the trees over-head. I was only aware of the jury standing before me, waiting for my culinary verdict. These were the kind of dudes who shot you just for looking at them funny. Imagine what they were going to do to an inexperienced Englishman stupid enough to 'diss' their beloved mother's cooking.

Please like this, Tom, and if you don't, make sure you look like you do, I told myself firmly.

But there was no need.

'This is good!' I mumbled through my first mouthful. And it was good, really good. Soft rice full of flavour, cooked in a rich chicken stock, mingled with fresh cilantro, hearty pigeon peas, chunks of salty pork and all impeccably spiced with those finely chopped chillies.

'Damn right it is! And now you gotta try my cousin Emilio's ribs.'

One thing the films do get right. Gangsters sure know how to eat. I soon found myself perched on the side of the small wooden picnic table, sandwiched between two enormous, sweaty men efficiently shovelling food into their mouths. In front of me, plates heaped with Puerto Rican rice; Emilio's perfectly mari-nated, sticky pork ribs; grilled New York strip steaks, rosy pink in the middle and oozing juices; long skewers of tightly packed grilled prawns, doused in fresh lime juice; a stack of fat, spicy sausages, bursting out of their skins; creamy potato salads and crunchy home-made slaw.

Now this is what I left home for.

I speared another sausage with my flimsy plastic fork.

This is culinary adventure.

As it turned out, my new friends were not ruthless gangsters. They were hard-working people with respectable jobs in construction and haulage. They were all family, all from Puerto Rico and had come to America to make enough money to return home and start their own businesses. Every Sunday in the summer they got together here in the woods to eat, talk, laugh, and it was an honour to join them.

I explained that my plans were to cycle to Rio de Janeiro, sampling the most delicious and authentic food I could find along the way. They were insistent that the perfect meal I was looking for would be found only in Puerto Rico, and their kind words and good wishes filled me with a new zest and optimism for the journey ahead. For the rest of the afternoon the sun broke through the trees in smoky shafts of light and the sweet smells of barbecue filled the forest. I was forced to take part in a post-lunch game of baseball, in which I performed uselessly, and as the charcoal embers gave off the last of their heat it was time to say farewell. A family-sized silver-wrapped parcel of leftovers was presented to me for eating later that evening, along with a crackly pillowcase of potato chips and a vast bottle of bright yellow fizzy liquid. Each of the men embraced me with a bone-crushing bear hug before going through a confusing collection of handshakes, knuckle taps and high-fives. Full of food and optimism, I waved goodbye, mounted my bicycle and made my way back on to the forest trail.

'Yo, brother! You ever write a book about this trip of yours, you better put my mom's rice recipe in there,' came a call from behind me.

'No problem,' I hollered back in my best New Jersey accent.

'And one more thing, if you're goin ta' Brazil, you goin' da wrong way. Rio de Janeiro gotta be south a here.'

This was not the last time I would be told I was going the wrong way. Leaving New York, my plan was to cycle north for the Niagara Falls and the Great Lakes before turning west across the country towards the Rocky mountains, on what I decided was the scenic route to Rio, via Toronto and Vancouver.

'I'm cycling to Brazil,' I shouted into the empty forest, buoyed with Puerto Rican rice, cheap American beer and naive self-assurance. Enjoying a long New England afternoon I made good time towards Nyack and the ominously named Bear mountain. The wide, slow-moving water of the Hudson river shimmered benevolently in the late afternoon sunshine. The dark green forested banks were dotted with whitewashed, clinker-built colonial houses, once homes to the wealthy merchants who managed the flow of New World commodities, fur, maple syrup, coal and buffalo, into New York. They stood as a reminder of the river's important role as an artery into the great city I had left behind earlier in the day. In the morning I had battled my way through the busy traffic, kamikaze cab drivers and beeping horns of Manhattan, but out here, cycling along the banks of this historic river, I could have been a thousand miles away from the energy and power of New York City. At last, I was on my way.

🚲

It didn't take long for my confidence to be undermined. The flat roads of the morning ride, which had stretched out before me making comfortable cycling, began to curve round the steep sides of the growing hills that now flanked the valley. The gradients increased and to keep my overloaded, 60-kilo bicycle moving forward became a hard and painful struggle. After leaving the shade of the forest trail, the heat of the afternoon sapped my energy.

I had only planned to spend five nights sleeping on a friend's couch in the Big Apple, but thanks to Natwest Bank's complete lack of customer service, and the epicurean charms of the city that never sleeps, I did not leave for five weeks. Any fitness I had gained labouring around Richmond Park had vanished after a lengthy intake of hamburgers, knishes, bagels and street pizzas, combined with late nights and riotous living. Now I was paying for it, hunched over my handlebars, dripping with sweat, making miserably slow work of the short journey to my first night's goal, Nyack State Park, where I hoped I might be able to pitch camp.

NYACK STATE PARK CLOSED
STRICTLY NO OVERNIGHT CAMPING!

If a squadron of mosquitoes hadn't been feasting on every bit of tasty skin that wasn't wrapped in sweat-drenched clothing, and if the tired muscles in my legs had not been contracting in complaint at their unexpected new existence, I might have obeyed the friendly sign that greeted me at the gates of the state park. Yet as the last minutes of twilight began to give way to gathering darkness and a distant growl of thunder warned me of the weather to come, I decided to risk the wrath of an angry park ranger and wheeled my heavy load up the last hill of the day. Finding a little corner of grass hidden between a large rock and a malodorous public toilet, I set about pitching camp. Pre-trip daydreams had been buoyed with romantic ideas about camping in the moonlight on the banks of foreign rivers, grilling fish over an open fire, but being able to count my previous nights under canvas on one hand, I was about to find out how immature this boy's own fantasy was.

🚲

'Ultra light' it declared on the bright label of my brand-new one-man tent as I pulled it from its tidy little nylon bag and rolled it out on the grass. Could have been a bit fucking lighter if you ask me, I muttered, while trying to decipher the complicated Swedish instruction manual.

'Grattis, du är nu den stolte ägaren av ett nytt tält'

The annoyingly efficient-looking Swede in the pictures instructed me that my first job was to link up the two sausage-strings of shiny, metal poles. Once connected, they had to be slid into their relevant holes before the whole tent could be pegged down. This was not dissimilar to knitting with a pair of eight-foot needles, but I managed, with an adequate amount of swearing and loss of temper, while being perpetually pestered by the biting and high-pitched whine of every blood-sucking insect in New York State, to get the right bits in the right places. And, as if by magic, my new home rose miraculously out of the ground.

It hadn't looked that small when I performed a dry-run erection on the living-room floor of the pokey, one-bedroom flat in London where I had lived for the last five years. But now, dwarfed by the immense trees and the public toilets of Nyack State Park, it looked pathetic. A London estate agent would have described it as 'compact and with a clever use of space', but as I climbed inside there was no escaping the fact that my accommodation for the next two years was inconveniently petite.

To rest my bones at the end of a hard day in the saddle, I had also invested in an expensive, ultra-light, self-inflating camping mattress. It too lived in an efficient nylon bag and, once removed, it unrolled itself like an asthmatic woodlouse, wheezing pathetically as it tried to 'self-inflate'.

That's it?

At that price, I had hoped that a plump and bouncy airbed would expand before my eyes, but instead a small, bright orange piece of foam that looked about as comfortable as a doormat materialised in front of me. 'Tat-tat, tat-tat-tat.' The sound of rain drumming away on the tightly-stretched nylon that now surrounded me didn't help lift my sinking mood. I made a dash through the escalating downpour to rescue my panniers and other bits of equipment, before retreating back into my bunker, soaking wet, to begin making plans for supper. My first-night fantasies of an open fire were literally washed away, and instead I would have to fire-up the most exciting item hidden in my bags. The camp stove.

I have no doubt that if you find yourself stuck on a freezing mountain at high altitude, somewhere in the Himalayas, and you fancy a quick cuppa, a high-octane jet engine is just the job for melting a few litres of snow and getting a good brew on, but if all you want to do is reheat some Puerto Rican rice and a couple of sausages, the violent little object I was now unpacking is completely unsuitable. Faced with a confusing set-up of metal cables and a bright red fuel tank that looked as if they were part of a bomb-making kit worthy of Al Qaeda, I unpacked the new toy that would cook my supper. Carefully following the English instructions, I obediently tweaked the levers and pumped the pumps. My shiny lightweight aluminium pots and pans were loaded with leftovers. I struck a match.

Booom – whoooooooooosh!

A yellow flame filled the entrance of my tent. My eyebrows sent out a smell of singed hair and, reeling back, I looked on in horror at the angry little object now roaring away with a ferocious blue flame in the tent porch. It seemed more suitable for stripping paint than cooking a light supper. Acrid black smoke invaded my living space. I plucked up enough courage to turn the thing off, then scraped away at the inedible burnt offerings welded to the bottom of my pans. I had to admit that the Hungry Cyclist's first night in the great outdoors hadn't quite gone to plan. I turned in, dirty, disheartened, dishevelled and hungry, wondering how and why I had given up a comfortable London life, an agreeable career in advertising and a beautiful girlfriend to be here alone, eating burnt sausages, camped next to a public toilet, in the pouring rain somewhere in New York State.

🚲

The following morning I awoke in the claustrophobic conditions of my nylon coffin, exhausted. I had all the gear but evidently I had no idea what I was doing. I climbed out of my tent, bleary-eyed, stiff and despondent. Strange calls and scratching had distracted me throughout the night and I had enjoyed little sleep. I needed coffee, and after rolling up my wet tent, gathering my belongings and getting back on the bike, I went in search of someone who might sell me one. Ten kilometres outside Nyack I found a busy café attached to a gas station. At just before six in the morning, it was full of dusty truck drivers and delivery men.

'Sit wherever you can find a spot, darling,' called a waitress busy filling coffee cups from a glass percolator jug.

But instead of taking a seat I headed straight for the rest room. I brushed my teeth, washed my face in the basin and took a sad look at the drained face that appeared in the mirror. I felt weak, demoralised and nauseous.

What am I doing?

The state I was in, I would have let somebody steal my bicycle, but I still found a booth next to the window where I could keep half an eye on my worldly possessions propped up in the parking lot. I ordered a tall stack of pancakes, which arrived dripping in maple syrup, and downed cup after cup of bitter coffee while I laid out my damp map on the table and made a plan for the day.

Now where am I? Nyack, Nyack, Nyack – here!

It took a few seconds to find the small red dot that signified where I was, and when I did, it was completely soul-destroying. In a day that had left me feeling physically and mentally drained, I had cycled no further than two-thirds of the width of my little finger. A pathetic thirty-seven miles. Looking north, the Canadian border and the Great Lakes were a stretched hand away. If I carried on at this pace Toronto would take two to three weeks and Rio de Janeiro was clearly impossible.

🚲

The next week was the stuff of nightmares. I was unfit, underprepared and it was very hot. The sun woke me from my tent every morning and soon became a merciless tormentor as I struggled further north into the Catskill mountains of Upstate New York. The rich landscape of pine-carpeted mountains and placid lakes should have been breathtaking but I had no breath to spare. As each day of hard labour came to an end, I was greeted with another uncomfortable broken night's sleep in my reeking tent, before having to start all over again at sunrise.

More than seven years of a nine-to-five existence in London

had left me completely unsuited to the hardships of life on the road. However I cut it, pushing a ridiculously heavy weight up a mountain in 30-plus degrees just wasn't fun. I was meant to be revelling in a newfound freedom. This was about as far from freedom as I could imagine. Dragging an oversized ball and chain disguised as a bicycle and trapped within a strange alter ego that called himself the Hungry Cyclist, I was meant to be cycling the Americas in search of interesting food and digging up local recipes. Instead I was surviving on chocolate bars, fizzy drinks and whatever else I could get my hands on at the sporadic gas stations that lined my route. I barely had the energy or enthusiasm to open a tin of beans. The Hungry Cyclist and his dream were both falling apart.

'Buy me; buy me,' called rusty station wagons parked in driveways.

'Take me, take me, look at my powerful motor,' goaded shiny, chrome-covered motorcycles with their fluorescent 'For Sale' signs.

And how easy it would have been to quit. To cash in my bicycle, dump the panniers and go on a real road trip in the land of the motorcar. The raw chafing between my legs would be a thing of the past. I could kiss goodbye to my aching buttocks and throw away my dirty, sweat-stained clothes. Covering as little as thirty-five miles a day, against the hundred I had projected, no more than a soul-destroying centimetre on my tatty map, I was making slow, painful progress on my way to Ithaca and the Finger Lakes. But as the long days and short nights gradually ticked over, the hills slowly became easier. It was revealing to see how body and mind learnt to deal with life on a bicycle, and I came to terms with the fact that this journey would not happen in the way I had imagined it would. After an initial few weeks of pain and suffering, I arrived in the town of Buffalo, famed for its chicken wings and the Niagara Falls. It was here that I would cross into Canada. I had cycled some five hundred miles after leaving New York. I was feeling fit, I was sleeping, I could operate my camping stove and I was almost having fun.

🚲

I was a cowboy. My sister was an Indian, hiding at the bottom of the garden in her wigwam that smelt of wet socks, doing whatever seven-year-old East Anglian girl Indians did. I would creep stealthily through the unkempt grass, in my finest hat, with a six-shooter at the ready, primed for an ambush.

'Yeeeeeeeeeeee ha!' *Pow! Snap! Pow! Snap!* Bursting into her peaceful camp, guns blazing, I ruthlessly fired off reels of pink caps while she ran for the cover of home, slapping the palm of her hand against her mouth, doing her best to warn me off with an unconvincing war-cry.

But cap guns and cowboy hats were soon replaced by a Walkman and a mountain bike, and the only contact I had with Indians was limited to over-imaginative, lustful thoughts provoked by Disney's buckskin-clad, leggy recreation of Pocahontas. As I matured a little, Daniel Day Lewis running bare-chested through the mountains of Upstate New York in his moccasins and Kevin Costner soulfully pursuing herds of buffalo across the Dakotas provided me with a little insight into the native tribes of the Americas. But shamefully, as I arrived on banks of the Great Lakes, apart from childhood and Hollywood fantasies I knew nothing about the great and tragic history of the land I was now cycling through.

Moving further into Ontario, surrounded by the waters of lakes Huron, Ontario and Michigan, it was clear I was in Indian country. Eagle feathers and dream catchers now hung from the rear-view mirrors of pick-up trucks, whose 'Support our Troops' bumper stickers also declared 'Proud to be Indian'. The patriotic posters that portrayed dust-covered New York firemen emerging from falling rubble under a red, white and blue Stars and Stripes, declaring 'These Colors Don't Run', no longer adorned the graf-fiti-covered doors of gas station toilets. Instead, dreamy, sepia-toned images of old men wrapped in blankets with feathers on their heads, gazing at the horizon, proclaimed you should 'Do what you know to be right'. But instead of taking their advice, buying a car and racing to Vegas, I continued cycling up the Bruce

Peninsula that bisects the shallow waters of Lake Huron and Georgian Bay.

A popular summer destination for those escaping the sweltering city heat of Toronto, the Bruce Peninsula's picturesque towns were well prepared for this seasonal boom. Pretty clinker-built houses, once home to wealthy fur traders, were converted into twee bed and breakfasts. Organic cafés, decorated with wind-chimes and lesbians, sold overpriced cups of coffee, and the famous Great Lakes 'white fish and chips' seemed to be sold in every one of the restaurants. Holidaying Ontarian families, towing caravans in long convoys up the Peninsula main road, licked ice creams and stared into the backs of digital cameras, but on the side of the road, the vendors sitting in part-time stands next to the highway selling wood carvings of eagles, feather-decorated dream catchers, buckskin moccasins and bags of wild rice to the passing trade told of deeper tradition in this bountiful corner of eastern Canada. Arriving in the port town Tobermory, given its name by Scottish fur traders, I caught the last ferry to Manitoulin Island. With my bike tied up below deck of the *Chi-Cheemaun* (big canoe) with the motorhomes and caravans, I sat above in the cool evening air watching the wake of the boat rip open the glassy skin of Lake Huron and began to feel thoroughly ashamed of my historical ignorance. I decided to take the very first opportunity to swot up on the First Nation culture of the Great Lakes. The next morning, after camping on the banks of the lake and full of campfire coffee, I rode to the Manitoulin Island cultural visitor centre for an education.

An impressive building with heavy wooden beams and a trian-gular roof, the centre provided me with vital information about how to stretch a tribal drum and weave a fish trap, and also gave me a potted history of the area I was in. I was in Ojibwa country, the largest and most powerful of the Great Lakes tribes and considered by many to be the most powerful in the North American continent. Occupying the lands around the Great Lakes and stretching as far west as North Dakota, the Ojibwa lived far enough north to have avoided the early flow of migration from Europe, but by the late eighteenth century they found themselves too close to the rapidly expanding trading posts of the Hudson Bay Company, and they were soon engulfed in a fur trade that was turning the Great Lakes into a war zone between the English and the French.

Beaver skins were big money back in Europe, and as demand for this New World commodity grew, the old rivals fought heavily to control the rivers, lakes and ports of the region. As outstanding hunters and trappers, the Ojibwa were unwittingly caught up in the Fur Wars, which continued well into the nineteenth century. Treaties were signed, alliances formed, alliances broken, and tribes were pitted against each other to best feed the appetites of smart Londoners and Parisians, who could not live without their fashionable beaver top hats. The Ojibwa traded with their new European invaders and, although the weapons brought wealth and power, the Ojibwa soon became dependent on French and English goods. The introduction of gunpowder, alcohol and small-pox would change the Great Lakes for ever. Changes in fashion brought a welcome end to the fur trade, but it was only replaced by a new hunger for lumber, copper and white fish, which tempted more Europeans to the area, where they pursued a policy of deforestation and overfishing that emptied the ancient woodlands and lakes of their harvest.

Like after any good museum visit, I found myself in the shop browsing for postcards, novelty pens, key fobs, moccasins and dream catchers, but to my excitement I also discovered a traditional Ojibwa recipe book. Until now the only regional dish I had found that Ontarians were at all proud of was poutine, a clumsy bastardisation of a French dish, consisting of a heap of greasy chips, topped with lumpy gravy and some rubbery cheese curds, normally sold from the hatch of a converted ambulance and served on a flimsy polystyrene platter. It had all the charm and sophistication of a late-night kebab. So to browse recipes of such exotic treats as beaver tail soup, boiled moose nose, white fish livers and manoomin (wild rice) was an exhilarating experience. As I left, the kind woman who sold me the book called after me to tell me that the Sagamok Anishinabek annual traditional pow-wow was being held at the weekend, and if I was lucky I might well be able to taste some of this traditional native fare.

Following the north shore of Lake Huron, I cycled deeper into the barren landscape of Ontario. Small one-café towns, surviving on the logging industry, provided well-needed breaks from the never-ending tarmac of Highway 17, romantically known as the TransCanada Highway. After two days I turned off this noisy road, which flowed with fume-belching logging trucks and made happy time along the pothole-infested back roads that wound their way under towering russet rockfaces and along the banks of placid lakes. Riding in silence, apart from my heart beat and the whoosh of my spinning wheels, I was alone. My imagination, overfed on Spaghetti Westerns, began to work overtime. I peered up at the cliffs flanking the roads and squirmed at the haunted calls and ominous shapes of the patient turkey vultures circling overhead. Rocks tumbling down precipices were no doubt misplaced by the warring redskin scouts who crept up on their bellies, primed to puncture me with arrows, and I could see the angular features of ancient warrior chiefs in every shadow and rock formation that surrounded me.

An hour before sunset I was still thirty miles away from where I hoped I would find my pow-wow and so decided to call it a day and cover the rest of the distance in the morning. A couple of miles along a disused, rust-stained railway track I hit on a good spot to camp, perched above the steep, rocky banks of Silver Lake. Hot and dirty after a day in the saddle, I stripped off, scrambled naked to the lake's edge and plunged into the cold clear water for a resurrecting swim. Before darkness fell I had failed to catch a fish for supper, but I had gathered enough wood for a small fire and prepared some lentils that had been soaking in one of my water bottles since the morning. The fire kept out the crisp chill of night and under a clear sky I lay back alone in this vast landscape.

The mocking laughter of loons echoed across the calm waters shimmering in the moonlight. At long last my bicycle was giving me real freedom, allowing me to find this perfect place, but after a month on the road I felt alone. For the first but not the last time I began to wish I had someone to share it with. It seemed a waste having it all by myself.

At sunrise I restarted my fire, brewed some coffee and cooked some oats before packing up, clicking my panniers into place and returning to the road. I did my best to make good time, before it got too hot, on a twisty road that ran between jagged rockfaces and thickets of tall pine. It wasn't until midday that I caught a glimpse of another human being. He was perched behind the wheel of a rusty old pick-up and wore a black felt hat that covered his long dark hair, which was stretched tight over his ears and gathered in a tidy ponytail behind. I offered a raised hand of acknowledgement, but the angular native features of the man did not flinch and he rolled slowly past until the mechanical clanking of his engine disappeared into the silence. Minutes later a beaten-up station wagon stuffed with several generations pulled alongside. Its occupants peered at me from the windows with blank, unwelcoming expressions.

⚲

SACRED GROUND OF THE OJIBWA SAGAMOK. STRICTLY NO DRUGS AND NO ALCOHOL.

Following the two vehicles I arrived at a clearing of dry, yellow grass on a small hill that looked out across the endless waters and small islands of Lake Huron. It may well have been sacred. It was certainly beautiful. A cool breeze swept off the lake and mingled in the leaves of the slender trees that cast long shadows towards the back of the clearing, where a line of twenty or so rusty vehicles was parked in the shade.

In the centre of this sacred ground a busy group of men and women were constructing some kind of circular shelter from felled trees. Their work filled the afternoon with the energetic sounds of hammering, chopping and sawing, but they stopped, one by one, and put down their tools to look at the English cyclist standing nervously under his Union Jack flag. I looked on, questioning whether I should be here. Eventually, after what felt like an eternity, a large-framed man approached me. He was dressed in tired blue jeans and a black T-shirt with a wolf's face peering out from the middle.

'You're here for the pow-wow?' he asked in a deep and flat tone. 'Camp over there. No drugs. No alcohol. The grand entry begins at seven.'

Still feeling the stares of a hundred pairs of eyes, I wheeled my bike clumsily towards a shady cluster of trees where a few more nylon domes had already been erected, and picked a good spot with a beautiful view across the waters of Lake Huron. I got my tent up quickly. I had become good at it, just like the little man in the instruction manual, and I got a strange sense of satisfaction out of being organised and efficient. By now it was the middle of the afternoon and, after making the most of a small picnic of two squashed bread rolls, a tomato and some uninspiring packaged ham, I lay back on the soft grass, rested my head on my rolled-up sleeping bag and shut my eyes. With the warmth of the sun on my face I began to enjoy my weekend.

'If you need to wash I am going to the lake.'

A deep voice woke me from my blissful slumber. I opened my eyes to the vision of a large bare-chested Indian towering over me holding a towel and a bar of soap. Without his wolf T-shirt it took me a few moments of sleepy confusion to recognise the man casting a long shadow across my body. He turned and walked away. I gathered the pathetic piece of material that had been sold to me as a quick-dry camping towel and jogged to catch up.

'My name's Tom.'

'John,' he replied. I had half expected him to be called Jumping Salmon or Silver Wolf.

I followed him in silence along a dusty tree-lined track to a small beach on the reedy, marshy banks of the lake. Our arrival was announced by a pair of ducks that burst out of a cluster of wild rice and scrambled across the surface of the water before taking off and flying into the distance. John took off his jeans, his white trainers and untied his ponytail. Standing naked, his long dark hair, which had been pulled in a smooth dome over his head, fell around his thick neck and muscular back like a curtain. He waded into the water and, after muttering some form of blessing, quietly sank his large frame beneath the surface, sending out no more than a few soft ripples. I peeled off my clammy Lycra, got out of my whiffy T-shirt and, feeling shamefully naked, quickly scuttled into the shallows. We both swam a little and the cool water seemed to wash away not only the dust and sweat of the last week's cycling, but also my tiredness and uncertainty. In an attempt to break the silence and show off the knowledge I had recently gained in the museum, I asked, 'What does the word "ojibwa" mean?'

'In the language of Ojibwa it means to pucker.'

John went on to tell me that the Ojibwa were given their name for the unique shape of their footwear, a buckskin moccasin whose edges 'puckered up' when sewn together. While I was wondering where I might be able to get my hands on a pair of these shoes, he went on with a second, more disturbing theory.

'There are those who believe it originated from a torturing technique used by the Ojibwa warriors who roasted their captives over fires until their skin puckered up under the extreme heat. Catch!'

John tossed me the soap and disappeared beneath the surface.

🚲

We walked back to the sacred ground in silence until the stillness of the afternoon gradually filled with the happy noise of the camp: the hammering of tent pegs, the chopping of wood, the calls of children playing. We climbed the last small hill and I looked out across the scene before me. The conical forms of traditional wigwams as tall as trees, children chasing each other through the encampment, men and women admiring each other's feathered headdresses, elders surrounded by eager listeners, a makeshift arena of planks and branches, and a busy group of women gathered around huge metal pots which hung above small fires filling the warm evening air with tidy plumes of smoke. I had to try and ignore the shiny chrome bumpers on the pick-up trucks, the unnatural forms of garish nylon tents, the baseball caps and the jeans, but looking out it was a scene from a childhood dream. I was looking at a real Indian camp and I was relieved that the fires being carefully tended and loaded with chopped wood were not puckering up captives. Instead they were heating cauldrons of bubbling chillied beef and wild rice.

Wild rice, also known as manoomin, which translates as the 'good berry' in Ojibwa, has played a major role in the lives of Ojibwa people for thousands of years. According to Ojibwa oral tradition, they were instructed to find the place where 'the food grows on the water' during their long migration from the east coast. This led them to the shores of the Great Lakes, where flowing fields of manoomin were found in abundance. Seen as a gift from the Creator, manoomin became a healthy staple in the Ojibwa diet. When harvested correctly, wild rice could be stored for long periods of time to be available when other foods were not. Besides being basic to the traditional diet, manoomin also developed cultural and spiritual resonance and remains an important element in many feasts and ceremonies today.

'The Sagamok Ojibwa tribal council welcomes all nations to the annual traditional pow-wow. Please join us for the opening feast. The grand entry will begin at seven,' screeched an announcement through the unsophisticated tannoy system. This triggered a scramble as people poured out of tents and rushed towards the small fires of the makeshift kitchen. Trestle tables laden with food were attacked by a growing swarm of women and children helping themselves to the food on offer. Paper plates were piled high with wild rice and deep ladles of steaming chilli on top of a golden hunk of Indian taco, a skillet-fried flat bread which was a staple among many of the Great Lakes tribes and given the name bannock bread by Scottish fur traders. It wasn't the feast of plump beaver's tail and boiling moose nose I had been hoping for, but I was hungry, I was happy and I was excited to be here at my first Native American pow-wow.

In the jargon-filled world of my previous existence in advertising, a pow-wow was an informal term for another dreary meeting, but its origins are deeply rooted in the Native American culture. Deriving from the Algonquin term 'pau-wau', which referred to a gathering of medicine men and spiritual leaders, it was anglicised to 'pow-wow' by the first European settlers. However, for the numerous plains tribes of North America and Canada, the Blackfoot, the Sioux, the Cheyenne and the Ojibwa, pow-wows were an important opportunity to gather together, trade, dance, celebrate and continue their culture, and eat.

Today the pow-wow circuit is in good shape and throughout the summer months traditional and competition pow-wows are held all over the continent. Competition pow-wows provide an opportunity for dancers, drummers and singers to perform for prestigious awards and big prize money. But the pow-wow circuit has not always been so healthy. Unsatisfied that starvation, land clearance and the introduction of western epidemics such as smallpox had done enough to decimate the indigenous tribes of the Americas, the invading white man, in all his wisdom, decided to prohibit the gathering of more than five native men in any one place at any one time. Afraid that any such meeting would lead to some kind of uprising, the American and Canadian governments imposed the Potlatch Laws of 1851 and 1857, which all but ended the traditional ceremonies that were vital to the survival of Native American culture, and saw the beginning of a generation of cultural prohibition. Clandestine pow-wows still took place but it wasn't until 1934 in the USA and 1951 in Canada that the respective governments were satisfied that Native American culture had been sufficiently weakened to no longer be a threat, and the Potlatch Laws were repealed.

㋕

I perched on a comfortable log on the edge of the arena, happily digesting my wild rice, chilli and Indian taco, as the dull thud of a large drum resonated in the air. The master of ceremonies announced the opening of the pow-wow across the tannoy system that crackled and squeaked from huge conical speakers hung in the trees. It was time for the 'grand entry', and the group of men seated around the large circular drum in the centre of the arena began to accompany the melodic beat with ululating tribal wailing.

The eerie noise grew in intensity, filling the sacred ground, and the crowd of about a hundred men, women and children seated around the makeshift arena took to their feet. In the falling dusk an opening prayer of single syllables was offered in Ojibwa, and those not wearing eagle feathers were asked to remove their head gear. My malodorous Boston Red Sox baseball cap had to come off. A line of dancers entered the sacred circle, led by elders and veterans proudly bearing flags and staffs: the Stars and Stripes, the Union Jack, the Canadian flag, signs of respect for Ojibwa braves who served their countries in Vietnam and the two world wars (where Canadian soldiers fought under the British flag). They were followed by the black, yellow, white and red inter-tribal Native flag, and then the mystical-looking eagle staffs adorned with feathers, eagle skulls and animal pelts, which represented a deeper allegiance, unknown to me.

Behind the elders came an energetic line of younger men dressed from head to toe in beads, pelts, buckskin and ornate displays of turkey fans and eagle feathers. They shook gourds and banged small drums. They shuffled forward, adding sporadic high kicks that threw dust into the air, while spinning deliriously in what looked like a pagan drug-induced haze. Dancers decorated in long grass dresses and fringes, which shook as if the wind was blowing through them, flowed behind, and every shell and every feather of the men's traditional dress seemed to follow the leading beat of the drum that kept this mass of colour and energy moving.

Native women and children now entered the arena. Their turquoise tunics hung with leather thongs, shells and tin cones that rattled and jingled sweetly in time with their slow and graceful movements. They carried delicate fans of goose feathers that twisted and turned in their fingers as they moved around the arena, skipping lightly in their Ojibwa moccasins. The drum beat changed and new drum groups were introduced and new dances announced: the corn dance, the trot, the crow hop, the horse-stealing song and the round dance.

More and more people took to their feet, and the arena became a confusion of black turkey feathers, bear claws, eagle masks, black-and-white skunk pelts, beaver skins, immaculate woven headdresses and the natural earth colours painted on the faces. As darkness fell the moon rose out of the water of the great lake and the tribal drum was still being hit. My initial anxiety and my English inhibitions slowly evaporated with every beat. I took to my feet and I began to shuffle gently in a small circle, and as my confidence grew I began to spin. I turned faster and faster, the drum controlling my every move, and I swayed forwards and backwards, catching glimpses of other dancers and costumes that flashed out of the shadows and spurts of firelight. The primitive beat resonated and invaded my system and I spontaneously began to wail like a brave.

The singing, dancing and drumming continued. In the moonlight I walked back to my tent and, untroubled by the usual frenzy of mosquitoes, put my head back on my sleeping bag and enjoyed the cool breeze that washed through this sacred and ancient place. The distant melodic pounding of the central drum continued to swell into the night, but far from being a disturbance, it was as if I was listening to a deep and distant heartbeat, while the haunting wailing of the singers carried into the star-filled sky. No words, no apparent plan, just the natural calling of grown men transfixed, concentrated, and singing as one. Their feelings translated into one true sound that needed no words to describe the sentiments and insights being expressed. Beauty, pride, honour, bravery, respect and the tragedy of the mighty Ojibwa people. This strange, abstract, wordless noise that had so much more meaning, more depth than words could ever convey, lulled me and I slept.

In the morning the pow-wow would pack up. The magnificent wigwams would come down. The traditional costumes would be packed away and the arena dismantled. One hundred and fifty years ago the Ojibwa would have finished their harvest of wild rice and maple syrup and moved west towards the buffalo-filled plains of the Dakotas. In the morning I too would roll up my shiny wigwam, pack a bag of wild rice and begin my journey west towards the Dakotas, the Midwest and cowboy country.

What is life? It is the flash of a firefly in the night. It is the breath of a buffalo in the wintertime. It is the shadow which runs across the grass and loses itself in the sunset.

Black Crow

Puerto Rican Rice

Serves 4
200g dried pigeon peas (black-eyed peas will do)
100g salt pork (or bacon), chopped into small pieces
1 small onion, chopped
2 garlic cloves, crushed
1 tablespoon olive oil
1 red bell pepper, cored, seeded and chopped small
1 green bell pepper, cored, seeded and chopped small
2 tomatoes, chopped
350ml chicken or ham stock
1 tablespoon annatto (achiote) oil
200g long-grain rice
salt and freshly ground black pepper
to garnish: cilantro (coriander), chopped chillies and limes

1. In a small pot, bring the pigeon peas and 700ml water to the boil. Cover, turn off the heat and allow to stand for 1 hour. Drain the peas,.
2. In a deep pan, sauté the salt pork, onion and garlic in the olive oil for a few minutes.
3. Add both bell peppers, cover and cook over a medium heat until the onion begins to turn transparent.
4. Add the tomato, drained pigeon peas and stock. Simmer, covered, over a low heat for 15 minutes until the peas are almost tender and most of the liquid is absorbed.
5. Stir in the annatto oil, rice, black pepper and 500ml cold water. Return to the boil then simmer, covered, for 15-20 minutes until the liquid is absorbed and the rice is soft and tender.
6. Add salt to taste and mix through a handful of chopped fresh cilantro, some diced chilli and a good squeeze of fresh lime.

Beaver Tail Soup

Serves 6
bones and tail from 1 beaver
2 large onions, sliced
3 bay leaves
2 large carrots, chopped
4 garlic cloves, chopped
salt and freshly ground black pepper
to garnish: sprigs of fresh mint

1. First you need to remove the tough skin from the beaver tail. This is done by toasting the tail over an open flame until the scaly skin peels off in one blistered sheet. This will reveal the tasty white meat underneath. Cut the tail meat into chunks.

2. Place the bones and pieces of tail in a large deep pan, cover with water (at least 2 litres), add a teaspoon of salt and bring to the boil. Lower the heat and simmer for 30 minutes, keeping the surface clean with a large spoon.

3. Add the onions, bay leaves, carrots, garlic and 1/2 teaspoon freshly ground black pepper, and keep simmering for a further 30 minutes.

4. With a large spoon, remove the chunks of beaver tail from the pan and leave to drain on a plate. Don't worry: these will be added back to the soup later. Carefully strain the remaining soup through a sieve into another large pan, being sure to remove any bits of bone. Now continue to boil until the soup reduces to roughly half of its original volume.

5. While the soup is reducing, cut the tail meat into bite-size chunks and add to the soup. Serve hot, making sure everyone gets some chunky bits of beaver in their bowl, and garnish with a few sprigs of fresh mint.

CHAPTER 2

rodeo ga ga

COWBOYS, CRITTERS AND BEAUTY QUEENS
IN AMERICA'S MIDWEST

> Mamas, don't let your babies grow up to be cowboys.
> Don't let 'em pick guitars or drive them old trucks.
> Let 'em be doctors and lawyers and such.

'Son, I drove cross-country once. The boredom near killed me.'

Plucking a couple of dollar bills from the pocket of his dishevelled checked shirt and tossing them on to the table as if placing a bet in a Vegas casino, the substantial man sitting in front of me then poured the remainder of his coffee into the mouth I had just witnessed demolish a breakfast large enough to feed a small nation for a month.

'But good luck to you all the same and God bless.'

He began to leave the diner booth we were sharing. No mean feat for a man of his size, who had to lever himself up on both hands while sliding a few inches sideways. But following three strenuous manoeuvres he was on his feet. He picked up his foam-fronted trucker's hat, pierced with the colourful feathers of prized fishing flies, and pulled it on to his round balding head.

'Thank ya, darlin'.'

'You enjoy your weekend, Pete.'

My eyes followed him through the rain-lashed windows as he did his best to hurry through the torrential downpour, dodging puddles on his way to a large brown and yellow pick-up truck. The engine rumbled into life, the windscreen wipers began their repetitive routine and he rolled out towards the highway. 'Born to Fish. Forced to Work' announced the sticker attached to his rear window. He waited for a juggernaut to thunder past, kicking up a violent swirling storm of surface water, rain and wind.

'What can I get you, darling?'

'A Hungry Trucker's Breakfast, please.'

'And how dy'a want your eggs?'

'Over easy, please.'

'Links or bacon?'

'Bacon, please.'

'Toast or muffins?'

'Toast.'

'What bread would you like?'

'Rye.'

'Home fries or regular fries?'

'Home fries.'

'Tea or coffee?'

'Oh coffee, definitely.'

Since leaving the Canadian Great Lakes and following the southern beaches of Lake Superior through Michigan, Wisconsin and Minnesota, I had become good at these small-town American diner exams, and with another multiple choice successfully completed all I had to do was wait for the results, and I really needed a good score. Americans don't like getting rid of their beloved gas-guzzling vehicles and the previous night, unable to find anywhere else to camp before nightfall, I had slept in a post-apocalyptic automotive graveyard, forced to pitch my tent amidst the rusty broken hulks of neglected station wagons, engine blocks, suspension shocks and other derelict metal innards.

Minnesota's state bird, the mosquito, had plagued me from dusk until dawn, and it had pissed with rain from the early hours and had no intention of stopping. Soaked through after a soul-destroying ten-mile ride through the wind and rain to where I now sat, this small-town, family-run diner, like all the others that fed me as I moved west across America, was a gift from God. A warm, comfortable, friendly sanctuary where, for a fistful of dollars, a hungry cyclist could take in enough calories to burn for a week. Eggs sunny side up, over easy, poached, boiled or fried. Thick pancakes in tall stacks drenched in maple syrup. Chunky waffles smothered in whipped cream and blueberries. Golden slabs of French toast dusted with icing sugar. Rashers of crispy bacon, sticky cinnamon buns, home fries, French fries, hash browns, English muffins, links of sausages, oats and coffee. American diners know all about breakfast.

With a mountain of cholesterol sitting in front of me, I took an essential gulp of coffee, refilled my cup and with a jammy piece of toast in one hand began to peel through the pages of the *Frazee Forum* the previous occupant had left behind. The quality of regional Midwestern journalism was as reliable as my break-fast and I entertained myself with the headlines that jumped off the page.

NARROW ESCAPE WITH HAY STACKER FOR LUCKY FARMER
GIANT QUILT KEEPS RESIDENTS BUSY
FRAZEE TURKEY LURES MISS MINNESOTA

Drawn in by an alluring picture of Miss Minnesota in a floral bikini, I read on. This weekend the town of Frazee was holding some kind of turkey festival, and the article informed me there would be a demolition derby, a mystery gobbler competition, a hillbilly horseshoe contest, a Turkey Dayz parade, a Miss Frazee beauty pageant and, most excitingly, a street dance.

At this point in the trip my contact with the fairer sex had been somewhat limited. The myth that an English accent in America would result in more amorous advances than a man could handle was still, sadly, a myth. I was by no means an ugly cyclist, I didn't think I smelt too bad, but, to date, the closest I had been to having anything to write home about was an over-eager, over-aged waitress who, bored with serving truck drivers for the majority of her life, cooed over my quaint English inflection.

I had barely seen a girl since leaving New York, but surely a weekend involving a street dance and a beauty parade would provide an opportunity. Farmers' daughters, beauty queens, beer and line-dancing were on the menu and, who knows, even Miss Frazee herself might fall for my pedal-powered tales of derring-do.

'More coffee, darling?'

The mental picture I had created was interrupted by the waitress hanging over me with two full percolator jugs of brewed coffee.

'Sure, thanks. Do you know anything about the Frazee Turkey Dayz?'

The waitress looked blank.

'Frazee Turkey Dayz?'

Nothing. I held up the article.

'Fraaaazeeeee. Suuuuure, they're good folk out that way. It'll be a blast.'

Ripping the article from its page, I screwed Miss Minnesota into my pocket and was on my way.

🚲

WELCOME TO FRAZEE.
TURKEY CAPITAL OF THE WORLD
AND HOME TO THE WORLD'S LARGEST TURKEY

You could smell Frazee before its giant cut-out cartoon turkey welcomed you there. The sour stench of mass-farmed poultry was repulsive and clung to the back of my throat. Cycling on Highway 10, parallel to the train tracks that cut an immaculate line through this featureless grassy landscape, I passed the huge sheds and cooling trucks that left me in no doubt what Frazee produced. Turkeys on an industrial scale. The town's distinctive water tower came into view and I followed signs for Main Street. Getting off my bike, I checked right and left and began lifting my load over the rusty railroad when a brown Willy's Jeep skidded to a halt on the other side with a smiling young man behind the wheel.

'Hey, I'm Paul, where you coming from?'

'England. Is this the right place for the street dance tonight?'

'That's right, starts at nine.'

'Is there anywhere I can camp in town?'

'Sure, Town Park, with our giant turkey. Follow me.'

If it smelt anything like the battery sheds I passed on my way into town, I wasn't sure I wanted to camp near the world's largest turkey, but obeying orders I followed the jeep through the suburbs to the town park: a scrubby piece of land with a few picnic tables on the banks of a small river.

'This is Big Tom – over twenty feet tall and weighing in at over five thousand pounds.'

I was staring in complete bewilderment at one of the ugliest things I had ever seen. An enormous fibreglass turkey, complete with snood and caruncles. 'THE WORLD'S BIGGEST TURKEY', announced a plaque. I wanted to point out that it wasn't a real flesh-and-feathers bird, but this was the Turkey Capital of the World and I didn't want to hurt anyone's feelings of civic pride, especially as Paul had now kindly invited me to camp in his garden instead of in the shadow of this monstrosity.

Paul and his family lived under the town water tower, a vast white object that, if decorated correctly, would probably become the world's largest upside-down onion. It towered above the town and 'FRAZEE' was proudly painted on its bowl, letting everyone know exactly where they were.

Paul's family took me in as one of their own and, after leading me through a garage full of fishing gear, invited me to pitch my tent on the tidy lawn behind their bungalow. At a small table on the porch, Paul's father, an elderly man in a grey T-shirt, denim dungarees and tidy white beard, patiently scaled and gutted recently caught sunfish that filled a plastic bucket. He dipped each one in a dish of milk and then flour before his wife ferried them into the kitchen where she was busy preparing for the invasion of her children and grandchildren, two of them, energetic twins, took great interest as I put up my tent, only to shriek in complaint at the fetid smell once they scrambled inside.

I was invited to join the family for supper, and ten of us crowded round their narrow kitchen table. After holding hands and saying grace, a feast of 'pot stickers', a type of Chinese dumpling filled with ground turkey and fried until they stuck to the pot, was served with heaps of rice salad and fried sunfish. After supper Paul and I wondered into town for the street dance. It was time for my 'Frazee Turkey Dayz' weekend to get under way.

🚲

In the centre of Frazee, under the orange glow of the town's street lamps, hundreds of residents and outsiders were gathering for the much-anticipated annual street dance. Bunting drooped from telegraph poles decorated with spirals of fairy lights and canvas banners hung over the street welcoming everyone to the town. A pleasant July evening, the day's earlier storms had cleared the air and under a star-filled sky a lively buzz of excitement resonated in this small Midwestern town. Frazee's Main Street had been closed off at either end by two enormous turkey-transporting juggernauts, and the space in between was quickly filling up with lively revellers. Leather-clad bikers revved the engines of oversized chrome-decorated motorcycles, clusters of burly men in cowboy hats and blue jeans attracted the admiring glances of giggling blonde-haired Daisy Duke look-a-likes, and from a makeshift bar set up in front of the town's magnificent fire engines, firemen clad in yellow trousers and tight-fitting Frazee Fire Department T-shirts handed out a constant stream of plastic cups brimming over with cold beer. Paul seemed to know everyone in Frazee, and as the drinks kept coming I was introduced as a continent-crossing cyclist on my way to Brazil. Turkey farmers and ranchers greeted me with roughened hands and ready smiles and impressed local girls asked to squeeze my prominent calves. It was going to be a good night.

The live music started and I looked out over an ocean of swirling, swinging, jiving Midwesterners. Willie Nelson, Travis Tritt, The Eagles and Kenny Rogers – with a feeble knowledge of Country and Western music, I was only able to recognise a few of the classics that kept the crowd moving and my feet irresistibly tapping. But I'd soon had enough of standing on the sidelines. The beer had numbed my shyness and as a new song was greeted with a wild 'Whoooop!' from the crowd, I waded into the action, introducing myself to a wholesome-looking girl with the clear completion and bright smile of someone who had spent most of her life outdoors. A flattering checked shirt was tied in a knot above her toned midriff and her big eyes and all-American white-toothed smile sparkled under the rim of her cream Stetson.

'I don't have a clue how to dance to Country and Western,' I called, trying to be heard above the music.

'Everyone can dance Country and Western,' she returned with a smile, and putting one hand round my rigid waist and clasping my unattractively sweaty palm in hers, she pulled me into the crowd.

The band played late into the night, interrupted only by the deafening clanking of the freight trains that rumbled through the town every hour, massive, mile-long mechanical serpents that passed so close you could see the driver ringing his bell in recognition of the jubilant mass of people below him. The crowd cheered. This was one hell of a Friday night. I had arrived in the Midwest, in a small town, and I was dancing under the stars with hundreds of happy people. The band kept playing. Travis Tritt was being covered by a group of seven elderly men performing on a trailer bed. They wore denim and Harley Davidson T-shirts, had bandanas and drooping moustaches and their paunches were supported by ornate belt buckles. With closed eyes and sweat-beaded faces they belted out the familiar chorus. The crowd loved it, roaring and twisting to the amplified metallic twang of the guitar and the whine of the harmonica. I had a beautiful cowgirl in my arms and at last life felt good.

I had never seen a snapping turtle. I didn't even know they existed, but they were a local Minnesota delicacy and Paul insisted, the next day, that I track one down. With the sort of half-hearted hangover that can only be achieved by drinking litres of tasteless American beer, I made my way accompanied by Paul to the local butcher. Ketter's Meat Market and Locker hadn't changed for a hundred years. It had one of those false flat fronts I had only ever seen before in Westerns, and a wooden deck raised a few feet above the street. On the counter stood a huge old-fashioned set of scales and bundles of sausage strings were hung up on the back wall. The dusty shelves were lined with bags of various types of jerky – air-cured slivers of marinated meat, the favoured chews of cowboys and cyclists – and disturbing jars of pickled turkey gizzards that would have looked more at home in the laboratory of a mad biologist.

The proprietor was an unhappy fellow who seemed too skinny to be a butcher. A blood-stained apron hung around his neck and in his large rubber-gloved hands was a menacing meat hook.

'Wal, this is a friend of mine. He wants to see your turtles.'

The butcher gave me an investigative look as if to establish I wasn't an operative for the CIA.

'Sure.'

Paul stayed back in the store while Wal led me behind the scenes into a cool concrete corridor lined with the mechanised heavy doors of refrigeration and lit by white fluorescent strips. At the end of the passage a set of damp concrete steps took us underground to another large metal refrigerator door, which opened into a dark, dank, musty cell. I began to recall a schoolboy production of *Sweeney Todd* and visualised the other unlucky tourists who had came down here to 'see the turtles' and who were now being sold upstairs as jerky and gizzards.

A single fluorescent strip hanging from the ceiling flickered to life like an injured insect and adjusting to the raw, unnatural light that now filled the small room I made out eight or ten monsters huddled on the floor around my feet.

'Keep 'em down here cos the cold makes 'em sleepy. They can get pretty frisky when their blood's up.'

I had expected to be shown a handful of terrapins paddling about in a dirty fish tank. These lifeless monsters were the size of coffee tables. Armoured horned heads with yellow eyes and ferocious pointed jaws peered out from thick, uneven, lichen-covered shells. Stiff, powerful arms with thick claws rested on the ground on either side of their grotesque faces. These things weren't turtles, they were prehistoric beasts. Stupidly squatting down for a closer look and a possible photo, I reached out a hand for a stroke. Before I made contact two strong arms grabbed my shoulders and I was yanked backwards, my buttocks landing on the cold hard floor.

'You wanna lose those little English fingers you're going the right way about it.'

'Sorry, it's just that I thought ... .'

The butcher took an old broom from the corner of the room and cautiously began prodding the head of an especially large specimen. I can't say I saw what happened next, it happened so fast, but after a powerful head movement on the part of the turtle the butcher's broom was six inches shorter.

'That's why we call 'em snapping turtles.'

'And these things live in the wild?'

'Sure. They make great eating too – four different types of meat per turtle. Makes a fine stew.'

We handed over a few dollars in exchange for a kilo of 'snapper meat' and headed home. Paul's mother was a snapper-stew aficionado and in her small kitchen, which was a confusion of pots and pans, recipe books and washing up, she went to work. The rubbery meat of different shades was cut into small chunks and browned on each side in a little butter before being added to a large pot. Thrown in with it were chopped vegetables – onions, potatoes, celery, carrots and tomatoes – cloves of garlic and plenty of seasoning. The contents were covered in water and left to stew over a gentle heat. Paul's house quickly filled with the sweet aroma of snapper stew and soon enough his family gathered around the kitchen table. Steaming bowls of this hearty Minnesota classic were passed from place to place, and after grace was said, the slurping began. Chewing on the subtly flavoured meat and drinking up the warming broth, I realised the butcher was right. These strange-looking creatures that lived in the swampy waters and ditches of Minnesota made a great stew.

⏚

'Leg or breast, Miss Minnesota?'

Taken in by the kind people of Frazee as something of a cycling celebrity, the next meeting on my Turkey Dayz agenda was to join none other than Miss Minnesota for a VIP turkey dinner before she crowned this year's Miss Frazee. The bikini-clad beauty that had been screwed up in my pocket for two days was going to become a reality. This would be something to tell the folks back home about.

The dinner was held at the substantial mansion of a prominent Frazee real-estate dealer. A recently built home in a traditional style, it boasted a grand hallway that led up to a sweeping stairway lined with wooden balustrades. The bathroom was encased with dark marble and in the living room a vast television beamed a football game to the owner's sons, who slouched in the expanse of an enormous leather sofa.

On a veranda that ran the length of the back of the house, a long table had been set up for the feast. Various journalists and people of local importance were there, and the finest Frazee spread was on display. Turkey soup, turkey fricassee, cold turkey breast, turkey Caesar salad, grilled turkey drummers and a large turkey hotpot. The people of Frazee were clearly proud of their town bird and loved eating it. I raced a couple of keen local dignitaries for the best seat in the house – next to Miss Minnesota herself. She ate as I expected, nibbling away daintily at a piece of turkey breast. I more than made up for her lack of appetite and as a result soon found myself in a strange, sweaty, post-turkey coma that left me completely unable to communicate with the Barbie doll beside me. Her teeth were whiter than white, her skin was free of any blemish, her hair perfectly blonde, and she said all the right things, mostly about her boyfriend, who came in the muscle-bound shape of the Minnesota state football team quarterback. We had an enjoyable evening. Miss Minnesota was pleasant on the eye and she never stopped smiling. She was kind enough to leave me with a signed photograph of herself to add to my collection. I was unable to return the favour. We wished each other luck and went our separate ways. Miss Minnesota was there to crown Miss Frazee and I was there to watch her at the greatest of American small-town events. The beauty pageant.

🚲

The Frazee high school gymnasium was packed. Neat rows of spectators ran the length of the hall, twittering with nervous anticipation. The question on everyone's lips was: who will be crowned Miss Frazee?

Shortly after I took my seat, the lights went down. A synthesised dance beat throbbed off the concrete walls and spotlights chased each other around the room. The crowd erupted. Bursting from behind a pink curtain decorated with tinfoil stars, five girls of all shapes and sizes, dressed in leotards, white tights and top hats, hurled themselves on stage. High kicks, tucks, twists and spins were all attempted as each girl struggled unsuccessfully to stay in time.

The initial excitement was soon extinguished as the self-important organiser took the stage to make a rambling speech about the virtues of beauty pageants. Each girl was introduced to a judging panel of local dignitaries who sat impassively at a desk at the foot of the stage.

Apparently the opening gambit of wobbling and gyrating had not been enough for the judges, and the first test in this gruelling contest was to be Modern Dance and Singing.

Each contestant returned individually to sing a chosen song while performing a choreographed dance routine. One by one Celine Dion, Elton John, Mariah Carey and Whitney Houston were all dishonoured, but it was contestant number five who got my vote. Dressed in fishnet tights, her ample proportions squeezed into a bustier, she performed a raunchy small-town rendition of Madonna's 'Like a Virgin'. Her puffing and panting was amplified around the hall by the microphone concealed in her corsage while she attempted a routine that managed to incorporate tripping, stumbling and belly dancing. She was greeted with proud applause by the enthusiastic audience.

The next round was designed to test that most important of female virtues: how to look good in a bikini. Eagerly anticipated by the male contingent in the room, who did their best to disguise their eager anticipation from their wives and girlfriends, the girls took to the stage in their finest beachwear to ripples of polite applause. Frazee is thousands of miles from the nearest beach and it was obvious the contestants had spent their winter evenings scanning home-shopping channels and catalogues in order to acquire the most alluring Californian beach swimsuits. Sashaying forward, each competitor attempted a pin-up pose, lowering their heads to smirk suggestively at the judges before turning with a final swing of their assets to leave the stage.

Each potential champion then re-emerged in a shiny evening dress made by their grandmothers for the battle of the ball gowns. More sauntering, more simpering, more posing, more cleavage, and more purposeful scribbling from the judges.

Last but not least the judges asked each of the contestants a series of taxing questions.

'What are your hobbies?'

'What do you think makes Frazee such a special place?'

'What are your plans for the future?'

Each girl did her best to remember her scripted answers, telling us how much she enjoyed working with children and animals and wanted to save the world. The final question, 'What are your views on America's involvement in Iraq?' was responded to in every case with patriotic fervour and roars of approval from the audience.

While the panel of judges discussed their decision in whispers, last year's Miss Frazee, as pink and plump as one of the town's prized turkeys, stood up. Predictably she burst into floods of tears, while trying to tell us through an onslaught of sniffling and blubbering how being a beauty queen had changed her life. She was followed by the sophisticated visiting Miss Minnesota, who drew astonished gasps from the crowd who had apparently never seen anything so beautiful.

Teasingly she peeled open the gold envelope holding the results while the five contestants and the whole of Frazee held their breath. In a slow Midwestern drawl, she announced:

'This year's Miss Frazee is ... Anna Hanson.'

The stage erupted in a tumult of shrieks and tearful hugging. The crowd rose to its feet in applause. At last the ordeal was over.

Or so I thought. Sadly, this was not the case. My buttocks, anaesthetised by three hours on a hard plastic seat, and my hands, weary from perpetual applause, would have to endure another forty-five minutes of crying, crowning and acceptance speeches before I could escape. At long last it came to an end and, mentally exhausted, I staggered from the hall. I had survived the rollercoaster ride of my first small-town beauty pageant, and Frazee had a new Queen.

☙

Paul's family wouldn't let me leave. After all, how could I possibly say goodbye to Frazee without enjoying the turkey luncheon and the Turkey Dayz parade? The previous night's dinner had pushed my annual turkey intake dangerously close to maximum and the thought of Christmas almost brought on a panic attack, but in the name of gastronomic research I promised to push on.

Held in the sterile surroundings of the Frazee event centre, the annual turkey luncheon was another excessive, no-holds-barred celebration of the town's bird. It took place shortly after the announcement of Frazee's mystery gobbler, in which the public had to identify a local dignitary from his warbling imitation of a turkey played out over the tannoy. The doors were opened and the townspeople shunted forward in an orderly line. A hard-working team of blue-rinsed female elders bustled around industrial-sized ovens, from which abnormally sized golden turkeys were produced. Other teams of busy Frazee doyennes set about tearing birds to pieces with alarming enthusiasm, piling the steaming meat on to large metal serving trays. Turkeys were being cooked, carved and served on an epic scale. Waiting in line with my flimsy paper plate, I inched closer towards the panel of old ladies serving up this gargantuan meal. Two heavy dollops of potato salad. An eight-inch gherkin. A turkey leg the size of a small child's arm. A ladle of gloopy gravy and a packet of crisps. My plate buckled under the weight of its load, my stomach gurgled in frightful antic- ipation of the suffering it was about to endure, and I tried to forget the rancid smell of the turkey sheds I had passed as I pedalled into town. I found a seat and did my best to dissect my genetically modified turkey leg with a plastic knife and fork.

The turkey luncheon was clearly a gathering of the Great and the Good of Frazee. On my table I was sharing conversation with none other than the deputy fire chief, the town sheriff and the local undertaker.

'And you must be Taaarm.'

Feeling a hand on my shoulder, I turned round to be greeted by a friendly-faced man with a large gold chain around his neck.

'I'm Mayor Daggett and people here tell me you're riding your bicycle to Brazil.'

'That's the plan.'

'Well, that's just wonderful,' he drawled. 'The people of Frazee would be honoured if you would ride your bicycle in the Turkey Dayz parade.'

Filled with a mixture of pride, nervous anticipation and turkey nausea, I accepted. With my turkey luncheon slowly working its inexorable way through my system, I fetched my bicycle and hurried to where I was told the parade would begin. A clipboard- wielding woman in a blue tracksuit gave me my orders.

'Taaarm, today you're riding in position eight. You have candy?'

'No.'

Rushing to the general store I grabbed two bags of synthetic lollipops and returned just in time. The Frazee marching band rolled their drums and crashed their cymbals, and the large trucks pulling the floats started their engines. At position eight in the parade I was riding behind none other than Miss Frazee, who was perched like a cake decoration atop a giant sequinned re-creation of a red stiletto-heeled shoe, being pulled by a tractor. In the position behind me was the Frazee Retirement Home float, a low-loader lorry with a few dazed octogenarians still in their beds, complete with swinging drips and catheter bags.

Whoop! Whoop! Whoop! Whoop!

An immaculately polished fire engine let out a controlled blast on its siren and the parade began to inch forward through the backstreets of Frazee before turning on to the main street. Frazee may only have had a population of 1,500 but her main street was lined with cheering residents and visitors. I rode with no hands and cycled in circles like a circus performer, rang my bell and waved to the crowds. The streets were lined with families and children who swooped like seagulls to pick up the sweets I tossed to them from my handlebar bag, like all the characters on the other floats were doing.

It was a surreal experience. Police cars and fire engines let off their sirens. The marching band played perfectly, while silver batons were tossed high into the air. Scantily-clad cheerleaders with turkey-fattened thighs ducked and dived, shaking day-glo tinsel pompoms. Clowns on stilts mingled with dancing turkeys, a group of fez-wearing old men in go-karts swerved crazily. Cowboys and cowgirls trotted on horses, their harnesses jingling. Vintage cars beeped their horns, children rode on the back of plump pigs, and the Hungry Cyclist rang his bell and cycled amidst this hallucinatory procession. I had no doubt that I would see some weird and wonderful things on my way to Brazil, but my weekend in Frazee would take some beating.

🚲

In the last two days all my Christmases had come at once and, never wanting to see a turkey again, I left Frazee and moved west towards North Dakota and Fargo, a large Midwestern town made famous by the Cohen Brothers' 1996 film of the same name. By all accounts the townspeople of Fargo could not have been more excited at having a feature film made about their beloved city, only to find that it portrayed them as group of backward, inbreeding maniacs who liked feeding people into industrial shredders. I didn't find any maniacs in Fargo, just car dealerships, endless strip malls and organised traffic patterns that cleverly led you to the doors of Burger King or Starbucks.

Less than happy with my stay, I turned northward for Grand Forks and got my first taste of the scale and emptiness of this rarely documented heart of America. Gone were the winding roads and the meandering highways that connected the small towns of Michigan and Minnesota. Here in North Dakota getting from A to B was much more functional and the straight roads on my map now looked like the national grid, a system perhaps left behind by the German farmers who settled here in the nineteenth century. Riding Highway 200, I was now on a straight road that would be my home for two weeks and carry me five hundred miles across North Dakota, from small town to small town without deviation. Day after day I moved gently, silently through flat fields that stretched as far as the eye could see, unbroken in every direction. I was cycling across the floor of a giant room. Take a pedal-boat cruise across the Atlantic and you will have an idea what it's like to move so slowly over such a vast distance. Gentle winds generated hypnotic waves through the corn, wheat and flax that surrounded me, as if an invisible giant was slowly dragging his hands over the tops of his crops. Perhaps it sounds monotonous, but this huge state, half the size of Europe with a population of no more than 650,000, held a unique peace and tranquillity all of its own, and as a tiny speck in this enormous landscape of land and sky I felt blissfully unimportant. I passed under herds of huge clouds moving gently across the deep blue sky, casting heavy shadows over the landscape like dark sprits. When I wasn't deep in thought, thinking about why I was thinking about what I was thinking about, I found ways to entertain myself on the never-ending strip of tarmac that passed beneath me. Mystified truck drivers peered down from their air-conditioned cabins in bewilderment at the strange Englishman pedalling across the state with a good book propped up on his handlebars.

More often than not they would release long, deep blasts of greeting from their air horns. The deafening noise would startle me from my book, forcing me to swerve and wobble as twenty tons of fast-moving cargo rushed past me in a violent vortex of wind and dust. Unlike the dirty and impersonal lorries of England, these huge juggernauts were palaces of polished metal, boasting rows of chrome-capped wheels, bright fenders and cabs personalised with flames, crossed pistols and semi-naked women, like those found on World War Two fighter planes. Tall vertical aluminium exhausts protruded like proud animal horns and their personalised slogans – *Got A Problem? Just Try JESUS!* and *Keep Honking I'm Reloading* – were the last words of wisdom they offered me before vanishing into the distance. Following slowly in their wake with my own heavy load decorated with stickers, flags and lucky charms, I felt an affinity with these kings of the road.

A water tower would appear in the haze on the horizon. Or was it another figment of my imagination? No, definitely a water tower. A symbol of life out here in this empty space. The sign of another small town with shops, a gas station and perhaps a diner. Incentives to up the pace a little. These small towns off Highway 200 were few and far between and could be over a hundred miles apart. Two days of cycling if the wind was against you, and ten hours in the saddle if it was on your side. Either way I would roll into town hungry, exhausted, but triumphant to have made it to another oasis lush with fizzy drinks, conversation, rest rooms, running water, milkshakes and hamburgers.

One-street towns, they all had their own local eatery: Tina's, the Prairie Rose, the Midwest Café. And in each one the décor didn't seem to have changed since John Travolta and Olivia Newton-John warbled at each other at the local drive-in. The daily specials, normally an item from the regular menu with 25 cents knocked off the price, were always a good bet, and the food was almost always fresh, home-made and served with a smile. Chunky home-made burgers topped with onions, mushrooms and any cheese you wanted as long as it was processed, turkey ruben sandwiches, well-stacked BLTs, plastic baskets of fries served on a red-and-white-checked napkin, malted milks, and always a home-made pie.

I do not normally have a sweet tooth, but riding an overloaded bike made my body crave sugar, and as I rode through North Dakota I got my daily fix from these pies, displayed in chrome and glass cabinets like prize exhibits in a museum. Peanut butter pie, apple pie, blueberry pie, Saskatoon pie, peach Melba pie, rhubarb and custard. These marvellous pastry-encrusted creations came with a dollop of vanilla ice cream as standard, and were washed down with a cup of coffee. The perfect post-lunch pit stop.

These small, friendly and cheap eateries that fed me every day determined my routine. Camping where I could – town squares, fields, farmyards and parking lots – I would grab a light supper at the local diner and then join the truck drivers and other men of the road sipping coffee while staring out of the windows at the sporadic traffic that flashed in the darkness like figures in an Edward Hopper painting.

'What time are you open tomorrow morning?'

'Five-thirty.'

'See you then.'

In the comfort of my tent I would drift to sleep anticipating the breakfast that waited when the sun came up. And rising at day-break I would make my way back to the same diner, already abuzz with hungry local farmers. Worn-out jeans, frayed checked shirts and braces pulled tight over a large frame. This was standard dress for these leather-skinned men of the land who would fill the tables and booths of the small diners. Eating together, drinking gallons of coffee and talking, always talking. Initially it was all too easy to categorise them as simple-minded rednecks who let the wrong people get into power, but every morning as I sat and munched my way through cream-topped waffles, syrup-drenched pancakes, crunchy hash browns, cinnamon buns and French toast, I would tap into their conversations with fascination.

'Flax seems to be coming through well this year.'

'Need to get my barley in before it gets too cold.'

'Could be an early frost this year, judging by the clouds.'

Farming in North Dakota is no easy task. Operating on such a grand scale means that changing crop prices, varied weather patterns, a wrong decision or simply some bad luck can make it hard to survive. These modest men had to be mechanics, meteorologists, botanists, gamblers, drivers and chemists, who worked tirelessly to feed America. Watching the harvests of wheat, flax and barley come in as I rode through their factory floor, I could only admire them.

Although the Midwest of America may host some of the most fertile land on the planet, after a week crossing the bread basket of America I began to wish that her farmers would grow some vegetables. Diner after diner in these small prairie towns pushed out endless carb-packed breakfasts, hefty daily specials and meaty evening meals, but the closest I got to any greenery was, in most cases, depicted in the pattern on my plate. Thus I became a skilled user of any all-you-can-eat salad bar I was lucky enough to come across. Not all diners offered such a luxury, and even if they did it was often hard to find anything genuinely nutritious among the mayo-dressed starchy offerings that prevailed. But if there was any vegetation, I would pounce, playing a precarious game of Crudités Jenga and making the most of the little ceramic real estate I was given on my one visit to the bar.

Feeling lighter and faster, I pushed deeper into North Dakota and the now-familiar crops of flax, wheat and barley began to be replaced by ranches dotted with cattle. I was getting to cowboy country.

⚴

This is looking good. This is looking really good.

I glanced down at my watch.

Could be a personal best.

A second time-check confirmed my excitement. Thirty-three minutes and seventeen seconds. I had sucked the same sour cherry drop for over half an hour, smashing any previous records, and I celebrated my proud achievement by popping another sweet in my mouth and continued pushing into a fierce headwind. Sapping every ounce of my strength, it howled in my ears and meant I had been crawling forward at no more than five miles an hour all day. My dry lips were peeling in large flakes, my knees complained with every turn of the pedals and the road sign for Stanton could not have come soon enough.

Stanton, North Dakota was another small one-street town that called itself a city. Three or four miles off Highway 200, it sat on the banks of the Knife river. Its dusty main street of flat-fronted rundown buildings was no different from all the other small towns I had passed through. The liquor store, the general store, the gun store and the diner. The place was deserted.

A guttural growl followed by a loud sound of spitting broke the silence of the afternoon. In a beaten-up blue Lincoln a man, apparently with nothing better to do, was busy topping up a puddle of brown tobacco-infused phlegm in the street. I cycled over to where he was parked.

A bald round-faced individual was slouched in the driver's seat. His dome-shaped belly swelled under a dirty shirt and a pair of braces while Willie Nelson sang about a 'Whiskey River' from a radio set hidden among the dusty papers and coffee cups on the dashboard.

'Good afternoon, sir. You don't know anywhere a guy can camp in Stanton, do you?'

'*Heeeeeeech papuut!* City Park, down by the river. Gonna get mighty busy though.'

'Yeah, why's that?'

'Stanton Rodeo.'

'Sounds fun.'

'If you're into that kinda thing. *Heeeeeech papuuut!*'

Another projectile flew from deep inside the man and landed perfectly in his puddle of spit. I thanked him for his information, steered wide of his phlegmy pond and rolled down the empty main street towards the river.

I unpacked and pitched camp in the shade of some large cottonwood trees with the muddy banks of the slow-moving Knife river only a few yards away. I slipped out of my sweat-stained T-shirt and my stand-alone padded Lycra, and waded into the river. The cool water washed away a week on the road and, after washing my clothes and hanging them up to dry, I put on clean jeans and a shirt and walked along the riverbank. The sun was setting in the west, painting the white bluffs of the distant Missouri river a soft orange. The silver leaves of the willow and cottonwood trees that lined its banks rolled gently in the wind. The town park provided basic brick grills, and once I had cleaned out the cigarette ends and incinerated beer cans from one, I set about collecting enough dry wood to see me through the night. With a small fire reduced to glowing embers, I unwrapped a large steak I had picked up in the general store and poured a tin of beans into my pan. I opened a can of Budweiser and lay back next to my fire to enjoy a peaceful North Dakotan Friday night.

The following morning I was woken from a deep sleep by the grumble of engines and the whining of generators. Peering from my tent I saw that the park was fast filling up with bulky pick-up trucks, trailers and oversized motor homes. Deckchairs were being spread out in designated camping spots and the park was abuzz with weekending Americans doing something weekending Americans do very well. Camp.

In the United Kingdom we don't know how to camp. Our idea

of a weekend's camping involves hiking to a cold, wet and desolate corner of the country, cooking an inedible meal from a ration pack, then spending a sleepless night cramped inside a smelly nylon shell designed for a hobbit. Americans, being Americans, do it very differently.

Motor homes the size of central London flats are plugged and plumbed into specialist bays. Reclining deckchairs with beer holders and sun visors are unfolded. Cold boxes the size of industrial freezers are unloaded. Smokers and multi-grill BBQs are constructed while sun shelters and gazebos are erected. The vast array of specialist camping gear available on the market allows Americans to recreate the ambience and comfort of their living room anywhere on the continent. Here in Stanton with my tiny tent and lightweight equipment I felt completely out-gunned, but I was only too happy to enjoy the hospitality of my new neighbours. Music played, beers burst open and another Midwestern weekend got under way. I was hanging out with the rodeo crowd, a faithful group of nomads who spend their summers following, and competing in, the various rodeos that take place across the States.

⚄

Rodeos are an important part of American culture. In the early eighteenth century, when the Wild West opened up, its grassy plains provided perfect cattle-grazing country. To feed the soaring population of the cities of the eastern United States, huge herds of cattle needed to be moved from west to east. For the cattle barons to get their commodity across country, long cattle drives were organised, and the skills of roping, branding, herding, horse-breaking and bronco-riding were vital to the cowboys who made these remarkable journeys.

The expansion of the railways and the introduction of barbed wire in the late nineteenth century meant that these roaming cross-country cattle drives were no longer possible or economically viable, creating a dip in demand for the specialist skills cowboys provided. Entrepreneurial ex-cattle hands, such as the famous Buffalo Bill Cody, began to organise Wild West shows that did their best to glorify and preserve the traditions of the fast-disappearing American frontier culture, and many cowboys found work in these shows that toured the country in what became an entertainment phenomenon. Part theatre, part circus, part competition, they recreated famous battles of the American Civil War and victories over Indians, as well as providing opportunities for cowboys to compete against each other for cash. Today Wild West shows still exist and the rodeo circuit is still strong, commanding large crowds, big prize money and a wide television audience. Stanton Rodeo, my first, was a low-key team-roping event. I leaned on the rusty metal fence of the enclosure as it got under way.

Two young cowboys on horseback waited behind a gate on either side of a terrified-looking young bull. At the sound of a klaxon the bull was released, nudged forward with a kindly jab from an electric prodder. Running in blind panic, the bull was pursued into a dusty arena by the two cowboys, who worked in a team swirling lassos above their heads.

One cowboy, the header, aimed his lasso for the young bull's head. His partner, known as the heeler, had to aim his lasso at the hind legs. Once head and legs were secured and the bull was immobilised, the clock would stop. Grown men on horseback chasing cows with long bits of rope may not sound like compelling viewing, but the whistling of rope lassos, the clatter of hooves kicking up dust and the hoarse cries of the men were enthralling. This team sport, which originated in the need to bring down cattle for branding, totally gripped the thirty or forty onlookers.

Team after team raced out of the gates. Heads were missed, cows escaped and horses bucked their riders as these highly skilled horsemen went to work. Involving amazing coordination and precise horse control, these immaculately dressed men in checked pop shirts and faded jeans charged across the arena, effortlessly manoeuvring their steeds into sharp turns and sudden skids. No helmets, no gum guards, no kneepads, no health and safety. Stetsons, a pair of boots, a Lone Star belt buckle, leather chaps and plenty of bottle were all that were needed here. These guys were real cowboys.

Surrounded by the smell of hot leather and hide, Marlborough men slept under large hats in the shade of trailers; others patched up bloody injuries and got on with the job. As these men strode between trailers, borrowing horses and testing lassos, I had no choice but to join the gaggle of giggling female rodeo groupies, local girls who had come to catch a glimpse of these rock stars of the rodeo circuit, men who were mad, bad and dangerous to know.

The contest came to an end and prizes were awarded. A few hundred dollars went to winners but most of the young men here didn't practise this dangerous sport for financial gain. Sure if you made the big competitions there was big money to be made, but the majority of the men I spoke to didn't have the funding. Most of them didn't even own a horse and had to borrow a ride from other competitors. Medical insurance was a laughing matter.

'Smashed four ribs, a pelvis and popped three shoulders. Still, no one wants to insure me.'

'Been concussed since I was fifteen – wouldn't have it any other way.'

'Drove three days flat to be here, and I ain't got plans to go to bed yet.'

Surfers follow waves around the world in a never-ending search for that next adrenalin-exploding ride. Rodeo junkies spend their summers driving from small town to small town in search of their next fix, covering huge distances to ride horses, local girls and live the dream. Sure a few hundred dollars might help pay a few bills and a bar tab or two, but these guys were here because they couldn't be anywhere else, they were addicted to this crazy way of life. And their energy was infectious. I wanted the hat and the confident swagger. I wanted the dirty old pick-up and a horse to ride. I wanted to chase women in smoky pool halls and ride out of town the next morning. I wanted to spend my days rumbling down prairie roads in a truck, kicking up a trail of dust and listening to Johnny Cash with a six-shooter under my seat. I wanted to wear the fitted checked shirts and the tight blue Wranglers with a huge buckle, I wanted a pair of lived-in cowboy boots, and I wanted to sit on my porch in a brim hat watching the sun set on the peaceful world around me. Cycling was suddenly very uncool. I wanted to be a cowboy.

⚲

Stanton's only bar was as unimpressive as the town itself and from the outside it seemed to be no more than an industrial-sized shed. A small neon light, advertising America's leading tasteless beer, blinked in the window of its only doorway but, excitedly, I followed my new cowboy buddies inside. The scene that greeted me was bathed in cigarette smoke and the faintly illicit red glow of neon advertising signs, while lively Country and Western music jumped out of a jukebox. A bar stretched the length of a room jam-packed with burly men in the usual faded jeans, cowboy hats and pop shirts. A busy gang of busty barmaids hurried from fridge to fridge, answering the demands of their rowdy customers.

I made my way to the bar and squeezed into a space between some Stetson-wearing ranchers. Behind the bar, surrounding the dusty bottles of Scotch and flavoured brandy, was a display of North Dakota memorabilia. A stuffed bear smoking a cigarette, sets of antlers, stuffed rodents, lost hubcaps, state flags, licence plates, worn-out saddles and prized Walleye fish. The rest of the room was decorated with the Stars and Stripes, posters of girls in hot pants draped over sports cars and flashing beer signs. Stern-faced men played cards at small round tables, players lent on cue sticks by a pool table, flashing video poker machines blinked erratically and a dated jukebox filled the space underneath a large screen showing men doing their best to hang on to crazy horses in a televised rodeo.

'What'll it be, sweetheart?' cooed a barmaid.

'I'll get a beer please.'

An ice-covered glass tankard was pulled from a chest freezer and filled with pale fizzy beer. I swigged and took stock of where

I was. The whole bar joined in with the chorus of the popular Country and Western classic that was being spun in the jukebox.

'Save a horse. Ride a cowboy.'

I sat at a table with my rodeo friends, who drank in the same way they rode their horses. Fast, and with total disregard for human safety. Tall story followed tall story, beer followed beer and busty girls in tight jeans and T-shirts tied at their midriff were passed from lap to lap. Perhaps I needed a hat or my jeans weren't tight enough but I kept getting missed out. It was clear that a cyclist, however far he had come, didn't cut the mustard.

The evening wore on in a continuing blur. As each drink arrived my determination to quit cycling and ride out on a horse became stronger, and by the time the bottles of blackberry brandy were being shot back I had as good as sold my bike. The problem was that apart from a few salty handfuls of popcorn salvaged from the bar, I had eaten nothing since breakfast. The cowboys were drinking faster and faster and if I was going to make it through the night and become one of them, I needed some ballast. I staggered outside, where my first lungful of fresh air was pure luxury.

As with all good drinking dens, a savvy local had set up a small stand within falling distance of the bar. Under a red umbrella a deep-fat fryer was sending a cloud of steam into the night and a home-made cardboard sign read:

FLEISCHKUECHLE $2

I rubbed my eyes, trying to make sense of the unreadable word.

'One flyschukehill, please.'

'Flesh licker. It's pronounced flesh licker.'

'One flesh licker, please.'

On a bicycle, moving slowly across the country, I was able to see and taste first hand the culinary effects that migration from Europe had on this country. In the same way that the USA's fast food favourite, the hamburger, began as the Hamburg sandwich, knocked together by a couple of wily Germans living in New York, here in the less glamorous surroundings of Stanton, North Dakota, I was enjoying a fleischkuechle, a relic left behind by the Black Sea Germans, who after fleeing oppression in Russia in the late nineteenth century began to look to the Americas, where some had already found freedom and land in the 1870s. Continuing through the 1890s and the early 1900s, the Black Sea Germans began to arrive in large numbers in the Dakotas, bringing their wheat-farming skills and culinary traditions to this fertile new land.

'Fleisch' meaning meat and 'kuechle' meaning little cake, this simple hearty snack was by no means a culinary masterpiece, but it did just the job after an evening of heavy drinking with cowboys, and it no doubt did the same after a hard day farming the fields in the bread basket of America. It turned out to be a folded pastry envelope the size of a pair of Y-fronts, filled with a well-seasoned beef patty. Deep-fried for four or five minutes in a large vat of oil until golden brown, they were left to cool just a little before being handed in a paper napkin to hungry customers. After two fleischkuechles, and suffering from first-degree burns to my mouth, I began to master the art of eating these napalm-filled pockets. One: carefully nibble away the top corner. Two: avoid the jet of hot steam that is blasted into your face. Three: gently squeeze your fleischkuechle a few times, drawing in some cool evening air. Four: nibble a little more from the corner. Five: insert a healthy squirt of tomato ketchup and a few scoops of sliced pickles. Six: devour. I don't know how many I ate, but for the rest of the night I seemed to commute between the bar and the stand outside. With a little food inside me I was able to keep up with my new fast-living comrades in a frenzy of dancing and drinking until a very large girl bought me a 'real cowboy' drink called a rusty nail.

Peeling my face from the dried puddle of drool that had accumulated on the plastic groundsheet of my tent, I enjoyed those fleeting blissful moments of memory loss before the previous night's excess came rushing home in a crashing headache and a violent wave of nausea. Still fully clothed, I had only made it halfway into my tent and pulling myself to my feet was embarrassed to find a damp patch around my groin. At the age of twenty-seven, I had wet my tent and now I knew I could never be a cowboy. With no other choice, I packed up my bicycle and rode out of town.

♾

> The party are in excellent health and spirits, zealously
> attached to the enterprise, and anxious to proceed.
>
> *Capt Meriwether Lewis, Fort Mandan, 7 April 1805*

In August 1803, Meriwether Lewis and William Clark, under the orders of the President, Thomas Jefferson, set out on an expedition to explore the Missouri river and try to establish a river route across the continent. Leaving Pittsburgh, Lewis and Clark led a corps of thirty-three men across America, and by Christmas 1804 were camped in for the long winter at Fort Mandan, a few kilometres outside Stanton. Having to endure skirmishes with natives, starvation, harsh winters and disease Lewis and Clark pushed deeper into what was then Louisiana. At last, finding the navigable waters of the Missouri river, they constructed a fleet of small boats and with the help of local natives followed the Missouri upstream into the ominously named Badlands of North Dakota.

With a terrible hangover, and my spirits low, I left Stanton following in the famous footsteps of Lewis and Clark.

Until now the changes in the landscape of the Midwest had been subtle but, as I entered the dramatic surrounds of the Badlands of the Theodore Roosevelt National Park, the changes became more dramatic.

'I grow very fond of this place, and it certainly has a desolate, grim beauty of its own, that has a curious fascination for me,' said President Theodore Roosevelt in 1883 and I could see why. For thousands of years the gentle flow of the Missouri river has carved out vast multicoloured canyons in the otherwise flat surroundings. Peculiar towering structures rise out of the ground as the sun highlights bright layers of sedimentary rocks built up over millions of years. I spent a wet and stormy night here, camped amongst the bison that roamed freely through the parkland. Staring up at the night sky, it was hard to imagine that these few hardy beasts once roamed the prairies in herds so big they would have been visible from space.

At the peak of their existence it is estimated that over sixty million bison, or buffalo as they are more commonly known, roamed the land between Mexico and Canada. As the great herds of buffalo migrated with the seasons, so too did the Native American tribes, such as the Lakota, the Sioux and the Cheyenne.

Considering their dependence on buffalo, it is not surprising that the Native Americans held the animal in the highest regard. Not only did the buffalo provide meat but almost every part of its body could be put to some use. Its hide for clothing and shelter. Its bones for tools and weapons. Its tough stomach as a vessel for carrying water. But the well-balanced relationship between the Native Americans and the buffalo would soon be lost for ever, changed by the introduction of white settlers. After Lewis and Clark, more and more white fortune-hunters began to head west in search of riches and glory. With horses and guns, buffalo were an easy target, and buffalo-hunting soon became directly associated with the adventures of life in the Wild West. Buffalo hides were used for leather while their tongues became an expensive delicacy, and white hunters left rotting carcasses strewn across the prairies.

The introduction of the railroads only added to the plight of the American buffalo. As railroads stretched into the western territories, buffalo provided meat for the hungry workforce, and once the railroads were complete the destruction became worse. Hunters could now take the train into the west on specific buffalo-hunting excursions, and locomotives would slow down so that passengers could take pot shots from the windows. The wholesale massacre of this proud animal only added to the demise of the Native American tribes who relied on the migration of the buffalo, and by the time the government prohibited hunting, the population in North America had dwindled from sixty million to eight hundred buffalo. The Midwest had been turned into a buffalo graveyard. Reports tell of piles of sun-bleached skeletons stretching as far as the eye could see in every direction, to be cleared up by 'bone pickers', who found a value in the bones as fertiliser.

🚲

Leaving the Badlands and North Dakota in August, I took Highway 2 and cycled west into Montana, Big Sky Country. More than three months on the road without much of a break meant that riding had become a Herculean effort, mentally and physically. My legs were empty and constant glances at the speedometer only revealed bad news. I was going nowhere slowly. The air was muggy and infested with mosquitoes that showed no mercy. If I didn't keep moving above a certain speed their sharp stings drew blood, forcing me to pedal faster as if stuck on some infernal exercise machine. Unable to shake off the permanent exhaustion that hung over me and with nowhere to stop and rest properly, my mood darkened.

I was also stuck in a culinary groundhog day. Breakfast, lunch and dinner, day after day, I was eating alone at the same table in the same diner. The same waitress was taking the same order from the same clipart-decorated menu with the same false smile and around me the same old farmers were having the same conversation about the same crops. Arriving in the small town of Williston on the border with Montana, I threw up my tent in the town park and, just about mustering the effort to get undressed, I climbed inside and collapsed, exhausted.

Waking from a deep sleep and not quite knowing where you are or what's going on can be a wonderful feeling. Waking like this to find a hard object growing into your back through the floor of your tent is a little confusing, and when this unknown growing object begins to gush water, you panic. Dazed and half asleep I scrambled about, trying to work out what was going on. Was it an animal, a giant insect, some alien being? After releasing a long, profane outburst, I began to piece together what was going on. This scene, a nasty cross between *Alien* and *Titanic*, had resulted from me pitching my tent on the town park's sprinkler system.

Wet and despondent, I packed up my damaged tent and waited for the small diner to open its doors. Sitting with a jug of coffee I picked at a stack of pancakes as the sun came up on another day on the road. After breakfast I queued up with grey-haired farmers' wives to use the dusty and slow computer in the town's library. An email from home lifted my spirits momentarily but I left feeling homesick once my half-hour limit was up. I got back on the road. If I was going to get over the Rocky mountains before winter set in, I had no choice but to keep moving.

All around me, buildings and farm equipment were left to rot. Schools, banks and libraries were boarded up and there were almost no young people around. With no work and few opportunities, the temptations of life in the cities were too hard to resist. As I moved from town to town along Highway 2, this social evacuation became more and more disturbing. Falling crop and beef prices led by cheaper imports had left farmers under huge pressure to compete. Market forces and expanding free trade had taken over and profit was king. Seemingly forgotten by their government, all it took was one bad year or a breakdown in machinery and a bigger farm would be willing to step in. Amid mega-farms the small ones couldn't survive. Family-owned farmsteads were being left in ruin or bulldozed down to make the most of the precious land on which they sat, and families were forced to move on. Just as the temptation of vast profit drove the buffalo to the edge of extinction, so it seemed the same was happening to the rural communities of America's Midwest.

On a warm Thursday evening I pulled into the town of Bainville, Montana, population six, feeling tired and dejected. The last two days had been a painful struggle against a relentless headwind, and without so much as a gas station in which to refuel, my meagre rations of peanut butter and beef jerky had run dry. Approaching the city limits, exhausted and under-nourished, my imagination began to run wild envisaging the possible treats that might await me in this small town.

Half of Bainville was drinking in the small characterless shed they called the bar. It didn't serve food. The town had no diner and no gas station, but the woman behind the bar, educating herself via the pages of the *National Enquirer*, pointed me in the direction of two dusty vending machines selling sweets. Appalled at the thought of dining on M&Ms and bubblegum balls, I pulled myself on to a stool at the bar and ordered a beer.

'You aren't from round here, are you, honey?' asked the barwoman, peering over the headline, 'Britney's New Drug Shame'.

'No, I'm from London,' I replied, with little patience for conversation.

'So what brings you to lil' ol' Bainville?'

'I'm looking for the perfect meal on my bicycle.' I popped a couple more M&Ms and washed them down with a second beer.

'Well, we like our beef out here. Ain't that right, Vance?'

She sent a glance to a solitary grey-haired figure in a black Stetson, sitting at the end of the bar. He didn't respond but emptied his glass of beer, and then began on another. I had been hearing about the legendary quality of beef in Montana since the onset of my journey, and in my last week it had been impossible to ignore the countless heads of healthy cattle that happily grazed the lush plains and hillsides of the Big Sky State. So far I hadn't found anywhere to eat this famous bovine treat.

Grabbing the barwoman's attention with a raised hand, Vance called her over and they exchanged a few whispered words, looking in my direction. The barwoman filled two more icy mugs of beer and placed one in front of each of us.

'Mr Anderson says he's got some steaks and oysters at home if you're interested. The drinks are on the house.'

I was bundled into the back of a pick-up truck with my bicycle and Mr Anderson's large panting German shepherd dog, and we turned off the highway a few miles out of town. We rattled and bumped down a dusty track through smooth rolling hills dissected by the unnatural straight lines of fence posts, which stretched unbroken across this vast landscape speckled with grazing cattle. Dwarfed by the steady form of two large buttes, whose steep sides and stubborn craggy summits broke through the grass-carpeted surroundings, Vance Anderson's ranch looked like a child's model. An immaculate, white wooden house sat next to a tall red Dutch barn, surrounded by a series of tidy fences. Horses with necks bent to the ground chomped and pulled on the yellow grass, momentarily breaking their feeding to acknowledge our arrival and the swirling cloud of dust that trailed behind us.

I was handed a cold can of Budweiser and took a seat on the porch. Mr Anderson emptied the remains of a sack of charcoal into half an oil drum and got a small fire going. We talked a little but Vance Anderson was a man of few words.

He lived alone but told me of his family, his work running a cattle ranch and the problems facing ranchers in Montana. His large farmhouse needed a family in it, but he told me there was no work in the area for his children so they had moved to the city. They weren't interested in cattle farming. With his grey handlebar moustache, deep weathered features, denim pop shirt and dusty boots, Vance seemed to represent the last of a diminishing breed. Perhaps the Midwest won't have any real cowboys in it in a few years. Cattle farming will have become automated, and men won't sit on porches shooting the breeze. The traditions I had seen at the rodeo and heard in the country music were fading away.

My protein-hungry muscles began twitching with excitement when Vance reappeared from the kitchen with a plate piled with two Flintstones-sized steaks, marbled with lines of yellow fat and smudged with the dark patches of aging, but I was mystified by the plastic bowl beneath the plate which was full of what appeared to be fleshy water balloons.

Splitting open a testicle brings tears to your eyes, even if it's not one of your own. Vance gave me a sharp knife and instructed me on the finer arts of peeling and preparing a calf's testicle, while he put a couple of potatoes in the oven. Otherwise known as Rocky mountain oysters, or prairie oysters, these tidy little bags were quite a bit bigger than my own pair but the whole process was still uncomfortably close to home. I had to make a delicate incision through the tough skin-like membrane that surrounded each ball before removing what lay inside from its pouch. Slicing the sac's pink contents through the middle, I dipped them in a little egg yolk, coated them in flour and dropped my balls into a hot skillet of vegetable oil that was spitting on the grill.

Three and a half months before putting a testicle in my mouth, I had left home on a bicycle in search of the perfect meal. I had not wanted to take the easy option of eating on my own in smart restaurants. I began the trip because I wanted to eat what ordinary Americans were eating, and so far that was exactly what I had done, from sharing Puerto Rican rice with gangsters in New York to gorging on turkey cooked a hundred ways in Frazee. And now that I was sitting here on Mr Anderson's porch eating Rocky mountain oysters, watching Montana's big sky smoulder in a fiery kaleidoscope of red and orange while the coyotes called into the night, I believed I might have found what I was looking for.

May your horse never stumble, and may your cinch never
  break,
May your belly never grumble, and your heart never ache.
Cowboy poem

Snapping Turtle Stew

Serves 6

1kg snapping turtle meat
150g salted butter
1 tablespoon cooking oil
1 medium onion, chopped
3 celery sticks, chopped
120ml dry sherry
2 cloves of garlic
1 pinch of dried thyme leaves
1 pinch dried rosemary
1 400g can lima beans
3 medium potatoes, diced
3 carrots, chopped
1 400g can tomatoes
1 tablespoon lemon juice
salt and freshly ground black pepper
to serve: 1 bunch of fresh parsley and your favourite hot sauce

1. Cut the turtle meat into bite-size pieces and brown on all sides in the butter in a frying pan. Remove from the heat and set aside.
2. Heat the oil in a large pot and add the onion, celery, sherry, garlic, thyme, rosemary, lima beans and a pinch of salt and pepper. Once the contents begin to sizzle and your kitchen is full of aroma, cover with water, bring to the boil and leave to simmer for 1 hour.
3. Now add the browned snapper meat and melted butter to the pot, along with the potatoes, carrots and tomatoes and lemon juice, a little more salt and pepper to taste if necessary, and simmer for a further 45 minutes.
4. Serve in deep bowls with a little chopped parsley and a shake of your favourite hot sauce.

Rocky Mountain Oysters

(Although the oysters I ate in Montana weren't soaked in beer I've learnt since that the process of soaking them tenderises the meat.)

Serves 6
1kg fresh calf's testicles*
2 cans beer
150g flour
salt, garlic salt and freshly ground black pepper
3 egg yolks
240ml vegetable oil
chilli sauce or a little chopped chilli

1. Using a sharp knife, split the tough skin-like muscle that surrounds each 'oyster' and remove the testicle from within.
2. Place the testicles in a deep bowl and cover them with beer. Leave to sit for at least 2 hours.
3. Now combine the flour with a pinch of salt and garlic salt and some black pepper and mix through. Remove each testicle from the beer and while still damp, dip in a little egg yolk and roll in the flour until well covered.
4. Heat the oil in a deep skillet or frying pan, seasoned with a little hot sauce or some chopped chilli. Drop in the oysters and fry them for a couple of minutes on each side until golden brown.
5. Leave them to cool on a bed of paper napkins and then enjoy them with a cold beer and a little chilli sauce for dipping.

---

* Be sure to ask your butcher for calf testicles, not bull testicles. Calf testicles are the size of a walnut and are much more tender than the larger bull testicles, which can be a bit of a mouthful.

CHAPTER 3

a rocky road

MOOSE BURGERS, BEARS AND AN UPHILL STRUGGLE

Behind mountains, more mountains.

Haitian proverb

Along with having to wear Lycra, and the inevitable chafing, there are three major downsides to cycle touring. The rain, headwinds and going uphill. Crossing the American Midwest I had been exposed to my fair share of lip-chapping, energy-sapping headwinds. The ending of the summer meant I had already been well watered, but until now the topography of my route had been sympathetic. A few unfriendly grades in Upstate New York had tested my early resolve but since then my legs had remained almost completely unproven at riding a 50-kilo bicycle uphill. This was about to change. Leaving the United States I had made it to Calgary, in Canada's oil-boom state of Alberta. Home to the annual cattle stampede, it stands where the Great Plains meet the Rockies. Examining my location on my soggy, worn-out map, the impending change in terrain was evident. To my east, the map's clean expanse of even green ink represented the flat ground I had just covered. To my west, a confusion of grey shaded crags seemed to rise out of the page, promising a very different type of landscape.

Beyond Calgary's silver skyscrapers the snow-covered peaks of the Rocky mountains shimmered against a cloudless blue sky.

From the safe distance of the city's coffee shops and busy streets they seemed calm, almost unreal, like the blue-screened scenery in an old movie. By all accounts I would need at least a month to get to Vancouver, and with the year moving on, if I was to make it 'over the top' before winter set in, I had to get going. Bike repaired, Lycra washed and bags packed, the weathermen gave me the green light, and on the first of September I rode off, excited and apprehensive, towards the Rockies.

ॐ

Cycling through Calgary's oil-rich manicured suburbs in the early morning I passed bleary-eyed commuters clutching briefcases and giant, insulated coffee beakers. They called their goodbyes to wives and children standing in the doorways of their prim cloned houses and climbed into shiny all-terrain vehicles parked in the tidy driveways. Row after row of identical houses sporting velvet lawns luxuriating under automatic sprinklers stretched in every direction, but as the houses stopped I began to ride uphill and the endless terrain of the Midwest closed in around me.

The wide-open spaces I had been used to became tight valleys with heavy, shadowed cliff-faces. Never-ending vistas shrank to dark dense forests. The water no longer meandered and gurgled in lazy riverbeds, it rushed and crashed in foaming streams. Within a day's cycling of Calgary, I was enclosed by mountains.

But far from being intimidated in these new surroundings, I felt strong and healthy, the air was crisp and clean and the climate cool and refreshing.

Gone were the slow-moving, nonchalant cowboys of the Midwest. Up here everyone I encountered at gas stations and small mountain cafés looked like a model from a camping catalogue. Ruddy-cheeked, clad in lumberjack shirts, heavy boots and efficient clothing with dozens of pockets, they had an infectious energy gained from their healthy mountain living. The Rocky mountains were an outward-bound paradise and after almost four months on the road I couldn't help but feel like the mountain alpha male, living rough and surviving on my wits. Under clear blue skies, surrounded by this dramatic new scenery, I rode confidently towards the mountain town of Banff.

⏚

Adding an uncomfortable coolness to my sweat-damp T-shirt, a chill wind whistled in my ears. As deep rumblings echoed in the distance, I looked ahead to the tops of the mountains that were enveloped in swirling white clouds. The sun was quickly obscured and without the picture-perfect backdrop of blue sky and bright sunshine the mountains took on a whole new character. The first few drops of rain fell on my arms and an explosion of lightning flashed behind the high ridges above me as I laboured up the last hill into Banff. I was losing a race against nature. From what I could hear, a storm was systematically moving from valley to valley, and as a blanket of black clouds unrolled above I knew I was next. I rode into one of Banff's large campsites with the cold rain now pouring down my face and battled with the unpredictable gusts of wind to put my tent up quickly. Deafening claps of thunder clattered round the mountains and each time the lightning snapped every detail of the valley was illuminated in brilliant phosphorescent light. Frantic to unpack my bike, I threw my panniers inside my tent, hurled myself in behind them and pulled the zip.

Like the snug comfort of being beside a roaring fire in a small cottage on a winter's day, rain beating against the windows, there is something strangely comforting about being in a tent during a storm. But this comfort soon turns to panic when your 'cottage' decides to blow away. My pathetic tent pegs put up no resistance to the gale-force winds that were now howling outside. My flysheet had torn away from the main body of the tent and, after transforming itself into an efficient mainsail, began dragging me around the campsite. Wrapped in a confusion of torn nylon, tent poles, sleeping bags, pots and pans and puncture repair kits, I tried desperately to locate the zip so that I could escape, but no sooner had I resigned myself to the storm's power than I felt a strong hand grab at me through the wreckage.

'You OK in there?' came a cry from outside.

'Not really,' I bleated in distress.

I was pulled from the wreckage and, after salvaging what I could, was rushed by my rescuer into the nearby safety of a motor home, where the confused faces of a young family seated around a small table at a game of Pictionary looked me over.

'We watched you come in. Didn't think you'd make it through the storm with your tent pitched where it was. Done much camping, have you?'

'Bits,' I muttered, embarrassed that my camping show had provided some light entertainment. 'I've cycled from New York,' I added, in an attempt to improve my credentials.

'Well, you're welcome to dry up in here while this storm passes through. Some fudge?'

The mother offered me a plate of home-made peanut butter fudge from the middle of the table where the family were grouped around their game. The Wendlebows were a family from Vancouver Island on vacation in the Rockies. In the snug comfort of the motor home, Paul, Emily and Erik, the couple's young children, eyed me up and down shyly.

Wrapped in a blanket, clutching a steaming cup of coffee and nibbling on a slab of fudge, I stared out of the steamed-up windows of the motor home and watched as the storm moved into the next valley. Suddenly downhearted in the midst of this comfortable family, I pondered my situation.

I had spent four months sleeping rough and cycling, and now the summer was coming to an end. I had almost crossed the continent but one last, seemingly insurmountable, hurdle remained, and after only a few days into the Rockies the weather had already got the better of me. My tent was in tatters and so was my morale. I imagined limping back into Heathrow and being met by a posse of friends and family offering polite congratulations.

'You did so well to get so far.'

'You should be really proud of yourself.'

'What a shame about the weather.'

At this point it was very clear how totally under-prepared I was for my mountain crossing, and I had at least another month ahead of me until Vancouver. For the first time the thought of failure was very real. I felt a long way from the heroic continent-crossing cyclist I was claiming to be.

The sky cleared and before darkness fell I was able to recover what was left of my equipment, which had been liberally scattered around the campsite. My tent would need to be patched up, I had lost four tent pegs and my inflatable mattress no longer inflated. The Wendlebows kindly invited me to join them for supper and after a comforting evening of Pictionary, hot dogs and corn on the cob, I crawled back into my weather-beaten tent, curled up on my deflated mattress and slept.

🚲

In 1885 the completion of the Canadian-Pacific Railway finally linked the east and west coasts of Canada, allowing passengers to travel the 2,500 miles across the North American continent in relative comfort. Passing north of Lake Superior, the tracks traversed the Great Plains of Manitoba and Saskatchewan before snaking into and over the Rocky mountains. A remarkable feat of Victorian engineering, which cost the lives of countless Chinese labourers, the project was spearheaded by the charismatic William Cornelius Van Horne. A rising star of the new industrial age, Van Horne not only saw the railroad as fundamental to trade and commerce, he also saw the potential of the Rockies' breathtaking scenery as a tourist attraction. 'Since we can't export the scenery – we shall have to import the tourists,' was his entrepreneurial boast before starting work on a series of luxurious mountain resorts where the super-rich of this new industrial epoch could come and take in the clean air and enjoy the views. Van Horne's vast chateau-style hotel, built on the convergence of the Spray and Bow rivers, was to be the jewel in the CPR's crown. A towering testament to industrialism, the Banff Springs Hotel quickly became one of the world's most prestigious getaways.

In bad weather, with its Gothic turrets and gables, it would have appeared like an impregnable cocktail of *Psycho*-meets-*Colditz*, but bathed in warm late-summer sunshine it was as reassuring as a Scottish baronial castle on the lid of a tin of Highland shortbread.

I pushed my bicycle up the long sweeping driveway, gazing at the towering façade with its backdrop of mountains. Then I walked into the imposing hotel lobby and, in my dirty shorts and worn-out shoes, I felt immediately and agonizingly under-dressed. Stone chimneypieces framed roaring fires, vast oil paintings of misty mountain scenery hung from the walls and the proud heads of deer and moose stared down at me with disdain. Colourful stained-glass windows lit up solid wood staircases and rich carpets, while busy staff scurried to attend to the well-to-do guests lucky enough to be staying here. I pulled off my bobble hat, revealing a shaggy head of unkempt hair, and approached the reception desk to enquire about brunch.

'Certainly, sir. Do you have a reservation?' drawled the concierge in a smooth Canadian accent.

'No, I'm afraid not.'

'Well, I'm afraid you need a reservation, sir, and we do have a dress code in the dining room. Resort casual.'

'Resort casual?'

'Yes, sir. Will that be all?'

A short ride back into town I found the nearest phone box and popped in a couple of quarters.

'I'd like to make a reservation for brunch please.' ... 'Today.' ... 'Just one, I'm afraid.' ... 'Eleven thirty? Perfect.' ... 'Tom.' ... 'Thank you.'

Back at the hotel's front door a polite porter offered to keep an eye on my wheels, and after I explained that I planned to be inside for quite some time he offered me the valet service.

'For a bicycle?'

'Don't see why not, sir.' Handing me a smart brass token, he wheeled away my overloaded bike.

I hurtled through the lobby, past well-dressed guests enjoying their Sunday, and made a beeline for the Gents.

It was an opulent room with yellow marble basins, golden taps, tall mirrors and, amid a baffling range of towels and scented toiletries, I went to work. I trimmed my wayward beard, added a few well-needed blasts of deodorant, put on a collared shirt and slipped into an almost clean pair of jeans.

The reflection that looked back at me may not have been wearing a pink Ralph Lauren shirt, chinos and a preppy blazer, but as I brushed my hair and eyed myself up in the large mirror I decided I was as close as I was ever going to get to 'resort casual'. Stuffing my dirty clothes in the small cupboard under the sink, I made my way to the dining room, leaving a trail of stubble and my own distinctive fragrance in my wake.

Like another of life's simple pleasures, eating is much more fun with other people. I gave my name to the maître d' and felt a momentary pang of sadness as I was shown to a single table, laid for one, in the middle of the large dining room, which was filled with families, groups of friends and the lively sounds of animated conversation. Eating alone is one of the downsides to solo travel, but determined not to dwell on my solitude I began to plan my brunch and activate my gastric juices.

'Do help yourself to the buffet, sir.'

Just hearing the word 'buffet' conjured up apparitions of metal trays filled with multicoloured gloop in cheap Chinese restaurants. It reminded me of cheapskate corporate functions with tables littered with cold cocktail sausages, plastic ham sandwiches, damp quiche, greying Scotch eggs and soggy sausage rolls. But as I stared at the galaxy of food laid out before me here, it was clear that they treat buffet very differently Stateside. This was buffet, but not as we know it.

Heaps of crushed ice were covered with pink lobsters, meaty crabs, fat shrimps and coral-coloured langoustines; there were sides of smoked salmon, trout and gravadlax; pepper-crusted pastrami, haunches of prosciutto, shiny maple-cured hams studded with cloves, salted hunks of beef, rolled pancetta, looped Spanish chorizo, slender salamis, chunky saucissons ...

Busy men in tall chef's hats and white jackets whisked eggs and made omelettes to order. Balls of pizza dough were thrown around like juggler's balls, stretched like chest expanders before being sprinkled with savoury ingredients. Headband-wearing sushi chefs patiently constructed flawless nigiri and sashimi while others tossed ingredients into hissing woks. Sous chefs with knives that could remove a man's arm at a single stroke dissected tender ribs with all the skill of a surgeon and racks of lamb and huge hams glazed with sticky honey were deftly sliced. Golden chickens rotated slowly on spits. There were salads of every colour and description. Baskets spilling over with fresh fruit and wild berries were next to towers of decadent pastries and puddings cemented with whipped cream and bejewelled with fresh fruit. It looked like the delirious fantasy feast of a starving man. After four months of living on the road, it was almost too much to take in. I wanted it all and yet seemed to be overcome with a strange sensual panic.

There is an art to eating a buffet of this calibre. I needed to be calm, disciplined. I needed a strategy. How many times you revisit a buffet on this scale is a private matter between you, the capacity of your stomach and your conscience, but the first rule of buffet is knowing where your enemy lies.

'Would like some bread, sir?'

Don't even think about it.

To gently ease my system into the impending feast, I began with a bowl of fresh Rocky mountain berries and natural yogurt, and sticking with the breakfast theme I then decided on eggs Benedict, an old favourite. I declined the offer of having it served on an English muffin and opted instead for a couple of rashers of grilled Canadian back bacon and a little wilted spinach.

My next stop was the sushi bar where a patient Itamae was practising his art. I briefly questioned whether I should be eating raw fish in the Rocky mountains, but the objection was overruled, and I returned to my table with a plate laden with beautiful nori, wrapped futomaki, uramaki made with Pacific salmon, nigiri zushi with shrimp and eel, and plenty of tender cuts of sashimi, all enjoyed with a little wasabi and pink ginger that rebooted my system perfectly for the next step.

Spoilt with cold sides of smoked Pacific salmon, sparkling gravadlax and fat prawns the size of giant's fingers, I loaded up yet another fishy plate with poached Bow river trout with a dill and caper sauce, and enjoyed it with some fresh asparagus dripping with butter. Fish is filling and, teetering on the edge of consciousness, I was grateful that I had had the foresight to bring a good book with me. After a visit to *Middlemarch* I was soon raring to go again.

Ahhhhhhh!

Roast loin of pork with morels, the sculptural mushrooms I had noticed growing on damp tree stumps and logs in the woods, served with a couple of boiled Yukon Gold potatoes coated in a little butter and fresh mint, and a couple of grilled peppers on the side. My mission was almost complete.

Unfortunately the Hungry Cyclist was on a tight budget, and this luxurious food had to be washed down with jugs of iced water and the complimentary fruit juices on offer. With each new plateful the black-dressed sommelier would approach to proffer his extensive wine list; each time he would retreat with merely a twitch to the corner of his mouth to show his disappointment.

He had much more luck with neighbouring tables, whose occupants changed two or three times during the course of my long-drawn-out brunch. By now I had been eating for over two hours. My brain was signalling frantically to my stomach and waves of dizziness washed over me. I began to feel increasingly light-headed and in a state of semi-delirium I mopped up the last of the meat juices with a lonesome potato. I needed to go back to *Middlemarch*.

After another chapter, I enjoyed some sharp Canadian cheddar and a healthy slice of Saskatoon strudel that had been flirting with me throughout the afternoon. I had reached my elastic limit and, sipping at a small espresso, I checked my time. Three hours and twenty-two minutes. I screwed up my napkin and triumphantly threw in the towel. Staggering out of the dining room I waddled through the labyrinth of the hotel like a sedated minotaur. The beast had been tamed. Stumbling across a cosy room with an open fire and a sofa the size of a family car, I slipped off my shoes, plumped up the cushions, let out a reassuring fart and collapsed.

Waking from a series of deep, cheese-induced dreams, I reluctantly made plans to return to the washroom to get back into my cycling clothes. In the lobby, excited fresh-faced guests were returning from the mountains and checking in for the night. How I wished I could have joined them. Instead I pulled on my woolly hat and walked outside into the cold. Reluctantly, like Cinderella returning from the ball, I gave the doorman my valet token and soon a young porter was struggling to push my bike to the front door. I shook his hand, slipped him a dollar for his efforts and pedalled out into the biting late afternoon.

'Thank you, sir. Enjoy your evening.'

♾

As I left Banff, the sun disappeared behind the dark green spruce that covered the mountains, and the warmth of the afternoon went with it. In the sunlight this snow-capped landscape was enchanting, but when you took away the sun it became a different place all together. Cold and imposing, the long shadows of the dark cliff-faces hung over me as if I was entering a whole new menacing world. The air chilled my face and icy drops of rain began to fall and to drip from the boughs of the dark trees that hugged the roadside. Cold and alone in this suddenly intimidating environment, my thoughts returned to the comfort of the hotel. It would be dark in an hour and I had no idea where I was going to sleep that night.

'Hey there, I'm Dave. Quite a load you have there, eh?' A man on a bicycle pulled alongside. 'I'm camping in the woods on the left, seven miles up the road. Come and join me. Can't delay, this rain doesn't look like quitting and I need to get a fire going, eh.'

Ending every sentence with the expression 'eh', it was clear Dave was Canadian, but other than his name and his nationality I knew nothing about him, and he and his old racing bicycle quickly disappeared over the crest of the next hill. Exactly seven miles from where Dave had raced past me, a narrow track, flanked on either side by tall trees and scattered with fallen pine needles, led into the woods. Away from the road the forest was densely packed and the thick evergreen branches almost completely blocked out what was left of the day's light. Rain poured down and heavy beads of water fell through the needles and branches. A mile or so up the track the light blue rainsheet of a small tent stood out in the darkness and working away behind it with a small hatchet was Dave, already busy splitting logs for a small fire that was sending a billow of thick smoke into the gloomy surroundings.

'Welcome, welcome,' he cried. 'Try and find a dry spot for your tent, eh.'

Fat drops of rain splashed from the high branches but the forest floor, a mix of old spruce needles and small twigs, was surprisingly soft and dry. I pitched my tent, prepared my sleeping bag and, still wrapped from head to toe in my claustrophobic waterproof carapace, joined Dave by the fire.

'Feather sticks,' he said, holding up a piece of split wood. 'Only way to get a fire going when the heavens open, eh.' He went back to working at the piece of kindling with his long hunting knife. 'You wanna try?' He offered me a piece of wood.

In a blue bobble hat that came down over his ears to the top of his well-kept beard, and wearing an old jumper and well-worn yellow waterproof jacket that would have been more suitable on a fishing boat, Dave was skinny and probably in his fifties, but the deep lines of his weathered features surrounded a pair of keen eyes that sparkled with the boundless energy of a teenager.

'So where are you cycling to?' I asked.

'Oh I'm jus' here on a little holiday.'

'And where's home?'

'Calgary right now, eh. But I'm kind of homeless at the moment.'

'But what do you do during the winter?'

'Oh, it doesn't get too cold any more. Perhaps minus thirty when there's a snap, and as long as I have my peanut butter and my marg, I do just fine.' Pulling a plastic tub from his bag, Dave proudly directed a heaped spoon of white margarine into his mouth.

'You want some?' he offered through a mouthful of margarine.

'Not for me, thanks.'

'Keeps out the cold, eh.'

I watched in disgust as the lump of margarine moved down his throat before Dave went on to repeat the process with his peanut butter. What little appetite I had after my gourmet lunch almost disappeared after witnessing this gastronomic monstrosity, but expecting a cold night ahead I offered to cook some supper and returned from my tent with my cooking staples – two ripe tomatoes, half an onion, a head of garlic, two bruised courgettes, a roll-up chopping board, a collection of herbs and spices stored in 35mm film cases, some chicken stock cubes, some brown rice, a little olive oil, two apples, a small bag of raisins and a plastic bear half full of honey, plus a couple of pans. The kindness of strangers and plenty of cheap Midwest diners meant I hadn't used them for a while. Producing my supplies, Dave's eyes almost fell out of his head.

'You cycle with all that gear on your bike, eh?'

'I like to eat.'

Placing a couple of flat and steady rocks around the fire, I sweated off some chopped onion with a little oil in one pan before adding chopped garlic and a couple of pinches of dried cumin. I added one cup of brown rice, which sizzled and cracked, and after a few minutes added two cups of water and a crumbled stock cube. Leaving the rice bubbling, I added the remains of the chopped onion and the rest of the garlic to the other pan and put in the courgettes, the rain hissing as it hit the bottom of the pan. The courgette began to colour and I added the tomatoes and some seasoning. The rice was ready. Dishing up a healthy portion on a plate, I added a little of what could almost be called Rocky mountain ratatouille and served it to Dave.

'Voila.'

'You sure like your food, eh.' Dave began attacking his supper.

'Oh, nothing special,' I said, ashamed to admit that only a few hours before I had been stuffing myself in one of the world's smartest hotels. For pudding I cored the two apples and filled the centres with a mixture of three damp digestive biscuits I found in a pocket, some honey, raisins and a pinch of cinnamon. I stewed them in a few inches of water and after a long wait while chatting over a strong cup of coffee they were ready, the piping-hot apples sticky and spicy-sweet.

We stayed up and talked a little about our respective lives on the road. A year before, Dave's mother had had to go into a nursing home and in order to cover the costs Dave had been forced to sell their apartment. Without a job he had no alternative but to camp for the ensuing year in a park in Calgary, from where he was able to visit his mother every day. This trip to the Rockies was his holiday. Before long the bitter cold sent us into the relative warmth of our tents. I stretched my balaclava over my head, pulled on my woolly socks and gloves and wriggled about for a few minutes to generate a little heat. It was no five-star hotel, but after my evening with Dave I was beginning to understand that comfort and discomfort were no more than a state of mind.

∝

The following morning I emerged wearily from my tent cursing the cold, frantically blowing into my hands and stamping my feet in an attempt to reboot my circulation. Dave was already up and about, chopping wood and successfully resurrecting the previous night's fire. My water bottles had frozen solid and after filling a pan in a nearby stream we brewed coffee and cooked oats. Then we said our goodbyes, and I was on my way to Lake Louise and the Icefields Parkway.

Fabled to be one of the world's most beautiful roads and tracing the spine of the North American continental divide, the

Icefields Parkway runs some 250 kilometres from the surreal turquoise waters of Lake Louise to Jasper National Park. Built by unemployed men as part of the 'make work' project during the Great Depression, it passes within viewing distance of seven upland glaciers. Dreamlike lakes the colour of scarab beetles sit peacefully below these vast fields of ice that cling precariously to the mountains, slowly dripping into the rivers that fill the air with the sound of rushing water and tumbling boulders. Cycling this road, where large trucks are thankfully prohibited, might be hard work but I have no doubt it is the best way to appreciate the outstanding natural beauty hidden in the heart of the Rocky mountains. Huge slabs of what was once the earth's crust have been smashed and thrust in all directions by violent seismic upheavals, creating the vast sharp-edged limestone mountains and splintered cliff-faces that surround you. Millions of years of slow-moving ice and rushing melt-water have done their best to tidy up this violent mess, carving out smooth valley basins.

Two days later, as I sweated inside my restrictive waterproof shell on a morning of slow uphill cycling in indecisive rain, the sun eventually broke through the thick clouds and the dramatic beauty of the valley I was cycling through became visible. Finding a peaceful clearing some way from the road I stopped for lunch beside the ominously named Mosquito Creek. I had not passed a shop since Lake Louise and my meagre rations dictated another lacklustre banquet of peanut butter and honey sandwiches, two bruised apples and a chocolate bar. Unsatisfied with lunch I lay out my damp clothes on a series of large boulders to dry in the afternoon sun and, doing the same to myself, began drifting asleep to the peaceful tune of the icy waters rushing in the creek. The warmth of the afternoon vanished as the sun hid behind the mountains and it was replaced by a sharp coolness that quickly reminded me where I was. It seemed a perfect place to camp, and deciding to stay put for the night I spent the next hour crashing around in the bushes collecting the driest wood I could find.

Organising my findings into three tidy piles, small, medium and large, I split some of the smaller branches into 'feather sticks' (of which Dave would have been proud), cut a strip of rubber from an old inner tube, covered it with smaller twigs and struck a match. On all fours, I moved around my fire. A directed blast of breath here. Another well-positioned breath there. Just move this stick a little to let some more air in ...

After ten minutes of concentrated tweaking, blowing and tinkering I was rewarded with the first comforting crackles and hisses of fire. I tenderly placed a few bigger sticks on the climbing flames and, swelling with primitive pride, I got to my feet and took in my surroundings. The wide creek ran away across the valley floor which was littered with sun-bleached tree trunks and heavy boulders, a reminder of its powerful potential. The broken peaks of the cold mountains rose hundreds of feet above the pointed tops of the densely packed trees that carpeted their slopes, and above it all the first star burst through the cloudless sky. It promised to be a bitterly cold night. In the gathering darkness my world was soon reduced to all that was illuminated by the dancing flames of my fire.

'Hey, Hungry Cyclist, why don't you come in here and take off my wrapper?'

'I'm rationing. Go away.'

'Oh come on. Come and wrap your lips around my sweet chocolate and caramel centre.'

'I'm saving you for tomorrow. Leave me alone.'

'But I'll taste so much better tonight.'

There is only so long you can sit in the bitter cold knowing that an uneaten chocolate bar waits for you at the bottom of a bag. After falling for the advances of Babe Ruth, I prepared to turn in and set about hanging what remained of my food in a nearby tree. Not only would this prevent me from decimating my rations in a fit of night starvation, it would also thwart the efforts of another hungry predator.

Ever since US President Theodore (Teddy) Roosevelt, the great conservationist, saved a baby bear from being shot on a hunting trip, humans have had a close affinity with these ursine creatures. We all cherish Teddy bears. We anthropomorphise them into likable characters, Paddington, Winnie, Balloo and Yogi, and a trip to the Rockies would not be complete without catching a glimpse of one of these majestic and lovable animals in the wild.

'Seen any bears?'

'Black or grizzly?'

'Any cubs?'

These are customary questions amongst visitors to the Rockies, and the traffic jams and tailbacks of eager tourists leaning from car windows and motor homes to capture a piece of moving bush on their digital cameras are testament to the important role bears play in the tourist industry of the mountains. But here lies a problem. Man and bear aren't the best roommates.

Every autumn, bears make the very sensible decision to get into a cave and sleep for four months, and before taking this long nap they go on a feeding frenzy to fatten up. As their normal food supply is depleted by the damming of rivers and deforestation, they have to look elsewhere, and thus they have developed a taste for easily found human food. Rubbish bins, local tips and campsites provide easy and delicious pickings. This means that bear attacks in the Rockies at this time of year are by no means unheard of. All visitors are advised to carry a bear bell, a pathetic little thing more suited for decorating a Christmas tree than scaring away a 600-pound ravenous beast, and park rangers, local people and road signs are full of advice on how to best avoid becoming a Teddy bear's picnic.

'Assess the situation you are dealing with. Are you dealing with a black or grizzly bear?'

'Climb a tree if available.'

'Don't announce your presence if a bear has not seen you.'

'Let the bear know you are of no threat.'

'If you come into contact with a bear, keep a close eye on its whereabouts.'

'Never look a bear in the eyes.'
'If attacked by a grizzly bear play dead.'
'If attacked by a black bear fight back.'

🚲

Startled from a sound sleep, this catalogue of conflicting advice scrambled in my brain. I could hear the rushing water of the creek but there was something else outside my tent too. I listened again. Perhaps it was just the breeze flapping the tent material. No, there it was again. Something big was in the bushes next to my camp. Bolt upright, motionless and hoping it was nothing more than a hungry racoon, I continued to tune into its movements, while my heartbeat pounded in my head.

That's some fucking racoon.

It was so close now I could hear the breath being drawn into its large hollow chest as it sniffed and scratched around the perimeter of my tent, its heavy paws pounding the ground inches from where I sat. I grabbed my bear bell, but was too scared to ring it. I sat paralysed by fear, and then remembered. My peanut butter.

Taking Dave's advice, I had taken a pot of the stuff to bed with me for those cold lonely moments.

The bear can smell my peanut butter ...

Trying to stay as still as possible, I fished the tub from the bottom of my sleeping bag and held it in front of me. There was only one thing for it: a sacrifice would have to be made. Slowly unzipping the front of my tent, I rolled the jar into the darkness. Terrified, I lay awake, not drifting back to sleep until the sun began to rise. Plucking up enough courage to get out of my tent, I saw that an immaculate white frost covered everything. My breath filled the air in front of my face, and I nervously inspected the camp. There was no trace of my peanut butter.

🚲

As I gained altitude, metre by metre, the air thinned and the temperature dropped. On hot sweaty climbs I peeled off layer after layer of windproof, waterproof clothing, only to put it all back on as the icy mountain air chilled me to the bone and stung my face on the fast, exhilarating descents through this literally breathtaking landscape. Childhood memories of queuing endlessly for a thirty-second roller-coaster ride returned to me as I spent hours trudging up steep climbs for only a few seconds of 'white-knuckle' decline, but as I continued my journey on the Icefields Parkway I rode with renewed energy towards the Columbia Icefields and the continental divide. A psychological milestone of the journey, it represented the highest point I would climb in North America, and the very top of the Rockies.

After a gruelling climb in driving snow, what I had been waiting for became visible through the whiteout in the valley below. Amid the snow, wind and glare the Columbia Icefields visitor centre appeared like an Antarctic base camp, surrounded by snow-mobiles, radio aerials and flashing lights. At 3,569 metres above sea level, I had crossed the continental divide. For months I had imagined this moment, standing tall on top of the world, blond hair and Union flag blowing in the wind as I surveyed the broken snow-capped peaks of the mountains spread out around me. Instead, wrapped up like a polar explorer, my snot-streaming red nose the only bit of skin exposed to the biting cold, I rode towards the visitor centre unable to see beyond the short distance of black tarmac that vanished into the whiteness only metres ahead.

As I waited outside the visitor centre, the snow blowing, a couple of young cagoule-clad hikers came and joined me.

'Come a long way?' they asked.

'London. You?'

'Devon. Sandwich?'

I took a damp triangle of bread and meat from a neat tinfoil parcel.

'Thank you.'

'We've been saving them just for this.'

And so, sitting on the continental divide of North America, I munched on a roast beef and horseradish sandwich. By no means the perfect meal, but as I huddled from the cold, the snow swirling in the white air, it tasted just great.

🚲

The melt-water from the vast Athabasca glacier rushes in three directions. To Alaska, to the Atlantic and west towards the Pacific. Having struggled in the opposite direction to the rushing waters that flowed east, I was now at last going with the flow and following the rushing rivers that poured west into British Columbia and the open waters of the Pacific.

Camped at the foot of Mount Robson in an area of deforested wasteland that resembled an abandoned battlefield, I was awakened at dawn by the all-too-familiar sound of rain on my tent. Looking at my map the Mount Robson visitor centre was close by and, if the other visitor centres were anything to go by, it would be open in a few hours and there would be some free over-brewed coffee there and possibly a rest room.

With my complimentary cup of stale yet reviving coffee, I sat on the steps of the visitor centre and waited for the rain to pass. Delving into my provisions I began preparing another peanut butter and honey sandwich.

'You're eating your way from New York to Rio, eh?'

'That's the plan.'

'You ever had a moose burger?'

'No, not yet. I seem to be living on these things at the moment.' I held up what remained of my sandwich.

'Well, that won't do. Why don't you come to dinner at my place tonight? I have a few burgers back home. I shot the moose myself, but I can't say that too loudly round here,' he finished with a conspiratorial whisper.

Scott was enthusiastic and optimistic, which is probably why he had got the job in the visitor centre. Aged about twenty-three, he lived in a trailer in a rundown trailer park on the edge of the railroad some thirty miles down the valley. I arrived early and waited on his porch, sketching for a few hours before Scott returned from work. As he pulled up in his rusty white Toyota truck, his round smiling face was a welcome sign.

'Come on in, come on in,' said Scott, opening the light screen door and leading me inside. I surveyed the chaos. The sink was overloaded with washing-up from another age, the walls were stained with damp and the floor was scattered with old newspapers and cat litter. I was quietly relieved when he apologised and said I should pitch my tent outside because he didn't have enough room to put me up.

'Shot the moose on the back side of Mount Robson last month and been saving the burgers for a special occasion,' said Scott, his head inside the filthy fridge that took up the majority of space in his small kitchen. Wrapped up in our warmest clothes, we sat on the tiny porch in front of his trailer. He grilled the burgers on a simple gas barbeque, while I sat spellbound by the tale of how he had stalked the beast before bringing it down with a quick kill to prevent the blood and adrenalin rushing into the animal's muscles and spoiling the taste of the meat. The moose tasted great, cleaner than beef, lean with a soft gamey flavour. Interrupted only by the passing freight trains that clanked down the valley on their way to Vancouver, we ate more burgers than we should have, washed down with plenty of the aptly named Moose Head Beer and a superb home-made blackberry port. Scott was quite the Rocky mountain gastronome, and before I said good night and crawled into my tent, he treated me to some potted smoke-cured salmon.

⍥

The Sockeye and Chinook salmon are some of our planet's most tireless journey-makers. Both members of the Pacific salmon family, they hatch from eggs in the interior lakes and rivers of British Columbia, often as far as a thousand miles upstream, then embark on a lengthy and treacherous journey downstream towards the salty waters of the Pacific. Once in the ocean they spend up to five years eating greedily and growing rapidly in the bountiful feeding grounds, building up enough strength and fat reserves for the long, uphill journey back, swimming against the current, into the Rocky mountains and their original spawning grounds to mate.

Rather like drunken men returning home from the pub, the way in which Pacific salmon return to the gravel bed in which they were born remains a mystery. Scientific thinking ranges from theories based on their having a highly developed sense of smell to following the stars, but either way after five years in the vast waters of the Pacific the salmon begin an arduous expedition back to their place of birth. These obsessive fish take on the ultimate aqua assault course. Dammed rivers, raging currents, hungry bears, waterfalls, fallen trees, patient fishermen and pollution are just a few of the formidable natural and man-made obstacles that ensure only the fittest of these magnificent creatures make it home. At this point the males do battle using their fierce hooked jaws, while females compete for optimum nesting space. For those that complete the mission, the ultimate prize awaits: sex and procreation.

I sat on the banks of the Fraser river where every inch of water was alive with bright pink salmon using the last of their strength to fight against the current and each other. Female fish thrashed in the water digging redds in which to lay their eggs, before waiting patiently for a lucky male to jockey into position, dump his milt and fertilise the nest. Once this journey and spawning is complete, both male and female fish die, having made the ultimate sacrifice for the continuation and strength of their species, and all along the riverbank, floating belly-up in the shallows, the lifeless, spent carcasses of those who have completed their mission waited to be cleaned up by the hungry bears and other scavengers whose lives depend on this natural food-delivery system. I watched in wonder at the climax of one of our planet's greatest migratory journeys, and one sacrilegious question raced through my mind. How can I get my teeth into some of this beautiful fish?

Scott had told me that the meat on the fish this high up the river was too far gone: worn out and lacking in flavour due to the depletion of fat. However, I was told that the local Simpcw people, a band of the Shuswap First Nation who have lived in the interior of British Columbia for at least 10,000 years, still fished the salmon this far upstream using traditional methods.

For centuries prior to the arrival of Europeans, the annual migration of salmon allowed the aboriginal people of what is now British Columbia to enjoy a high standard of living and economic prosperity. Salmon were deemed vital to physical health and spiritual wellbeing, and played a huge part in the cultural identity of these people. The salmon's return was celebrated, its arrival assuring the renewal and continuation of human and all other life, and the Native Americans developed sophisticated weirs to harvest the annual salmon run, drying and smoking their catch to preserve the fish in preparation for the fierce winters. However, the arrival of the white man meant that this reliable food supply was threatened.

After the discovery of gold deposits in the Fraser and Thompson rivers in the mid-nineteenth century, prospectors poured into the area and a brisk trade in salmon sprang up, driven by the demands of hungry miners. Coinciding with advances in shipping and the introduction of the canning process, ironically given to the world by the self-proclaimed guardians of gastronomy, the French, during the Napoleonic wars, it was now possible to pack the British Columbian salmon into canisters (cans) and send it all over Canada, the United States and Europe. By the end of the nineteenth century, canneries had sprung up along the lower stretches of the Fraser and the Thompson rivers as more and more investors got in on the 'salmon rush'. The huge demand for canned food during the First World War meant fish stocks plummeted and the very existence of the salmon on these mighty rivers, and the lives that relied on their annual migration, came under threat.

I spoke to a local journalist on the *North Thompson Star Journal* and was advised that if I was going to get to sample some of this salmon, the man I needed to find was Chief Nathan Mathew, who lived on the Dunn Lake reservation. The journalist kindly scribbled down some directions. Leaving the Yellowhead Highway at the small town of Little Fort, I cycled some way down a rundown road that ended at a simple platform ferry, just big enough to hold a pick-up truck, moored in the sun on the banks of the river. On deck a skinny man dressed from head to toe in faded denim slept in a fold-up chair.

'Is this the crossing for the Dunn Lake reservation?'

Opening his eyes he reluctantly pulled himself from his chair. 'Sure.'

He started the small engine, a series of heavy gears turned together and, as the rope slung from bank to bank passed through the mechanism, we slowly traversed the running waters of the Thompson river. On the other side, I rolled my bike down the gangplank, thanked the operator and set off up the steep rocky track that led into the woods. Cresting a hill I looked back over the river below me, the ferryboat and its operator both happily returned to their original positions. Enjoying a beautiful day, I followed the dirt road that weaved into the dense woodland. The further I rode into what locals referred to as 'the high country', the steeper the gradient became. The track I was following didn't exist on my map, and other than some crude directions scribbled on a piece of paper I had little idea where I was. Loose rocks skidded under my tyres, doing their best to tip me off, and at the start of another long climb I admitted defeat. I got out of the saddle and began to push. A pale blue pick-up rolled up behind me and came to a stop.

'Hot day for climbing hills. You want to pop your bike in the back. We'll take you up to the top.'

'Sure. Thank you.'

The kind couple were in their sixties, and would both have been beautiful when they were younger. Gordon looked like a more wrinkled Robert Redford, if such a thing were possible, and Gloria would have been the spit of Britt Ekland. Both still had blond hair and bright blue eyes, and their truck was a dusty, old-fashioned beast. From the rear-view mirror hung a collection of feathers, dried flowers and dream catchers, and the sweet smell in the back of the truck was overwhelmingly familiar. Like Burgundy in France, a region synonymous with its intoxicating export, British Columbia, with its perfect outdoor conditions, is increasingly known for the premium quality of its marijuana, known amongst those who know about these things as 'BC Bud'.

'We're just going to a favourite spot of ours, what with it being such a fine day.'

They came to a stop at the top of the hill and we took a short walk into the woods until we came to a small clearing and a pristine little lake. We sat on the ground, our backs against a large fallen tree. Gordon pulled out a leather pouch bulging with BC Bud. Never one to recommend cycling under the influence of anything stronger than a good cup of coffee, but being of a curious nature, I took a couple of puffs as we passed around the neatly rolled joint.

The warmth of the sun on my face and body became magical, and as my tired muscles relaxed the faultless beauty of the sky and the trees reflecting on the surface of the water captivated me, the image disturbed only by the delicate ripples sent out by insects that sculled above the surface, and a fish rising for food. The breeze caressed the leaves, translucent and glowing green in the rays of the afternoon sun, and the almost inaudible creaking of the boughs of the trees played as a backdrop to the careful footsteps of a small black water bird, tiptoeing through the shallows with a strange mechanical gait.

'Well, we best be moving on.'

I had no idea how long I had been sitting there, my mind wandering freely in the enchanted place, but after giving me a lengthy list of verbal directions to the reservation, Gordon and his wife said goodbye. As the sound of their engine faded into the forest, the first seeds of doubt were sewn in my mind. The directions I could remember were fighting each other for validity. I didn't know where I was or where I was going, but feeling good and with a smile on my face, I cycled on into this perfect afternoon.

The coolness of dusk crept up and what had been a blissful afternoon ride became a journey surrounded by the sinister calls and long shadows of the forest. I arrived at a small fork in the track, and the voices in my head all agreed that I was completely lost. However, the faint glow of lights in a dip in the valley ahead lifted my spirits. I hoped it was the reservation.

Dogs barked and howled as I got nearer. Glancing up a narrow, tunnel-like track flanked by high verges and dense undergrowth, I could make out the shape of an old homestead, illuminated by a single light on its porch. I cautiously cycled closer as the barking intensified. Then two wolf-like beasts came out of the gloom and charged down the track towards me, barking frenziedly, their pale coats and vicious snarling faces caught in the light on my handlebars. Panicked, stoned and terrified I leapt off my bike and clumsily turned it around. I jumped back on, scrambled for my pedals and took off while white fangs flashed at my ankles and panniers.

Back on the main track, my pursuers left behind, I continued, shaken and trembling. I came to a collection of simple houses and hoped that this, at last, would be the Dunn Lake reservation. There were no shops, no gas station, nowhere to ask for directions, and standing alone in the darkness I was only too aware of the curtains being pulled back as inquisitive faces sought a glimpse of the intruder.

Sod the salmon, this is simply not meant to be, I told myself, while another voice in my head told me to stick with it. After all, I had come all this way. I plucked up enough courage to knock on the door of the nearest house, and an impatient female face appeared in the tight gap that the door chain allowed.

'Good evening. I'm looking for the home of Chief Nathan Mathew. Any chance you can tell me—'

The door slammed shut.

'Who is it?' came a deep muffled voice rising above the din of the television.

'Some guy looking for Nathan's place ... I don't know. He's on a bicycle.'

The door opened again.

'Up the hill on the left, second turn on the right.'

Back among the shadows of the forest, I followed my orders, repeating them over and over like some Buddhist mantra, terrified of forgetting them.

Up the hill on the left, second turn on the right.

Up the hill on the left, second turn on the right.

Up the hill on the left, second turn on the right.

Up the hill on the left, second turn on the right.

Following the second turn on the right, I carefully approached a tidy log cabin.

'Good evening, is this the home of Chief Nathan Mathew?'

'It is. And you must be Tom.'

Welcomed into the warm house by Nathan's wife and his mother, I was encouraged to hear that Nathan had gone fishing. The journalist I had spoken to had tipped them off about my arrival, and when Nathan returned he was carrying a large salmon. Tall and well built with aquiline features, Nathan had a wise face. He was wearing a check shirt and jeans but every gesture he made and every word he spoke marked him out as a chief.

In the calm, warm surroundings of the Mathews' log cabin, which Nathan had built himself, my head began to clear. I explained the purpose of my trip and my desire to unearth local cuisine. He invited me to take an inviting and well-needed shower and then we sat down for a traditional Secwepemc meal of the salmon he had caught that afternoon with his dipping net, which leant by the front door.

In the soft electric light, Nathan's mother, a wizened but dignified old woman, said a few words of thanks in her native tongue and we began to eat. The salmon was cooked on an A-frame over coals in the yard. Nathan explained that by using a dipping net he was able to select the best fish from those making their way upstream, and he had chosen well. The smoky meat was dense and full of flavour. Hungry after the day's earlier exploits, I relished every mouthful.

My spirits soared when I was told we were having Indian ice cream for dessert, but when Nathan produced a bowl of small red berries I was confused. I watched in astonishment as he turned the handle of an old-fashioned whisk. These inconspicuous dark red berries quickly peaked into a pink cream as firm as any beaten egg whites. He added a little sugar and gave me a bowl. I spooned in my first mouthful of this fluffy flamingo-pink foam. It was sharp, almost as though citric acid had been added to a bowl of blackberries, but the texture was wonderful. The foaming nature of the berries was no doubt what led early European settlers to call them soap berries. Native people call them honshu, and Nathan's mother explained that they were rich in iron and often eaten fresh as a cure for stomach upset.

I popped one of the seemingly harmless berries into my mouth and my face puckered up in disgust at the bitterness. Without the addition of sugar they were uncomfortably sour.

Lying in a comfortable bed in the Mathews' guest room, I wondered who had made the remarkable discovery that these otherwise nondescript little berries could froth into a delicious creamy mousse when whipped. Other thoughts rushed through my mind too. What a day it had been, and what an ending. I had left New York on a bicycle nearly five months ago and here I was now only days away from Vancouver and crossing the great continent of North America. I had left Manhattan in search of the perfect meal, and tonight I had indeed eaten one. I had cycled past the glaciers that filled the rivers with fresh water. I had watched the beginning and the end of the salmon's epic journey, and here, with Nathan and his family, I had eaten that salmon, caught and prepared by the chief of an indigenous people whose culture, identity and very existence is reliant on the fish's annual run. I had enjoyed a perfect meal born of a faultless and yet fragile system and I had no doubt that on my journey this would be hard to beat.

In the Big Rock Candy Mountains there's a land that's fair
and bright
Where the handouts grow on bushes and you sleep out
every night
Where the boxcars are all empty and the sun shines every
day
On the birds and the bees and the cigarette trees
Where the lemonade springs where the bluebird sings
In the Big Rock Candy Mountains

Harry McClintock

Moose Burgers

Makes 6-8 burgers
1kg freshly minced moose meat*
1 onion, finely chopped
2 garlic cloves, crushed
1 egg
2 tablespoons soy sauce
1 tablespoon chopped fresh basil (dried will not do!)
1 pinch fresh thyme
1 pinch fresh rosemary leaves, chopped
1 teaspoon finely chopped fresh chilli
1 teaspoon salt
1 teaspoon freshly ground black pepper
to cook: a rasher of bacon for each burger
to serve: buns, Canadian cheddar, lettuce, tomato and sweet
    relish

1. Mix all the ingredients together in a large bowl using your hands. Take a good handful of the mixture and shape into a thick patty, then flatten to about an inch thick and set aside while you make the rest of the burgers.
2. Cook some rashers of bacon in a heavy frying pan until they have released their fat. Remove the bacon and set aside.
3. Place the burgers in the same hot pan and cook on each side for 3–4 minutes. The bacon fat will add a wonderful flavour.
4. Serve each burger in a bun with a chunky slab of Canadian cheddar, some sweet relish, tomato and lettuce.

*Fortunately for me, but perhaps a little less fortunate for the moose, my taste buds have been able to feast on such meat. However, it is impossible to find in butchers' shops, so if you want to indulge in a bit of moose you need to find a local who hunts or has access to a hunter. And to be in a country where moose live.

Indian Ice Cream

Serves 4 small portions
1 handful honshu (soap berries)
sugar to taste

1. Put a handful of honshu (soap berries) into a bowl. Add a little water and a heaped tablespoon of sugar and whisk until it foams into a salmon-pink mousse that peaks when you remove the spoon.
2. Add more sugar to suit your sweet tooth.

CHAPTER 4

california dreaming

OYSTERS, DUCKS AND DOGS ON THE LONG ROAD SOUTH

> I hate nature!
>
> *Chunk, The Goonies*

Unless you find yourself clutching a lavatory seat with your doctor's index finger two knuckles deep in your arsehole applying a suppository, there is no such thing as a bad oyster. Having left Canada, south of Vancouver, I was now cycling for food in Washington State's Olympic Peninsula, a cold and wet corner of America where the brackish, nutrient-rich waters and long, narrow inlets of the Puget Sound and the Hood Canal provide perfect feeding conditions for the most flavoursome and cleanest oysters on the planet.

Cycling through the fir forests that line the banks of the Hood Canal, a glacier-carved fjord with steep sides and deep cold waters perfect for growing meaty Pacific oysters and the area's home-town hero the Olympia oyster, I was desperate for a mollusc fix. I began to follow a series of home-made signs nailed to the telegraph poles along with tatty bags of old shells.

Tom Farmer Co. Oysters and Clams. 10 min

Tom Farmer Co. Oysters and Clams. 5 min

I pulled into a yard at the top of a hill where the ground was covered with years' worth of sun-bleached oyster shells. A boat sat on a trailer between two sheds, one of which had see-through rubber curtains hanging in its doorway. A radio played inside.

'Hello.'

A short man in dirty work jeans and a brown hooded jacket came outside. On his head was a squashed bobble hat. His face was rosy from the cold.

'Tom Farmer,' he said, holding out a calloused hand with short fat fingers.

'Tom.' I shook his wet hand and explained why an Englishman on a bicycle had just ridden up his drive with the aim of trying some of his oysters.

Behind the rubber curtains, a bored teenager was working through deep plastic baskets brimming over with jagged shells, checking each specimen before tossing them into another basket.

'These are Pacifics,' he said, pointing at one load, 'and these, our very own Olympias.'

He went on to explain that the Pacific oysters, *Crassostrea gigas*, were an import from Japan, which had been farmed in Washington State since the early 1900s. Big and hardy and less susceptible to disease, they accounted for the majority of the oyster production in the area, but it was clear from his enthusiasm that the second pile, the smaller Olympia oysters, *Ostrea lurida*, with delicate round shells, was a superior breed.

'This is the best oyster in the world,' he said, holding one aloft, before sliding his stubby shucking knife inside the small fluted shell and prising it open. 'One of those Arab princes has these guys flown wherever he wants 'em, on his own friggin' jet – I shit you not!'

And all I have to do is pull on the brakes, I thought, taking the shell I was offered, sipping the pale flesh into my mouth and swallowing. Mr Farmer wasn't wrong, and after telling me a little more about the ins and outs of farming these hermaphrodite bottom feeders, I ordered a dozen. He filled a net sack with twelve of these local bi-valve beauties.

'And you better take a dozen Pacifics too so you can tell the difference,' he said, adding them to the load and sending me on my way, refusing to take any money. 'I'll bill that Arab!' he called as I rolled down his driveway with two dozen of the world's greatest oysters strapped to my panniers. I was in for a good night.

☙

Loggers are an endangered species too

read the tatty bumper sticker that clung to the rust-infested chrome fender of a beaten-up maroon pick-up truck, which rumbled to a halt in front me. A pair of busy wipers cleared water off the large windscreen and rain beat a disorganised rhythm on the domed roof of the cab.

'You're sure leaving it late to cycle the peninsula,' said the bearded man in denim dungarees and a chequered shirt who leant from the passenger window. 'There some big ol' storms lining up out there.'

He was right. The sensible cyclist journeys the west coast of the United States in late summer. When the days are long, temperatures balmy and the beaches are dotted with sunbathing beauties. But paying the price of a delayed exit from New York, a lazy pace set in the Midwest and a lethargic crossing of the Rockies, I was now in Washington State in early winter. The days were short, it was cold and wet, and if anyone was wearing a bathing suit it was hidden beneath a hard exterior of chequered shirts, work clothes and heavy beards.

In late October in Washington State it rained and rained. Even when it wasn't raining, the water came down. Dribbling from sodden lichen and dripping from the branches of towering trees, collecting in glass beads along the coarse fronds of giant ferns and saturating cushions of dense moss. It spilled off roofs in neat streams and leaked from broken gutters, and it hung in the air in clouds of vapour spewed from the heavy wheels that screamed and span underneath the overloaded logging trucks roaring past me.

Cycling the long dark corridors that cut through tightly packed forests, I rode to a soundtrack of dripping water, my tyres hissing on the wet tarmac and the rhythmic rustle of my watertight garb, until disturbed by the scream of a chainsaw or the chilling crunch and crack of a falling tree. As well as oysters, western Washington is also logging country, and great trees were being ripped out of the ground with ruthless efficiency. Optimistic timber-company billboards did their best to persuade me that this systematic rape of Mother Nature was being done in the best possible way, but the steady routine of logging trucks piled high with the severed trunks of vast trees and the stump-littered wastelands stood as constant reminders of our insatiable appetite for profit at nature's expense.

I witnessed scenes reminiscent of First World War battlefields where monstrous muddy machines went to work, and felt the force of the overloaded, dirty beasts that engulfed me in a turbulent microclimate of wind, rain and woodchip as they roared past. It was hard to believe that the logging industry was in decline. But since leaving Seattle, with its comfortable coffee shops and shiny office blocks filled with affluent geeks, I was seeing a different corner of Washington State. Starbucks and software may bring billions to the city's manicured suburbs, but a few miles off the freeway I was seeing the other side of the Evergreen State.

As I followed the Hood Canal, the dishevelled towns I stopped in for coffee and food revealed the level of poverty in this hidden corner of America. Buildings were boarded up and left to rot. The rusting carcasses of abandoned vehicles filled junk-littered yards and, not for the first time on this trip, the cruel and destructive grip of crystal meth was mentioned in hushed tones.

'You be sure to watch out for those tweakers if you're sleeping rough,' advised the driver of the maroon truck, not lifting his hand from the large steering wheel when I asked where I could camp.

'You can take most forest trails into the woods, only watch out for dogs. People up here can be mighty funny about what's theirs. This might keep out the cold.'

He handed me a bottle of dark beer from a case between him and his dungaree-clad passenger on the sofa-like front seat. I peered through the small opening of my waterproof hood, thanked the men and said goodbye.

The bumper sticker disappeared into the gloom. Perhaps the last surviving pair of loggers had just given me a beer.

ڶ

Following a muddy trail a mile or two into the forest, so as not to be seen from the road, I unrolled my tent in the quickening darkness and bundled inside. It was just after 5 p.m. In torchlight I carefully organised my oysters into two neat piles. The Pacifics with their deep cupped shells, and the small Olympias, flat and elegant with fragile fluting.

With no shucking knife stashed in my panniers, I took my multi-tool penknife in one hand and wrapped a stale T-shirt around the other. I carefully inserted the blade into the hinge at the rear of my first Olympia, applying a strong twist and a light wiggle, so as not to damage the cargo inside. The stubborn muscle gave way and with my head torch shining down, I feasted my eyes on the flawless blue-beige flesh resting amongst the emerald hue of its pearly case.

They really are perfect, I thought, before sipping gently. *Sluuuuuuuuuuurp!*

Oh fuck, that's good!

Having been strapped to my bike for a couple of hours the oysters were the perfect temperature. A glorious briny flavour filled my mouth followed by a unique coppery finish and a light taste of vegetables. I savoured the creamy texture and wonderful taste of the ocean that kissed my lips before swallowing the goodness that filled my mouth. Without question it was the best oyster I had ever eaten, and I still had twenty-three to go. Popping the lid of my beer I took a short swig, and with the alcohol rushing through me I slipped into a wonderful oyster delirium. Alone in my tent until sunrise with two dozen oysters and a bottle of beer, I had the best oyster-and-porter house in the world.

⚙

After my one-man oyster festival I woke the next morning with energy restored. The entrance to my tent looked like the mouth of a sea otter's cave, and climbing over my discarded shells with the saline taste of oysters still on my lips, I packed and cycled west for Willapa Bay, another world-renowned oyster field, where I hoped to get my first view of the Pacific Ocean.

The back roads that cut through the forest eventually brought me to the grey wetlands of Willapa Bay. Oystercatchers and other needle-legged birds picked their way through shallow pools left behind by the retreating tide and the sinister silhouettes of cormorants perched on the rotting pillars of once busy docks. The ribbed skeletons of forgotten trawlers lay lopsided on the rippled mud and a large blue heron, disturbed by my passing, rose clumsily into the air, flapping oversized wings before taking off in lolloping flight and gliding to safety. The haunting laughter of other sea birds mocked me as I passed and what little sun there was broke through the heavy cloud and reflected purple and blue on the placid surface of water that collected around thick clumps of reeds. Channel markers blinked red and green, a sign for those needing to find their way through this treacherous network of mud and water.

Elma, Brady, Raymond, Bay Center. In the small hamlets of this coastal region, bright-coloured floats and buoys hung on the sides of shabby houses. Tangled nets and wire pots lay redundant by overturned dinghies. Crooked, hand-painted signs advertised oysters and clams, smoked and boiled, and hard-faced men in rubber dungarees, woolly hats and plastic boots worked on their trawlers in dry dock, or cleaned weed and barnacles from huge wire oyster cages.

As I crossed the wetlands on to Highway 101, the mud ceased, and in its place windswept dunes covered the peninsula like untidy grey sheets. Outside the small town of Long Beach I pushed my bike across the sand and on to an enormous beach, from which the town and this stubborn spit of land took its name. Wrapped in my balaclava, I took in the expanse of smooth grey sand, its wet surface mirroring the seagulls that swooped and dived in the gusting wind. Beyond the beach an ominous rolling mass of aggressive sea repeatedly thumped the deserted coastline.

'*Mare pacificum*,' declared the Portuguese explorer Ferdinand Magellan when he first laid eyes on this great ocean, but from where I was standing there was nothing pacific about it. It roared and growled and blew salty spray in horizontal sheets. Nervously I introduced myself. Almost six months before I had sat bare-chested on the wooden pier of Coney Island, New York, chewing a hotdog smothered in onions and mustard, the summer sun warm on my face, while looking through sunglasses across the blue waters and white horses of the Atlantic. Now I was standing wrapped head to toe in waterproof clothing squinting at the Pacific. I had crossed America and, allowing sentiment to get the better of common sense, I decided to camp in between the tall dunes behind the beach, where I would be lulled to sleep by the sound of the ocean that would be on my shoulder all the way to South America.

In a basin between two tall dunes, my sleeping bag was warm and the sand beneath my tent made for a soft mattress. Eager to have a basic grasp of the language before entering Mexico, I popped in my headphones and went through a few audio lessons of teach-yourself Spanish.

Me llamo Thomas.
Me llamo Thomas.
Vivo en Londres.
Vivo en Londres.
Quiero una hamburguesa.
Quiero una—
Pa tat ta pa ta pa pa ta.

The light pitter-patter of rain interrupted my studies.

Not to worry, a little rain won't hurt, I thought, and went back to class.

Pa tat ta pa ta pa pa ta.

As the drumming rain rose to a crescendo, the wind section joined in. The conductor waved his arms. The sides of the tent flapped and cracked. Not enjoying the tune, I turned up the volume again on my Spanish lesson.

Tengo un hermano y una hermana.

Pa papa pa papa a whoooaaaaaar phuppuppa reeeearch poing.

Powerful gusts pulled, tugged and ripped. I saw that my repairs were not holding up. The sound of tearing canvas accompanied violent cracks and flaps. The orchestral storm plucked the tent pegs one by one from the sandy ground. My Rocky mountain needlecraft was in tatters and my gaffer tape had given up. I was taking on water and it was time for a decision. Go down with the ship or scram.

Vamos vamos vamos.

Outside I could barely stand up. One defiant tent peg held on to my flysheet. The rain was horizontal, a fierce wind blasted sand into my face and, with my torch strapped to my head, I gathered everything I could, haphazardly strapped it to the bike and made a run for town. As I pushed over the dunes the deep sand worked with the wind to bring me down, but after an uncomfortable struggle I found the road.

Arriving back in Long Beach was like cycling on to a film set. Trash cans rolled in the street. Shops signs swung on their hinges and neon lights blinked in the darkness. Encouraged by the light and the muffled voice of Bob Dylan seeping from a small bar, I staggered in. A few washed-out old men acknowledged me before returning to their mugs of beer, as I made a puddle on the floor. I hoped the owner might take pity on the shipwrecked creature washed in from the storm, but he didn't and I turned back into the night.

'Some of the drifters sleep out by the baseball field when the weather turns but don't let the law catch you in there.'

Drifter indeed!

Opening the gate of the baseball field I sloshed through the puddles of the outfield to a wooden shed, similar to a bus station. It offered little shelter from the gravity-defying rain and a couple of beer cans already swam in the inches of water that filled its floor. But I lay down on the thin bench and, exhausted but unable to sleep, waited for the storm to pass.

The rain didn't stop, but the wind died down and at 6 a.m. I went in desperate search of coffee. On the road out of town a small diner came to my rescue. Passing the trucks parked out front, I waddled in. The Beach Boys sang from the kitchen about good vibrations while the wind rattled the large windows that looked out across the road to a video store and launderette. Taking a booth next to the window, I ran my tired eyes over the menu.

'What'll it be, sweet'art?' asked a middle-aged waitress in a soft low voice, turning over my thick china mug and filling it with steaming black coffee from a stained Pyrex jug.

'I'll take the Hangtown omelette, please.'

'You sure look like you need it,' she muttered sympathetically, before hollering at the kitchen with what little enthusiasm remained at the end of her long season. 'One five-egg Hangtown with wholemeal and home fries!'

'Thanks.' I handed back my menu and waited.

🚲

When gold was discovered in north-western California in 1850, the rush was on. Thousands of migrants crowded into the remote region in search of riches and a new life, and the effects of this mass migration were considerable. San Francisco grew from a tiny hamlet of tents to a boomtown, and roads, churches, schools and other towns soon followed. The supply of raw materials could barely meet the demand and before long the vast trees of Washington's forests were felled and shipped south. Sending ships north to pick up lumber, these vessels often returned to San Francisco supplementing their ballast with Olympic oysters. Once wealthy prospectors got a taste for these delightful little molluscs they became almost as valuable as the gold itself. So great was their popularity that, according to folklore, when asked what he wanted for his last meal, one condemned man in Hangtown, an insalubrious district of San Francisco, demanded the three most expensive ingredients in town.

'I want Olympia oysters, bacon and eggs,' he ordered, awaiting the noose.

A jail cook heated all three ingredients together in his only skillet, and the 'Hangtown fry' was born. Word spread amongst prospectors of this lavish dish, and before long it had became the meal of choice for those who had struck gold in the fields and mines of California.

After my miserable night I felt I deserved a treat, and as an enormous five-egg open omelette was placed in front of me, decorated with oysters and rashers of crispy bacon, I knew I had struck gold. It was crispy at the edges and gooey in the middle. I admired its yellow-brown colour and then began digging.

With a clean plate in front of me, I stared through the window, quivering in some kind of post-egg, caffeine and oyster trance while unnatural murmurings and loud bubbles resonated deep within me. The sign on the door of the Laundromat was at last flipped over and, dazed and confused, I meandered across the road. Stripped down to a well-worn pair of Marks and Spencer boxer shorts, bundled almost all my belongings into the drum of a huge tumble dryer and shut my eyes, mesmerised by the warm drone of Laundromat machinery. Marvin Gaye, grapevines and memories of Levis adverts came rushing home as I drifted to sleep.

The Astoria-Megler bridge across the Columbia river, connecting the states of Washington and Oregon, should be in a theme park. An aged metal structure, it runs flat across the river estuary, then climbs abruptly in an impossibly steep hump, hundreds of feet above the water, to allow tall ships to pass underneath.

As gale-force winds rushed down the river estuary, whistling in the squeaking metal girders around me, white horses kicked and reared on the water hundreds of feet below. Terrified, I took on the outrageous gradient of this big dipper that at six-and-a-half kilometres seemed like some cruel rite of passage, or, last examination of resolve before I could enter the Beaver State. But with five eggs powering my engine, I paused at the crest of the bridge only to peer up at the small sign riveted to the rusty framework:

Welcome to Oregon

Oregon had been well advertised and I was looking forward to my visit. I was now riding Highway 101, the road that would carry me all the way to the Mexican border, only 1,000 miles away. If people's descriptions of the coastline were accurate I was in for a stunning ride, but no sooner had I arrived than I was reminded of how far north I was this late in the year. Autumn was officially over and I was being punished for my laidback time-keeping. I am sure people had kindly held back on telling me about the bad weather I was heading into, but day after day and night after night the heavens opened, dumping their damp payload on me and my possessions.

Perpetually wrapped in waterproof jacket, trousers, gloves, hood and pixie-like booties, I sweated and steamed inside my plastic skin up and down the steep rolling hills of Highway 101. My worldly belongings were wrapped in a series of ziplock bags and bin liners, but rain being rain, it found its way everywhere. Maps turned to papier mâché, clothes were fungal and fetid, food was ruined and my permanently wet and wrinkled feet would not have looked out of place in a morgue. But as the only other option was to sit in my tent until March, when it might stop raining, I had no choice but to continue south in search of the sun.

Pitching my wet tent night after night and folding it away every morning, my one-time enthusiasm for camping waned. The days were short and there was little time for anything but cycling.

It seemed that after only a few hours of waking, darkness fell and I had to slip back into my mouldy, nylon bunker and sit out the long hours until sunrise, reading, writing and wondering what on earth I was doing. Resting during the day in cafés, shops and gas stations, I would stare blankly at TV screens showing cheerful men in suits standing before giant maps and satellite pictures that looked like disturbing baby scans.

'Looking at this system just here off the coast we can expect more rain, with some parts of northern Oregon seeing heavy rain, and some coastal areas getting as much as six inches overnight. This storm front gathering here will bring some strong winds gusting to 60 and 70 miles per hour ...'

After another broken night's sleep in an abandoned state park north of the Nehalem estuary, wondering whether or not my feeble repairs and long-suffering tent pegs would hold out against another storm, I woke to the familiar sound of rain tapping on my flysheet. Pulling on my saturated socks, I slipped into my wet shoes, which released their usual squelch, and tried to ignore how bad I smelt. Unzipping the front of my tent, I began the tedious routine of repacking everything I had unpacked the night before.

Back on the road, high above the shoreline, I could peer at the swelling water crashing around the towering sea stacks below, the rock formations that were stubborn testament to the land's losing battle against the elements. Heavy waves reared up before thumping down on smooth sandy beaches, spewing rolls of white foam towards heaps of washed-up lumber and debris. Violent gusts of wind did their best to blow me off course, firing sharp rain that stung my face, forcing me to squint tightly to see where I was going.

'Yeeeeeeeeee haa!'

Cresting a hill above the Nehalem estuary, I heard whoops of delight echo out of the low-hanging mist that clung to the coast. But no one in their right mind would be outside on a morning like this, let alone enjoying themselves. This was a day for Americans to sit on their sofas, clutching bags of potato chips while watching adverts on their televisions. How I wished I could join them. And yet, pulling over the next hill I was astonished to see a flotilla of motorboats zipping around the estuary, rushing between a series of bright orange buoys that burst through the gloom.

It was cold, wet and windy, but there is one advantage to cycling the Oregon coast in November: the abundance of Dungeness crab lurking beneath the rough waters. Found from central California to southern Alaska, these large crabs are prized for their sweet, tender meat. The cold waters of winter mean their flesh is dense and meaty, but more important still, the buttery fat cells that make Dungeness crab such a treat are full to bursting. A month before the commercial fishing season opens, the *Cancer magister* are plentiful and locals get their fill, fishing for their share of this local delicacy from docks and small motorboats.

Negotiating a steep downhill run of broken asphalt, I arrived in a rundown boatyard where lopsided rusty trawlers sat redundant and a couple of clinker-built huts stood on stilts over the water. Except for the fluorescent orange buoys that hung on walls or lay next to coils of old rope, plastic barrels, crates and nets, the place was colourless.

Private dock
NON-SLIP SHOES ONLY
MOVING DOCK CAN BE WET AND SLIPPERY

warned a faded sign. Beyond it a network of jetties zigzagged across the surface of the estuary. The laughter and cheering was coming from a few figures at the other end dressed from head to toe in bright yellow and orange uniforms. As the water slapped at the wood under my feet, I slipped and slid across the wet duckboards.

'You here for the crab?' a man in orange oilskins with a thick moustache asked as I drew closer.

'Sure.'

'Six bucks for a pot off the dock or I'll take you out in the boat for twenty-five.'

Pointing at a small aluminium motorboat, where an empty, family-sized bottle of Wild Turkey floated in the water collected in the hull, I decided my crab would be caught from the relative safety of the jetty. The man handed me a round crab ring, the size of a dustbin lid, knitted together with metal wire mesh, netting and rubber tubes. He picked a couple of decaying fish carcasses from a bucket and tossed them inside.

'Plenty crab down here, son,' announced one of the other men fishing from the dock, and with a clumsy throw I tossed my crab pot on to the water and watched as it slowly disappeared, leaving a floating trail of fish scales and guts.

'Turkey?'

One of the other waterproofed men handed me a half-litre bottle of bourbon. I took a polite swig.

'Thanks.'

After twenty cold minutes I was ordered to pull. Heaving in forty pounds of crab and fish guts on a cold wet rope, my soft office-job hands stung in complaint. Noticing my discomfort, my inebriated fellow crabbers mocked my every tug.

'Pull, you limey pussy.'

'What are you, French?'

To add injury to insult my pot emerged from the murky depths with nothing worth keeping. It was writhing with females but Oregon law states that only males of a certain size are good for the pot, and seeing as all my crabs had a furry flap between their legs, which determined they were of the fairer sex, they were allowed to crawl free. Pull after pull, insult after insult, I had nothing. After three hours standing in the rain being abused by drunk fishermen, I was finally blessed with a male Dungeness crab worthy of being boiled alive.

Invited back to the boatshed to cook my catch, I sat with the others around a shaky table, while our crustacea and a net bag of oysters were lowered into a deep cauldron of boiling sea water.

Drying off, we waited for our crabs and oysters to rise to the surface. Plenty more whiskey was passed between us and, surrounded by floats and hooks, motors and oily tools and faded photos of prize catches, I listened to the men's glum predictions for the forthcoming season. Twenty impatient minutes passed and up came the crab.

I feel very sorry for the Dungeness crab. While the great creator was kind enough to give it a perfect suit of armour to run around sideways in, she also created a creature that is just designed to be eaten. Cooking, cleaning, cracking and shelling crab may be a chore, it may be a little hard to dig the sweet flesh out of the claws, but the crab's shell makes the perfect dipping bowl, and the Dungeness crab has its own fat pockets that provide a buttery dip to die for. Bursting these sacks of golden fat into my inverted top shell I tapped in a couple of drops of chilli sauce and went to work. With a newspaper laid out in front of me, I ripped off limbs, breaking claws in my teeth to reveal rich hunks of rubbery claw meat, which I dipped into the golden liquid. I snapped and sucked leg cavities and scraped out the flaky flesh hidden within, before dipping half a dozen boiled Pacific oysters in what remained of the buttery puddle in the shell.

'Don't miss the heart,' advised one of the fishermen, piercing the crab's tiny ticker with a cocktail stick from my discarded wreckage of orange legs and broken claws. I dipped it, and popped it in and it tasted superb. Relishing the knowledge that I had caught this crab, each mouthful was worth every cold, wet mile it had taken me to get here, in a boatshed amongst fisherman, wrapped in my waterproofs, swigging Wild Turkey on the Oregon coast.

㚶

Fish & Chips, Broiled Steak and
Whole Deep-fried Chicken – best on the coast

Thus read the signs on the front of Garibaldi Pub some twelve miles down the coast, where my new fishermen friends said they would be drinking for the rest of the day. But inside the pub was deserted. A long wooden bar with a brass foot rail was dotted with empty stools. On the back wall a few video poker machines flashed and blinked with garish lights and beside them a jukebox sat silent next to a pool table with worn blue felt. On two televisions attached to the ceiling a group of cars raced round and round an oval track. On the walls, black and white photos of trawlers and bearded men with crabs hung next to posters of smiling blondes with big breasts and slender hips leaning over fast cars advertising beer. See what you get if you drink Budweiser.

Fat Tire, Mirror Pond, McMenamin, Rogue. A line of chrome taps ran half the length of the bar behind a couple of ashtrays, a bowl of peanuts and three dollars in tips left by the last customer. At the far end was cutlery wrapped in paper napkins, salt and pepper pots, mustard and ketchup. Two men stood idle behind the counter. One young, the other older and overweight and dressed in a grimy white chef's jacket. Perhaps he deep-fries the chickens? I took a stool and the young barman was chatty and engaged me with the usual 'what's your name and where do you come from'.

He poured me a pint of Mirror Pond IPA but wouldn't take my money, and I spent the rest of the afternoon drinking beer, good beer, drying out and shooting the breeze. The barman's name was Ken and he said I could sleep on the floor. The only downside was I had to stay until closing. But Ken and I got on well. He hadn't lived in the area long, but had an infectious charm and enthusiasm that made him instantly likable. He had lived here and worked there, and I enjoyed his stories. The afternoon became the evening and the bar filled up with locals.

'Well, what have we here?'

Ken's eyes lit up and turning on my stool I checked out the gang of women who had rolled into the bar.

'Looks like you're my wing man tonight.' Ken filled my glass again and went to work.

Blame it on the crabs, blame it on the oysters, blame it on the succession of lonely nights or most likely the litres of Mirror Pond and Wild Turkey sloshing in my system, but after Ken introduced me as a heroic English cyclist, the amorous advances and sultry looks I was getting from one of these women was too much to resist. She couldn't get enough of my tales about hungry bears, drinking with cowboys and sleeping rough in the wilds of her country and, as the evening progressed, while nibbling my earlobe she whispered the words I longed to hear.

'So are you gonna come back to my place?'

I had a think. Wake up on the peanut-shell-littered floor of the Garibaldi Pub, surrounded by the stench of stale beer and deep-fried chicken? Or wake up in a huge soft bed, next to a beautiful woman to the smell of brewing coffee?

'Let's go.'

At this stage Ken was getting on rather well with another of the girls, and after buying some beer to go, we piled into a truck and the party moved to a house set back in the hills some way from the coast. We were led through a large garage, full of fishing gear, skis and other American garage paraphernalia, to a living room with a huge television set in front of an enormous leather couch. Stuffed heads mounted on the wall peered at me with questioning glass eyes as I, tipsy on beer and lust, allowed myself to be taken upstairs.

🚲

I don't know what happened to Ken but I next saw him when he burst into the bedroom.

'Taarm, we gotta move.'

'But, but, I'm just ready to ... why?'

'Gather your shit, we're going.'

'But I—'

'Your girl here ain't quite as sweet as she makes out. Her friend tells me her husband is out hunting with his buddies and due back any time soon.'

'Husband? Buddies? Hunting?'

The enormous TV, fishing gear and animal trophies began to

make sense and, determined not to end my trip mounted with the other unfortunate beasts above a pretty brass plaque saying 'English Cyclist', I grabbed my clothes, jumped into Ken's truck and headed back to town. In the early hours Garibaldi was still dark. Behind the black form of the hills that ran to the coast the sun was introducing itself to the day, turning the night sky grey and purple. Making the most of the remaining cover of darkness, I thanked Ken and rode out of town.

After I left Garibaldi, the skies cleared and for a couple of happy days the rugged natural beauty of the Oregon coast was plain to see and, although it was still bitterly cold in the evenings, I was able to enjoy my first Pacific sunsets and they were every bit as beautiful as I had imagined. In front of a red, orange and purple sky the misty tree-covered hillsides ran down to endless empty beaches where the waves of the Pacific crashed on the shore. The rain and storms would torment me again but I began to understand why people raved about this unspoilt section of America's west coast.

⚄

Along with The Beatles and David Beckham, football hooligans are, alas, one of England's best-known exports. In almost every country I cycled through, my quiet announcement of where I was from was invariably followed by bad renditions of 'Love Me Do', questions about my relationship to David Beckham and whether or not I was a hooligan. It was the same in a mountain village in Colombia as a deserted town in the American Midwest. English football fans, or dare I say soccer fans, are infamous across the world for their over-zealous endorsement of their chosen team. But while English football fans may have the edge over their colonial cousins when it comes to aggression and passion, they have been completely outclassed when it comes to pre-match feeding habits.

The typical English football fan, with his one-size-fits-most team shirt pulled tight around his tattoo-decorated gut, might appease his pre-match hunger with a microwaved meat pie and a pint or two of powerful continental lager. The American football fan's pre-game feasting is as different as the football they play.

Cycling through the United States, explaining my pedal-powered culinary mission to anyone who would listen, I was told by a large number of folk, mainly big men in big trucks listening to rock music, that I need look no further.

'No need for you to pedal that bike to Brazil. You just need to get yourself to a tailgate party.'

'What's a tailgate party?'

It was kindly explained to me that before big sporting events in the United States, rival fans got together in the parking lots or fields near the stadium to eat, drink and be very merry.

'A bit like a picnic?'

'Well, yeah, but bigger.'

I was excited to discover that my time in Oregon coincided with the state's biggest football game of the year, between its two rival universities, the Eugene Ducks and the Corvallis Beavers, in what is romantically coined the 'civil war'. Cycling a hundred kilometres inland, I made for the university town of Eugene to stay with an old friend and to try and hunt down a ticket for the game and some tailgating.

Unlike in England, university football in America is big, big business. Games are televised to millions, players are bought and sold at huge cost and the Eugene Ducks play in a stadium of 60,000 seats that would be the envy of any Premier League English football club. But for all the abundance of seats I arrived in Eugene a week in advance and the game was already a sell-out. Tickets were not being passed on for love nor money, but having cycled almost 5,000 miles to be there I was not giving up without a fight. Putting on my best English accent I made a call.

'This is the press office of the Autzen stadium.'

'Good afternoon. My name's Tom and I'm riding my bicycle around the Americas in search of the perfect meal.' ... 'London, England.' ... 'Yes, I'm interested in writing an article about tailgating for a magazine in London.' ... 'Sure, thehungrycyclist.com.'

Giving the nice lady a white lie, a link to my website and the number where I was staying, I waited.

'Hi, Taarm, this is the director of hospitality at the Autzen stadium.'

'Oooh! Hello,' I replied, excited by the word 'hospitality'.

'I've been looking at your website and your trip sounds interesting. Why don't you come down here on game day and we'll show you how we tailgate out here? Say 10 a.m.'

🚲

Armed with pen and paper I stared up at the bowl of the Autzen stadium, a vast multi-storey construction surrounded by metal crowd fencing and with numerous bulky security officials who spoke to each other ostentatiously on walkie-talkies. Explaining who I was there to see, I was led through the bowels of the stadium, in and out of various elevators, before arriving at the director of hospitality's office.

'You must be the Hungry Cyclist.'

'Hi.'

Given an official-looking plastic pass to wear around my neck, which I was assured would take me wherever I wanted to go, I was introduced to a photographer and journalist from the university paper, the *Oregon Daily Emerald*, who wanted to write an article about the English cyclist's first tailgating experience. As I looked out from the office window, I began to understand what I had let myself in for.

I was expecting to see a couple of hundred cars lined up with a few well-heeled football fans standing around the boot handing out sausage rolls and Scotch eggs, but then I was forgetting this was America. First of all, a car would have looked totally out of place. For a big picnic you need a big vehicle, and stretching as far as I could see was row after row of pick-up trucks, vans, coaches and motor homes, all lined up next to each other underneath the green and gold flags and standards of the Ducks, which mingled in the breeze with the smoke of a thousand grills. Apparently over 80 per cent of American families own a grill or barbecue. From what I could see they were all here in Eugene. And so, armed with a pass, a photographer and my very own journalist, I went to join them.

Down at ground level the scene before me kicked off every one of my senses and I hadn't even put anything in my mouth. The sweet aromas of grilling meat and charcoal hung in the air. Huddles of singing men with painted faces banged their chests and roared at each other as they barged past me on their way to a gaggle of smiling blondes in skin-tight green and gold T-shirts and figure-hugging jeans. Bags of ice and charcoal were ripped open, canvas chairs unfolded, gazebos erected. Previous games' highlights were played out on huge flat-screen televisions attached to the sides of buses and motor homes, while grey-haired veterans sat in deckchairs discussing plays and formations. College kids looking for an extra buck walked amongst the crowds selling beer-coolers, scarves, balloons, hats and T-shirts. People greeted each other with powerful hugs and high fives. Rousing rock music competed with the heavy hip-hop beats that thumped from car stereos. Bear-like men in baggy football shirts played catch, spinning their pigskin high in the air. Kegs of beer were rolled from the backs of trucks and men dressed in aprons stood over smokers, grills and griddles discussing football tactics and cooking techniques.

Bloody T-bones, ribs and briskets were pulled from cooler boxes and laid down on piping hot grills, releasing angry hisses and billows of thick smoke. Spatchcocked chickens with golden skin and limbs akimbo sat on smoky griddles while sausages popped and spat, their hot fat causing flames to leap into the air. At this time-honoured gladiatorial contest the grill was king and virile men tended their fires while wives and daughters set up long tables with salads, slaws and pickles. Bottles of whiskey were passed between camps while others worked at the hand pumps of kegs of beer that foamed and frothed into plastic beakers. The whole place was brimming over with macho pride and it was only 11 a.m. Big men, big trucks, big grills and big cuts of meat. Wherever I looked food was being prepared and eaten on a grand scale, but overwhelmed and intimidated by this multitude of football-crazy, asphalt-dwelling omnivores, I didn't know where to begin.

A well-used Ducks apron wrapped around his swollen gut and beady sweat clinging to his forehead, a balding man of 300 pounds plus painted the inside of a rack of ribs with a dark syrup. Glossing the contour of each rib like a master craftsman, he then lay down his brush, turned the sizzling rack over with a pair of tongs and repeated the painstaking process on the other side. Next, the tongs were transferred to the handle of his half-drum grill while he meticulously fed soaked wood-chips in between the bars, like a child feeds an animal at a petting zoo. Thick smoke rose around his meat. He lowered the barrel lid and a tidy plume of smoke spiralled out of a hole at one end. After a long swig on his beer, he crushed the can in his hand, wiped his substantial forehead with the inside of his arm, sat down on the fender of his large Toyota truck and ripped the top off another beer.

'Excuse me, sir, I'm here from London England, doing some research on tailgating. Would you be able you tell me a little about your ribs?'

He eyed me up and down, taking special note of my Ducks baseball cap.

'Sure, you wanna beer?'

'Thanks.'

'Honey, this kid's come all the way from England, get him a beer.'

Peeling the metal foil off a sticky stack of ribs he had prepared earlier, he offered them to me. I picked out a meaty-looking pair with my fingers.

'Been marinatin' 'em for almost three days,' he announced proudly. 'But it's the cider-soaked hickory I smoke 'em in that gives 'em that sweet smoky flavour.'

From the moment my teeth ripped at the flesh on my first rib, my taste buds were sent on an epicurean adventure. Paprika, cayenne pepper, cumin and garlic, and then at the end the sweet, dry smoky flavour that lingered in my mouth. The man was a genius. Pork ribs are not easy to cook. Leave them on the grill for too long and you end up gnawing on dried-out pig flesh, the majority of which gets stuck in your teeth. Undercook a ribrack and you are left with a mouthful of slimy swine. The meat on these slender curved bones was sticky and tender. Taking another brace, I chewed, the photographer clicked and the eating began in earnest. So did the speculating.

'I think he's some journo from England.'

'Goes around on his bicycle.'

'Some limey from the Food Network or the BBC I think, looking for tailgate recipes.'

'He kinda looks like that naked guy with the funny accent.'

Never let the truth get in the way of a good story. As news of my false fame mingled with the grill smoke wafting around the park, I was happily commandeered from tailgate to tailgate.

'Been slow-cooking this brisket since two a.m.,' said one man, proudly revealing a bloody slab of meat then cutting me a couple of strips that were succulent and full of flame-charred flavour. Another handed me a juicy pulled-pork sandwich, a traditional southern treat of slow-cooked pork shredded and served in a bap. It was dripping in a fantastic barbecue sauce.

'Wow! What's that sauce?' I asked, chewing on a mouthful of pig.

'I tell you, I gotta' kill you,' replied the man, looking like he would. I said no more.

'Shrimp on the engine,' yelled another man, unwrapping a foil parcel to reveal a cluster of pink shrimp, marinated with chilli and garlic, which he claimed had been cooking on the engine of a school bus he drove over in, but they were delicious with no hint of diesel. He took me on a guided tour of the bus he had lovingly converted into a yellow and green shrine to his beloved team. The man was clearly mad.

I was given my first oyster burger, a firm pâté of Pacifics seasoned with cilantro and lime zest that tasted so much better than it should have. The donor was so impressed with my trip he led me halfway around the parking lot to try a friend's clam chowder.

'Karl, give this boy a cup of your victory clam chowder,' he bellowed at his friend, swinging an arm over my shoulder and pulling me under the gazebo attached to the side of the vast motor home, where I was given a warm plastic beaker of creamy gloop. I took a sip. It was smooth, creamy and delicious.

'It's the nectar in razor clams that makes it so special,' added Karl quietly, and I took his word for it.

Being close enough to the coast, this wasn't a primitive meat feast. Other fish and shellfish were also being smoked in custom smokers around the car park, and a tender hunk of smoked Albacore tuna was the nicest thing I had ever put in my mouth, until I tried one of same man's slow-smoked scallops.

'You gotta soak the plank for three or four days so when it gets hot it releases that sweet-tasting steam into the fish,' explained a man with a Ducks baseball cap pulled backwards on his head, concentrating on a 20-pound King salmon steaming on a plank of wood laid over his hot coals. He pulled away a side of pink flesh and offered me some. I took a bite and he was right, the flavour of the wood had infused the succulent pink meat and it was amazing. Moving from grill to grill this 'fan-fare' kept coming. A tenderloin of beef was pink and tender inside a smoky blackened crust; coils of bratwurst sausages simmered in deep skillets topped up with beer; warm Buffalo chicken wings were so sticky I thought I would be licking my fingers for days; chilli bubbled in electric cauldrons. Bear-hugged, slapped, chest-pumped and man-handled from grill to grill, tailgate to tailgate, for five happy hours I sampled the very best that Oregon's game-day gourmets could throw at me. But there was a problem. For every tailgate I gate-crashed, American hospitality insisted I toast the home team.

'Go Ducks!' I raised a beer.

'Go Ducks!' Another beer.

'Go Ducks!' A whiskey chaser.

'Go Ducks!' A shot of Jägermeister.

'Gwo Dushks.' More beer.

After five or six hours I was a broken man and unable to take any more. I waddled about the party marvelling at the sights, sounds and smells of this glorious American feast. Sure, for the latte-sipping liberals in the US who are desperately trying to shed the stereotype that their countrymen are a bunch of gas-guzzling, loud-mouthed, meat-eating sports fans, tailgating is going to be about as popular as a midweek Klan meeting. But for those who believe American culinary culture is dying due to the pandemic rise of Walmart and fast food, tailgating is testament that it is not. Because if you replace the motor homes and SUVs with horses and chuck wagons, change the multi-level gas smokers and Pac-light gazebos for open fires and canvas tents, this is how Americans were eating when they first settled in the west. People travelling far and wide, coming together for a common cause to eat fresh food, made from local ingredients, and prepared using techniques of smoking, curing and broiling that are as old as Oregon. Like it or not, a tailgate party is a great opportunity to see that, contrary to popular belief, Americans are deeply proud and passionate about the food they so enjoy eating.

The band started to play, the rowdy army of beer-swilling tail-gaters were primed to cheer the on-field exploits of their daring young gridders and, en masse, they marched for the Autzen stadium. Drunk and bloated I was swept up in the advance. Inside the stadium a hundred-strong marching band were going through their immaculate synchronised repertoire, while leggy cheerleaders in pleated skirts flipped and twisted, their green and gold pom-poms bouncing in time to the music. An eight-foot furry duck mocked an eight-foot furry beaver and, as I took my seat in the stands just behind the home bench, the beloved Ducks charged on to the field. The roar of 60,000 fans blew my head apart. This was the civil war, the biggest game of the Oregon season and, surrounded by 60,000 crazed sports fans, I didn't have a clue what was going on, but I cheered the Ducks home to a convincing victory.

> We are strangers in this far off land and those who inhabit
> it and the beautiful ... which surrounds us in Oregon, but
> could you see our land of enchantment! Though the coun-
> try is new we have no aristocracy and no high style of
> living. Still we enjoy life as those who roll in luxury ... 'tis
> not wealth but contentment conscience clear of offense
> that makes the sum total of this life.
>
> *Eugene Skinner 1860*

No sooner had I finished digesting the delights of my first tailgate party than another traditional American festival of eating beck-oned. Thanksgiving weekend.

In 1620 the *Mayflower* landed in Plymouth, Massachusetts with around sixty passengers who had made the perilous journey from Plymouth, England in search of a new life in an apparently resource-full New World. But their fortunes were short-lived. Completely ill-equipped to deal with the harsh climate of this strange new land, in the winter of 1620 almost half the colonists' party perished.

But aided by the friendly Wampanoag Indians, who taught them how to fish, hunt and plant this new land, by the winter of 1621 the pilgrims' circumstances had improved. With enough food stored to see them through the winter, they put on a harvest supper to give thanks for their bounty and, inviting the Wampanoag, they feasted on corn, pumpkin, lobster, fish and wild turkey.

Since that very first turkey dinner in 1621, Thanksgiving has remained a time-honoured American family-feast and on the third Thursday of November each year Americans get together to munch their way through over 45 million birds. Thanksgiving was a dinner date on the American calendar I didn't want to miss, but unless I wanted to share it with myself, a reconstituted turkey burger and a pumpkin pie McFlurry, I would need to impose my malodorous person and ravenous hunger on an unsuspecting American family and, thankfully, the hospitality in Oregon was warmer than the weather.

Resting from the rain over a cup of coffee on my way to Eugene, I was divulging to a pretty waitress my tales of culinary derring-do when my ramblings were overheard. As well as triggering a tedious recitation of the girl's English heritage and whether or not I knew her second cousin, who she believed lived in Manchester, they also sparked the interest of the kind couple sitting next to me, who invited me to stay for Thanksgiving, promising turkey, pumpkin pie, beautiful women and rock stars. How could I possibly refuse?

After a wretched night camping behind the public toilets in a highway rest area just north of Roseburg, I arrived the next day, dirty and dishevelled, on the Arnesons' doorstep. Armed with a couple of bottles of Californian wine and the ingredients for bread sauce, I rang the bell. After a brief wait the front door opened to one of the happiest weekends of my journey.

Enjoying a well-needed night's sleep on their sofa I was woken, on my inaugural Thanksgiving morning, to the sound of a busy kitchen. Two monstrous pink-skinned birds were being removed from a brine soak, and once cooked would provide the all-American centrepiece of Thanksgiving dinners from New York to San Francisco.

The bald eagle, a striking and powerful bird with sharp eyes and menacing talons, is the national bird of the United States, but looking at history it's arguable that the turkey has claims to the illustrious post. Admittedly the fat, feathered fowl with its ugly purple snoods and wattles would not have the same awe-inspiring presence as the elegant eagle, and perhaps announcing 'The turkey has landed' would not have had the same heroic impact when *Apollo 11* plopped down on the moon, but the modest turkey, an indigenous fowl of the Americas, surely has a case. Even the founding father and sixth president of the USA, Benjamin Franklin, was a keen advocate of the gobbler. He wrote to his daughter when considering the attributes of the turkey over the eagle:

'I am on this account not displeased that the figure is not known as a Bald Eagle, but looks more like a Turkey. For the truth the turkey is in Comparison a much more respectable Bird, and withal a true original Native of America ... He is besides, though a little vain & silly, a Bird of Courage, and would not hesitate to attack a Grenadier of the British Guards who should presume to invade his Farm Yard with a red Coat on.'

I was yet to be attacked and sent running from my tent by an irate wild Tom, but having spent a weekend in Frazee, the turkey capital of the world, I was in no doubt of the turkey's prominent place in American history. After helping truss and stuff the Arnesons' birds, I was put to work converting their garage into a Bedouin Tex-mex Thanksgiving grotto. Rugs were laid on the floor, fairy-lights hung from the ceiling and colourful drapes covered every wall. Enough tables and chairs were unfolded for thirty hungry Thanksgivers, and as the day drew on the Arnesons' house filled up with friends, family and the smell of cooking. With each ring on the doorbell another friendly face appeared and another dish was added to this pot-luck feast.

Orange hunks of sweet potatoes, creamy heaps of mashed potato, shiny glazed carrots, cranberry sauce, green bean casserole, gravies and pumpkin pie. Everything was laid out for the feast. And not wanting to be outdone, and feeling a good 'Red Coat' recipe was lacking, I put together my bread sauce. After a few initial jibes that all I had brought to the table was some Dickensian gruel, my greying gunge received rave reviews. Feeling like a Lycra-clad Marco Polo introducing pasta to Europe, I revelled in pride as the vegetarian contingent of the party delighted in the clove and onion-infused grey gloop that they said would ...
'Go great with our tofurkey.'

'Toffwhat?' I asked. Was this some rare fowl yet to grace the supermarket shelves of London?

'It's a turkey made of tofu,' replied one chirpy veggie.

I half expected a lifesize faux turkey sculpted from tofu to be unveiled from under the tinfoil, but instead I was presented with a thick brown log filled with what I'll admit looked like very tasty stuffing.

'May I?'

I cut a thin slice, chewed my first mouthful and winced in disgust. It was like eating the sponge used to clean the oven on Boxing Day. It had all the flavours of turkey but what I had in my mouth had absolutely no meat-like characteristics.

'Interesting,' I returned, not wanting to get bogged down in a debate on animal cruelty and the celestial qualities of bacon sandwiches, but I was left wondering what the pilgrims who landed in Plymouth in 1620 would make of this strange man-made mongrel. Either way the tofurkey had certainly landed, and with all the trimmings ready and everyone in place it was time for the real stars of the show to take centre stage. Two plump, golden, turkeys were unveiled, one roasted in the oven, the other on the barbecue. The men of the house began probing and prodding, saying 'hmmm' and 'ahhh' like mad scientists, until removing their digital meat thermometers and other surgical instruments they announced the birds 'done'.

It would be fair to say that my fondness for the traditional Thanksgiving plate goes about as far as my love for an English Christmas dinner. Turkey, mashed potatoes, cranberry relish, bean casserole, pumpkin pie and a little bread sauce will never, in my eyes, be a perfect meal, but throw in the vital ingredients of good friends, family, laughter, tradition, wine, music and a little tequila, and you get pretty close to perfection.

All over America families and friends were gathering just like we were, perhaps not in a garage, but they were getting together to give thanks just like their forefathers had done in 1621. Giving thanks for friends, for family and for the food they were eating. While my knackered digestive system mulled over the tryptophan-rich turkey sitting in my stomach, I began to digest my journey to this happy point. Without the unlimited kindness of strangers such as Jim and Pat Arneson, this trip would be very different, if not impossible. This was food at its most powerful and I had much to give thanks for.

'No. It can't be. They must have shrunk in the wash ... but I haven't washed them. I've cycled almost five thousand miles on an overloaded bicycle. I'm an athlete!'

Bathroom scales never lie, and glancing down, over a well-rounded gut, I came to the embarrassing realisation that I must be the first person in history to cycle across the American continent and gain weight. After a few quiet words of reassurance to convince myself that a man pedalling the world in search of the perfect meal should be a little soft at the edges, I said goodbye to the Arnesons and cycled into another damp Oregon afternoon. After the kindness and warmth I had received over my Thanksgiving weekend, the world outside seemed bleak and cold. The sunshine of California was still some way away and I needed to start putting in some miles and get south.

My first night back under canvas, after a three-night Thanksgiving rest, was a stark reminder of how cold and lonely life on the road could be. The sun disappeared behind the hills of Oregon, the biting cold that had plagued me since Vancouver returned, and in a sodden field in the rundown logging hamlet of Porter Creek I pitched my tent before deciding to take a few hours' refuge in the general store glowing in the darkness beyond.

No different to any other small-town American store, it sold large amounts of beer and little else. Candy, razor blades, aspirin, Alka Seltzer, cigarettes, a few lonely tins of ravioli, a dusty pack of Fig Newtons, some glow-in-the-dark fishing lures and a jar of fluorescent pink objects claiming to be pickled sausages. But it was warm in there, and at five in the afternoon, I killed a few hours before I could go to sleep. To the dull hum of the beer refrigerators I drank cups of filthy over-brewed coffee, wrote my journal and listened to the rambling tales of the owner.

Bald apart from a few tufts of grey hair that sprouted from behind his rubbery ears, his chinless face small and ruddy, he wore a thick chequered shirt, open at the collar to reveal a T-shirt underneath that might once have been white, and a pair of jeans pulled high up to his navel.

'There's things in my brain they don't want people knowing about,' he whispered as I handed over a damp dollar bill for a refill of the stale coffee that was sweating in a dusty percolator, and a pink sausage.

'Oh yeah?' I replied with an ounce of intrigue as he fished in the jar with a pair of dirty plastic tongs.

'I designed the computer program that can locate every nuclear submarine in the US fleet ...'

'Wow, how does that work? I mean ...'

He secured a sausage. 'I might have to be whisked away and flown to a nuclear submarine to fix their circuit boards at any minute.' He held out the flaccid pink object.

'Cool.' I took it and bit in.

'Just thought you should know.'

The sausage tasted like pickled plastic. I dropped it in the trash can.

A little later I said goodnight. I returned to my tent, put on my beloved knitted socks and did my best to get warm and to sleep, ready to take on the hills that would lead me back to the Pacific coast and Highway 101, but all the time expecting the imminent whirr of rotor blades.

Welcome to California – The Golden State

informed the blue sign just north of Crescent City, but in the drizzle and low-lying cloud of early December it felt more like oxidised lead than precious metal. Owing to misspent teenage years mesmerised by TV shows based in the Golden State, I assumed that simply by crossing the state line into California I would cycle into a land of endless sunshine, where bottle-blondes with blow-up boobs drove red convertibles along twisting palm-lined coastal highways while listening to The Beach Boys. But as I cycled into the redwood forests, David Hasselhoff and his bevy of bathing suit-clad beauties were nowhere to be seen and the cold, wet reality of my arrival could not have been further from my puerile fantasies. Charming Victorian logging towns now converted into summer tourist traps would have been a heaving mass of semi-naked flesh during the summer, but in December they were inhabited by a few bearded locals with bad teeth, who grumbled when I asked if I could use the rest room. Northern California was everything but the paradise I had been dreaming of, and yet for all my yearnings and forlorn grumblings, on my first night in the Golden State I didn't sleep alone.

Pulling into the Talowa Downs State Park, I picked a spot hidden amongst the towering trees where a thick carpet of pine needles and bracken were relatively dry, unrolled my tent and in apparent solitude went through the unthinking process of assembly. Inside, patterns of mould decorated the lining and the floor was shiny with stale moisture. The airless environment smelt like a post-rugby match laundry basket. As I climbed in unenthusiastically, I heard a voice behind me.

'Matt,' said a young man of about my age.

'Tom,' I replied.

Matt was homeless, and camping in the park with his girlfriend, Lisa. He asked if I had plans for supper.

Mentally I went through the contents of my front-right pannier: tin of tuna, half a head of garlic, red onion, pasta, tired hunk of cheese, two apples ...

'Nothing special,' I replied.

'Well, come and join us.'

In my waterproof clothing I followed Matt through the forest, rustling like a wet packet of crisps, until we arrived at their impressive camp hidden amongst the thick tree trunks. As well as a spacious tent, they had a small area in which they cooked and ate that was protected from the rain by a large green tarpaulin. On a park table they had an impressive collection of pots and pans and a small gas stove-top with two burners. A gas lantern covered everything with a warm glow. As far as homeless folk went they seemed to have it pretty good. Sharing stories, we prepared supper and Matt explained their predicament. Having been unable to keep up the payments on their home back east they had moved to California to find work and a place to live. They had been camping in the woods since summer, which they said was perfect (and I could believe it), but now they said the rain was starting to get them down.

Their selection of food was remarkable, and as my eyes widened at the bars of chocolate, tubs of peanut butter, bags of rice and fancy jars of pesto that materialised from their tent, they both noted my surprise and explained the wonders of California's food banks. Nonprofit, charitable organisations, food banks receive food from manufacturers, wholesalers, supermarkets, restaurants and the general public, which is then distributed to needy families, children and individuals free of charge.

But the pride of Matt's abundant larder was a collection of wild mushrooms he had picked while walking his dogs in the woods, which included bright yellow trumpet-shaped chanterelles and wrinkle-capped morels. Pooling our resources, we enjoyed a hand-some supper. A simple salad niçoise, only let down by my tinned tuna, was followed by heaped bowls of pasta topped with the meaty morels and the earthy chanterelles sautéed in a little butter.

This couple may have been without a home, but they certainly had a kitchen, and they knew how to use it. The superb campsite supper was topped off with a bar of unusually good American chocolate and a pot of organic coffee, to which Matt added a healthy glug of whiskey.

'The food banks give you whiskey too?' I asked, warming my hands on my mug, having already decided that I needed to visit one of these charitable bounties.

'Afraid not. We just have this to keep out the cold.'

Which indeed it did. But only for so long, and succumbing to the bitter temperature we retreated to the relative warmth of our sleeping bags. The cold earth seeped through my damp camping mattress and I had to wriggle around in an attempt to generate a little warmth, but the whiskey served its purpose and I drifted into some kind of sleep.

'Hey, Taaarm – you awake?'

Matt's voice caught me somewhere in that blissful no-man's-land between consciousness and sleep. I took a few moments to answer.

'Um yeah – kind of.'

'You warm enough in there?'

'Um yeah – kind of.'

'You need some company?'

From what I had determined at supper, Matt and Lisa were a couple, but his late-night proposition had me befuddled. This was California after all. I'd once been offered a blowjob by a perfectly respectable-looking Frenchman while cycling in the back country of France, so you never knew your luck.

'Ummm … ' I mumbled, unsure how to respond.

'Well, suit yourself, but you're welcome to have Chewbacca for the night.'

Opening my tent, I found Matt there with Chewbacca at his heel. A glorious 200 pounds of slobbering Newfoundland.

'Wow! OK, thanks.'

Dutifully wandering into my tent, Chewbacca lay down next to me in what little space there was. Curled up next to his thick black hair, with my head resting on the warmth of his heaving chest, I slept. Apart from some lusty snoring, unsavoury breath and drooling on the pillow, Chewbacca was the perfect gentleman. I enjoyed one of my most comfortable nights under canvas, but when I unzipped my tent in the morning he left without a word, and with numb fingers I packed up alone.

TREE DOWN
NO through traffic
Road closed

warned the sign at the entrance to the Avenue of the Giants, but being a typical cyclist I ignored the traffic signal and wheeled my bicycle under the black and yellow tape. Having come this far in the wind and rain, I was not going to miss my chance to ride this world-famous road through the ancient groves that are home to the largest remaining virgin redwoods on earth.

It was like cycling into one of Europe's great cathedrals. The wide trunks of thousand-year-old trees ran skyward like stony pillars, their dense branches vaulting out to create a ceiling hundreds of feet above me. Rays pierced the dense foliage overhead sending shards of light through the shadows, highlighting the intricate mosses, creepers and ferns that decorated the floor of this immaculate habitat. These mighty trees have towered over northern California for millennia, withstanding generation after generation of natural and human disasters, and with the road closed I had the largest living organisms on the planet all to myself. America may not have buildings of any great age but the giant redwoods of northern California more than make up for that. Passing in among their shadows I felt blissfully unimportant.

But for all the natural beauty that surrounded me, it was hard to keep my spirits up. Riding a bicycle can be the perfect remedy for the blues, you can pedal them right out of your system, but being alone with your thoughts for so long can have the opposite effect. Soon I began to question the validity of my whole journey.

I could have a career, a relationship, a home. What can I possibly gain from all this? Why have I created this strange new identity?

I had no answers to the questions I was asking and my mood plummeted. I rode alone through the dark days and at night vivid dreams of friends and family entertained me while I slept only to be smashed into a hazy reality when I awoke. For a few blissful seconds I had been home again, life was normal, but staring up at the stale interior of my tent I was reminded where I was, trapped in this trip. Mustering enough enthusiasm to unzip my tent to a new day, I stood exhausted, staring at my loaded bike, wondering how I ever got into this mess. Another day of up and down beckoned. Like the day before and the day before that. What was I trying to prove and what was this all for? Charity, pride, vanity?

Cycling a loaded bicycle uphill is hard enough. Riding with a heavy heart only added to the burden.

How many Mexicans does it take to push a van through a tree? As well as the abundant drive-through restaurants, banks and coffee shops that allow Americans to carry on with their day-to-day lives without having to leave the comfort of their climate-controlled, air-bag protected, globally positioned sports utility vehicles, they also have a few drive-through trees. No, really. On my last day amongst the Redwoods I arrived at Leggett's Chandelier, a famous Drive-Thru Tree, a towering 300-foot sequoia whose gaping trunk had on this occasion resisted the ambitions of a blue panel van. Behind the vehicle a team of red-faced Mexicans were doing their best to push the vehicle through. Propping up my bike, I joined in.

'Un, dos, tres!'

'Un, dos, tres!'

After some wheel spinning and gear crunching the van came loose, minus a wing mirror. The Mexicans cheered and as a reward for my efforts I joined the men for a picnic of burritos and beer. I was given a bulging wrap the size of child's head. The folded tortilla was packed tight with rice, tender strips of grilled beef, refried beans, guacamole, sour cream and plenty of cilantro. Washed down with a cold bottle of Corona, I had my first real taste of Mexico and my new friends, a lively group of dishwashers, cooks and mechanics from Los Angeles, buoyed me with positive tales from their homeland. They waxed lyrical about the kindness of the people, the beauty of the women, the lively music and they enthused endlessly about the food.

Rallied by these words of enthusiasm and full of beans, I rode through the Chandelier tree again before giving each of my new amigos a turn on my bicycle. Ringing the bell we each rode through the trunk of this great tree, which seemed to act as a gateway to happier times. Saying goodbye amid warm wishes for my journey, I made the satisfying climb to the top of the Leggett Hill. I came out of the darkness and cool shadows of the forest and the sun, reflected off the swelling silver surface of the Pacific, dazzled me. The mist that normally clung stubbornly to the bluffs had burnt away, and following a perfect stretch of road I could see the coastline stretch for miles ahead of me into a hazy horizon. I breathed in the smell of the ocean, tasted its salt on my lips and rejoiced at the warmth of the sun on my face.

After such a long, cold ride through the north-west states, I needed a drink. I turned away from the Pacific and cycled inland into the rolling hills of the Anderson valley, Mendocino County. Located in the coastal belt about a hundred miles north of San Francisco, this quiet wine-producing region is only fifteen miles from the cold waters of the Pacific, and being so close to the ocean, it enjoys a varied range of daily temperatures. From the saddle of my bicycle I was only too aware of the bitterly cold nights, misty mornings, balmy afternoons and chilly evenings that allow the wine growers of the Anderson valley to develop the acid and sugar formation of their grapes, producing some of the best pinot noir in North America, as well as superb gewürztraminer and Riesling.

Narrow roads meandered in and out of valleys where the early morning fog shrouded the world, until the sun went to work evicting the sea mist to reveal the twisted limbs of ancient oaks that lingered against this grey backdrop. After the last wisps of sea mist evaporated, a verdant landscape was unveiled. Healthy-looking sheep pulled at damp grass in the shade of misshapen leafless trees, whose roots grew out of the steep-sided gullies and basins, while the shallow slopes supported neat rows of empty vines that ran over the hills like the weave of a fine material. Pieces of wood nailed to trees advertised family-run wineries that lay hidden at the bottom of bumpy lanes overgrown with hedgerows. Here I found friendly wine-makers who were only too happy to lubricate my cracking knees and aching muscles with the fruit of their labour. Camping where I could, I wobbled from vineyard to vineyard. Slowly falling in love with the Anderson valley and the easy life of pedal-powered wine-tasting, I slept through the cold nights that made this region so unique, while during the day I felt the same sun on my face that helped develop the sugars in the grapes. I'm sure the county sheriff would disagree, but cycling and wine-tasting were a perfect match.

Leaving the rustic charm of the Anderson valley, the road led into the affluent heart of American wine-making, Napa, and as if an excess of alcohol had affected my vision, rusty pick-ups morphed into European sports cars, lumberjack shirts were replaced by designer labels and weathered faces changed to unnaturally smooth complexions. Rustic family-run wineries became enormous grand enterprises round which minibuses full of wine fans trooped on organised tours. It was wine-tasting Disneyland, and heading to Yountville I hoped I might get a table with Walt, who goes by the name of Chef Thomas Keller.

If, as many believe, the French Laundry is the American culinary Mecca, then Chef Thomas Keller is the prophet Muhammad. By all accounts it is the finest restaurant in the USA, if not the world, and reservations need to be made months in advance. I had no table booked, but having cycled across the continent I believed I had made my pilgrimage. However, arriving in my dirty cycling gear after months sleeping on the road, I didn't rate my chances. It was only a couple of weeks before Christmas and the place was completely full. Standing outside, looking like a post-apocalyptic cycle courier, I watched for hours as limousines with blacked-out windows and stern-faced chauffeurs delivered men in sharp suits with big watches and trophy wives.

I found my way to the press office, where they could not have been more helpful, and after explaining my mission I was promised that I was at the top of the list should there be a cancellation. For the next couple of days I killed time in the local area doing some more wine tasting. I bumped into Mo, a bon viveur, wine boffin and former restaurant manager from San Francisco, who took me under her wing. She said I could stay with her while waiting for a table. Back in her beautiful kitchen decorated with dried herbs, strings of garlic, pots and pans and postcards of beautiful places, we dined on roast chickens, bright orange roast yams and juicy persimmon salad. We drank bottles of Stags' Leap merlot and chatted about food and travel late into the night. After a rib-sticking breakfast of eggs, snap-in-your-mouth bacon and pancakes drenched in maple syrup, I left with an invitation to spend Christmas with Mo and her bar-owning restaurateur friends in San Francisco.

My first Christmas away from my family could not have been more different from the one they were enjoying back at home. Dim sum replaced turkey at lunch in San Francisco's Chinatown, and in the evening Mo's hard-drinking, food-loving friends got together to eat and drink. An Albacore tuna tartar with wasabi and ginger was followed by a Dungeness crab and blood orange salad. A huge prime rib of beef was perfectly cooked and served, surprisingly, with Yorkshire pudding, and all washed down with wine of a quality I am unlikely ever to drink again. It being my first Christmas away from home I missed my family hugely, but it was a blissfully happy Christmas.

A table never became available at the French Laundry. I will have to wait for my chance to enjoy Chef Keller's culinary creations. I was somewhat disappointed, as I am sure it would have been a highlight of my journey, but I found myself wondering whether it would have been a perfect meal, spending five hours making my way through a fifteen-course tasting menu alone? I think not. By this stage of my trip I was only too aware that food tastes better when shared and enjoyed with another human being, be it a cowboy, a lumberjack, a fisherman or a beauty queen, a best friend or a total stranger. The best chef on the planet and the very fresh-est of ingredients cannot compensate for a lack of good eating companions. Without good company food is simply a fuel. It is no surprise that the very word 'company' derives from the Latin *cum pane*, 'with bread', and describes the joyous sharing of food.

It was New Year's Eve when I first laid eyes on Amir. He was sitting on a bench sheltering from the pouring rain under the eaves of a youth hostel roof in Santa Cruz. Two middle-aged women in leather jackets sat either side of him, one clutching a spent bottle of vodka in her limp hand, the other with her head between her legs, her hands on her knees, while her body buckled with the effort of forcing a line of viscous bile to dribble from her lips, connecting her mouth to the floor. The woman with the bottle was trying to flirt with Amir. Dressed in a wet tank-top and shiny black Lycra that wrapped the bulging muscles of his tanned legs, Amir did his best to politely shun her advances while she stroked his thigh and whispered alcoholic nothings into his ear. The youth hostel didn't open until 6 p.m. and, as I wheeled my load through the small gate, Amir jumped to his feet.

'I am Amir from Israel,' he said in a strange accent, thrusting a hand towards me.

'Tom,' I replied, 'from London.'

'You are riding a bicycle also!' he proclaimed, seemingly astonished that there was another idiot out there cycling in this miserable weather. 'I have ridden from San Francisco.'

'New York,' I returned. 'Where you headed?'

'Panama City, and you?'

'Brazil, where the nuts come from,' I answered, but the joke didn't hit home.

'Then we shall ride together,' he said boldly.

Later Amir and I saw in the New Year in a small restaurant before gate-crashing a riotous house party. We got on well, we had much in common and the next day, after sharing a bunk in the hostel dorm with a shifty Mexican who tried to sell me his tatty leather jacket and a grey-haired Polish man whose snoring made the windows shake, we decided to ride south together. I relished the company.

As cyclists go we could not have looked more different. Amir was a tall, dark and well-built Israeli. I was a short, pale and well-rounded Englishman. Amir was athletic, strong and confident, but by this stage of my trip I was tired, road weary and lazy. But we carried more or less the same load, travelled at more or less the same pace and got on well. Until now I had adopted the policy that he who travels best travels alone, but the serendipity of our chance meeting was too strong to ignore, and I soon discovered that Amir was the answer to my low spirits. After six years in the Israeli navy (I didn't think they had one either), he had had enough of boats and had decided to hang up his lifejacket and cycle from San Francisco to Panama. His six structured years in the navy held comparisons with my previous five years working for an advertising agency in London, and just having him ride next to me gave me a well-needed shot of enthusiasm. His passion for travel and life on the road reminded me of my early gusto when I left New York seven months before, and how I had almost forgotten how exciting life on the road could be. His permanent smile and toneless Hebrew songs, which he bellowed as he rode, blew a well-needed gust of wind into my tatty sails. Amir was a blessing, and at the end of our first day cycling together into southern California I wrote in my diary:

'The Hungry Cyclist is no longer alone.'

With a healthy competition running between us, we rode hard and my pace picked up. We carried each other over the steep hills that snaked along the coast and willed each other on in those last few testing hours of the day. We made good time during the day and at night we camped in the state parks that overlooked the ocean or in farmers' fields. At last, I had someone to cook for. Cooking is a performance, I enjoyed having an audience and I revelled in the applause. Preparing hearty suppers of grilled fish, meaty steak, beef stew and home-made pizza, over campfires under the stars, sharing stories – this was the life on the road I had been longing for.

If driving is to the Americans what eating is to the French, a drive along Big Sur, the 200-kilometre stretch of the Pacific Coast Highway that runs from Monterey to Los Angeles, is the equivalent of having your lunch cooked personally by Alain Ducasse in Paris. A twisting two-lane road hugging the mountain ridges that plunge into the Pacific in a dramatic encounter between land and sea, it is considered to be one of the world's great drives, and Amir and I had arrived on our bicycles.

The road, cut into the cliffs, snaked and weaved ahead of us, tracking every feature of the coast, sometimes hundreds of feet above the ocean, sometimes close to the water's edge. Open-topped cars cruised past us, beeping their horns in encouragement, but we had the best seats in the house, with nothing but mountains above us, sea below and empty tarmac ahead. Under blue skies and sunshine, my waterproof uniform could at last be put away for another rainy day, and my sunglasses could come out of hibernation. This was as close to perfect as cycle touring can be and at last I felt like a man on the move.

On our last day riding Big Sur, before the narrow concrete miles carried us into the suburbs of Los Angeles, we stopped for lunch at the aptly named Big Sur Deli. Smoked hams, cured beef, roast beef, chicken, salami, pastrami and smoked turkey all sat plastic-wrapped behind the glass front of a gently humming cooling counter. Metal trays of various salads, pickles, tomato and cucumber waited next to baskets of bread rolls, brown, white, wholegrain and flat, speckled with different seeds. Above the counter hung a plastic-lettered menu with a hundred combinations of the ingredients before me.

'I'll take a roast beef, with dill, red onion, Swiss, lettuce, mustard and extra mayo on a pumpernickel, please,' I put in, in what now was a favourite order. After carefully building my sandwich, the man behind the counter squeezed it in a plastic-wrapped hand and, with a bread knife in the other, cut through the middle, revealing colourful strata of fresh ingredients. He wrapped the bun in waxy paper with speed and grace, then the neat package went into a brown paper bag with a couple of napkins. He spun the bag twice between his hands and handed it over.

'Gracias.'

'Nada.'

Packing my lunch into a pannier with a couple of cold beers, I spared a thought as to how much I would miss my American deli stops with their cornucopia of fresh ingredients and generous fillings.

A mile or two down the road we pulled over on to a driveway that led to a headland that looked out over the Pacific. A couple of hundred feet above the ocean, we sat on the grass and unwrapped our sandwiches, comfortable in our T-shirts with the California sun warm on our faces. Above the gently rolling silver mass of the Pacific, I stared south at the road that cut into the jagged cliffs and disappeared south into a hazy horizon towards L.A., San Diego and the Mexican border, which was now only days away. Popping the tops of our beers we clinked the necks together.

'Mexico!'

'Mexico!'

Everything works out for the good.

Amir Rockman

Hangtown Fry

Serves 1

half a dozen live oysters
2 eggs
2 tablespoons double cream
2 tablespoons bacon dripping
4 rashers streaky bacon
salt and freshly ground black pepper
to garnish: a little fresh parsley, chopped

1. Shuck the oysters and pat them dry with paper towels.
2. In a small bowl, beat the eggs and cream and set aside.
3. In a small skillet or heavy frying pan, melt the dripping and cook the bacon until crispy. Take out and set aside on a warm plate.
4. In the same hot skillet, sauté the oysters in the remaining bacon fat for 1 minute. Watch out for spitting!
5. Now pour the egg/cream mixture over the oysters, and season to taste. Cook over moderate heat for 2 minutes or until the eggs are set.
6. Remove from the heat and flip onto a warm plate. Garnish with parsley and serve the rashers of streaky bacon alongside. Wash down with plenty of strong coffee.

Snickers in a Twist

Serves 2
2 bananas
a knob of butter
cinnamon
as much tequila as you can lay your hands on (mezcal will suffice)
1 Snickers bar
1 pack of fresh flour tortillas

Cooking for someone else is always better than cooking for one, and cycling together Amir and I never ate badly. This is an easy campfire favourite we developed in Southern California, where tortillas and tequila are easy to come by.

1. Slice the bananas into centimetre-thick slices and fry in the butter with a little cinnamon until beginning to brown.
2. Add a good slosh of tequila and flambé your bananas before cooking off the alcohol.
3. Chop the Snickers into small chunks and add to the banana-tequila mix.
4. In a separate pan, start to warm the tortillas.
5. Once the chocolate has almost totally melted, spread your chocolate-banana mix over a tortilla and wrap it up. If you were feeling very fancy you could add some whipped cream at this stage.

CHAPTER 5

cycling the baja

DON'T WORRY – IT'S JUST LIKE GAZA

> The man who sleeps on the floor never falls out of bed.
> *Bedouin proverb.*

From a dusty, litter-strewn hilltop in Tijuana, north-west Mexico, I took one last look at the immaculate silver skyscrapers of San Diego. A symbol of opportunity and a promised land for the tens of thousands of Mexicans who try to jump the heavily guarded border every year, but for me a last view of the western world for a long time. Simply by embarking on an almost effortless one-hour bike ride I had transported myself into a new world, and from the summit of my first hill in Mexico it became very clear that the world I had entered was very different to the one I was leaving behind. For months the public of America had been filling my naive head with negative propaganda and horror stories, which had left me suffering from a nasty bout of Mexicophobia.

'You wanna' go to Mexico on a bicycle! You won't last ten minutes.'

'I sure hope you're packing a gun.'

'The police down there are worse than the criminals.'

If the stories of corruption, kidnappings and theft were to be believed, I had just cycled into a lawless world where every man was a criminal, every woman a pro and every policeman bent. And my time on the road counted for little more than a nice pair of legs and a suntan. A friendly policeman waving us on was translated into a lifetime in some grim dungeon. Every passer-by was a potential mugger, and when a smiling man appeared from behind a graffiti-decorated wall asking me to donate a few dollars to aid his attempt across the border that very evening, I was convinced my time was up. I was petrified, and never more grateful to have Amir cycling beside me.

'It's just like Gaza,' he announced cheerfully, but his words hardly filled me with confidence. At only twenty-five, his six years of military service meant he had worked checkpoints on the West Bank and reprimanded suicide bombers. For him this was a cake-walk, and once again I was reminded of my inexperience of the world. This was Mexico. New rules, new faces, new language, and a whole new adventure.

With our overloaded bicycles and garish flags we nervously plotted a course through Tijuana. The busiest international land-border in the world, a favourite haunt of underage American drinkers and junkies in search of cheap prescription drugs, and home to ten million Mexicans. Its labyrinth of dusty, rundown suburbs seemed to go on forever. On almost every corner vibrant little stands sent tantalising smells into the midday heat, advertising their fare, and it wasn't long before we were lured in for lunch.

Deciding on a stand that seemed busier than most, set up in the shade of what appeared to be a butcher's shop, we leant our bicycles against a tired tree and made our way across a dusty wasteland towards a huddle of parasols and plastic furniture where various generations of Mexicans were enjoying a roadside Sunday lunch. Traffic rumbled across the treacherous pot-holes in the road, energetic music jumped out of a car radio parked close by and, as Amir found a seat, I went in search of our first meal in Mexico.

Donning a pristine white apron pulled tight around his large belly, a broad-shouldered man pulled long rubbery-looking coils from a plastic bucket and lay them on a round griddle heated by a gas ring attached to a large red gas canister. After vanishing into a hissing confusion of steam and smoke, he tossed some already cooked pieces of what looked like a fleshy inner tube on to a huge tree trunk of a chopping board and began immaculately dicing and slicing with a huge cleaver, while continuing to joke with his customers and bellow orders at his young staff.

Chicharrón, carnitas, mondongo, sopas, carne asada, tripitas

I eyed the menu scribbled in black ink on a piece of fluorescent orange cardboard and it meant nothing. This was Mexico, but where were the burritos, the fajitas, the tacos? Reverting to the age-old technique used by foreigners in far-off places, I pointed at the juicy heap of sizzling rubbery meat in front of me.

'Cuántos quiere?'

If what I was pointing at tasted half as good as it smelt, I was on to a winner. I cautiously ordered: 'Dos, por favor.'

Behind the butcher a teenage girl rolling golf-ball-sized pieces of dough in her hands placed four in a crude wooden device lined with cling film. She pulled down a handle and four small semi-translucent tortillas appeared. They were doubled up, tossed on to the other side of the hotplate and as they began to levitate and brown a little, they were scooped with a spatula on to a clean plastic plate. A healthy amount of unknown meat was placed in the middle of each tortilla along with a good pinch of fresh cilantro and some diced onion.

All the same, it was a meagre offering for a couple of hungry cyclists and so, taking my lead from the woman in front of me, whose opulent curves told me she knew what she was doing, I began loading my tacos. A small spoon of green salsa; a drizzle of red salsa; a dollop of guacamole, and a few pieces of sliced radish and cucumber sprinkled with a pinch of salt and a squeeze of lime.

'Don't eat it all at once,' I quipped, placing the plate in front of Amir.

'That's it?' he returned. 'What is it?'

'It's a taco.'

'I can see that. What is this meat?'

'Not sure.'

Pinching the sides of the soft tortilla and releasing a stream of meaty juice and salsa down my T-shirt, I took my first bite. Warm, meaty flavours filled my mouth, followed by a stimulating burst of salsa. The rubbery meat's strong taste mingled with the fresh cilantro and the smooth guacamole, then came the cleansing rush of the lime juice.

It was love at first bite. I was head over heels. On the edge of a dusty highway in the suburbs of Tijuana I had fallen in love; returning to the stand I ordered us each two more, and while my tacos were prepared I enquired what it was that I had just enjoyed.

'Qué es eso?' I pointed at the pile of meat, sizzling and spitting in front of me.

'Tripitas.'

I looked blank.

'Trip-i-tas,' he said again, snaking his finger over his large belly before pulling the hairy snout of a pig from a bucket under the table.

'Intestino de cerdo.'

The first thing you notice about cycling in Mexico is the state of her roads. The Mexican government, understandably, has better things to spend its money on than cycle lanes for the self-important few who decide to bike the Baja. Having been spoilt by over 5,000 miles of smooth, wide-shouldered American highway, daydreaming in the comfort of California's faultless hard shoulders, I now had to manoeuvre my load in the three inches of tarmac that separated me from erratic local drivers on one side and a sharp drop, of at least a foot, into a gutter littered with broken glass and roadkill on the other.

The second lesson for the novice riding his bike in Mexico is that Mexican dogs do not like cyclists. Unlike their American cousins who are quite happy to bark at the passing cyclist, Mexican dogs seem to adopt a 'bite first ask questions later' policy. Having just about mastered the tightrope cycling act needed to stay on the road, I panicked when, from out of nowhere, a fast-moving pack of wild dogs eager to get their fangs into a pound of tender British flesh erupted upon us.

'If you show fear they will only chase you harder,' advised Amir.

'Fear? There's a pack of feral dogs trying to take chunks out of my legs. I'm bloody terrified!'

After an afternoon of being chased by rabid dogs, menaced by heavy traffic and exhausted by an oppressive heat, we limped tired, dusty and dirty, into the coastal town of Rosarito. We hoped to find an idyllic little fishing town in which to celebrate our first night in Mexico. Instead we cycled into a swarming resort town that seemed to be designed purely to satisfy the desires and vices of young weekending Americans. We pedalled Rosarito's neon-bathed main street, where loud electronic beats pulsated from a never-ending row of bars. Swaying topless men in oversized sombreros swigged pirate-fashion from bottles of pale beer and multi-coloured margaritas, while their equally inebriated partners hung from their shoulders. Broken glass and empty bottles littered the sidewalk of this adult theme park, and from every corner eager local businessmen badgered us. There were no well-kept state parks to pitch our tents in here. We would have to look for a room.

Amir picked out a faded piece of cardboard nailed to a lamp-post that advertised rooms by the month, week or night. It was the first place that wasn't charging by the hour and we were quietly hopeful. We knocked on the heavily barred glass in a thick door. An apathetic man in a sweat-stained white vest eyed us up and told us it was thirty dollars for the night. 'Twenty,' replied Amir, and the heavy door was unbolted. Amir waited with the bikes and I followed the owner down a long dank corridor. He switched on a naked bulb, which revealed a small room with filthy tiles lining every surface. There were no windows; the majority of the floor space was taken up by an old, yellowing mattress that looked like an incontinent dog had spent its last days on it. The room next to it, which the man called a bathroom, resembled a deserted torture chamber.

'You'd have to pay me to sleep in there,' I declared unadventurously to Amir on my return.

'Well, we must sleep somewhere,' he snapped. It was clear we had both lost patience with the situation and we had little left for each other.

Returning to the centre of town we followed a cobbled backstreet away from the main strip and tried our luck on the beach. On a dusty plot of land set back from the beach a few scruffy chickens pecked at the dirt, while a collection of mangy dogs, sleeping in the shade of two vintage caravans precariously propped up on bricks, tyres and bits of lumber, acknowledged our arrival. If the booze-riddled American who gave us directions was to be believed, we might be able to camp here. After we'd knocked on the door of both caravans, an elderly, bare-chested man appeared and we negotiated that we could both sleep there for six dollars. There was a hose for washing, the toilet was a hole with an adjacent bucket, and, exhausted, we gave each other a tired and knowing look and decided enough was enough. Our first night in Mexico would be spent here between two old caravans on a dusty piece of wasteland somewhere at the back of Rosarito beach with a pack of dogs.

As the tide withdrew into the horizon and the large orange sun slowly slipped behind the Pacific, the crowds of margarita-swilling American weekenders evaporated and Rosarito took on a new life. Small groups of local men and women gathered around beach fires dancing to music played on the stereos of pick-up trucks parked close by. The vast beach was now all but empty except for a few opportunist combers and dogs that searched the sand in the hope of finding whatever booty the tourist trade had left behind. On the tide line the silhouettes of men digging for clams stood out against the fiery sunset. Hungry after a gruelling day, Amir and I made our way to a small shack set up at the back of the beach in the hope of finding something to eat.

A tatty canvas wall kept out the chill of the evening breeze and a driftwood fire burnt steadily in an old oil drum in the corner. The solemn tones of a mariachi band crackled out of a small radio held together with overlaid generations of tape, and the proprietor stood behind his stand rapidly chopping chillies, red onion, cucumber, tomatoes and cilantro before turning his attention to a bucket of huge white clams. He prised each one open and all the ingredients were put into a tall glass and doused in the juice of a handful of limes. He mixed the contents with a long spoon and placed the glass in front of us with a tall stack of fresh tostadas, a toasted tortilla not dissimilar to a poppadom.

'Ceviche de almeja. Quiere una cerveza?'

We ordered two cans of blissfully cold Tecate beer and, perched at the bar of this small makeshift eatery, toasted our first day on the road in Mexico. It had been an exhausting assault on all of the senses and Mexico would clearly take some getting used to, but munching on fresh clam ceviche to the sound of the ocean, the barman chopping his ingredients and the unintelligible banter of the clam fishermen sitting next to me, I had no doubt Mexico and I were going to get on very well. In fact, I liked it already.

✈

Baja California is a thousand-mile-long, finger-like peninsula that protrudes from the north-west side of Mexico. Flanked on one side by the crashing waves of the Pacific and on the other by the rugged fish-filled waters of the Sea of Cortez, it is bisected by the infamous Transpeninsular Highway, a twisty, narrow, two-lane, shoulder-less road that weaves its way through the cactus-filled deserts, deserted beaches and barren mountains of this unique corner of the world. A road trip through the Baja is considered by many to be one of the world's greatest driving adventures, but whether it offered the same rewards on a bicycle remained to be seen.

Our first days on the Transpeninsular Highway, with its thundering lorries, dead dogs and non-existent shoulder, had left us both frustrated. Neither of us had come to Mexico to cycle a mundane strip of tarmac and, in the hope of finding more tranquil roads, ocean views and quiet fishing villages, we decided to follow a series of back roads along the coast. We would avoid the worst of the main road, which we could rejoin before heading into the desert. But it became very clear, very quickly that there are two types of road in the Baja: the Transpeninsular Highway, and the washed-out, sun-baked, cactus-infested dirt roads that make up everything else. The road we had chosen barely existed and for three days and three nights we followed a maze of donkey tracks and dried riverbeds carved out in the dirt between the endless fields of exotically shaped cactus.

When the plants have to arm themselves with spikes the size of knitting needles in order to survive, you know you are in a harsh environment, and almost as soon as we left the tarmac we were both attacked by the cyclist's worst enemy. From New York to San Diego I had suffered no more than two punctures. Less than a week in Mexico and my tally had rocketed to eighteen. My arrogantly marketed 'thornproof tyres' put up little resistance to the fierce Mexican cacti spines that littered our route. On an almost hourly basis, the life would slowly seep out of one of our tyres, signalling yet another tedious hold-up. The bike was unloaded, tyre removed, puncture located, patch applied, glue dried, wheel back on, tube pumped, bike reloaded. All ready for the next flat. Our three-day excursion into the wilds of the Baja was a disaster. From now on we would stay as close to the highway as we could.

After our unsuccessful shortcut, the feeling of the Transpeninsular Highway's smooth asphalt rolling under our wounded tyres was a joy. We cycled away from the coast, the road's shiny black surface flowing over the rolling hills of dry scrubland. Climbing what would be our last hill of the day, Amir came to a stop and I pulled alongside. In silence we looked down at the view that spread out below us. Far off in the distance the cobalt shades of the distant mountains stood ominously behind a vast tundra of beige, russet and ochre. The late afternoon sun bathed everything in a soft light. Against a flawless blue sky, the harsh and barren terrain of the Desierto de Vizcaíno was a highly coloured picture of tranquillity. The trivial black thread of the highway flowed across this enormous space, disappearing into the mountains that shivered in the heat. The hot air clung to the land. In the foreground a cluster of small buildings stood dwarfed by this vast landscape, their black water tanks and shiny metal roofs glittering in the sunlight.

The dot on our map had had us believe that El Rosario was a thriving little town that would provide us with a well-needed shower, a bed and an opportunity to load up on the necessary supplies needed for our crossing of the Desierto de Vizcaíno. But from our vantage point above the collection of derelict buildings and abandoned vehicles that flanked the road, our dreams of showers, clean sheets and well-stocked shops evaporated into the heat. El Rosario was no more than a few decrepit shacks, a rundown gas station and a few other businesses that did their best to survive on the passing trade of the highway. There was nowhere to stay in El Rosario, but it did have two taco stands and, after enjoying a couple of carne asada (grilled beef) tacos, washed down with a refreshing hibiscus flower cordial, we took the advice of the proprietor and pulled up outside a crude corrugated-metal hut with a cross on its roof. We waited for the rapt evangelical chanting and clapping of the small congregation to come to an end, then in broken Spanish explained our predicament to the local parson, who kindly agreed to let us sleep on the floor of his church. A small but surprisingly well-stocked shop provided us with our essential desert supplies: water, rice, chocolate biscuits, boiled sweets, coffee and Pepto-Bismol. We topped up our tyre pressure in the local garage, revisited the taco stands and then turned in, determined to get as much rest as possible before heading into the desert in the morning.

The grinding gears and grunting air brakes of trucks heading into the desert and Amir's volcanic snoring, however, kept me from sleep. Unable to rationalise in the early hours, my mind raced erratically from thought to thought. What if we ran out of water? What if we got sick? I had never been in a desert before. Such were my nerves about the days ahead that I didn't get to sleep until the early hours.

'Up, up, Tommsy, we need to get going,' ordered Amir, kicking me lightly as I lay huddled on the simple church floor in my sleeping bag. It was shortly before 5 a.m. and the town was dark and quiet, the air full of cool moisture. I was tempted to beg for a couple more minutes but Amir was right, we needed to get going. I slipped into my Lycra, still damp with yesterday's sweat, and we lit a small fire and brewed a Thermos of strong coffee. Apprehensive, we set out into the darkness.

It wasn't long before El Rosario was no more than a collection of feeble lights flickering on the shady horizon behind us, while ahead of us the silhouette of the mountains was lit from behind by the orange glow of another day arriving. A sun-faded blue sign with a couple of clichéd bullet holes told us that the next gas station was 350 kilometres away in the town of Guerro Negro.

∞

By the late morning we had reached the mountains. As we pulled up the swerving switchbacks that snaked into the hills, each treacherous corner and blind bend was decorated with the small white crosses and sun-bleached plastic flowers that commemorated those whose luck had run out. The heat of the sun was immense and, far from providing life, out here it seemed to sap the energy from everything it touched. Wiping the sweat from our eyes at the peak of each gruelling climb, we were greeted with another endless stretch of arid, rock-strewn desert. Boulders the size of buildings littered the landscape, all that remained from a glacier long ago. Thriving in the little shade they provided, the towering forms of 'cowboy film' cacti provided perches for menacing turkey vultures, wings spread out, drying the night's moisture from their feathers, ready for another day scavenging in this fruitless environment.

'Is that what I think it is?

'No, it's just another truck.'

'Come on – it's not moving.'

Closer still and you could make out a little colour. Some red, a splash of white, a logo.

'Last one there buys the drinks.'

No more than an advertising sign for another Mexican beer, or the colourfully painted wall of an adobe hut, the sight of these unannounced pit stops emerging from the haze had us sending whoops of joy across the desert. Unmarked on the map and little more than a scattering of crude corrugated-metal and wooden shacks put together amongst the cactus and rocks, these rundown desert hamlets with their rusty and sun-faded advertising signs became our oases. They offered shade, a stale bun, a noxious cup of coffee, some refried beans wrapped in a stale tortilla and perhaps some water. But above all they offered a break in the monotony and a chance to rest. Hidden in the shadows of the makeshift buildings we read, drank coffee and slept alongside whoever else had come to a stop at these simple settlements. An underfed family of dogs roaming the dirt for whatever scraps they could scrounge from the passing trade, a truck driver on his back patiently working on his tired rig in the hope of bodging a repair that would get him to the next town, the stripped-down carcasses of other, less fortunate vehicles – all were stark reminders of the unforgiving nature of this desolate place. We camped where we could amongst the cactus, in disused buildings, anywhere out of sight of the road, and as the sun disappeared in a kaleidoscope of colour behind the slender silhouettes of the cactus forests, the desert came into its own. It came alive. The coyotes, buff-coloured geckos and owls that sheltered from the sun during the day filled the cool night air with strange calls. Sitting around our small fires we cooked our simple suppers of rice and beans while sharing stories of home and our plans for the future, sleeping under the stars before waking in thick desert mist to begin another day cycling in the heat.

🚲

Since leaving the cold and blustery conditions of northern California, I had been cycling along the Pacific coast of what the Spanish Crown in 1519 had named Nueva España, through what began as mission towns: San Francisco, Santa Barbara, San Luis Obispo, Monterey, Santa Monica, San Diego. In over two months of cycling through these testaments to a once immense Spanish empire, none pleased me more than the vision of San Ignacio in modern-day Mexico.

A natural oasis and ancient resting place for all who make the long pilgrimage through the Baja, San Ignacio was like a dream. Leaving the highway we passed over the underground river that bubbled into the quiet lagoon of the oasis. Red grass-like reeds leaned out over the water's edge, shaded by the bushy heads of date palms bending under the weight of their fruit. Water birds disappeared under the smooth surface of the lagoon and citrus trees filled the tidy walled gardens along the shady road to the town centre. Pastel-coloured colonial buildings surrounded a sleepy plaza, its centre point the Mission San Ignacio de Kadakaaman, whose heavy walls made from local volcanic rock were emblazoned with plaster reliefs and draped in the vibrant pinks and blues of bougainvillea. It was all a shocking contrast after the lifeless shades of the desert.

We made the most of our time here. We restocked our supplies and pitched camp on the edge of the Laguna San Ignacio. Then we swam in the cool, palm-lined waters and washed away our days in the desert. The sun went down and as the darkness filled with the rapid-fire bullfrogs' chorus we lounged by our fire, popping sweet sticky dates into our mouths like Arab princes.

I was as surprised as Amir to come across dates in a Mexican desert. The Spanish, introduced to the fruit by the Moors, then took it to the New World. The lush palms of San Ignacio had been brought here as seedlings by the Jesuits, who established the mission in 1728. Amir was very familiar with dates, but until that evening my contact with this fruit had been limited to the dusty capsule-shaped box, featuring camels and palm trees under a lurid sunset, that was unearthed every Christmas. My father always ate a couple of these strange fruits, neatly packed in shiny rows like the eggs of some giant insect. I never touched the things and was only too happy to see them disappear back into the cupboard with the neglected cracker toys and carefully folded wrapping paper for another year. But here under the shady palms of San Ignacio I was won over. Sweet, fibrous and packed with sugary energy, this was the perfect desert cycling food. Amir and I loaded up with kilos of it. With bags hanging from our handlebars we rode back into the desert the next day, our route easily tracked, like Hansel and Gretel's through the forest, by the trail of stones spat out on our way across the Baja peninsula towards the fabled Sea of Cortez.

Besides a sunburnt Englishman, an Israeli ex-naval captain and the numerous tweaked-up Mexican truck drivers, who hauled their dilapidated freightliner rigs up and down the hills of the Baja with almost as much trouble as we did our bikes, the main travellers heading south were the North American and Canadian snowbirds. A warm-blooded species, identified by white, grey or purple hair, they migrate southward in large herds, moving at no more than 30 kilometres an hour in search of warmer climes to escape the bitter winters of their natural habitat. They travel in gas-guzzling mobile homes, fully equipped with climate control, so they don't get too warm, wide-screen televisions so they can watch the Super Bowl, cooking facilities so they don't have to eat local food and a well-stocked fridge of tasteless beer. Reminiscent of the wagon trains of old, they snake their way through the Baja in never-ending convoys, their brilliant white RVs standing out against the natural colours of the landscape like rows of shiny teeth.

Apparently suffering from the same Mexicophobia that gripped me in my first days, and convinced that stopping or even slowing down would result in certain theft, rape and murder, these octogenarian nomads are a cycle tourist's nightmare.

'Weeeeee caaaaant get passt yooooou!' they holler from the comfort of their air-conditioned living rooms while yanking on their deafening air horns. Only to receive a firmly raised finger and a cocktail of the finest English and Hebrew abuse, to which they retaliate by forcing us into the cactus and boulders in a cloud of dust and red mist. The heat, vultures and rabid dogs of Mexico are not the cycle tourist's primary concern. For those brave, or indeed foolish enough to bike the Baja, the biggest threat to your life expectancy is the senile snowbird who has forgotten to fold up the steps to his motor home.

Climbing the sweeping switchbacks through the hills north of Loreto, the destination of this bizarre nomadic community at last became clear. Riding the coastal road that twisted and turned high above the clear turquoise waters of the Sea of Cortez, we had crossed the Baja, and from high in the hills, we saw the cactus marching down towards perfect golden beaches on which stood row after row of gleaming white motor homes. This is where the snowbirds migrated.

Picture the kind of beach shack that Robinson Crusoe and Man Friday might have hung out in and you have an image of a palapa. A traditional Mexican hut used by fishermen, it is a crude construction made of local lumber and thatched with palms. It offers shade from the sun during the day and at night shelter from the cool winds that blow out of the desert. We found an abandoned palapa at the end of Playa El Coyote, where the rough road meant we were a suitable distance from the whirring generators of the geriatrics, and we took the unanimous decision to take a few days' rest and enjoy the beach. Woken by the rising sun over the Sea of Cortez, we spent days watching the pelicans dive for their lunch as well as diving ourselves for our own. Fan scallops hid in the sand between the rocks. We prised open their stubborn shells, cut out the hockey-puck-sized flesh from their centres, and washed them down with a squeeze of lime juice and a dash of hot sauce. The horn of a passing pick-up truck announced the arrival of meals-on-wheels, another entrepreneurial local arriving to sell fresh fruit and vegetables to this part-time community of snowbirds and cyclists.

We could have stayed forever, and staying longer than we should our recuperation on Playa El Coyote coincided with Amir's twenty-fifth birthday. Having spent his last six birthdays cooped up on an Israeli patrol boat with fifteen other men, camping on a beach with an army of pensioners didn't equate with the birthday plans he had hatched before heading out on his great adventure.

'Tomorrow is my twenty-fifth birthday and we have no girls – this will not stand, my friend,' he moaned. I understood his predicament. Staying on a beach populated by Americans old enough to be his grandparents wasn't ideal but, after setting aside our differences with the local snowbird community, we set about putting together the best Mexican birthday we could.

A Mexican birthday party would be incomplete without a piñata, a brightly coloured papier-mâché container filled with sweets and modelled in the shape of a star, animal or person. You hang it from a nearby tree, and the idea is that the blindfolded birthday boy, or girl, has to beat the piñata with a stick until the sweets are scattered for all to share. Now this seems to me like about as much fun as a person can have with a stick and some papier-mâché, but Amir, fuelled on cheap tequila, could not quite see the fun in it all. Standing blindfolded in front of thirty jeering geriatrics, demanding he beat the effigy of a young girl until her head exploded, seemed to throw him. I took things into my own hands. The sweets were scattered, and later, sitting around a well-stocked fire eating grilled fish with our fingers, we toasted Amir and the continuation of our journey.

Along with the corrupt cops and merciless bandits, the doom and gloom mongers living north of the Mexican border also take great pleasure in warning the inexperienced traveller about the perils of eating in Mexico. More than happy to fill their cake holes with reheated Tex Mex slop, they revel in counselling you that Mexico is a germ-infested hygiene nightmare, where eating fruit, drinking water or eating on the street will result in a certain slow, uncomfortable and messy end to your travels. Perhaps cooped-up inside an air-conditioned motor home or languishing in a five-star beach resort you can insulate yourself from the local cuisine, but on a bicycle, thankfully, you are exposed to it. Baja California is a fish lover's paradise. Hard to believe when surrounded by the arid expanse of its cactus-filled deserts and mountains, but it boasts over 3,200 kilometres of fish-packed coastline and its mellow towns and fishing villages are abundant with clams, lobster, octopus, marlin, scallops, manta ray, prawns and crabs, all served in what many would argue is the quintessential dish of the Baja. The fish taco.

Sold from numerous colourful street stands, the fish taco relies totally on the quality of its ingredients, and contrary to the rumours, Mexicans take great pride in using only the freshest of produce. With the majority of taquerías unable to afford the luxury of refrigeration, food is prepared with basic equipment in primitive conditions. But don't let this put you off. The lack of refrigeration and storage ensures the food is always fresh. The fish hasn't been sitting in a freezer for days; it has come straight from the boat. The salsas have not been made en masse the night before, but are made that morning, and the tortillas, far from coming out of an air-sealed packet, are rolled and pressed in front of you. In the Baja it is reassuringly impossible to buy a fish taco on the street after midday, and for anyone to travel the length of the Baja without experiencing the total joy of a fish taco is nothing short of sacrilege.

Back on the Transpeninsular Highway, we crossed the Baja again and, hungry after a night sleeping in the desert, rolled into the dusty agricultural town of Ciudad Constitución and began looking for breakfast. Already alive with the bustle of commerce and rumbling traffic, the town had no shortage of taquerías. Reverting to our primal instincts, we begin to search for where other beasts were feeding, and glimpsed a particularly busy little stand dwarfed by a pair of enormous trucks. We had found our spot.

Truck drivers the world over know how to eat. The vehicle owners were easily recognisable propped up at the bar with a collection of dusty rancheros in tight jeans and cowboy hats. Inside the stand, over-decorated with a collection of gaudy catholic kitsch, the young owner, baseball cap pulled backwards on his sweaty forehead, worked comfortably, operating cooking utensils in both hands with the precision of a drummer. Finding some space amongst the other animals, our presence was acknowledged with a gentle raise of the eyebrows.

'Cuatro pescados, por favor.'

Pinching four golden hunks of battered fish from the large shallow vat of bubbling oil he was working over, the owner delicately placed each piece away from the oil to cool a little, and apparently without thinking he had already taken another handful of succulent white fish, dipped them in a creamy batter and tossed them into the oil where they disappeared in an eruption of spitting bubbles and foam. Diverting his attention to a lightly oiled griddle next to him, where a neat row of home-made corn tortillas were at various states of readiness, he doubled up a couple with his spatula and flicked them onto a pair of plastic plates. Placing a piece of golden battered fish in the centre of each tortilla he handed us our breakfast. 'Buen provecho!'

Presented with a few small pieces of lightly battered fish served on what is little more than a grilled corn pancake, you might wonder why such a simple dish warrants such a cult following but, like its meaty cousins, assembly is everything when eating a taco, and the fish taco is transformed with the do-it-yourself application of the salsas and salads that line the bar of any self-respecting taquería. Deep bowls of refreshing tomatillo salsa, made from the green cousin of the tomato; mojo de ajo, a flavour-packed blend of grilled garlic and fiery chillies; various grades of tongue-curling red salsas riddled with jalapeños; a creamy mayonnaise, gently flavoured with garlic and smoky grilled chipotle, a vital addition to any fish taco; translucent sliced radishes; diced habañeros, the powerful chillies that must be handled with extreme care. And more. Bowls of loosely chopped tomatoes and jalapeños mixed through with cilantro and red onion, known romantically as pico de gallo, or rooster's beak, perhaps because of the chilli that pecks away at your taste buds. Smooth guacamole; essential crunchy salads of shredded cabbage, preferred in the Baja over lettuce for its ability to hold up in the fierce heat, and forget at your peril that squeeze of fresh lime.

Make no mistake, dressing a fish taco is an art. It requires time, practice and patience. Overload your taco and the ingredients will landslide down your front. Add too much spice and you will be weeping like a child. But once you are delicately pinching your tortilla between thumb and forefingers and directing your very own personalised parcel of flavour into your mouth, implementing a light sucking action and then taking that first magical bite, all the messy practice and research is worthwhile. You are eating a masterpiece. The batter is light and as good as any tempura. The cabbage has crunch and is delightfully peppery. The fish is fresh, firm and succulent. The chipotle mayonnaise is smooth and soothing, the chilli salsa fiery and aggressive, the squeezed lime and cilantro clean and refreshing, and then there is the luxurious texture of the guacamole. Pure bliss!

ठ

The dictionary definition of a tachometer is the device used to determine the speed of rotation of a vehicle's axle. The Hungry Cyclist's definition is the average number of tacos consumed in a day while cycling in Mexico; and after little more than three weeks in the Baja my tacometer was moving dangerously close to triple figures, but I had yet to find out how the succulent fish I was eating day after day were getting from their comfortable ocean home into my mouth, via a guacamole and salsa-drenched tortilla.

Following the quiet coastal road close to the calm waters of Baya Magdalena it seemed like a perfect spot to make camp. The high ground ensured we would be safe if the tide came in and a rundown pair of pangas, typical clinker-built Mexican fishing boats, provided a good rest for our bikes and shelter from the sandy breeze that blew in from the sea. We had lit a small driftwood fire and begun to prepare supper when the rumble of a truck, just audible above the roar of the ocean, grabbed our attention.

'You can hear that?' asked Amir.

Police (federales), locals looking for easy pickings, the chances were it was nothing sinister, but not wanting to take any risks we hurriedly buried any incriminating evidence, cameras, credit cards and the majority of our cash in the loose sand and then watched apprehensively as the glow of headlights moved behind the dune towards where we were camped. The truck rounded the bend. Caught like a pair of rabbits in the headlights, we got to our feet. The doors of the truck opened and the silhouettes of six large men came towards us, their long shadows cast before them.

'Buenas noches.'

'Buenas noches.'

It soon became clear that we had pitched our tents on a spot in active use by a team of local fishermen. Working together, the six men lifted another small boat from a trailer behind the truck and after placing it with the rest they joined us around the fire.

'Quiere café?' offered Amir, and accepting silently the six men of various ages passed our small enamel coffee cup between them, the eight of us eyeing each other up in silence in the flickering half-light of the fire. This was an opportunity.

'Es possible para mí voy contigo a mañana?'

A confused look spread across weathered faces staring back at me.

'Quiero ir contigo a mañana. Es possible?'

'A donde?' replied the captain.

'A pescar.'

'Porque?' came a confused reply.

'Para mirar.'

The fishermen looked at each other in confusion and Amir joined them.

'Pues, bien – mañana a las seis.'

The captain handed me the empty coffee mug. Saying goodnight, the men followed him through the darkness back towards the truck.

'If I understood that conversation correctly, you are going fishing tomorrow. Well, you are on your own, my friend. I have had enough boats for one lifetime.'

🚲

The last people I ever expected to spend a Valentine's Day with were a six-man Mexican fishing crew, but shortly before six in the morning on 14 February the rumble of the fishermen's pick-up truck woke me from sleep and my dates had arrived. The bay was shrouded in a thick mist and as the shabby truck pulled up I walked towards the burly men, who were clad in a collection of bright-coloured rubber dungarees, nylon swimming shorts, white Wellington boots and worn-out trainers from which toes protruded. With my backpacker sandals, sunglasses and figure-hugging Lycra shorts, I felt decidedly underdressed.

The captain, a short man who introduced himself as Capitán Bin Laden, much to the delight of his crew, put me to work cleaning and repairing the mountain of nylon netting stored under the panga. I had no idea how to repair a fishing net, but while the other men entertained themselves with what I guessed was Mexican fisherman's banter, I began removing the crusty bits of seaweed and stubborn crabs that clung to this never-ending tangle of netting. After an hour my hands were an aching mess of tiny cuts and scratches, aggravated by the saline dust that coated everything I touched.

We turned over the panga and lifted it on to its flimsy trailer, folded the cleaned net and placed it into the boat, then we all bundled into the back of the rusty pick-up truck. After Gustavo, one of two large brothers, did some rewiring with his big fish knife, a multi-tool in these parts, Capitán Bin Laden successfully started the engine and we rumbled off down the beach, the suspension in the stripped-down truck a distant memory. We crossed the small spit of sand that protected the calm waters of the Bay of Magdalena, where I thought we would be fishing, and turned on to a vast, empty beach that faced the crashing open waters of the Pacific Ocean. We came to a standstill. After thoughtfully eyeing up the shoreline, Capitán Bin Laden spoke.

'Desayuno.'

Initially intimidated by this burly group of rough and ready men, when each one produced a breakfast, neatly wrapped in a colourful hand-embroidered handkerchief, my fears disappeared. As each bundle was opened, a colourful spread of warm corn tortillas, refried beans, home-made salsas, bunches of bright-red radishes, fresh limes and hibiscus cordial was laid out on the bonnet. I could not have imagined a more picturesque breakfast. Under a perfect blue sky, the seven of us sat in the sand, eating breakfast and staring at the ocean. This was my kind of fishing. I felt like a real fisherman. But then the captain got to his feet, and it was time to start work.

We reversed the panga into the surf, lifted it from its trailer and the captain ordered me in, then followed along with two other men. He yanked the engine into life and we began cutting through the foaming waves of the shallows. Pointing a telling finger at the sea, like an explorer at the first sight of land, it was clear where the captain was taking us. The engine revved, the bow of the panga lifted out of the water and I held on tight. The neat coil of rope on top of the net span out behind us and on the beach the other men took the strain. Our small boat skipped over the rolling foam towards the towering waves ahead. The captain pulled on his plastic hood, the two men next to me ducked into the hull and, after taking one last look at the huge wave about to convert us into a box of matches, I did the same. Pitched at a terrifying angle, the small boat charged up the face of the wave, the engine whining in resistance as we struggled to climb the wall of water bearing down on us. The hull came down with a loud thud – we had made it over the top. But no sooner had I peeped up above the parapet than we were charging at the next roller moving towards us. Heads down, revs up, we climbed again as water rushed over the bow of the boat until once again we heard the reassuring thump on the other side.

Rolling on the smooth swell behind the break the captain cut the revs and, turning the boat, we began bundling the net into the water, trailing it behind us as we ran parallel with the beach. After dragging some 200 metres of net behind us, we turned for the shore. All that remained in the boat was another coil of rope and it quickly dawned on me what the plan was. Back on the beach the hazy figures of the other men had one end of the huge drag net secured and we had to close the loop. The captain pushed on the tiller and pointed our bow towards the beach. He revved the engine, I ducked back into the hull, and, like a surfer catching a wave, the captain timed his run back to the beach, navigating us over the waves as they exploded behind us.

Relieved to be back in the shallows, I couldn't get out of the boat fast enough and leaving two men to hold the rope, the captain and I dragged the panga on to the beach before joining the others securing our end of the net. The hazy figures of the other men way down the beach, waiting on the rope like a tug-o-war team, acknowledged our readiness. The captain raised his arm and we all began to pull.

'Vamos, vamos,' called the crew, our hands crossing in rhythm as we pulled against the ocean. My legs sank into the wet sand, my hands slipped on the damp rope, but the first edge of net at last became visible and soon we were dragging it on to the beach. The gulls and pelicans swooping and squabbling overhead signalled our success and as the net was hauled on to the sand our catch became visible, the bright silver flashes of jumping fish catching in the bright sun as they made one last bid for freedom.

We set about collecting our catch in plastic crates. There were well-camouflaged bottom feeders similar to a sole or flounder; round-bodied white fish, cousins of the hake and the cod, flipping to free themselves; colourfully spotted rays with venomous tails that flapped on the sand. Slimy catfish with strange investigative whiskers wriggled in the netting while wide-mouthed monsters flashed their aggressive fins in protest at being touched and puffer fish sat inflated in complaint. The crew, of course, had their own names for everything we gathered: ratón, sierra, lisa, corvina, caballito. And nothing was wasted. What didn't make it into the boxes was tossed to the unsure brown pelicans, with their strange flabby gullets, who waddled and jumped at a safe distance. It wasn't long before the huge net was empty and the floor of the truck a lively harvest of exhausted marine life gasping for air. Not a bad day's work, I thought.

'Bueno. Otra vez.'

The boat ride had terrified me, my back ached in protest at the hard work and my hands were a tender mess of cuts and blisters, and we had to do it all over again. I alternated between waiting on the beach and taking the white-knuckle ride in the panga as the fishermen repeated the exhausting dragging process four more times before stopping for lunch, another wonderful truck-bonnet affair. Four large, still wriggling ratón, a streamlined oily fish rather like mackerel, were skilfully gutted, skinned and filleted. The raw flesh was diced with the same knife used for rewiring the truck, and after it had been mixed through with plenty of fresh cilantro and doused in lime juice, we scooped it on to crispy tostadas and into our mouths. Served with a little sliced cucumber, diced habañero and radish, fish had never tasted so good or so fresh.

We made four more exhausting drags after lunch, working our way up and down the empty beach with the expectant flock of gulls and pelicans cautiously following our every move. The sun moved across the sky, we pulled the net and the truck slowly filled with fish until at six in the evening the captain signalled we would make our last energy-sapping drag.

There was no room in the truck on the way back, and beaten up, exhausted and sunburnt I collapsed on top of the damp net in the boat with the other men as we bumped along the sand back to our camp. I smelt like a fishmonger's bin, my hands were cut and blistered, my back was tight in complaint and my eyes and face stung with sunburn. The boat was unloaded. I said goodbye to the crew, who still had to sort their catch and get it to the market by the early hours. The truck rumbled into the distance and I collapsed on the sand by the small fire.

'How was your day fishing?' asked Amir, but I was already asleep.

♲

The vision of La Paz, the capital city of southern Baja, could not have come soon enough. Amir had been reunited with a love interest, so on my own, sunburnt, exhausted and longing for rest, I rode the last few miles on the Transpeninsular Highway into the busy streets. Good fortune introduced me to a little old lady who was happy to rent me a small room in the northern quarter, next to the city market.

In the mornings the sun lit up the pink bougainvillea flowers and lush papaya leaves of the small garden below my window, and woken by the market's tannoy system sending the day's special offers into my room, I was soon lured to one of the lively cantinas for a long breakfast. Chiles rellenos, menudo, pizolé, huevos rancheros, sopes. In the bustling Mercado Municipal I began to experiment with some of the flavours I would be finding on the mainland, but it was hard to break my allegiance to my beloved tacos. Returning to bed for well-needed siestas away from heat of the afternoon, I would wake hungry and cycle about town in search of new haunts to sate my taco addiction. It wasn't long before I knew all the best taco stands and they all knew the strange blond gringo on his bicycle who would appear at all hours for a quick fix. My daily schedule was simple and effortless and a world away from the routine of hauling my bicycle up and down hills. After nine happy nights, La Paz begin to feel like home. But the show had to go on. The bizarre show of pedalling, eating, sweating, loneliness, uncertainty, pain and adventure. Now well rested,

I was quietly longing for a return to the nomadic charms of life on the road.

🚲

The eighteen-hour ferry crossing to mainland Mexico set sail at three in the afternoon, and arriving at the port in good time I found a small beach and lost myself watching the squadrons of pelicans dive for their lunch while frigate birds soared effortlessly on the thermals high above. Time came to board and I pulled myself away from my postcard writing and dusted the sand from my shoes. The beast of burden was ready and waiting, and, having almost forgotten how much she weighed when fully loaded, I clumsily wheeled her into the dark, fume-filled hold of the ferry that would take me to Mazatlán.

With a dull blast of her fog horn, the tired-looking ship pushed away from the dock just before dusk. The lights of La Paz soon blended into the sunset behind the mountains. To my surprise, and contradicting the many horror stories I had been fed, she was a clean vessel bustling with a friendly cargo of families, soldiers, a couple of backpackers and plenty of truckers. Doing my best to enjoy an uninspiring meal of refried, reheated beans and some exhausted tortillas, I took in an hour of a somewhat tactless movie about a naval disaster that was blaring from the televisions hanging on the walls. The ship went down, the credits rolled and within minutes the ferry transformed into a glorified refugee camp. Under garish blankets, bodies sprawled on every available floor space. Lorry drivers snored loudly, babies cried in complaint at the sticky heat, while everyone else did their best to catch that moment of broken sleep that would make the next day a little bit more bearable. A child's electronic toy played an out-of-tune version of 'London Bridge is Burning Down', and sick of the collective smell of over five-hundred sweaty passengers, I decided my best chance of catching that cherished moment of sleep might be found on deck. Rolling out my sleeping bag I lay back under a star-filled sky and with the gentle rumble of the ship's engines beneath me, fell into a peaceful sleep. Tomorrow I would enter Mexico proper.

A wonderful bird is the pelican,
His beak can hold more than his belly can,
He can hold in his beak,
Enough food for a week!
I'm damned if I know how the hell he can!

Dixon Lanier Merritt

A Perfect Fish Taco

Serves 5

500g very fresh fish fillets cut into chunky strips (good fish for
*   tacos are firm ones like swordfish, shark and cod)*
1 white cabbage (or iceberg lettuce), finely shredded
white wine vinegar
1 ripe avocado
1/2 lime
10 fresh flour tortillas
cooking oil
150g plain flour
1/2 teaspoon baking powder
1 teaspoon sugar
240ml Mexican beer
salt and freshly ground black pepper
to serve: hot sauce, red salsa, finely chopped red onion, chopped
*   fresh cilantro (coriander), fresh limes*

1. First prepare the cabbage and avocado. Put the cabbage in a small serving bowl, sprinkle with a splash of white wine vinegar and a healthy pinch of salt and mix gently with your fingers. Peel the avocado, remove the stone and spoon the flesh into another small bowl with a small pinch of salt and the juice from the half of lime. Mash with a fork until you have lumpy paste – this is the guacamole.

2. Now unless you have been brave enough to make fresh tortillas, your shop-bought tortillas will need to be warmed and softened. To do this, heat a well-seasoned skillet or heavy frying pan to a medium heat and add a teaspoon of cooking oil. Place your first tortilla in the pan and as it sizzles, flip it with a spatula. Continue to flip and turn with your fingers until the tortilla begins to develop air pockets, then remove from the pan and place flat on a warm plate. Continue until all the tortillas are warmed then wrap the plate in a tea towel or napkin.

3. To make the batter, put the flour, baking powder, sugar and beer with a teaspoon of salt into a mixing bowl. Whisk until you have a smooth and creamy batter. Place the fish chunks in the batter and make sure each piece is well coated.

4. Fill a heavy saucepan with 1 ½ inches of cooking oil and heat to 180°C (a small piece of bread will brown in 30 seconds). Lower the battered fish into the hot oil and fry for 3-4 minutes until golden brown. Remove with a spider or slotted spoon and set aside to cool slightly on a paper towel.

5. The perfect fish taco is all about assembly and everyone has their own technique. Here are the basics. Take a warm tortilla in the palm of your hand. Add a spoonful of guacamole, a couple of fried fish chunks, a squeeze of lime, a pinch of cilantro, a drizzle of red salsa, a small pinch of red onion and a large pinch of cabbage. Shake on a little hot sauce and demolish.

San Ignacio Date Cake

After days of gruelling cycling in the vast Desierto de Vizcaíno, San Ignacio was a truly welcoming sight for us. A local woman added the metaphorical icing by delivering a freshly baked date cake for us to enjoy with our first cup of campfire coffee.

150g plain flour
2 teaspoons baking powder
200g sugar (or date honey)
4 eggs, separated
1 teaspoon vanilla essence
350g dates, pitted and chopped, plus extra to decorate

1. Preheat the oven to170°C/Gas 3.
2. Sift together the flour, baking powder and sugar. Beat the egg whites until stiff and fold into the flour.
3. Add the egg yolks and vanilla, and mix well. Now add the chopped dates, and the date honey if using instead of sugar. Mix thoroughly. Pour into a greased baking tin and bake for 35–40 minutes.
4. Decorate the cake with a few sliced dates.

CHAPTER 6

¡ándale! ¡ándale! ¡arriba! ¡arriba!

MENUDO, MOLÉ AND THE MEXICAN MAINLAND

> Las penas con pan son menos.
> *(All grief is less with bread.)*
>
> Mexican proverb

Bweeeooorr. Bweeeeeeeooooorr.

The blast of an air horn gatecrashed my brain, sending my body into a startled spasm. My bicycle swerved and wobbled beneath me. I kept my head down and did my best to stay on the extreme edge of what was left of the eroded strip of asphalt.

Bweeeeeeeooooorr. Bweeeeeeeeeeooooorr.

Oh FUCK off! Where am I supposed to cycle?

I glanced over my left shoulder and made eye-contact with the enraged driver gesticulating at me with a clenched fist from behind the wheel of the gigantic juggernaut. Unable to lip-read the series of Mexican expletives being fired at me, but making an educated guess, I returned my eyes to the road ahead.

Bwaaaaaaaaaaaaaaaarrn.

On the other side of the two-lane, pothole-riddled highway, a truck of equal size was charging towards me, being equally tuneful

167

with its horn. The road simply wasn't wide enough for the three of us. Outsized and outnumbered, I released my own collection of expletives, picked what looked like the softest part of the soft verge, turned right, held tight, shut my eyes and careered down a steep bank into the waiting wildlife. To the sounds of engine brakes, rushing wind, air horns and cracking branches, I disappeared into the undergrowth.

It was the third time I had been forced off the road that morning. Removing the twigs and leaves from my wheels, I counted my spokes and my blessings, straightened my helmet and gathered my thoughts before pushing my load back up to the road to continue on this hellish leg of my journey.

Reminding me of my lowly position on the Mexican highway hierarchy, and filling the sweltering air with the rotten stench of death, the flattened faces of animals less fortunate than myself stared back at me from the asphalt. In dark mood I cycled south, wondering what I might look like completely squashed, before my self-pitying thoughts were averted by another long blast from a truck's horn.

Here we go again...

Since landing in mainland Mexico two and half a days earlier, I had been struggling along the same polluted artery between Mazatlán and Tepic, immersed in the perpetual flow of heavy traffic that coursed and rumbled over its worn-out tarmac. I was dirty, exhausted, sunburnt and scarred, and to add insult to my various undergrowth-induced injuries I was also desperately lonely.

Amir, my ally since our fateful meeting in Santa Cruz, California, over two months before, had at long last met somebody of the fairer sex and he was making the most of it. While he basked on the beach in the arms of a beautiful woman, I suffered in the tropical heat surrounded by fume-belching trucks and road kill. Cycling alone in Mexico for the first time, I was made well aware of how much I appreciated his company and how vulnerable I felt without it. Whether we were collecting wood, starting a fire, cycling uphill or eating tacos, a friendly competition had spurred us on in almost every aspect of our daily routine, adding discipline and efficiency to our journey. Together we were a team, partners, compadres. I had taken for granted our systems, catch-phrases and routines, and I quickly discovered that without them, and without Amir, the very day-to-day routine of living on the road was far less enjoyable.

Leaving Amir in La Paz, I foolishly believed that the liberal pleasures of riding a bicycle alone, which I had enjoyed in the United States, would return, but I was forgetting one very important detail. My audio lessons and time in the Baja had improved my grasp of Spanish, but it was limited to conversations about where I was from and who would win the World Cup. I was no more fluent than a local three-year-old, and very quickly I longed for the interaction that went beyond ordering food and asking for directions. Unable to communicate, I felt insecure. I was treated differently, and in turn I reacted differently.

Without the luxury of someone to fall back on or hide behind, I became suspicious and felt totally exposed. I was unable to see the beauty in my situation and, after only a few days in Mexico, my mood darkened. My morale deteriorated and the questions returned about the very purpose of my trip and my ability to continue with it. My months with Amir seemed like a happy holi-day, and now I was back at work. Back to the mundane routine of covering small distances very slowly in a strange place. I stopped to rest in the middle of the day, sat by the side of the road and stared at my map, trying to work out how far I had to go. With stretched fingers, the days became weeks and the months became years. Mexico seemed like an awfully big place, and my target of Brazil totally unattainable.

🚲

It would be fair to say that my on-road relationship with Mexico's truck drivers was less than cordial. I was always in their way and they did their best to run me off the road while suffocating me with fumes. But we had much in common. We each belonged to our own nomadic species. We were away from home and we were always on the move. We endured hours of tarmac-induced monotony and we spent those hours fantasising about the hearty plates of home-cooked food that waited for us at the end of the day.

In England, the invasion of big business and a desperate desire for profit has driven the once abundant privately owned roadside restaurants and truckers' caffs to the edge of extinction. What used to be institutions of no-frills English cuisine, where a man could feast on plates of bubble and squeak, toad-in-the-hole and a real full English breakfast, have gone the same way as village shops, greengrocers and local butchers. They have been replaced by generic, controlled environments, where the best a hungry traveller can look forward to is a few polystyrene sandwiches filled with plastic ham, a greasy salami wrapped in a condom or a bag of maize-based orange objects shaped like Shrek, covered in toxic dust and costing about the same price as a weekend break in Spain.

However, in Mexico, freshly made, cheap roadside cuisine still plays an important role in the culinary culture of the country, and Mexico's road-weary truck drivers provide a perfect guide of where and what to eat. Rarely at home, they rely on the ladies who work tirelessly in the simple kitchens of roadside cantinas for their next fix of home cooking. The majority of truckers may look like extras from a low-budget, Latino porn flick, but don't be put off. Dirty hands, oily clothes and sweat-stained T-shirts are the preferred get-up of these freeway foodies, and they are the very best guide to the independently run cantinas, where competition is fierce and standards are high. Riding the same dusty roads year in, year out, they know every turn, every hairpin, every pothole and every good restaurant. Pick a place with a handful of trailers parked outside and you know you will be well fed.

I also discovered that the majority of roadside restaurants, as well as providing me with a well-needed feed at the end of a long day's cycling, were only too happy to let me spend the night once I had invested in some hearty fare. In my first week on the Mexican mainland I felt unsafe camping alone, so I organised my days to make sure I ended up in one of these restaurants each night. Instead of eating bland campfire rice alone in my clammy tent, I dined on home-made Mexican food with the kings of the Mexican highway. Sharing stories, we showed each other photos of our families and homes and we argued about who would lift the World Cup. They scrutinised my maps and told me the best routes south, and we talked a lot about food.

It began as lengthy games of Pictionary on the backs of napkins. We sketched and guessed various animals, vegetables and minerals, and slowly I was introduced to the traditional ingredients and dishes of the Mexican kitchen. As I was advised on roads to take and cities to avoid, so my inventory of must-eat Mexican food expanded. In Mexico City I had to eat escamoles, fried ant's eggs; in Puebla I had to try chapulinas, crickets marinated in lime and chilli; and in Oaxaca I should drink pulque and mezcal, two potent beverages made from fermented maguey cactus. Huitlacoche was a fungus that grew on corn, a delicacy described as the truffle of Mexico, and superb in quesadillas. Barbacoa was a traditional way of slow-cooking lamb in central Mexico, and chile en nogada was the local delicacy that should not be missed when I passed through Puebla.

I spent my time at the tables of these small homes from home, in the company of these admirable men of the road, and my Spanish began to improve, albeit riddled with dirty trucker's slang. With it grew my knowledge of Mexican culture and cuisine, and my confidence returned. Although I was still alone, I felt that I belonged to this mobile community who, like me, spent their days riding the roads of Mexico.

At the end of another hot and thankless day, I limped into a roadside hamlet, a jaded-looking village bisected by the disturbance of the highway. On the edge of its main street women sat under parasols in front of improvised wooden stands, selling small woven baskets of mangoes and papayas and bags of dried shrimp to the never-ending stream of customers who passed throughout the evening.

Set back from the road on either side, rows of once bright-coloured buildings, now faded by the sun and traffic fumes, housed the typical small-town businesses. The verdulería displayed tired-looking vegetables in wooden boxes; a dulcería's shelves were stacked with garish bags of sweets and strung up with flamboyantly decorated piñatas; the carnicaría exhibited bloody cuts of meat and offal that hung above tidy piles of yellow-skinned chickens, and the panadería filled the evening with the smell of fresh baking. Beyond the shops, trucks and trailers lined each side of the road like a busy border crossing, dirty men working patiently underneath their rigs. Bright blue flashes of welding torches lit up mechanics' yards and tyre shops, and while stray dogs slinked between parked vehicles, a group of children chased plastic bags blown into the air by the turbulence of the traffic. It was another bustling highway town, whose very existence was determined by the passing trade that Mex15 provided.

I cycled up and down the main street, narrowing down my options of where to invest some pesos in exchange for supper, and perhaps a place to sleep. Hidden behind a dozen vast trucks, I spotted an open-fronted establishment lined wall-to-wall with large, sweaty, feeding beasts. It was perfect. My arrival was acknowledged with a gentle nod by a few oily men, who I guessed had seen me labouring up the last hill into town. They removed their cowboy hats from the table.

'Buenas noches.'

I sat down to join them and in a few minutes a waitress was waiting impatiently for my order. I pointed at the appetising plate of the man in front of me and asked what it was.

'Chile relleno con salsa de tomate y camarón.'

The man held up his thumb and forefinger in a loop to signify it was good.

I ordered one, and a glass of agua de jamaica, a cordial made from hibiscus blossoms.

Before long a deep plate filled with a puddle of warm tomato salsa was placed on the colourful plastic tablecloth in front of me. Swimming in the red sauce were a few small shrimps, which I assumed were the ones being sold on the roadside, and half submerged in the middle, like a wallowing hippopotamus, was a plump poblano chilli stuffed with cheese and potatoes. The chilli had been grilled until soft, hollowed out and stuffed with cheese and potatoes, before being dipped in a light egg batter and shallow fried.

As I sliced into the flaccid sack of the chilli, deliciously gooey cheese spilled out. I cut a bite-sized piece of dark green flesh and batter, speared a shrimp with my fork and wrapped it in all in a stringy strand of cheese. The men at the table watched and waited for my reaction. Would the gringo on the bicycle like their food? He would. It was superb! The sweet flesh of the poblano chilli sat perfectly with the slightly saline flavour of the soft cheese and the subtle fishy flavours of the salsa.

My chile relleno didn't last long and I was soon unwrapping a stack of warm tortillas from a round basket and mopping up what remained of the sauce, while watching in admiration as the jolly team of sisters, mothers and daughters worked the tables, serving plate after plate of this classic Mexican dish. I have tried to make chile relleno since that evening and have struggled to succeed, and yet these queens of Mexican cuisine were knocking them out perfectly on an industrial scale, with only the most basic of apparatus.

One by one the drivers said goodnight and returned to their cabs to sleep, and in the balmy heat I sat by the side of the road, mesmerised by the long beams of the headlights that came and went. A crudely built, open-fronted restaurant on the edge of a traffic-clogged highway in Mexico may not sound like the location for a perfect meal, but in the same way that starched white tablecloths, waistcoat-wearing sommeliers and immaculate service are quintessential elements of a Parisian restaurant, a Mexican truck-stop cantina wouldn't be the same without the stray dogs, overweight flatulent men, thundering traffic and the smell of unburnt diesel. Rolling out my sleeping bag on the concrete floor, I settled down and drifted off to sleep, a happy man.

⚲

Horses, not seen in the Americas since the prehistoric ice age, began to be shipped across the Atlantic from Spain soon after the explorer Hernán Cortés landed in 1519. They were a crucial means of transport, vital in controlling the new colony and subduing indigenous armies.

As Nueva España expanded, a demand for beef and leather amongst its new inhabitants grew and, as well as horses, domesticated cattle were also introduced to the New World. Enterprising and wealthy colonial landowners filled their new ranches with cattle but, far too important to do the work themselves, they trained local men in the skills needed to control these swelling herds on horseback. These cattle hands became know as vaqueros, and as the enterprise of cattle ranching extended further into central and northern Mexico, so did the gutsy traditions and colourful folklore of these men.

During and after the Mexican–American War in the 1840s, the customs of the vaquero were absorbed by settlers in California, Texas and the southern United States, who borrowed their ranching skills, distinctive and functional attire and their vocabulary. The term 'buckaroo' is the anglicised pronunciation of vaquero.

Months before pedalling into the northern states of Mexico, I had experienced first-hand the hard-drinking, hard-riding, testicle-chewing cowboys of America's Midwest, and I thought I had seen the real McCoy. But cycling further into the state of Sinaloa, on Mexico's north-west coast, it became very clear I was now riding into real cowboy country.

Today the vaqueros of modern Mexico are known as charros, and when I wasn't being passed by open trailers packed tight with baying cattle trailing their rich stench of manure, posses of hard-faced, moustachioed men clip-clopped past me on proud horses, decked out in black or white sombreros, gleaming spurs, high-cut boots, leather chaps and ornate belt buckles. Sitting bolt upright in their worn saddles, they controlled their steeds with gentle tugs on the reins with one hand while the other arm hung nonchalantly behind. The machetes, lassoes and blankets that hung from their saddles made it clear these men were working cowboys. Their horse was their livelihood and their weather-beaten, worn-out attire was not a costume worn at weekends as a testament to a dying culture, but the most practical clothing for days in the saddle, driving cattle under a blazing sun.

⚲

Cantina de Vaquero. Carne Asada. 4km

It was the end of a steamy day's cycling, and the abundant cattle flies and mosquitoes had begun their evening blood hunt. Fed up with the perpetual stings and bites, I pulled off the road and followed the dusty trail away from the highway towards the Cantina de Vaquero, in the hope that it might be a suitable place to eat and sleep.

At the end of the track six horses and a dusty pick-up truck were parked in front of a simple thatched barn, open on all sides. A large, smoking grill filled the air with the magnificent odours of grilled beef, and an antiquated jukebox pumped loud Banda, a traditional brass-based music favoured by charros, into the warm evening.

The only other customers, a gang of charros, sat around a table, their impressive collection of beer bottles littering the floor. This drunken cowboy choir mimicked every tune from the jukebox in pitch-perfect baritone voices, before accompanying the trumpets and trombones of the chorus with a succession of high-pitched shrieks and cat-calls.

To my huge disappointment the grill was no longer serving food, but after eyeing me up and down suspiciously, the woman in charge said I could pitch my tent on a piece of scrub behind the restaurant. Content with a good day's cycling and happy to have found what looked like a safe place to stay, I began the mundane ritual of unpacking and setting up camp. From behind me, as I forced a stubborn tent peg into the dry earth, I heard the unmistakable offer of a beer. Having cycled over sixty miles that day, at the end of a hot, hard week, I accepted. I joined the men at their table, drinking Michelada, a gloriously refreshing cocktail of ice-cold beer, lime juice and chilli. It was soon dark. The owner of the restaurant had had enough and apparently so had we. The plug was pulled on the jukebox and next on the agenda was a local charreada in a nearby village. I was assured my bicycle would be safe hidden behind the toilets and, encouraged by plenty of beer and the chance to see a rodeo Mexico-style, I climbed into the back of a beaten up pick-up truck and we shot off in a cloud of dust.

Climbing out of the truck, I stood there with my blond hair, cycling shoes, blue jeans and camping-store fleece and felt the stare of a hundred dark eyes home in on me, accompanied by expressions that seemed to say, 'What the fuck is he doing here?' The burst of fresh air from the truck ride meant my beer-induced confidence was fading fast and in the dim light my friends from the restaurant seemed to have been cloned by the dozen. I began to question why I hadn't stayed with my tent but instead was standing alone in a small rural village somewhere in the state of Sinaloa, northern Mexico.

In the glow of a couple of failing streetlights I watched as swarms of charros swigged from cans of Tecate beer and exchanged macho greetings. Men on horseback sparred with each other, pulling off sharp turns, twists and other equestrian trickery, while others showboated their horse-handling skills, galloping around the crude plaza before pulling on their brakes, forcing their horses to skid across the cobbles, then sharply turning tail, whooping with drunken bravado and joyriding back into the darkness. Amongst the crowd broad-shouldered men in all their charro finery of matching boots, belts and hat straps strutted about parading their women on their arms, while those without partners stood puffed up like fighting cocks in the hope of attracting the attention

Taking on the Manhattan traffic and flying the flag (upside down)

Traditional dress at the Sagamok Anishnawbek Pow Wow

A cold start crossing the Rockies

Getting to grips with Dungeness crab in Oregon

Having a rest in the hills of southern Mexico

Big vats of molé in the market of Oxahaca

Tom and Amir

Heading into the mist in the mountains of Guatemala

Taking lessons from Piney in cooking Ron Don in Costa Rica

Harvesting coffee in Columbia

Torsten the German

Fishing for supper
on the Rio Napo

'Siempre Adalante' – the boat that was home for a week

Loading buffalo – Amazon style!

The flamboyant chefs on the boat to Brazil

Sleeping arrangements on board

A local delicacy – armadillo

Glorious Brazilian mud

Bahaina Brazil

I had finally arrived!

How to prepare a guinea pig

Step one:
Dip in boiling water

Step two: Pluck

Step three: Gut and
season the insides
with garlic and cumin

Step four:
Roast and enjoy!

of the pretty girls in tight-fitting jeans who swung their hips and giggled in the shadows. The place was bubbling over with machismo. Suffering from a serious bout of testosterone deficiency, I went to look for another beer and something to eat.

Making the most of the faint orange light, a team of enterprising locals had set up a taco stand under one of the village's working lamps. The red plastic tables and chairs were full of customers. They were doing a roaring trade, feeding the alcohol-induced hunger of the crowd. I got happily in line.

A man with a weighty cleaver chopped and diced sticky heaps of meat on a large wooden chopping block, and a woman worked pressing fresh tortillas from round balls of dough. But something was different about this taco stand. There was no hissing grill covered with cuts of meat. There were no shallow vats of oil sizzling and spitting with short lengths of intestine. Instead the meat was being cooked on a round metal plate, domed in the middle, that puffed steam from numerous small holes punched in its surface. Slimy grey heaps of meat were cooked in the middle of the plate by hot vapour, and tortillas were warmed on the edges, slightly marinated in the sticky juices that seeped from the well-kept meat. Waiting in turn, I listened intently to the orders of the people in front of me, trying to determine what I was about to eat, but my beer-dulled brain failed me. I tapped the shoulder of the man in front and asked him what the meat was.

'Cabeza.'

I must have looked blank. The man tapped a finger on the edge of his black hat.

Head. Of course!

Taking me by the shoulder, the man pointed at the different textures and colours of meat. 'Labio,' he said before touching his lips. 'Ojo.' He pointed at my eyes. 'Cachete.' He pulled on one of his cheeks. 'Sesos.' He tapped his temple again. 'Lengua.' He stuck out his tongue. This was a mad-cow-disease pick 'n' mix, but before I could decide which cut of a cow's head to choose from, my tutor ordered for me.

'Un mixto, unos sesos, una lengua y uno cachete.'

I thanked the man and, holding my plate of four neatly packed tacos, I went to work on the no-frills selection of condiments. A classic salsa verde, some finely diced onion, chopped cilantro and a deliciously smooth guacamole. None of the vibrant red salsas, radishes and pico de gallo I was used to, but the subtle greens complemented perfectly the grey tones of the meat and the translucent hue of the tortillas. In the half light it was hard to tell which meat was which, but I think I started with my brain taco, and the first thing I noticed was the wonderful texture of the steamed tortilla, soft, damp and chewy, like the skin of dim sum. The flavours of the various head parts were rich and meaty with a tender texture. To hell with bovine spongiform encephalitis. These tacos were great.

Feasting on offal, I watched the crowds and listened to the invigorating tones of Banda music that jumped from a simple tannoy system attached to the roof of a van until they were replaced by an undistinguishable announcement. The crowd suddenly drifted away, and swept up with them I too arrived at a large circular arena encircled by a high metal fence. Pick-up trucks and tractors were parked tidily all around the edge, acting as both improvised seating and lighting. The vehicles' headlights filled the ring with a brilliant light, casting long shadows of the men and women climbing onto the roofs, bonnets and fenders for the best view.

'Pssssssssssst – eh, gringo!'

It was one of the men from earlier in the evening. I was pulled on to the roof of a truck and squeezed into a row of tequila-enriched charros. I took a long pull on the bottle offered to me, and after the initial hit of the cheap tequila, a rush of calm coursed through my veins.

A loud announcement, followed by a chorus of wolf whistles and cheers, signalled that the charreada was about to get under way. On the far side of the ring, a teenager in thick leather chaps and a sombrero nervously mounted a gigantic bull, its broad neck and heavy frame a mass of muscle. Wriggling into his desired position and gripping a rope tied round the bull's forequarters, the young man lifted one hand in the air, signalling to a man with an electric cattle prodder that he was ready to roll. The prodder was pushed through the bars of the fence towards the bull's hind legs and then *Zap!*

What had been a docile and tidy collection of beef cuts was transformed into a wild, angry mess of muscle, horns and mucus, charging, bucking and kicking its way around the dusty arena, dismounting its rider after about five long seconds and sending him scrambling through the dirt for the fence and safety. While the victorious bull pawed the ground and acknowledged the adulation of the crowd, a team of men lassoed him in, ready for the next competitor.

Men were tossed high into the air. Others hung on for seemingly impossible amounts of time. Bodies were hurled effortlessly into the railings, while others ran scared, throwing themselves over the fence in the nick of time. There was no ambulance, I had no idea how far the nearest emergency room was, and I watched in amazement as these apparently fearless men clambered aboard. I wasn't sure whether I felt sorrier for the young men being flung around, kicked and charged like worthless ragdolls, or for the bullocks who had to withstand 200 volts being zapped into their backsides. Either way, it made compulsive viewing. The bulls kept bucking and the riders kept coming, as did the bottles of cheap tequila and cans of beer.

🚲

The scratchy call of a cockerel exploded in my head and I woke, startled from a shallow, inebriated slumber, with no idea where I was. Scrambling to my feet, I took in my surroundings. Shafts of sunlight pierced a rusty metal roof. A few mangy chickens pecked at the dirt floor and a litter of whimpering dogs huddled together on a sackcloth bed. Topless, but thankfully still in my trousers, I was drenched in sticky sweat, and the plastic beer crates I had been sleeping on had left a strange geometric rash across my chest. In a fearsome one-two combination, an excruciating pain in my head and an overwhelming feeling of nausea threw me back on to the floor. The stale taste of alcohol on my breath and my parched mouth triggered my memory, and slowly a few broken fragments of the previous night began to materialise. The restaurant; the cowboys; a long ride in a truck; the rodeo; beer; tequila ...

My bike! Where the fuck is my bike?

I had no idea where I was. I had no idea where my bicycle was. I began to curse my stupidity. My trip of a lifetime was meant to end on a beach in Rio, not languishing in a hungover mess on the dirty floor of a shed in Mexico.

Heeeeeeeraaaaaaarch ... putt!

The hideous noise came from the other side of a tatty, hessian curtain, and the ensemble of deep-throat retching was followed by a combination of spitting, coughing and cursing, all culminating in a disturbingly loud expulsion of wind. Whatever lived behind the curtain was not well.

The curtain was drawn back to reveal an overweight, hairy, semi-naked, sweaty and very muddled-looking Mexican. The expression on his face conveyed his thoughts exactly. 'Why have I got a semi-naked gringo lying on my floor?'

This silent standoff continued for a few more moments while he put his pieces of the night together and, after kicking a few chickens out of the room, he put on a shirt, picked up a worn-out leather saddle from the floor and threw it on the back of his tired horse, tied up outside. He signalled with a grunt that I should climb aboard, and at the mercy of a crippling hangover, and with equestrian skills that went no further than piloting a doped-up donkey on a beach as a child, I tried to obey. With one foot trapped in a stirrup, I hopped up and down trying to get my leg over, until the man from behind the curtain pushed a shoulder under my buttocks. With all the grace of a man climbing out of a small window, I clambered on board. The man from behind the curtain jumped on behind me and with our bodies sandwiched together in the saddle we wound our way through a cobbled maze of pathways and the simple adobe buildings of his village.

Apart from the steady clip-clop of the hooves on the cobblestones, and the occasional bout of retching, we suffered in silence, trotting past the confused faces that peered out of the shadowed doorways of the village. We rode into a sun-scorched pasture, dotted with heavy cattle. At length, climbing a gentle hill, I could hear the drone of the highway, and was relieved to see the restaurant where I hoped I would be reunited with my own trusty steed.

'Adios.' The man from behind the curtain trotted back the way we had come.

Mercifully, my bicycle was where I left it, and against my better judgement I rode it slowly through the heat of the morning, suffering from the kind of soul-destroying hangover that makes you swear never to touch alcohol again. Wearily, I counted the miles to the next town on my map, where I hoped I might find my cure.

In pre-revolutionary Mexico, poverty was chronic. The unfair distribution of wealth meant that the best cuts of meat went to the wealthy landowners, while the campesinos and vaqueros had to survive on cheaper cuts. Having to make do with offal, brains, heads, tails and hooves, these became the foundation of Mexico's cuisine, of which menudo is one of her most celebrated recipes and a famed hangover cure. Overcome by waves of nausea, the thought of swallowing down slippery chunks of tripe hardly helped my delicate condition, but having heard about the magical powers of this miracle dish from numerous truck drivers, it was now my only hope.

Limping into town, I headed straight for the mercado municipal, a boisterous and stifling labyrinth, heaving with people. Behind tables piled high with produce, men and women shouted above each other. Boys pushing loaded sack-barrows ordered me out of their way and the sound of butchers thumping heavy cleavers down on chopping boards echoed in my head. The screeching and crowing of chickens in metal cages was amplified alarmingly. Swept up in the slow-moving current of people, I was pushed past tables of reeking fish buzzing with flies and on through alleyways of smoking grills and steaming pots that filled the already stuffy air with pungent smells. On any other day I would have loved this place, but in my state of disrepair it was all too much and, like a poisoned man with only minutes to live, I searched desperately for my life-saving antidote.

At the heart of the market a huddle of small fondas or temporary kitchens was busy with women, each with their own speciality, cooking local delicacies from the freshest of market ingredients. Lining one side of a long table, a line of black and white sombreros indicated the heads of men hunched over steaming bowls. On a chalk board above them were the magical words.

Rico menudo, fines de semana.

I had found what I was looking for. Drenched in sweat, I squeezed into this hungover line-up, the only man without a hat and well-kept moustache, and asked for some menudo.

Bubbling under the lids of four metal vats was the magic potion. After lifting the lid, the woman spooned three large ladle-fuls into a bowl and placed it in front of me, along with a plate of warm tortillas, two halves of lime, a plate of chopped cilantro and diced spring onion and a small terracotta dish of tiny red and yellow chillies.

The menudo smelt unusual, like a wet animal, but after stirring it through with a healthy pinch of cilantro, and wringing every last drop of vitamin-packed juice from the limes, I dropped in a pinch of chilli and took my first spoonful. Like my mother's hand on my forehead, it was immediately comforting. The soggy texture of the tripe soothed my parched throat, nursing every inch of my insides as it found its way south, and with every spoonful I could feel my damaged system recovering. The stew was spicy enough even without my addition of extra chillies to begin flushing out every drop of the previous night's excesses. I was crying like a teenage girl at the end of the film *Titanic*, rivers of mucus poured out of my nose, saliva dribbled from my lips and every pore of my skin was emitting fluids. I was a sniffling, drooling, sweat-drenched mess of a man, but peering with bloodshot eyes down the line of vaqueros on either side of me, I knew I was not alone. I didn't have a wide-brimmed hat, I didn't have a fancy belt buckle and I couldn't ride a horse, but with my own ride tied up outside, enjoying this perfect hangover cure, I felt at one with the real cowboys who surrounded me.

⌚

> But to me, a dreamer of dreams
> To whom what is and what seems
> Are often one and the same,
> The bells of San Blas to me
> Have a strange, wild melody,
> And are something more than a name.
>
> Henry W. Longfellow, 'The Bells of San Blas'

On 6 March the bells of the small coastal town of San Blas welcomed in my twenty-seventh birthday. It was my first birthday on the road, and after my lonely weeks of solo cycling, I was presented with the best birthday present I could have wished for. Waiting on the corner of the town's sleepy plaza was the immediately recognisable figure of Amir with his loaded bicycle. We had only been apart for a few weeks, but we sat in the sand for hours drinking cold Pacifico beer and regaling each other with our tales from the road. Young surfers pulled tricks on the barrelling waves, squadrons of pelicans glided in tight formations, folding their wings before diving for fish, and as the sun went down we camped behind the beach next to a small restaurant.

The following morning the restaurant was full of activity. Tables were being arranged, chairs lined up around them and endless cases of beer unloaded into a deep chest freezer brimming with ice. A team of cooks had their heads down in the open kitchen, chopping and dicing fresh ingredients, and the owner's daughter rushed about bellowing orders at her staff, in preparation for her mother-in-law's seventy-third birthday party. By midday a rowdy gang of thirty grey-haired local women, dolled-up in their finest floral dresses, had descended on the restaurant. They were seated at a table that ran the length of the room, swigging from bottles of beer, gossiping and laughing with the verve of women a third of their age. Strolling through the restaurant after a long swim, the owner's daughter announced to the banquet that we almost shared a birthday, and from then on there was no escape. The party introduced themselves to me with a round of passionate and whiskery kisses, and I was ordered to sit next to the birthday girl, the only man at this boisterous table of juiced-up geriatrics.

The food arrived to rapturous applause from the table, and it was well deserved. There were trays heaped with plump, grilled shrimp drizzled in lime; platters of warm octopus mixed through with tomatoes, red onion and cilantro; bowls of squid, swimming in oil infused with garlic and chilli; meaty fillets of smoked marlin, barbecued red snapper and whole sea bass baked in foil with various herbs, which released clouds of fishy steam when they were unwrapped. There were wooden bowls of smooth guacamole, home-made salsas, translucent slices of scarlet-edged radishes and, of course, baskets of warm tortillas. Filled with bliss, I stared down the long table, across the beach and towards the rolling turquoise ocean. Plate after plate of vibrant fresh ingredients was brought to the table. The intricate patterns on the ladies' dresses, the happy smiles on their knowing faces, the lively twinkle in their eyes, the gold flashes in their smiles, all enhanced by the shafts of bright sunlight breaking through the thatched roof of the palapa. I could not have imagined a more beautiful meal if I tried.

In the middle of the afternoon, a three-man band arrived. Dressed in wide-brimmed sombreros, sequin-trimmed trousers and tight little jackets, they played their guitar, double base and violin faultlessly and, buoyed by good food and cold beer, as they struck up another song I offered the birthday girl my arm for her first dance. Kicking off our shoes, we danced in the sand to the gentle rhythm, and the rest of the party gathered around clapping and singing us to the end of the song. Then the fighting began. Fuelled on beer, this once genteel group of respectable old ladies evolved into a determined squabbling mob, all desperate for a turn with the young English cyclist. Apparently, I was hot property, and, pulled from lady to lady, I blushed my way through the afternoon, disturbed by what women of that age could do with their hips. I lost count of the amount of times my buttocks were firmly groped, to wild cheers from the rest of the mob, but by six o'clock I admitted defeat. Exhausted and completely out-danced by women old enough to be my grandmother, I took a well-needed rest. Back at the table, I made a belated birthday wish that on my seventy-third birthday I would have a party like that, surrounded by close friends and family. And who knows, if I played my cards right there may even be a 27-year-old Mexican señorita to grope.

🚲

Back on the road side by side with Amir, we made good time, crossing into the Tropic of Cancer and cycling south into the rich jungles that blanketed the hillsides running down to the coast. Unlike the parched, lifeless landscape of the Baja, with its aggressive cacti and sun-baked earth, our surroundings were now verdant and jumping with life. Huge palms fanned out with sharp fronds, thick-trunked mango trees hung with ripe fruit, all entwined by tangles of creepers and twisting tendrils that ran between the wide green leaves of papaya and banana.

I had never been to a tropical country before. Now plants I had only ever seen in botanical gardens were growing all around me. Hidden in their dense foliage, birds with strange and exotic songs reminded me of my long-forgotten mobile phone, only ever allowing me a flashing glimpse of their colourful plumes as they flew from tree to tree.

Passing through the small communities that lived in this generous natural landscape, modest houses sold their surplus on small wooden tables, their children running out to take a few pesos in exchange for a plastic bucket of the freshest fruit. Until now every mango, pineapple or banana I had put in my mouth had spent at least a month holed up in the metal hull of a container ship, but here they were growing right in front of me. Resting in the shade of dense trees, Amir and I sat like a pair of monkeys, juice running down our faces, munching on the fibrous flesh of sweet mangoes, before cycling away, plucking ripe bananas from the bunches strapped to the back of our bicycles.

Sleeping rough at night, beaches, dried-up riverbeds and abandoned buildings became our homes, and together we could carry enough food so that we always ate well. The nights were balmy and with no need to sleep in the airless conditions of our tents, we slept by our fires after dining on fried peppers, grilled chicken and sautéed beef. We made fresh guacamole, hearty stews of lentils and beans, heaps of well seasoned rice all served with warm corn tortillas, and spicy salsa.

🚲

As the sun rose each day on this beautiful country we ate fresh fruit, made huevos rancheros and brewed strong coffee before cycling into the heat of the morning. By the middle of the day even the mad dogs of Mexico, which normally took great pleasure in chasing the Englishmen through the countryside, found a shady spot to sleep, and we were only too happy to join them. Tired after our mornings of excursion we picnicked in plazas of small towns and villages or on the banks of languid rivers before sleeping it off with a blissful siesta in the shade of fragrant bushes of bougainvillea.

As the shadows of the afternoon lengthened, the people re-appeared and Mexico came back to life. The metal shutters of shops were rolled up, music was played from every building, shoe shiners come out from wherever they were hiding and well-kept leafy colonial plazas filled with Mexicans of every generation.

Every so often when we felt we deserved it, we slept in these small towns, where a cheap hotel would provide us with a well-needed shower and where we could also leave our bicycles in our room and take to the town on foot. Mexico was at her most beautiful in the early evening. Flocks of chattering birds would swoop from tree to tree feasting on insects, churches opened their doors and rang their bells, gangs of well-groomed teenagers in counterfeit US designer clothes joked and flirted, old men sat on their favourite benches watching it all pass by. And, of course, of special interest to hungry cyclists, all manner of street food became available from the portable carts that opened for the evening trade.

In a short stroll along cobbled streets, and with no more than a handful of pesos, you could eat a four-course al fresco meal of the very highest quality in the most beautiful surroundings. Elote, a cob of grilled corn served in its husk, smothered in queso fresco and chilli flakes, made a perfect starter, followed by tripe, adobe and carne asada tacos, washed down with refreshing glasses of agua de jamaica. For pudding, a paper bag of warm churros, deliciously light deep-fried sticks of batter dusted with sugar and cinnamon, followed by a warming cup of arroz con leche, a Mexican rice pudding.

When we weren't dining under the stars in the Mexican countryside, we were eating out on the streets and plazas of old colonial towns. In this temperate climate, and with Amir as companion, the nomadic lifestyle was without fault.

🚲

By now, Amir and I knew each other's strengths and weaknesses as well as we knew our own. Cresting a large hill in the dry heat of the afternoon to the sight of a sun-faded Coca Cola sign on the other side, there was no need for communication. We both knew when we needed to pull over for a rest. We were well practised in answering the routine questions too. Where did we live? Where were we going? Every time we reeled off the list of towns on our proposed route, as soon as we proudly announced we were planning to ride into Mexico City, eyes would widen and jaws drop.

With a reputation for crime that spread even further than its ever-increasing suburbs, it was clear that cycling into Mexico City was not recommended. Cycling into any big city is an exhausting, unpleasant experience involving litter-strewn highways, dirty traffic and pollution, and the thought of entering the biggest city on earth on a bicycle was just too much. It would involve at the very least a day of riding through some of the city's less desirable districts, and after a little discussion we both decided to load our bikes on to a bus and cheat our way into Mexico City.

With our bicycles cruelly dismembered and loaded into the cavernous belly of the bus, we took our seats. Vents above our heads blasted cool air on our faces, while levers allowed us to recline for a nap to help pass the time. Dated action movies starring Jean-Claude Van Damme blared from televisions that hung from the ceiling, and when a uniformed stewardess offered me a cold can of soda and a packet of American crisps, I wanted to get off.

What would have taken three days of tough, hot cycling flashed by in a matter of comfortable, air-conditioned hours, but I longed to be on my bike.

🚲

The moment of wisdom that guided Amir and me into Mexico City, however, failed to find us when we decided to leave, and on a scorching Friday morning we saddled up and cycled into the rivers of traffic that poured out of the world's largest metropolis. We found ourselves trapped between a concrete wall on one side and eight lanes of fast-moving traffic on the other. Powerless over where we were going, we were sucked out of the city in a torrent of cars, taxis, buses and trucks.

We cycled over and under graffiti-covered concrete flyovers holding more congested streams of traffic. We pedalled past the giant warehouses of soulless industrial parks and next to the polluting pipes and funnels of oil refineries. The road was lined with rundown, laundry-decorated tower blocks and littered with foul-smelling rubbish. At times it seemed as though the impoverished suburbs of this megalopolis would never end. But at last, with tired eyes that stung from hours of exposure to choking exhaust fumes, we looked back at the hazy yellow dome of smog that hovered over Mexico City like a dirty forcefield. Ahead of us the misty blue layers of Mexico's central highlands stretched into the horizon.

No sooner had we escaped the modern plagues of pollution and heavy traffic than a volley of hail-stones burst from the heavens. Bouncing off the tarmac and our helmets like sizzling popcorn, it stung our arms and legs before morphing into driving rain. While we both rushed to unpack the waterproof jackets and trousers that had been lurking for months, unused, in the bottom of a pannier, a large white van came to a halt on the shoulder ahead of us. The driver's door opened and, using a plastic bag to shelter his head from the rain that fell in biblical proportions, the driver jogged towards us. Explaining that he was a keen cyclist, he said that we should put our bikes in the back of his van and stay at his house. Amir and I gave each other a knowing look. A total stranger was asking us to bundle our worldly belongings into his van, before taking us wherever he wanted. It might not have been the logical thing to do, but we got in. Amir climbed into the cab and I was packed into the complete darkness of the back along with the bikes.

↺↻

What remained of the daylight burst in through the open doors of the van and woke me from a contorted and uncomfortable sleep. I had no idea where I was. The air was cold and fresh, and the hills I could see in the distance were densely carpeted with dark pine trees.

Mateus, the driver, was outside, demanding to know if I was all right.

I said yes, as I did my best to pull myself up on a pair of numbed, lifeless legs. Amir and I heaved our cumbersome bikes out of the lorry, and Mateus showed us to a small room next to his family-run clothes factory. It was a confusion of sewing machines and rolls of bright material. We were offered some dinner but, exhausted, we declined and were both soon asleep.

The following morning we chatted over coffee, and I admired the shiny trophies, clusters of medals and proud photos that decorated Mateus's modest living room. This man was a real cyclist, and when I explained I was also collecting recipes, it became clear we shared a love of food too. Suddenly becoming excited, he insisted we couldn't leave town without trying a local barbacoa. Pulling out one of his beloved bicycles, a shiny thoroughbred machine with slender wheels that made me long for a faster ride, the three of us raced through the streets of his small town on our way to the barbacoa.

Due to the apparently unstoppable rise of supermarkets in the United Kingdom, customers have become almost completely detached from the animals they eat. Any blood or guts or reference to the butchering process has been well hidden behind a veil of shrink wrap, fancy packaging and advertising.

As a result, generations of Brits are being brainwashed into not eating anything unless it looks just the way the adverts have sold it to them. Trying to get a British child to eat a vegetable is hard enough. Try to tempt them away from their Disney-endorsed burger and chips with a bowl of tripe or tasty plate of tongue, and you are likely to be told you're a bad parent, before a restraining order is slapped in your lap. For over a generation the British public has been told to eat what it is sold, and we are almost totally conditioned. It is impossible to buy ox tongue in Sainsbury's or tripe in Tesco because meat has to be branded. Beef must be pink, chicken must be white, and if what we are buying doesn't look exactly like the image in the adverts there must be something wrong with it.

In Mexico, butchery is thankfully still a celebrated and integral part of culinary culture and there is no better display of the way meat should be prepared and eaten than at a traditional barbacoa. This method of slow-cooking turkey, game and fish in shallow fire pits covered over with maguey leaves dates back to pre-Colombian Mexico. Following the introduction of cattle, pigs, sheep and chickens by the Spanish in the sixteenth century, the barbacoa evolved into time-honoured carnivorous feasts that take place every weekend in the towns and villages of Central Mexico. We propped up our bikes under the large imposing sign that hung on the front of a military-sized hangar, and there was no doubting what was on the menu. Underneath a painting of a stout ram with spiralling horns were the welcoming words:

Barbacoa los Cordovas.
Exquisita barbacoa de carnero de horno

The building was a simple construction of breeze-blocks and girders roofed over with corrugated metal. Admittedly it looked more like a bus depot than a restaurant, but inside rows of trestle tables with multicoloured plastic chairs provided seating for generations of Mexicans, who filled this glorified shed with an atmosphere of unbridled enjoyment. Rosy-cheeked waitresses dressed in red-and-black-checked aprons worked the tables, and Mateus was greeted like an old friend by the owner. After being introduced as a continent-crossing cyclist searching for food, I was taken to the pits.

Behind the restaurant, a row of huge dome-shaped mounds of earth seeped smoke like dormant volcanoes. On the top of each improvised oven, the earth was less compact, and digging at it like an archaeologist excavating a hidden tomb, the owner scraped away a thick layer of mud to reveal folds of thick maguey leaves. The long fronds of this giant member of the agave family were peeled back like heavy sheets of green rubber. I peered inside.

Initially knocked back by a strong waft of heat and steam from the deep pit, I was quickly engulfed by the magical sweet smells of slow-cooking lamb. As the vapour cleared, a mass of tangled sheep parts emerged from the misty darkness. Legs, ribs, hooves and heads had all been slow-cooking in the horno, the name for this traditional oven of earth and maguey leaves, for over seven hours. Reaching inside the horno with a long metal hook, the owner removed cut after cut of steaming, sticky meat and quickly went to work hacking, shredding and cutting on a butcher's block, so well used it had its own topography.

We ordered a kilo of tender meat for the three of us, which I thought was a modest amount until we were presented with a mountain of viscous flesh. My hungry muscles flexed with excitement. With all the grace of a starving Neanderthal, I filled a fresh tortilla with juicy meat, splashed on a little salsa, cilantro and a squeeze of lime, carefully manoeuvred the loaded tortilla towards my mouth and took my first bite.

Boooooom! My senses exploded in what appeared to be some kind of orgasm. The meat was unfathomably tender and each bite released ambrosial juices into my mouth. It was a dream come true, and I truly believed I had found the perfect meal. But in a land where meat is a luxury, nothing was put to waste, and my carnivorous feasting had only just begun. Mateus insisted that I try everything, and so in the name of culinary research I went to work on a steady flow of meaty delicacies.

A plate of tacos de sesos, a crunchy deep-fried maize tortilla, filled with soft sheep's brains marinated in a powerful chipotle salsa, was followed by a bowl of caldo de pata, a surprisingly subtle and refreshing bowl of stock, made from sheep's hooves that had been slow-roasted then boiled. Panza de carnero, a sheep's stomach prepared as a type of haggis, stuffed with diced intestine, chipotle chillies, garlic and herbs, was slow-cooked in the oven and served in tortillas. A row of deep earthenware bowls, heated gently on a charcoal grill, held spicy molita de panzita, a rich offal stew similar to menudo but made from the sheep's lengthy intestine, which floated on the surface like a nest of pale snakes. Sangre de carnero, sheep's blood, was boiled until solid like our black pudding then served swimming in a rich red mole of pasilla chillies. Mixiote, a type of boil-in-the-bag barbacoa, was made from tender cuts of lamb seasoned with pasilla and guajillo chillies, cumin, thyme, cloves and garlic, wrapped in small parcels made from the tough paper-like skin of maguey leaves. Even the drinks at this meat-eater's festival were meaty. To quench my thirst I sipped at warm mugs of lamb consommé made from the rich juices collected by a small pipe that ran from the base of the fire pits.

In almost a year of cycling I had developed a fierce metabolism, and it was rare for me to turn down food, but at my first barbacoa I honestly thought that if I swallowed one more mouthful I would collapse. As more and more meat was placed in front of me, I could feel my brain blinking as all the blood in my body raced to deal with the emergency in my stomach. This was medieval eating, a carnivore's paradise, but just when I thought I could take no more, Mateus had arranged for one last treat.

The maguey cactus that is used to wrap the meat for the barbacoa is a hugely important part of the culinary culture of Mexico's central states. Although not eaten as a specific dish, its hearts are roasted and fermented to make tequila's evil twin brother, mescal. Its sweet sticky sap is lightly fermented to make the vitamin-packed tipple called pulque, and during the rainy season the maguey's giant leaves make an ideal home for gusanos de maguey. These plump two-inch grubs live inside the damp leaves, protected from predators by the leaves' sharp spines. Packed with protein, they are a Mexican delicacy that has been popular for thousands of years.

Picking one up in his fingers, Mateus showed me how it was done, popping the ribbed white grub into his mouth and chewing away with wide eyes of pleasure. Amir, in his wisdom, politely refused. Staring at the plate of unfortunate giant maggots in front of me, it was a while before I was able to select my first candidate. Tentatively placing it in my mouth, I closed my jaw and waited for the instinctive gag as the abdomen exploded, filling my mouth with an unknown viscous substance. But there was no explosion, and having been shallow-fried with chilli and garlic, these crunchy grubs made surprisingly good eating.

Going against our better judgment, Amir and I got back on the bicycles after this gargantuan breakfast and cycled towards the city of Puebla. Since just before Mexico City, Amir and I had been discussing the pros and cons of cycling alone, and although we greatly enjoyed one another's company, I was keen to spend more time in Mexico looking for food, while Amir was keen to push on south into Central America. We didn't need to say anything, but we both knew the time had come to separate.

My time with Amir had been one of the highlights of the trip, but the more we cycled together the more we understood that we each had our own agenda. The barbacoa would be our last meal together. On arriving in Puebla we said a sad goodbye, planning to meet again in Guatemala.

Alone again, I left Puebla and rode south for Oaxaca. Dense groves of aged mango trees blanketed the valleys and the roads were peaceful. Apart from the occasional passing vehicle all I heard was the wind disturbing the dense leaves of trees and the crashing of mangoes falling from their branches before landing with a soft thud on the ground. Mangoes were everywhere, and the air was filled with their sweet aroma and the drone of the insects that feasted on their sweet meat. In the middle of the day, I would scout for a handful of plump fruits, before sitting in the shade of the trees, peeling back the skin and slicing off slabs of ripe flesh with my sticky penknife. As I sucked at the flesh of the large stone, the sweet juice would run down my chin and the long fibres of the flesh would get stuck in my teeth. For three days, on the road to Oaxaca, I ate mangoes for breakfast, lunch and dinner, and never once got bored. Instead of protecting my head, my helmet hung from my handlebars, loaded with delicious ripe fruit, and at the top of each long climb I sat on the side of the road admiring the views across the valleys of Oaxaca and eating mangoes.

Two days' ride south of the colonial city of Oaxaca, I stopped in a small market for breakfast. Studying my map over a delightful breakfast of quesadillas de flor de calabacita, a folded maize tortilla generously filled with courgette flowers and stringy Oaxaca cheese, I began discussing my route with a dust-covered construction worker perched at the fonda next to me. Scribbling down a list of villages that didn't appear on my map, he assured me that in the last few days a route connecting the mountain villages had been bulldozed through and if I didn't mind 300 kilometres of dirt road, I could loop through the Oaxaca highlands and arrive at the same spot that the mundane main road would take me to.

I asked him was it really possible on a bike.

A long pause was followed by the typical hissing sounds that Mexican men make when they are mulling something over. Looking me up and down, then studying my bicycle, he declared it was possible.

His thoughtful pause didn't fill me with confidence, but the idea of perhaps being the first person to cycle this newly broken route through the mountains did. Loading up with a few essential supplies of rice, lentils and honey, I set off into the hills, looking for adventure.

🚲

Three days later I had found my adventure, but the feeling of excitement had long been forgotten and replaced with the darker, more purposeful emotions of cycle touring. At nine in the morning I had been cycling uphill on a single-lane dirt track for over two hours. My legs seemed to weaken with every turn of the pedals; the pain in my lower back screamed at me to stop. The red-earthed track I was following ribboned across the steep slope of the valley before disappearing into the dense white clouds that obscured its summit.

It must be downhill after this climb. I willed myself on.

Reaching the top in an exhausted sweaty mess, I stopped to catch my breath and savoured the cool breeze that rushed up the enormous valley in front of me. Leaning on my handlebars, I stared at the blue-grey shades of the far-off slopes and ridges that faded over countless miles into the hazy distance, before blending into the skyline. Like a meandering crack in the landscape, the dusty trail I had been following for days zigzagged into the horizon of this otherwise untouched landscape, promising more of the same.

It felt good at the top. It always does. Every ounce of effort accumulated into a wonderful glow of accomplishment, and in this most beautiful of places, feeling blissfully insignificant, the hardship of the morning vanished and I set off down the other side.

Even going downhill in this wild country was exhausting. There was no racing down through sweeping hairpins of well-kept tarmac. Just prolonged, treacherous descents over broken rubble and loose sand, never daring to let go of my brakes or pick up speed for fear of disappearing over the vertigo-inducing cliffs that waited for my mistakes.

'Go on, let go, just for a few seconds. Rest your tired hands. It'll be fun to pick up some speed. Take a risk,' said a little voice in my head, but it was overruled. I knew only too well, from numerous near misses, that one rock hit at speed could send me out of control and into the abyss. And who would ever find me? Other than a dust-covered construction worker, nobody knew where I was. Hell, apart from a list of names scribbled on a scrap of paper in my pocket, *I* didn't know where I was.

With my wrists and hands still aching from the aggressive vibration caused by the rough terrain of the descent, I had reached the bottom, and what remained of the trail had disappeared under a shambles of broken boulders, rushing water and fallen mud. After splashing a few handfuls of water on my face, I unclipped my panniers. Carefully stepping from boulder to boulder, I ferried my belongings to the other side. Reloaded, I looked ahead. It was time for my mind and body to return to the opposing disciplines needed for a climb. Concentrating on the ground directly in front of me, I began to pick the most efficient passage through the loose rubble and gravel that skidded underneath my wheels. Standing in my pedals, I pumped my legs, and with each exhausting rotation the bicycle pulled me forward a few more precious inches while I went through the various mantras that helped me onward.

One inch at a time, if that's what it takes. Just don't look up.
Inch by inch is a synch.
Slowly, slowly, catchee monkey.
You chose this. You chose it.

As I rounded another hairpin bend, the imprint of footsteps distracted me. They were too small for a man. Could be a child. Maybe a woman. I wonder if she's pretty...

Around the next switchback the owner of the footprints was revealed, dwarfed underneath a huge pile of wood. Slowly making her way up the mountain, she moved forward with a determined rhythm. On the steeper parts of the hill the distance between us grew, but as the trail levelled out I caught up and came alongside.

'Buenos dias.'

The small woman stopped and slowly turned her head to face me. A sackcloth harness, which took the considerable weight of the bundle of wood on her back, was pulled tight around her forehead. Her features were wide and angular, but I was unable to put an age to the craggy face that looked back at me. It belonged to a woman possibly in her sixties or seventies, but I had seen girls as young as eight or nine carrying equally large bundles of logs up these hills, and she could have been much younger. I offered another timid 'buenos dias' but knew I was unlikely to get a response. 'Mixe' is the first language and the name of the indigenous people who inhabit the eastern highlands of the Mexican state of Oaxaca. Our brief encounter ended and we both continued up the trail. Each with our different objective. The woman who owned the footsteps was providing vital fuel for her family to survive the impending rainy season. I wasn't sure what I was doing.

🚲

The strong scent of wood smoke and the increase in shoe and sandal prints in the dirt told me I was getting close to another village. The last mountain community I had passed through was two days behind me, and enthused by the idea of edible treats that might be waiting for me, I picked up speed.

The village was no more than a shabby collection of wood and metal huts and crude adobe and concrete buildings that clung to the steep hillside, connected by muddy pathways and steps cut into the mountainside. Laundry hung from a tangle of power lines, along with the remains of multicoloured paper bunting that fluttered in the breeze. Some black-haired pigs sniffed and grunted in the dirt. I disturbed a brood of scrawny chickens, who darted up the hillside, clucking as they went. Throughout the village was evidence that its inhabitants were preparing themselves for the rainy season.

Cobs and kernels of drying maize were laid out in the sun in front of homes. Thin strips of scarlet flesh and yellow fat hung from lines over doorways, like some form of witchcraft, along with bloody hides and coils of entrails. Tidy stacks of lumber were piled high under every possible shelter and the endless sound of chopping wood echoed from the surrounding dense forest. The village's only shop was a clinker-built hut decorated with a few plastic advertising signs for fizzy drinks. Inside it was dark and musty. Spread out on the floor in plastic crates were a few dusty onions, some muddy eggs and a cluster of overripe tomatoes, being enjoyed by a small swarm of flies. On a basic set of shelves a few packets of stock cubes sat next to some bags of rice, boxes of matches, light bulbs, tins of tuna fish and a large plastic jar of lurid lollipops.

Clutching three eggs, a tin of tuna and sucking a wonderfully sweet lollipop, I began thinking about where I might spend the night. The sun dropped behind the hills and the temperature with it, and the sound of distant thunder made my mind up. The shopkeeper sent me in the direction of the municipal building, a characterless concrete structure with a cell, a small office and a large open balcony, where a portly police officer said I could sleep on the floor.

He locked his office and bade me goodnight. Leaning on the balcony I stared into the gathering darkness at the faint flickering lights of the village, which ran down the dark hillside like hidden diamonds, while the night chorus of muffled voices, crying children and barking dogs reminded me where I was. I heard some strange greetings in an abrupt language in the street below, and followed the sound of the accompanying footsteps. Two men climbed the stairs of the balcony. Acknowledging me with a subdued nod, they pulled a pair of heavy blankets from their bag and laid them down on the floor. A woman followed, with a basket of yellow mangoes, then a young couple with a small child wrapped in a shawl. Within an hour the balcony had filled up with people and their lively conversation. As well as Mixe they used some Spanish, and I understood that they were all waiting for the bus to Oaxaca at 4 a.m. the following morning.

The last people to come up the steps were a robust, broad-shouldered woman and two girls who I assumed were her daughters. They wore square-cut blouses of dark red and turquoise embroidered with geometric patterns, and were weighed down with large baskets wrapped in colourful woven material, as well as a metal urn and a stack of plastic mugs and bowls. With the kind of efficiency that revealed they had done it a hundred times before, the family team set up shop. Two men sitting on a wooden bench were told to move. The women unwrapped the cloths and laid them on the bench, then lifted the lid on a large aluminium pot that had been hidden in one of the baskets, releasing a cloud of steam into the cold evening air.

A huddle of customers quickly gathered around this efficient trio, before returning to their spaces on the floor clutching deep bowls of pozole, thick maize tortillas and cups of atole. I waited in line and was given my own bowl, cup and tortilla. Leaning against the wall, I ate my impromptu supper.

The pozole in my bowl was a gloopy gruel-like substance, made from thrashed kernels of maize, boiled into a glutinous stew with trotters and other cheap cuts of pork and flavoured with lime juice and cilantro, the slimy offcuts and knuckles adding a rich meaty flavour. I sipped at my plastic mug of warm atole and mopped up the remains of my pozole with a warm maize tortilla so thick and earthy you could almost taste the bare hands that had made it. In the cold evening the atole, a traditional Mexican hot drink made from finely ground maize brewed in hot water and flavoured with chocolate and cinnamon, warmed me to the core. The hearty and nourishing food I was eating in this police station somewhere in the hills of Oaxaca was totally different to the Mexican food I had been enjoying previously.

Indigenous American societies have cultivated maize for millennia and it was the staple of the Aztecs, the Incas and the Maya people. But after the Spanish conquest and during the colonial period, Mexico's cuisine changed dramatically. With the conquistadores came new flavours and imported ingredients, and people developed a taste for them.

The food I had been eating until now had been a blend of the original indigenous fare and Spanish techniques and ingredients. But in the police station, surrounded by the wide faces and strange language of these ancient mountain people, I was lucky enough to be eating a meal as old as the mountains I had been cycling in. I had seen the maize growing in the small plots on the hillside, I had cycled past the kernels drying in front of the simple homes, I had witnessed the effort needed to carry the wood up the steep hills to fuel the fire that cooked this simple and ancient meal. It tasted very special. These recipes and techniques were vital to the survival of these people and, passed from generation to generation, they were as important to their identity as the Mixe language they were speaking.

In spite of the seismic snoring and murmurings of the other bodies curled up next to me, I slept well on the concrete floor of the police station, before waking with the others for the Oaxaca bus. Watching the passengers climb on board in the dim light of the morning, I quietly wished I could join them. My fifth morning in these mountains. I had no idea how much longer my little mountainous detour would last and I was exceptionally tired. Staring at the next impossible climb that twisted over the mountains as I left the village, I felt angry and despondent. On my first days in these mountains I had felt clean, powerful, efficient. But now I was tired, dirty, weak and defeated, I came to a standstill, stood astride my bike and quit.

If there had been a magic cord to take away the pain, to take away the tiredness and take me home, I would have pulled it, but as far as I knew I was at least a week's ride from a sizeable town. I had no choice but to go on. A few refreshing drops of rain landed on my arms, momentarily improving my mood. Dramatic dark clouds filled the sky and the village I left became obscured in a blanket of thick white mist. The rain quickly lost its refreshing charm and the dark mountains and oppressive sky began flashing and cracking with electric energy. The rain poured, small muddy streams began to find their way down the road and my wheels slipped in the mud and on the shiny wet rocks. I had no choice but to stop and wait.

One elephant, two elephants, three elephants...

The seconds between the sharp cracks of lightning and the rolling thunder drew closer. The rain made a great noise as it hit the leaves around me, splashing violently in the puddles that were filled by gurgling russet rivers running down the hillside. Above the assorted din of the storm the sound of an engine grunting and revving its way over the broken road filled me with hope. A muddy truck laboured around the bend. Slowing to a halt next to me, the driver unwound his window and offered me a ride.

Shouting at me through the rain, he explained that the weather was not going to improve but, cold and sopping wet, I didn't need persuading. I lifted the red tarpaulin on his truck, and six blank faces stared at me. My heart sank. There wasn't room for me and the bike, and glumly I explained I would push on. The driver barked a few sharp words at his passengers, the truck was rearranged and heaving my bike inside I climbed in after it. For over three hours we bumped and jolted up and down the mountains, sealed underneath the red tarpaulin. Shortly after the rain stopped, we pulled over. The tarpaulin was lifted to reveal bright sunshine and the simple whitewashed church of Santa Isobel. I looked it up on my map.

'Santa Isobel, Santa Isobel! I got it!'

I was back on the map, and the relief of being able to pinpoint my location was enormous. I no longer relied on the sacred scrap of paper the construction worker had given me almost a week before. A few hours beyond Santa Isobel, the road returned to levelled asphalt and when it finally became smooth black tarmac I let out a loud, long whoop of relief that echoed off the hills. By the evening I had made it to the town of Ixtepec, and after booking into one of only a few rundown hotels, I carried my bike up the stairs into the squalid little room and collapsed after the hardest week of my trip.

🚲

'Gaaaaas, gaaaaaas,' sounded below my window. Accompanied by the cacophony of a selection of hollow, metal objects being dragged from his rear bumper, the gas man's loud-speaker hollered its message into the morning, advertising canisters of propane gas.

'Aaaagua, aaaagua.' An old man selling home-made fruit sorbets from a tricycle rang continuously on a small high-pitched bell to make himself heard. From the shops lining the street opposite, three of Mexico's current pop hits were being pumped into the street. The energetic rhythm of salsa rose above the pulsing thump of Reggaetón and, depressingly, James Blunt's high-pitched warble overtook them all.

Confused at how the evils of the UK top forty had managed to find me hidden in a grim hotel room in a ruinous railroad town in southern Mexico, I looked at my watch. At just before seven in the morning, tired and aching from the uphill struggle of the previous week's ride, I craved just a few more moments of dreaming, but amid the continuous din there was no chance. Climbing out of bed and opening the window, I turned up the volume on the busy street below, where the urban orchestra had been accompanied by a stubborn red-faced policeman blowing hopelessly into his whistle in an impossible attempt to direct the chaotic traffic he had deceived himself into thinking he was controlling. He seemed to believe that by defiantly blowing harder and faster into his feeble mouthpiece, he would bring some order to the gridlocked pedestrians, cars, buses and bicycles that swarmed about him.

Revitalized by a delightfully cold shower, I stepped out into the street in search of breakfast. Bicycles weaved in all directions through traffic and pedestrians; women strode purposefully past me carrying overloaded baskets of colourful produce; thick, meaty smoke bellowed from the grills of the nearby taco stands; and a young man pushing a sack barrow, precariously loaded with fresh papayas, did his best to knock me off my feet on his way to the market.

I decided to find the market myself and set off in pursuit of the sack barrow. My man with the papayas, moving fast through backstreets crowded with street vendors, vanished into the dark maze of dim alleyways and corridors that was the town market. I followed.

Huge sacks spilled over with every of variety of dried chillies; heaped baskets of dry hibiscus blossoms lined the floor. Fruit sellers shouted out their prices, hidden behind mountains of ripe mangoes and pineapples and beneath hanging bundles of hand-made baskets, next to shiny cooking utensils and aluminium pots and pans. Women in traditional dress sat in front of large plastic vats of milky-looking liquid chocolate, whisking it into a thick foam with a strange-shaped rattle, while chatting in their strange dialect to other women who were peeling the spiky skin from brilliant green cactus pads. Steam rose from cauldrons of bubbling mole, heated on makeshift charcoal stoves, while grey-haired women in their finest aprons stirred them with giant wooden spoons. Row after row of deep wooden bowls were filled with freshly prepared salads of cactus, chillies and beans. Thick-armed men poured milk from dull silver urns, while others pulled at long bands of rubbery local cheese, shredding it into stringy mounds. Heaps of cows' stomachs were bundled up like wet towels next to organised rows of hooves and trotters. Heavy cleavers came down on the heads of plucked chickens and men in bloody aprons removed the flesh from gruesome skulls. Strings of scarlet and orange chorizo were hung up next to sides of bloody beef, and long blue tongues were pierced by menacing metal hooks. Stepping over trussed-up turkeys and geese, I pushed forward, resisting a persistent old lady doing her best to convince me to buy a bag of fried crickets flavoured with lemon and chillies.

'Chapulinas, señor, chapulinas.'

At the nucleus of the market a huddle of small fondas were busy serving breakfast to hungry locals. Fonda Maria. Fonda Bonita. Fonda Violeta. Each stand had its own distinct sign, and behind busy worktops, the namesakes were busy preparing home-cooked local treats for their loyal customers and whizzing up fresh fruit in liquidisers. After four months in Mexico I recognised most of the dishes being prepared: chile relleno, menudo, nopales, pozole, gorditas, sopes, quesadillas, but at Fonda Lupita I found what I was looking for. Doing my best to be polite, I took a seat between two plump women on the metal bench. Grabbing the attention of a large woman I assumed to be Lupita, I placed my order.

'Tres sopes e uno jugo de piña, por favor.'

With the speed and efficiency of an arm-wrestling champion, Lupita immediately went to work forcefully extracting the juice from a pineapple, while her young daughter, who should probably have been in school, delicately prepared three maize tartlets in her hands, the *pat pat* of the soft dough music to my ears. Piled high with shredded beef, refried beans, fresh local cheese, a little white cabbage and tangy green tomato salsa, each tart was placed delicately on the oily griddle in front of her and after a short wait I was handed my plate.

A squeeze of lime, a little salsa and the sopes were sublime. Completely content I loudly sucked up the chunks of pineapple that had collected at the bottom of my glass. After the hardships, highs and lows of the last week, life suddenly tasted very good.

A year to the day earlier, I had arrived with my bicycle in the sterile, lifeless environs of JFK Airport, and in twelve months of travel my bicycle had carried me here to this unique, colourful temple of gastronomy in southern Mexico. Considering the date, I looked around me and wallowed in the sights, sounds and smells of Mexico.

> Paradise is not where you go but how you feel for one moment of your life.
>
> *Anon*

Menudo: Mexican Tripe Soup

Serves 8
1kg beef tripe, cut into bite-size pieces
6 garlic cloves, finely chopped
1 large onion, finely chopped
1 pinch dried oregano
1 pinch chilli powder
4 tree chillies (chile de arbol)
4 jalapeño chilli peppers
1kg hominy (canned is fine)
salt and freshly ground black pepper
to serve: chopped spring onion, chopped fresh cilantro
  (coriander), limes

1. In a large pot, bring 3 litres of water to the boil. Place the tripe in the pot and reduce the heat. Simmer for 2 hours, making sure to skim off any fat that rises to the top.

2. Carefully drain off the water through a colander, reduce the heat and pour in 3 litres of fresh water. Bring to the boil then simmer the tripe for 1 hour, and drain a second time.

3. Pour another 3 litres of fresh water into the pot with the tripe, and bring to the boil. Stir in the garlic and the onion, season with oregano and chilli powder, and salt and black pepper. Reduce the heat, and simmer for a further hour.

4. Preheat the grill to hot. Arrange all the chilli peppers on the grill and cook until they begin to scorch. Remove from heat, slit lengthwise and scrape away the seeds.

5. Put all the chillies in a food processor and blend into a rough paste. Mix into the pot with the tripe and continue cooking for 1 hour over low heat.

6. Now mix the hominy into the pot. Continue cooking for a further hour. Serve in deep bowls with a couple of pinches of spring onion, chopped cilantro and some squeezes of lime juice.

Chile Rellenos: Stuffed Poblano Peppers in Tomato Sauce

Serves 6
6 large poblano chillies
300g cheese*
50g flour
1 large potatoe, boiled and chopped
3 large eggs, separated
cooking oil
salt

The tomato sauce
1 large onion, finely chopped
olive oil for cooking
8 ripe tomatoes, chopped
1 large bunch of cilantro (coriander), chopped

1. First make the tomato sauce. Sauté the onion in a little oil until clear. Add the tomatoes and cook for another 5–10 minutes until the liquid has evaporated. Season with salt, add plenty of cilantro and pour into a blender. Whiz until you have a smooth, thick sauce.
2. Roast the chillies under the grill or over the gas ring on top of the stove. Once the skin has blackened and blistered, place in a plastic bag and set aside for 20 minutes.
3. Take the chillies from the bag and peel off the blackened skin. Insert a sharp knife into the top of each chilli, just under the stem, and slice downward about halfway. Using a spoon or a knife, scrape the seeds and the white membrane from inside, trying not to tear the chilli flesh.
4. Cut the cheese into 6 pieces that will fit snugly into each chilli, and carefully place them inside with a few bits of chopped potato.
5. Put a little flour on a plate and roll the chillies in it before

sprinkling more flour on top, making sure the entire chilli is coated. Dust off the excess flour and set the coated chillies aside.

6. In a deep mixing bowl, whisk 3 egg whites until stiff and then slowly fold in the yolks, a pinch of salt and the rest of the flour.

7. Fill a heavy saucepan with 1½ inches of cooking oil. Heat the oil to 180°C (drop a tiny bit of batter in the oil – if it sinks, the oil is not hot enough) and then, one at a time, dip the stuffed chillies into the batter and then into the hot oil.

8. Once the batter is golden brown, carefully remove the chillies with a spider or slotted spoon and drain on paper towels. Serve each stuffed chilli in a shallow bowl swimming in hot tomato sauce.

*Any cheese will do. I like Monterey Jack and goat's cheese with this recipe.

central america

FEELING FRAIL ON THE GRINGO TRAIL

> The best traveller has no plan and is not intent on arrival.
>
> *Lao Tzu*

'This way, Thomas, this way,' whispered the toucan without opening her sharp orange beak. Naked apart from a digital watch, a pair of sandals and a small backpack, I did as I was told. The beautiful bird flew with its distinctive lolloping flight on to another branch deeper in the tropical forest and, stepping over the smooth, unstable rocks of the stream-bed, the cool water rushing around my ankles, I followed the bird. Above my head the heavy jungle canopy all but blocked out the daylight and only a few sharp rays of sunlight cut through the shadows, landing on the intricate lattice of silver spiders' webs and attracting pairs of fragile butterflies that danced in the sunbeams.

Thick tendrils corkscrewed around the broad trunks of ancient trees that soared towards the sunlight, while the limbs of their exposed roots wandered the forest floor overgrown with enormous prehistoric ferns. Running water continued to splash and gurgle amongst the smooth rocks around my feet. I stared open-mouthed at the roof of this perfect tropical habitat, where, amongst the confusion of intertwined creepers and foliage, a troop of howler monkeys whiled away their day lounging in the high branches of the jungle canopy. With their long supple limbs, females swung calmly through the boughs, gathering and peeling fruit, handing it to the young that clung to their chests, while their male counterparts roared at each other like heavy-metal rock stars, flexing their thick necks and peeling back their gums to reveal vicious jaws. Every part of this verdant habitat seemed to have a voice. Above the penetrating calls and squawks of birds and primates, the giant trees creaked and groaned in the light breeze. The jungle pulsated and grew in front of my eyes and even the smooth biomorphic forms of rocks and boulders throbbed with a deep, hidden energy.

Distracted again by a flash of colour, my toucan flew to another branch. She was trying to tell me something and I followed her away from the river and into the jungle.

Ruben's hand on my bare shoulder startled me and brought my addled mind some way back to reality. It'll be dark in a couple of hours, he said, before offering me some more of the contents of a small paper parcel. 'Mas ongos?'

He was right. It was getting late and if we wanted to find the ancient ruins before dark we had to keep walking. I took a small handful of the mushrooms he was proffering, removed the muddy stalks, popped a couple of soft heads into my mouth, took a long pull on my water bottle and continued following the stream we had been tracking since sunrise, in the hope of finding the ancient Mayan city of Palenque.

🚲

The day before, after a gruelling journey from San Cristobal, Chiapas, I had arrived in the modern town of Palenque, a muddle of ramshackle concrete buildings that had grown out of the jungle, feeding off the tourist trade that arrived by the busload to visit the ancient ruins some ten miles away. Promptly set upon by gangs of greedy gringo-hunters flogging jungle lodges, jungle treks, waterfall excursions, guided tours, and whatever else they could sell to the fresh meat being delivered by huge air-conditioned coaches, I evaded their aggressive tactics and approached a scruffy man sitting on the pavement, unsuccessfully trying to sell a selection of home-made jewellery.

I asked if he knew of a cheap place to camp near the ruins. Happily for me, he rattled off some instructions. I bought a tacky bracelet by way of thanks and with my simple directions I set off towards Palenque.

Hidden in the jungles of the Tumbalá mountains, the ancient city of Palenque is one of the finest Mayan ruins in Mexico. First occupied around 100BC, it reached the peak of its power in about AD700 before being mysteriously abandoned. Built in an area that receives heavy rainfall, the ruins quickly became overgrown by dense jungle, where they remained hidden for centuries until they were discovered by the Spanish in the mid-eighteenth century. Containing some of the finest architecture, sculpture, roof-comb and bas-relief carvings the Maya produced, with its imposing jungle setting it is one of the marvels of Mexico.

According to many, the Mayans' well-chronicled obsession with, and deep knowledge of, astronomy and the solar system ensured that the city was built at an epicentre of cosmic energy and, arriving at where I was told I could camp, I found some pretty cosmically charged people wandering about. I was shown to an open thatched hut on the edge of a murky swamp that I could share with a couple of Spaniards for a few pesos, and after unpacking my things I accepted their kind invitation to a communal evening meal.

Sitting round a smouldering fire on a collection of logs, tatty furniture and seats salvaged from scrapped vehicles, the other members of this small community had gathered to smoke pot, play drums, weave jewellery and wait for the blackened pans sitting on the embers of their fire to heat up and cook their supper. In the flicker of the small flames that jumped in the fire, the features of the characters flashed in the shadows.

Squatting on his feet, a wide-faced man, with oily black hair and earlobes stretched around thick disks of bamboo, mumbled unintelligibly between taking swigs from a dirty plastic bottle of chicha, a powerful home-brew of fermented pineapple.

The stocky man next to him tapped a gentle rhythm on a bongo held between his thighs, Aztec and Mayan motifs etched into the sweaty skin of his toned torso. A young mother, her face embellished with metal piercings, breastfed her child wrapped in a gaudy woven shawl, while next to her an emaciated man in a dirty open shirt turned his long matted hair in his fingers. A girl in her twenties, with a clean-shaven head and big sparkling eyes, took charge of the cooking, peeling dark-skinned yucca root to reveal its brilliant white flesh, before slicing it into chunks and adding it to the pot. My two Spanish roommates, with their dark eyes and ponytails, sat together on the back seat of a car, chatting quietly in Catalan that I could barely understand.

It was hard not to be intimidated by this animated community of real travellers. Individuals who had truly stuck two fingers up at the system, cut loose and lived on the road. Men and women who had no plans, no start and no finish. They had no iPod and no bank account and amongst these seasoned nomads I felt like a fraud. A half-hearted voyeur, unwilling to make any real sacrifice. A tourist taking a brief glimpse of this transient existence, until I had had enough, only to return to the comfortable world I was ultimately unable to leave. These artisans made their living selling jewellery and trinkets made from feathers, shells and bones to people like me, a tourist, whom they chastised for turning the sacred place I had cycled to see into an overpriced Mayan theme park.

I sat on the ground by the fire, the steady beat of the drum blending with a chorus of frogs and the rolling drone of cicadas, and in silence I ate my over-cooked rice, picking out chewy chunks of yucca in my fingers, doing my best to avoid conversation until the man I met in town questioned me about my trip. Uneasily I explained where it started, where I hoped to finish and about my interest in unearthing local food.

'You must try the flesh of the gods,' announced the man with stretched earlobes, excitedly jumping to his feet and taking another pull from his bottle of chicha.

Sheepishly I asked what that was.

'Ongos,' replied one of the Spaniards I was sharing the hut with, before the man with matted hair explained that there was substantial evidence, found in stone carvings and stucco reliefs, that ancient Mayan shaman and medicine men ritually dosed up on potent hallucinogenic psilocybin mushrooms to give them a hotline to dead ancestors, gods and other supernatural creatures.

Intrigued by this celestial twist in my culinary research, I asked eagerly where I might find some of these mystic fungi, at which point my two Spanish friends offered to take me mushroom hunting the next day. The man with the pierced earlobes then insisted we hike to the ruins, and after scribbling down a crude map that would take us around the back of the mountain and into the ancient city, avoiding the entrance fee, we said goodnight and returned to our hut. Nervous and unable to sleep in the tropical heat, my mind played out the adventures that awaited me the next day, but at no point did I imagine that I would be standing naked in the jungle talking to a toucan.

⬥

Walking all morning and most of the afternoon, following as best we could the broken lines of blue ink on our simple map, we stopped to check our location, talk to birds, nibble more ongos and swim, before continuing to follow the network of rivers and streams that took us deeper into the jungle.

In what had been a magical hike, in every sense of the word, the rivers we were following had taken us under and over crashing waterfalls that fell into natural swimming holes where we swam naked feeling no need to put our clothes back on. Fast-moving streams babbled and gurgled under huge fallen logs that carried endless streams of worker ants marching in organised lines carrying bright cuttings of fallen leaves. Water sprayed off rocks in immaculate patterns, each drop sparkling in the sunlight that broke through the canopy then continuing its journey downstream over boulders and rocks, sculpting and smoothing them into polished steps before falling in crystal curtains in front of deep grottos lined with damp moss.

Marching deeper into this enchanted jungle, following the stream and munching the carne de dios, we became totally involved in our surroundings but none of us had the good sense to admit we were lost. Then, just before sunset, we drew back some branches to reveal a small pavilion. We had found the ancient city of Palenque, and feeling like a young Indiana Jones, albeit with no clothes on, I peered through the foliage. There wasn't a bum-bag-wearing tourist in sight. The place was ours!

We wandered alone in the shadows of enormous stone pyramids and turreted palaces, the angular faces of Mayan deities peering from ornate bas-reliefs that hung to walls. The russet lichen that spread over the carved stones was like the blood of a thousand sacrifices, and climbing slowly to the top of a small pyramid I stared, mesmerised at the view.

In tall mahogany trees troops of howler monkeys disturbed the overgrown vegetation that had all but engulfed this ancient city, while pairs of toucans flew in the clearings between the combed tops of pyramids. Sitting on the cool steps I lost myself in the hazy view that stretched from this standing testament to a once great civilisation, across the misty treetops towards the Yucatan peninsula, and the Gulf of Mexico.

⏚

'Oi!'

A loud voice burst through the serenity of the evening and shattered my euphoric state. Scrambling up the pyramid towards me, a red-faced federale in military fatigues was pulling himself up the steep stone steps with one hand and brandishing a small firearm in the other. In the courtyard below me, I saw that his colleague had already apprehended my two Spanish friends, who were kneeling in front of him with their arms behind their heads. I was overcome with a fierce wave of guilt, the complete stupidity of my situation suddenly horribly clear. I held my hands up, then put on some clothes and was marched aggressively down the steps of the pyramid. At ground level the other soldier had already found a substantial amount of ongos in Ruben's backpack and was now busy trying to get through to his headquarters on his shortwave radio. We were fucked.

Tales of run-ins with the police and being able bribe your way out are a staple amongst travellers in Mexico. A bag full of weed; jumping a red light; pissing behind a tree after too many tequilas. If the hostel stories were true, it was apparently possible to pay your way out of any sticky situation. But being caught naked, in possession of hallucinogenic mushrooms, having broken into Mexico's finest archaeological site was the equivalent of scaling the walls of Windsor Castle naked on LSD, and I wasn't sure I had the funds. Spending the next few years of my life trussed up in a seedy Mexican jail was a real and vivid possibility.

I too knelt on the ground with my hands behind my head, embalmed in a confused state of mushroom-induced delirium. The dense jungle and great Mayan temples had turned macabre and spine-chilling. My Spanish accomplices had gone to pieces like a couple of jigsaw puzzles, and I was barely holding on to the reality of our situation. Hurriedly I tried to string together enough Spanish to politely ask an angry man with a gun if he was open to bribes, before he made contact with his headquarters and the situation spiralled dangerously out of control. I stuttered my clumsy, desperate sentence.

After a brief pause there was a reply.

'Cuanto tiene?'

Emptying our wallets we scraped together just short of 600 pesos. The soldiers split the cash, tucked it in their pockets, but it wasn't enough. The shortwave radio went back to work. I pulled a small pair of binoculars from the side pocket of my backpack. I made an elaborate play of exhibiting their performance and after passing them back and forth, the federale added them to the pot. But clearly miffed that a pair of binoculars doesn't divide up between two people, one of the soldiers pointed at my watch: a technical-looking Timex, with various screens and buttons that I had no idea how to use. It looked like our last chance.

I demurred, saying it was far too expensive, exaggerating the worth of a timepiece I had picked up for fifty cents in a thrift store in Minnesota months before.

'Démelo!'

I played my poker-face a little longer.

'Démelo!' he barked.

Unstrapping the watch, showing just enough reluctance to be credible, I handed it over. The desperate ploy had worked. They took our cash, they took my binoculars and my watch, and we were escorted in shame from the ruins. A movement disturbed the branches above the road. A toucan landed on a branch above us.

'That's enough from you!' I muttered, turning away from the ruins.

棶

In hindsight, the sultry red and black decor that lined the corridors of what was advertised as a motel should have rung some alarm bells. The satisfied look on the face of the overweight trucker who barged past me on the steep stairs doing up his flies should have been evidence enough too, but as a very confused-looking 'Madame' took in perhaps the first sweat-drenched cyclist to darken her door, the penny still hadn't dropped.

I asked politely how much it was for a night. Eighty pesos by the hour, she replied.

It still took a few more seconds before I realised what kind of establishment I had wandered into. Since leaving Palenque three days earlier, my imagination had put together the perfect scenario for my last night in Mexico. I wanted to sit in the leafy plaza of a picturesque colonial town, listening to mariachi while munching tripe tacos and swigging cold bottles of Pacifico beer. Being kept awake by the lustful soundtrack of an over-zealous truck driver venting his frustration on an eight-dollar hooker was not what I had in mind.

Politely turning down a bed in the brothel, I returned to the muddy street of this small town, some 30 kilometres from the border with Guatemala. But 'town' is too generous a description.

This place was nothing more than a few rundown buildings from which locals flogged cheap sunglasses, mangoes and steering-wheel covers to the drivers of the vast dilapidated trucks along the potholed stretch of highway.

The humidity only added to the gloomy nature of this typical Mexican whistle stop, which only existed because of its proximity to the border with Guatemala, and amongst the acrid smell of smouldering rubber and exhaust, I was left with no other choice but to pitch my tent on a piece of dirty ground behind the petrol station. Surrounded by the rusty carcasses of broken-down buses, I squeezed my last tent peg into the soft earth and the heavens opened.

Drops of rain exploded violently off the surface of the road. Skipping to the other side, I seized a plastic chair from outside a small open-fronted restaurant, tipped the puddle of dirty rainwater out of the seat and sheltered inside. Thick clouds of water sprayed from the wheels of the heavy goods traffic that roared through the night, and from behind the clean lines of rainwater that ran off the roof, I tried to enjoy my last evening in Mexico.

A woman with wide cheekbones and a flat nose, dressed in a vivid huipil (Mayan blouse) embroidered with flowers, submerged green, leaf-wrapped parcels into a steaming cauldron of water that sat beside a second pot where boiled corn floated on the murky surface. I asked what was inside the tamales, and she answered, 'Carne.' It seemed rude to enquire any further, so I placed an order.

Fishing one of the tidy, green parcels from the steaming water with a long metal spoon, she placed it on a plastic plate and handed it to me.

'Gracias.'

Back in my wet chair, with my plate in my lap, I untied the tidy knot of twine that held my tamales together, carefully unfolding the damp maize leaves to reveal a well-formed pillow of steamed maize dough. Breaking the masa with my fork, a few fatty offcuts of what I think was pork revealed themselves, along with a slice of soggy tomato and a waft of minty steam. My last meal in Mexico wasn't going to be the taco I dreamt of, but cycling in southern Mexico I had come to enjoy the subtle flavours and soft texture of tamales, a staple of the Maya people, and this woman knew what she was doing. Trying not to be put off my supper by the hairy shoulders and dirty vest of the restaurant's only other customer, a pot-bellied Mexican who was busy consuming a cob of corn with the efficiency of a plague of locusts, I ate.

Through a mouthful of corn, the hairy-shouldered man asked if I was travelling by bike.

I was.

His next question came accompanied by a shower of half-chewed kernels. Was I going to Guatemala?

I was.

'You'll have to be careful. The place is full of thieves.' He nibbled at the thin end of his corn before sucking at the ravaged core like a famished baby at the breast. 'And guns.'

I thanked him for his warnings but I had heard it all before. In the same way that Americans had warned me about the perils of cycling alone in Mexico, Mexicans were now doing the same for their southern neighbour. God only knew what kind of lawless hellhole Panama would be if this apparent domino-effect of badwill continued, but here I was after five months' cycling and camping in Mexico and I had only good things to say about the place. I was in no doubt there were bad people out there, but they are heavily outnumbered.

The previous evening's heavy rain had expelled the humidity that made cycling sweaty and exhausting, but it had left behind a thick blanket of cloud and mist. I crossed the border into Guatemala, the air around me damp and chilly. What little I could see of the road disappeared into a white oblivion. Moving slowly and unsurely into this invisible country, I listened to muffled conversations spoken in an unknown tongue and the perpetual thud of wood being chopped. The damp air carried the sent of burning pine, and every so often the escalating roar of combustion warned of the arrival of heavy trucks and buses, which burst out of the mist then disappeared as suddenly as they arrived, leaving behind a stench of burnt fuel.

The road I had been tracking since crossing the border twisted and turned up and down steep hills. I heard powerful rushing water dislodging the boulders in the bottom of deep canyons, but without a view I was completely disorientated. I wasn't lost, I just had no idea where I was. Trapped within this heavy mist that engulfed the mountains, what little I could see of Guatemala was pallid and colourless, as if the sun's disappearance had sucked the pigment out of the world. The vibrant colours of Mexico now left behind, my initial perceptions of Guatemala were black and white.

When a man appeared at a fork in the road, slowly emerging from the surrounding gloom, the orange hilt of his machete evident, I should have been alarmed. But he could not have looked any less threatening. Standing next to a hessian sack almost as tall as he was, he wore a thick woven skirt, not dissimilar to a kilt, under which were what appeared to be red and white striped pyjamas. On his feet were a pair of oversized black boots, and to keep out the cold he wore a blue 1970s ski jacket, a beige jumper and a pork pie hat. I had barely seen another soul since my passport was stamped, and being confronted by this character, whose fashion sense seemed to be influenced by Andy Pandy, Robert the Bruce, Eddie the Eagle and Frank Sinatra, was somewhat surreal.

I greeted him with a smile, my spirits lifted by the very sight of him. He nodded his head gently. Pulling out my damp map I tried to ask for directions to Huehuetenango.

The man shook his head.

I wrapped my tongue around various other possible pronunciations, but received the same silent response. With this bizarre encounter going nowhere, I said goodbye and continued up the hill, leaving the man to vanish like a ghost into the mist.

After a cold night camping in a clearing by the side of the road, I came out from my tent to find that a bright morning sun had all but burned away the cloud and mist of the previous day's white-out, and only a few stubborn billows clung to the roof of the densely packed forests that stretched across the steep hills and valleys below. I had no idea I had climbed so high. With the clean scent of pine smoke in my nostrils, I got back in the saddle and set out for the small mountain town of San Francisco. No longer broadcasting in black and white, Guatemala was now showing in full glorious Technicolor.

Hand-me-down American school buses, as lavishly decorated as fairground rides with their religious effigies and football colours, charged carelessly round the twists in the road, blaring their tuneful horns to advertise their service, before pulling over without warning to pick up customers who materialised from the steep muddy hillsides. Pine-covered mountains and flat-topped volcanoes stretched into a hazy blue horizon. Steep canyons gushed with icy water. Wide, gold-toothed smiles on kind local faces greeted me from every community and the air was cool and crisp. In well-kept fields lines of yellow courgette flowers were radiant in the sunshine, while men and women in heavy boots and traditional dress bent their backs to work the rich, dark soil. Men sat astride long-eared mules, loaded with wicker panniers brimming with produce, and as I drew closer to town, the number of people on the road increased.

Arriving in San Francisco late in the morning, I moved with the crowd, wheeling my bike through a maze of crooked cobbled streets to the town's main square, where a lively scrum of Guatemalans from surrounding villages was converging.

The town square was a free-for-all of colour and activity. Specimens of striped watermelon, sweet-smelling pale mango and plump yellow papaya were cut open to advertise the quality of the bright coloured flesh inside. A fat woman poked a gnarled finger into a melon to test its ripeness, provoking a tirade of abuse, before a pair of flies made the most of the sweet, exposed flesh.

Boys perched on flimsy wooden crates, next to delicately balanced towers of scarlet tomatoes being sold for a quetzal a stack. Shiny blackberries were sold in small plastic bowls. Young girls clutched dense bunches of fresh mint, cilantro and dark green spinach. Sacks of pine needles and other medicinal roots and leaves filled the fresh mountain air with clean odours. Clusters of men in red and white trousers, checked skirts and pork pie hats leant against the turquoise and brown walls of a hardware store negotiating, smoking tobacco and catching up with news, while wide-hipped, gold-toothed women knelt on woven rugs on the pavement, peeling the pale green beans that spilled from wicker baskets.

Cooked food was on sale too. Mothers and daughters with dark eyes and jet-black hair sat in the tall doorways selling paper bags of thin-cut plantain crisps, dressed with salt and chilli, while others turned golden cobs of maize on blackened grills made from recycled wheel hubs. Under the red, yellow and blue glow of parasols, men fried pieces of chicken in deep metal bowls, cooling the cooked golden meat in white enamel trays before handing them to the line of hungry customers who had also been attracted by the whiff of frying oil, accompanied by tidy paper bags stuffed with expertly cooked chips.

I waited in line for a bag of chips and then visited a woman with a hamper of warm tostadas, fried maize tortillas, generously topped with chojin, a salad of radish and fried pork rind. I bought a bowl of mora (blackberries) and then sat on the steps of the church, blowing on the chips before popping them into my mouth. They were exquisite. Better than any chippie back home. The radish salad was crunchy and peppery, and the blackberries stained my fingers with their tart juice.

I enjoyed this perfect picnic lunch surrounded by the faces, language, flavours and colours of this beautiful Guatemalan market. My mind returned to the man I met by the side of the road the previous day, whose clothes, in the misty grey surroundings, had seemed garish and out of place. But watching the men and women of this market and the food that surrounded them, the inspiration for the designs and colours used in their traditional clothing became perfectly clear. The red of the radishes, the orange of the papaya, the pale green hues of the beans, the vibrant yellow of the courgette flower, the deep mauves found on my blackberries. Every one of these rich colours was replicated in the clothing of the Mayan people around me.

Tucked underneath Guatemala on the Pacific coast, the tiny country of El Salvador is, curiously, one of the world's biggest consumers of Worcestershire Sauce. No mean feat for a country the size of Wales. Its inhabitants can't get enough of the Lea and Perrins lightly piquant, slightly fishy and certainly fruity condiment, but unable to wrap their Latino tongues around its apparently unpronounceable name, they have rechristened it Salsa Ingles. With this in mind, after fourteen months on the road, El Salvador seemed the perfect spot for the Cyclista Ingles to take a break, and with my younger brother Ed visiting from England, I would hang up my Lycra and take a few months' rest from the road.

Thanks to a fierce civil war, which ended in 1991, El Salvador is sadly still talked of in hushed tones by many of the travellers of the Gringo Trail, but on our first night in its capital, San Salvador, notorious for its gang rule and violent crime, the city seemed positively sleepy. Sitting in a shabby street-bar sipping cold bottles of Regia beer – the only relief in the stifling tropical humidity – my brother and I caught up on a year's news before taking to the streets in search of food. We were damp with sweat after walking only a few deserted blocks of this mysteriously empty city. Even though a refreshing drizzle began to fall, we glumly decided enough was enough and turned round. While we were on the way back to our hotel, a bulky American-made pick-up truck rumbled to a halt next to us. The steady sweep of its wipers washed rain from its blacked-out windscreen, and after the driver rolled down his window, an unusual American accent, that seemed honed from a hundred American action movies, drawled, 'You guys looking for help?'

I replied in my peculiar Spanish, honed from a year on a bicycle, that we were just looking for something to eat.

'I drive you best place... Jump in.'

Now perhaps this wasn't such a good idea, but he had a trustworthy face and a young family lined up next to him on the front seat, so we tossed caution to the wind and increasing drizzle, and clambered into the back.

We raced through the streets of San Salvador, our faces blasted by the light rain and warm air. Illuminated office buildings blurred into a succession of rapid flashes. Empty flyovers were trimmed with flaring lines of streetlights and images of vast pale-skinned beauties with seductive eyes, advertising shopping malls and beachside condominiums, stared out from tall lit-up billboards. Tired security guards leant on their shotguns in the entrances of opulent international banks, and continuing into what was clearly an affluent corner of this central American metropolis, we came to a standstill on an empty four-lane highway, bathed in unnatural light. Towering over us like garish, capitalist totems were the golden arches, a slowly rotating blue, red and yellow burger and the impudent wink of a colossal Colonel Sanders. My heart sank.

I believe the identity of any culture fundamentally lies in its food. So what did this day-glo line-up of fast-food chains say to our new friend about my brother and me? Did the kind man who had delivered us here really believe that in the West we lived on milkshakes, quarter-pounders and chemically enhanced chicken? What was perhaps more upsetting, in this corner of the world with its own deep traditions, was that the worst components of our capitalistic society were being advertised as sophisticated and glamorous. The companies whose bright lights now burned my retinas were successfully managing to convince the people of Latin America that eating their nutrition-less excuse for food was something to aspire to.

'Is good, yes?' asked our kind driver as he trotted round to the back of the truck, shielding his head from the rain with a magazine.

Tired, wet and hungry in a strange place, it would have been easy to say yes. After all, this generous man had already driven us across the city, but I couldn't bring myself to do it. After a year on the road, dedicated to unearthing culinary excellence and local cuisine, I had not brought my beloved little brother 8,000 miles and halfway around the world to spend the evening picking greasy bones from the bottom of a family bucket or chewing on Whoppers and reconstituted chips.

I took a deep breath, thanked him sincerely but told him what we really wanted were pupusas.

'You want pupusas?' His face was painted with surprise.

He climbed back into the cabin of his truck, and we listened as a heated argument broke out between him and his wife. We were uncomfortably certain that she had had enough of providing an unpaid taxi service to a couple of wet gringos, but it quickly transpired that they were arguing about where to find the best pupusas in San Salvador. The truck was slipped back into gear, the wheels skidded on the wet asphalt and the golden arches vanished behind us in a neon blur.

As we continued through the city, our surroundings became more rundown. Shiny office blocks became dilapidated tower blocks. Glowing multinational banks turned into scruffy corner bars propped up by shady-looking men, and scantily clad women with shiny wet skin advertised their curves in the shadows of side streets. We pulled up in front of a small restaurant where the word 'pupuseria' was hand painted in tall letters above a vibrant red and yellow awning.

The family waited in the truck while my brother and I went inside. Generations of Salvadorans were hard at work stuffing themselves on thick, hand-made corn pancakes stuffed with cheese, beans and deep-fried pork. It looked like a Latino pie-eating contest, and we were only too happy to join in. We found a table and ordered six pupusas between us. I picked up my first ice-hockey-puck-sized maize cake and took a bite.

I yelped in pain.

I might as well have bitten into a Cornish pasty filled with napalm. I ejected a nugget of pupusa from my scalded mouth, while Ed collapsed in a fit of laughter.

'It's not funny – the thing's hotter than the sun,' I barked through seared lips, while puffing frantically into what remained of the steaming pupusa in my hand. Quickly learning that patience and a generous topping of curtido, a slimy relish of pickled cabbage, onion and carrots, served from huge glass jars, went some way to chilling the boiling lava that lurked inside these maize pockets, I carefully ate my way through my share. Surrounded by the happy babble of conversation and the steady pit-a-pat of fresh pupusas being moulded by hand and tossed on to a piping-hot griddle, we enjoyed this real Salvadorean fast food. Fresh, home-made and healthy. At the end of a long day, eating pupusas with my brother in San Salvador was very special indeed.

歠

Next day we left San Salvador and headed to the sweltering Pacific coast. For three dollars a night we rented a small room that overlooked a perfect beach and together we learnt how to surf. We slept, we played Scrabble on a set made from bottle tops and a T-shirt and we ate our bodyweight in pupusas. For six happy weeks I didn't touch my bicycle. But the day of departure slowly arrived and it was time to move on. Seeing my brother had made home feel incredibly close. Saying goodbye and cycling into the claustrophobic heat of an El Salvador afternoon, it was hard to comprehend that another year of cycling and sleeping rough lay ahead. As I stopped where the rubble track that led to the beach met the clean tarmac of the highway, the enormity of the task ahead became horribly real.

Just a sequence of day rides, Tom, I told myself. Take each one as it comes.

With tears in my eyes, I willed myself on, stubbornly turning right on to the black strip of tarmac that rolled over the hills of the coastline. Unsurely and unhappily, I pedalled south for Honduras.

歠

The reality of being back in the saddle hit me like an unseen pothole, and at the end of a daunting first day back on the road I pulled into the sleepy Salvadorean town of Santiago Nonualco. Not ready to face the inside of my tent, I searched in vain for a cheap hotel. As the rain that rumbling thunder had earlier promised began falling in heavy sheets, I hurried over the town's slippery cobblestones and found shelter in a large doorway under the eaves of a metal roof. A shout made me jump.

Materialising from the rain like a pair of limbless drones, two soldiers draped in dark ponchos and clutching heavy rifles demanded to know what I was up to.

They ran the beam of a powerful torch over me and my belongings, thumbed through the pages of my passport, then ordered me to follow them. Around the corner a pair of tall wooden doors opened to a reveal a cloistered courtyard that echoed with the sound of water gushing from its roof. I was told to wait.

This I did, until an officer approached me, clearly pissed off at being dragged into the rain to deal with a Cyclista Ingles. He was of imposing size, with a functional military haircut and a craggy face that had forgotten how to smile. His military fatigues were neatly tucked into a pair of heavy leather boots. This man was the evil general from a thousand movies. Only too aware of the role of the military in El Salvador's vicious civil war, my imagination went into overdrive. Loose electrical wires became implements of torture. Echoed laughter from within the building lost its innocence, and sinister scenarios of ill-treatment and interrogation lurked behind every closed door.

I tried to explain that I was travelling through the country by bike.

'Porque?' he replied.

Always a good question and one I was still mulling over myself.

'Donde vive?' His next question was easier to answer.

'Londres, Inglaterra.'

'Gusta helado?'

'Eh?'

By this stage in the trip, my Spanish was passable, but I was being interrogated in the pouring rain in a barracks in El Salvador. I ran over his last question again. Had he really just offered me an ice cream?

'Si?' I replied tentatively.

A shaven-headed private was sent running and returned clutching a blue box of choc ices. Taking a seat on a bench at the edge of the courtyard, the officer and I carefully nibbled at the brittle milk chocolate casing, and the officer's fierce persona melted as fast as the sweet vanilla ice cream within.

'American ice cream,' he proclaimed proudly, showing me the maker's mark on the wrappers, explaining that they were supplied by the American military in exchange for El Salvador's help in the war in Iraq. I was sure it was more than just ice creams that had won his country's allegiance.

It continued to pour while he talked passionately about his family, his work in the army and his hopes for El Salvador's future after its troubled past. But he had more important things to do than eat ice cream with an Englishman, and we said goodnight. He kindly showed me where I could unroll my camping mattress.

A little later, lying back on the cold concrete floor on the edge of the courtyard, I did my best to ignore the rain that poured off the roof in steady streams and splashed violently on the earth a few feet from where I lay. On the underside of the roof a line of fluorescent strip bulbs flickered like dying insects, and every hour on the hour, the rhythmical steps of a patrol officer's boots beat on the concrete floor. I was back to sleeping rough. Six months ago this kind of spontaneity had filled me with the spirit of adventure. Now it had lost its charm. It seemed that just that small taste of sedentary life in the company of my brother had weakened my resolve. Unable to sleep and unable to make sense of the anxious thoughts that flailed around in my tired mind, once again I began to question the very purpose of the trip. I used to have a job, prospects, friends and a place to live. Now I was alone with a bicycle and four panniers of wet belongings, trying to sleep on the floor of a barracks somewhere in El Salvador. My spirits were as damp as my clothes.

After what seemed like only a couple of hours of what might be described as sleep, I was woken at sunrise by the shrill warble of a bugle. Loading up my bike unenthusiastically, I watched shaven-headed young men rushing about for morning inspection while stern-faced officers barked orders at them. Cycling into a beautiful cool morning I saw that the previous night's rain had filled the trees with life, and underneath a cluster of mango trees that twittered with birdsong, a gaggle of women was selling pupusas, coffee and fresh mango juice to the morning trade. The shouts and pointless stamping of the young men echoed out of the barracks while I, sitting on the kerb, ate my breakfast with the early sun on my face, studying my map for the best approach into Honduras. Perhaps I didn't have it so bad after all.

☙

With its damp cloud-filled mountains, sweltering tropical coastline and totally unpredictable weather, Central America can be a thankless place in which to cycle alone. But one of its benefits is the manageable size of its countries. It had taken me nine months to get around the United States, five months to traverse Mexico, but in this relatively small strip of land that connects the two great continents, I was crossing countries in a couple of days, and nothing lifts a traveller's spirits more than watching an overweight, sweaty border official ink up his rubber stamp before bringing it down with a satisfying thud on a clean page of your passport.

After two days of cycling in El Salvador, I arrived at her southern frontier with Honduras. A high concrete bridge spanned the Río Goascorán that bisected these two countries. On each side double-dealing money changers, with bundles of dirty currency, dodgy calculators and a little sleight of hand, fed off the traffic heading north and south. Changing a few clean dollars into grubby lempiras, I entered Honduras as Honduras entered a record-breaking heatwave.

The sun flared and beat down on an arid landscape of dusty fields. Limp crops surrounded rundown communities of wooden shacks. Their inhabitants hunkered in the shadows, avoiding the unforgiving cruelty of the heat outside. Shimmering in a mirage ahead of me, the dark surface of the Pan-American Highway cut through the scorched landscape like a dirty infection, and slowly and painfully I nibbled away at the hundred kilometres that lay between me and the border with Nicaragua.

Antiquated freightliners spewed foul-tasting fumes. Minibuses driven by maniacs and bursting with passengers swerved in front of me to pick up customers, then repeated the process a few yards down the road. Tired mules plodded along heads hung low, skin pulled tight around heaving ribs, while their drivers on makeshift trailers loaded with bunches of plantain urged them onward. Dusty bicycles laden with drums of water, bundles of sugar cane and extra passengers creaked past me, each one greeted with a quick *ding ding* from my plastic hamburger bell, which I also rang for the delight of children who chased me in bare feet.

'Gringo, gringo! Gringo, gringo!' they called until, losing interest, they returned to play in the dust and rubbish that littered the roadside. Every moving thing on this hideous road lifted a little more dust into the hot air, and it filled my nostrils and stung my eyes. Immersed in dirt, fumes and heat, however hard I willed myself on, my enthusiasm waned in equal measure. I had no interest in what was happening around me. I had no interest in my bicycle. In a permanent state of dirty exhaustion, my mind entered that strangely satisfying and self-pitying hole that human nature saves for times like this.

How can I get out of this? Maybe I could suffer a broken ankle while being run off the road by a geriatric farmer on a donkey. Perhaps an unpronounceable stomach bacteria picked up while eating some crazy local dish would provide a viable excuse. Or, better still, how about being trussed up by a gang of machete-wielding bandits, only to fight my way to freedom with my bicycle pump and puncture repair kit?

It was while I was masochistically wishing for a turn of events that might justify a return home that a pair of cyclists pulled alongside me.

In Central America the bicycle is a working vehicle. Totally efficient, simple to maintain and cheap to run. If a man or woman in these parts owns a bike they can get to work faster, cover greater distances and they can carry plenty of cargo. Every morning and evening I was accompanied by fleets of flip-flop-clad men riding robust, single-speed beasts with thick frames and chunky wheels to and from work. So you can imagine my surprise when, as I was slaving up a steep hill some 25 kilometres short of the Nicaraguan border, a pair of shiny aerodynamic racing bikes bearing Lycra-wrapped collections of muscle and sinew zipped passed me in a flash of colour. They looked as if they would be more at home sprinting through a crowd-lined Champs-Élysées than battling with the roadkill and fumes of the Pan-American Highway. They slowed down for a conversation, but I was far too busy wallowing in a deep puddle of self-pity to make idle chat. I replied curtly to their interrogations about where I was from and the various components of my bicycle.

As this almost one-way conversation about what gears I was running and the construction of my front forks continued, it transpired I was being chaperoned by none other than the former cycling champion of Honduras, Melvin Betancourt, out for a training ride with his younger brother, and in the presence of such pedal-powered glitterati my mood began to improve. As we rode together towards the border with Nicaragua and Melvin's home, they kindly invited me to spend the night.

Excited by my invitation, my imagination began working overtime as I put together the kind of luxury an international cycling hero might return to after a hot day's training. Multi-speed power showers that washed down weary muscles; towering fridges bursting with healthy food and energy drinks; a trophy room stuffed with precious metal; a personal gym with all sorts of muscle-bending machinery, a swimming pool, a hot tub, a massage table... Cresting a hill a few kilometres short of the border, Melvin pointed to a gathering of crude buildings set back from the road amid a cluster of plantain. 'Es mi casa.' My delusions of luxury evaporated.

The house was built of traditional earth bricks and topped with a metal roof. It was clear that cyclists in this part of the world did not command the pay cheques they did elsewhere. Entering into the cool darkness of Melvin's home I was introduced to his mother, who pedalled gently on a sewing machine, and his father, who was lying in a net hammock slung across the length of the room. He was staring blankly at the black and white interference and unintelligible images that flashed from an ancient television set, crudely wired to a car battery. It was hard to tell whether he was in fact watching the TV or admiring the shelf of metallic cycling trophies reflected in the screen.

Coated in a layer of sweat and Pan-American Highway grime, I asked Melvin where I could freshen up. He led me into the garden, past chickens, ducks and an ugly turkey that scratched at whatever it could find in the dirt. At the back of the garden, outside a foul-smelling outhouse, was an old oil drum filled with water, on whose surface a broken plastic bowl bobbed up and down. I would have to wait for my power shower.

Honoured to be invited to have dinner with the cycling champion of Honduras, after washing myself I changed into my best, and only, pair of trousers and a relatively clean T-shirt and joined his mother, who was preparing supper in the glow of an oil lamp in her kitchen, which was set up under a simple lean-to on the side of the house. A stove made of mud bricks filled the air with thick smoke. In the lamplight, Melvin's mother flipped thick maize tortillas from hand to hand before laying them on the grill of a stove next to a steaming, soot-blackened metal cauldron. On the walls around the stove a cleaver, bunches of herbs and a few other well-used kitchen utensils were visible in the light. As I took a seat on a plastic stool, an emaciated mongrel with drooping nipples barred her teeth while releasing a prolonged growl.

Melvin's mother raised her hand and let out a few angry words, and the dog slinked back into the shadows.

Earlier in the day, Melvin had explained that he had less than a month before his next race, the Pan-American Cycling Championships, and so I assumed that a carefully controlled, high-performance recovery meal would be on the menu. I was not disappointed. Energy-packed carbohydrates were provided by the chunky maize tortillas. A ladle of protein-packed black beans and a small heap of scrambled eggs would replenish his tired muscles, while grilled slices of plantain would supply plenty of natural sugar, vitamins and potassium.

It was a perfect cyclist's supper. Afterwards we sat in the lamplight drinking coffee sweetened with sugar cane and exchanging stories of cycling heroes past and present. Armstrong, Basso, Ulrich and Lamond were all gushed over, but later, as I lay on an old mattress on the floor of Melvin's bedroom, which he shared with his brother, I knew I had a new cycling hero.

The next morning, after another meal of tortillas, eggs and refried beans, Melvin and I rode for the border with Nicaragua. Melvin had to go to work, mixing cement for the new customs office, and I had to pedal for Granada, the country's old colonial capital, where I hoped to find a ferry to carry me the length of Lake Nicaragua to San Carlos and the border with Costa Rica.

撶

I was expecting something a little more substantial than the tired, rust-stained vessel that waited for me at the end of Granada's long concrete pier. Pumping thick black smoke into the heavy afternoon sky, her engines rumbled from somewhere deep within and she made a sad sight, rolling on the choppy grey swell of Lake Nicaragua.

Bouncing up and down the gangplanks that bridged the wide gap, a rowdy crew of 'Nicas' hurriedly loaded cargo, making ready for the thirteen-hour journey across the lake. Watching as heavy bunches of banana and plantain made their way aboard on the shoulders of the crew, I worried as their attention shifted towards my bicycle.

'Cuidado, cuidado,' I shouted.

As they lifted my bike with the same disrespect they applied to the bananas, I was convinced my journey was going to end watching my worldly possessions disappear into the murky depths of Lake Nicaragua, but with no other choice than to leave my wheels to the mercy of the crew, I made my way to the top deck as she disappeared beneath a mass of produce.

Locals who had made the crossing countless times before had wasted no time in grabbing their prime hammock real estate and the deck was a tangled web of ropes, woven material and passengers bedding down for the long night ahead. I hadn't the foresight to carry a hammock, so I rolled out my sleeping bag and camping mat on the damp metal. As the growl of the engines increased, we pulled away from Granada, and the heavy forms of the volcanoes that surrounded the lake blended into the darkness.

Although I lacked the planning to invest in a hammock, I had, like a good Englishman, packed a picnic. Rushing around Granada's dirty labyrinth of a market before setting off, I had picked up a parcel of bajo, a traditional Nica delicacy.

An amalgamation of plantain, banana, sweet potatoes, yucca, tomatoes and meat, the ingredients were wrapped in plantain leaves and slow-cooked in a huge pot for hours until the contents had formed into a sticky mess of meat and veg. In the market it had looked and smelt delicious. But unwrapping my leafy parcel in the dim light cast from a single light bulb that throbbed on the power of the boat's generator, I might as well have been looking at the forgotten gubbins in the bottom of a wheelie bin. The meat was no more than a few slimy offcuts of fat and gristle and the vegetables had congealed into sludge. As we rolled on the swell that smacked our hull, sending showers of cold spray over the deck, waves of nausea surged in my stomach. Picking through the mess with my fingers, I admitted defeat. Shamefully I tossed my plantain-wrapped bajo overboard.

Through the night, we navigated in and out of the small, volcanic islands that dotted the lake, and at each stop the surreal alarm call of opportunist children selling their bread, coffee and sweet tamales would wake me from confused and shallow sleep. Each time, I pulled myself up from the cold deck and in the darkness kept a tired eye on my belongings down below. Sipping sweet cups of coffee and nibbling delicious tamales filled with raisins and almonds, I watched more cargo and more passengers come aboard from the small stone piers of these tiny island communities, making the most of this once-a-week connection with the world beyond the lake.

In the cold half-light of dawn, before the sun had reappeared from behind the vast expanse of the lake that shimmered like beaten steel ahead of us, our destination came into view. Initially no more than a few gently flashing coloured lights breaking through the mist, as we pushed forward the broken and rundown forms of San Carlos became visible. A huddled collection of wooden shacks, perched on stilts connected by gangplanks and muddy streets, it might as well have been the end of the world.

There were no roads connecting San Carlos to the outside world, and after a few tedious hours waiting for a self-important passport official to finish his breakfast, I bought a hammock, added another stamp to my passport, climbed into a motor-canoe and headed south on the Rio Frio for Los Chiles and Costa Rica.

It was far less exhausting than pedalling, and with my bicycle and bags carefully balanced in the bow of the slender boat, dense jungle-lined waterways led us upstream through twisting channels of dense mangrove.

Bare-chested men cast hand-nets across the water, steadying their svelte dugout canoes that rocked in our wake. Small thatched communities sat on stilts above the water where women washed their clothes. Basking crocodiles wriggled from the mud banks, disappearing into the brown water where brilliant white storks with sharp black beaks stood one-legged on submerged logs waiting to strike. The scratchy roar of howler monkeys announced our arrival to long-haired sloths that moved in relative slow motion up the trunks of tall trees. Smaller white-faced monkeys chattered in the canopy overhead. With a cool breeze washing over the boat, and making good time, I relished this change from the tarmac, but within hours it was over. Heaving my bike out of the canoe in the small town of Los Chiles, it was back to work.

Although I had eaten well in Central America, by the time I arrived in Costa Rica, it would be fair to say that that my culinary research had been dominated by two ingredients. Rice and beans. Whether I was camping, eating in roadside restaurants or dining with families, this double act just kept coming back, and so you can imagine my delight when entering Costa Rica to see a dish called gallo pinto now advertised on the menu.

Literally 'spotted rooster', my mind raced with visions of chewing on the slow-cooked meaty limbs of the loud-mouthed birds that woke me from my tent every morning. Or perhaps it was a Costa Rican version of spotted dick. But my dreams of a Central American coq au vin or sticky pudding evaporated when I discovered that gallo pinto was no more than the same old rice and beans.

Locals proudly informed me that their national dish derived its name from its resemblance to the speckled markings on the neck of a rooster. I could sympathise with the young Tica (Costa Ricans are known as Ticas, in the same way that Nicaraguans are called Nicas) who, while playing with yet another helping of this dreary dish, muttered in a moment of rice-and-bean-induced boredom, 'Suppose it looks a bit like the pattern on our cock.'

Call it what you want, rice and beans is rice and beans and I had had my fill. My Lake Nicaragua short-cut meant I was now on the eastern side of the Central American isthmus, and the river and streams that rushed through the verdant landscape were heading to the warm water of the Caribbean. Only too happy to join them, I cycled for Puerto Limón, where I hoped my culinary fortunes would improve.

With its tropical heat, impregnable mangroves and mosquito-infested swamps, the Atlantic coast of Costa Rica was left largely unexplored by Spanish settlers. But in the late nineteenth century, as the demand for coffee grew amongst Europe's booming industrial classes, the construction of an ambitious railroad began that would connect the coffee plantations of the Costa Rican central highlands to the Caribbean sea. Puerto Limón was chosen as the site of a major port from where Costa Rican coffee could be shipped to the world.

The construction of the railroad was to change the Atlantic coast of Costa Rica for ever. The freed, English-speaking, Jamaican slaves who were shipped in as cheap labour to build the railroad, settled on the coast and quickly introduced their island culture to the area. And bananas. The bananas planted alongside the tracks, as a source of cheap food for the workers, soon surpassed coffee as Costa Rica's predominant export.

Cycling through the lush lowlands on my way to Limón I could see, hear and taste Caribbean culture everywhere. Towering banana plants laden with fruit flanked the muddy corridors that ran through the plantations, where teams of black workers in shabby nylon clothes and Wellington boots gave me directions. In the small towns and communities, wooden shanties were painted sky blue, banana-leaf green or the bright turquoise of the clear waters of the Caribbean, and their roofs were painted russet red. Tidy gardens bloomed with bright flowers and the blouses that dried in the sun belonged to the voluptuous women in tight pants or billowing floral dresses who walked around sheltered by lace-trimmed parasols.

Each morning I enjoyed slices of pan bon, a dark sweet bread filled with local fruits, with a morning coffee. I chewed on limbs of jerked chicken on the roadside and my handlebar bag was rarely without a couple of warm, deep-filled, spiced beef patties or some sweet pineapple empanadas. But until I arrived in Puerto Viejo, the real delicacy of Costa Rica's Caribbean coast, the ron don hearty fish stew made from whatever the cook could 'run down', had evaded me.

❀

A small tourist town a little south of the rundown city of Limón, Puerto Viejo looked like a postcard. Tall palm trees stooped over pristine white beaches that ran into crystal waters where happy, holidaying couples kissed and frolicked. Skinny locals with tanned bodies and long dreadlocks meandered the sandy high street, rolling to the calming pulse of reggae reverberating from the red, yellow and green bars that served cold beer and fresh fish.

With the right person this Caribbean gem would have been paradise, but alone it was all slightly nauseating. A few overpriced tourist restaurants would happily make me a ron don, but it was hardly going to qualify for my perfect meal if I had to eat it surrounded by sunburnt American love birds, listening to a Bob Marley look-a-like sing 'No Woman No Cry'. So instead I propped myself up in an empty fisherman's bar, feeling sorry for myself, listening to the real thing on my iPod. Determined to hunt down a traditional ron don, and buoyed by a few glasses of cheap rum, I pestered the barman about where I might be able to find one, and after I bought him a drink, he told me to wait for a fisherman called Piney, who would be sure to come by later.

❀

'Piney, this bwoy wants to make a ron don wid you.'

A short man had come to the bar. He was lean and muscular, his sweat-drenched skin shone, and his clean-shaven head, LA Lakers tank top and heavy metal necklace encircling a trunk of a neck gave him the stature of a man three times his size. I bought him a drink and went on the offensive.

'Apparently you can cook a good ron don.'

'Maaaybee, depends who's asking.'

I explained a little about my trip, and my quest for the perfect meal, and he seemed a little bemused. But at the end of the night after a few more glasses of rum, he gave me my orders.

'We got plenty fish, but you bring da rest and enough rum and beer for da bwoys. Come to my place tomorrow round seven.'

Yammi, plantain, sweet potatoes, yucca, coconut, cilantro and scotch bonnet chillies. Piney reeled off a long list of ingredients that in my rum-drunk condition I had no chance of remembering. Before he left I asked where he lived.

'You just axe. Everybody here know Piney.'

⚄

The following day I woke late in my tent, sweaty and hungover. I went for a long medicinal swim, slept on the beach and then jumped on my bike for the local shop, a small collection of wooden crates filled with various dusty ingredients. With the help of the young girl who worked there I remembered what I needed, and weighed down with a case of beer, a litre of potent-looking rum and various bags of heavy Caribbean vegetables, I wobbled and swerved around the potholes and backstreets of town, stopping at each corner to ask for directions to Piney's place.

'Left at the next blue house and he's the one three down with da dish under da cables.'

Eventually I found Piney's place. A clinker-built wooden building with torn mosquito nets in the windows. Inside, his kitchen was surprisingly big, and around a large table two men with tight curly grey hair sat sipping dark rum from glass jars.

'Piney, ya boy be here now,' one hollered before topping up his glass. And after an anxious wait, Piney appeared. He was closely followed by an attractive woman called Elizabeth, whose satisfied demeanour and sweat-coated skin left me in no doubt what they had been doing. Piney examined the ingredients I had placed on the table, pulled a bucket of fresh fish and lobsters from his old fridge, and put me to work chopping two heads of garlic, a couple of onions and a bunch of celery.

'Ya boy can cook,' declared Jesus, one of the two old men, apparently impressed as I diced the garlic efficiently under a heavy blade without removing the tips of my fingers.

'I can chop,' I replied.

A healthy glug of cooking oil went into a heavy aluminium pan heating on one of only two gas rings, the chopped garlic, onion and celery were tossed in next, quickly filling the kitchen with a powerful aroma as they sweated in the hot oil.

'Ya know how to juice a coconut?'

'No,' I replied, unsure whether coconuts had juice. I was promptly sat down on a wooden stool and a flat plank with a serrated metal blade on one end was placed under my buttocks, the sharp end thankfully protruding from between my legs. Given two halved coconuts, I began scraping the inside of each shell on the serrated edge between my thighs. As I grasped the technique, flakes of rasped white flesh began filling the metal bowl at my feet.

With a substantial drift of grated coconut in the bowl, Piney poured in a pint of water and began squeezing the flesh to extract its milk. Slowly adding more water his black hands were soon immersed in an opaque white liquid, and repeating the process until the bowl was full of coconut milk he strained the flesh through a fine sieve. Pouring the coconut milk into the pan, he sprinkled in a couple of tablespoons of dried shrimp stock and gave it all a stir.

While all this was going on, the other old man, whose name was Alonso, went to work on the vegetables and the bottle of rum. Chatting to himself and anyone who would listen, he peeled the skin of the yucca and yammi and sweet potatoes, before cutting them into meaty chunks. The vegetables were added to the cauldron, which was simmering gently, the aroma of garlic replaced with the smell of sweet coconut. Piney seasoned the pot with salt and some ground black pepper, then tossed in a bunch of fresh thyme.

'I take it ya like spice?'

Handing me four innocent-looking, red, yellow and orange scotch bonnet chillies, I was ready to start chopping when a strong hand grasped my shoulder.

'Hold up, hold up! You tell me ya could cook. Ya never chop this type a chilli. Ya burst it.'

Taking a chilli between his thumb and forefinger he held it over the steaming pot and squeezed. The chilli burst open and he dropped it in the pot.

Gutting and washing a large jack fish, Piney hacked off its head and tail before removing the skin and filleting the fish, chopping the white flesh into healthy pieces. These were seared in a little oil and put in the pot followed by two halved lobsters. I chopped a bunch of fresh cilantro and stirred it through the ron don. It looked beautiful. The creamy white milk of the coconut, decorated with floating red chillies, green cilantro, orange sweet potatoes and pink lobster claws. Leaving the ron don to stew for half an hour, we drank cold beer until Piney announced, 'It is eeeating time now. Where Jesus at?'

'He falled asleep like he always do after too much rum,' said Elizabeth, shaking her head.

'Stop your frettin', woman. There be more for us.'

The ron don was stunning. The rich cream of the coconut was smooth and sweet and had worked its way into the cavity of the lobster and the meaty chunks of the jack. The plantain and sweet potatoes were chewy and gave the dish real substance, while the chillies added a punch that left us all dripping with sweat. Once we were all done trawling chunks of fish and vegetable out of the creamy soup, and sucking at the claws and tails of the lobster, we slurped at the rich liquid in the bottom of our bowls. With our shirts sticking to our sweaty backs, we sipped magically cold bottles of beer, and when that ran out we sipped dark rum from used jam jars. Reggae songs rolled out of the radio on top of the humming fridge and, amazed by the meal I had just enjoyed, I asked Piney where he learnt how to cook like this.

'You don't have to study to be smart,' he replied in his strong Caribbean accent, and it was good enough for me.

🚲

After enjoying the sights, sounds and flavours of Costa Rica's Caribbean coast, I rode for Panama. Crossing a disused railway bridge, I cycled into the last country that stood between me and

South America. On my second night in Panama, I pulled into a fire station, where the chief kindly allowed me to camp on the floor behind his bright orange engines. I unrolled my sleeping mattress, hung up my mosquito net and began preparing my supper on my camp stove, a young bombero watching my every move.

I took a bunch of green plantain from my helmet, peeled a couple, chopped them into chunks and began frying them in a little oil. Once golden on each side, I placed them in a plastic bag and carefully crushed each one flat under my foot. Peeling the discs out of the bag, I seasoned them with a little salt and pepper, which I kept in used film cases, and placed them back in the hot oil for a second fry. While each gold and crispy disc, which the locals call patacones, cooled, I mashed an avocado into a smooth guacamole.

My patacones were as good as any I had eaten by the side of the road, and although exhausted, I enjoyed a small sense of satisfaction. I offered one to the young bombero who had sat silently watching me cook this Panamanian snack. He accepted and seemed impressed. Then he gathered his courage to ask me, very politely, was I MacGyver?

I was amused by his question, but I felt very far from the all-action TV hero he had mistaken me for. I may have had all the gear, and the rugged look of a man who had been living on the road, but inside I was finished. Lying under my mosquito net that night, while hungry mosquitoes tested it for weak points, I studied the map of South America that had remained hidden in my left-hand rear pannier, somewhere between a damp photocopy of my driving licence, some brake cables and a few snaps of my family, for over a year. In the last few days I had been spending more and more time staring at the vast continental mass that I planned to cycle into.

Until then, Rio de Janeiro had been no more than a thoughtless, routine answer supplied to the curious when they asked where I intended to finish this trip. Now, while I did my best to comprehend the vast continent ahead of me, the fluorescent orange sticker that signified Rio de Janeiro and my destination seemed further away than ever. Huge distances, the snow-covered Andes, the never-ending green expanse of the Amazon basin, it all scared the hell out of me. I had never felt so far away from the city that would reunite me with friends, family and the normal life that I had now learnt was so special. Hot, tired, bored and homesick, I was totally adventured out. Panama City lay only a few days away down where the Pan-American Highway came to an end, and perhaps this would be as good a place as any to call it a day. I had cycled a little over ten thousand miles. Panama was a natural dead-end before I had to find a way into South America. Maybe this was the night to admit defeat, give up and go home.

> Stop worrying about the potholes in the road and
> celebrate the journey.
>
> *Fitzhugh Mullan*

Pupusas with Curtido

Makes 8
oil for shallow-frying

The dough
300g masa harina (corn flour)
240ml warm water

The fillings *(use separately or mix them up for pupusas revueltas)*
grated cheese (pupusas de queso)
deep-fried bacon chopped into small pieces (pupusas de chicharrones)
refried beans (pupusas de frijoles refritos)

The curtido
½ cabbage, finely shredded
1 onion, chopped
120ml water
1 carrot, grated
120ml white wine vinegar
1 Serrano chilli, chopped
salt

A night with a couple of pupusas will leave you exhausted, hot and sweaty but ultimately satisfied...

1. First make the curtido. (Curtido is a simple cabbage salad traditionally served with pupusas. Large jars of curtido are kept at room temperature in restaurants, which gives the dish a nicely fermented flavour similar to sauerkraut.) Mix the ingredients in a bowl with 120ml water and 120ml white wine vinegar and a pinch of salt, and set aside ready to serve with your pupusas.

2. Then make the dough for the pupusas. In a large bowl, mix together the flour and most of the water and knead well. Gradually knead in more water, a tablespoonful at a time, until you have a moist but firm dough. Cover and set aside to rest for 5–10 minutes.

3. Roll the dough into a log, cut into 8 equal portions and roll each portion into a ball. Press a hole in the middle with your thumb. Put 1 tablespoon of filling into each ball and fold the dough over to enclose it completely. Press the ball out with your palms into a disc about 2cm thick, taking care the filling doesn't escape.

4. Heat a little oil in a skillet or heavy frying pan over medium-high heat. Cook each pupusa for 1–2 minutes on each side, until lightly browned and blistered. Remove to a plate and keep warm until all your pupusas are done.

5. Serve on a plate with a heap of curtido.

6. Take your first bite, but be careful – the contents will be hot!

Ron Don, Costa Rica

Serves 6

1kg yucca
2 sweet potatoes
2kg yammi
4 coconuts (or 3 x 400ml tins of coconut milk)
1 head of garlic
2 celery sticks
1 large onion
3 red bell peppers
3 large plantains
8 green bananas (unripe)
1 bunch of cilantro, chopped
1 bunch of thyme
2 scotch bonnet chillies
3kg fresh fish: snapper, Jack and corvina (sea bass) are all good
4 tablespoons chicken stock powder or granules
2 tablespoons freshly ground black pepper
oil for frying
2 lobsters
to serve: cilantro (coriander), chilli sauce and limes

1. Clean and peel the yucca, sweet potato and the yammi, cut into large chunks and leave to soak in a bowl of cold water.

2. Now you need to juice your coconuts. Grate the meat of the coconuts into a large bowl (you really need a specially adapted device for this) and add 3 litres of water. Get your hands in and squeeze the juice out of the coconut meat. Strain through a sieve until the water is the colour of milk. If you can't get good coconuts and are a little short on time and specialised coconut graters, buy some tins of coconut milk.

3. Pour the coconut milk into a large pan and bring to a gentle boil.

4. Smash, peel and chop the garlic, reserving 4 cloves. Chop the

celery and onion, slice the peppers and add the lot, apart from the reserved cloves, to the coconut milk. Simmer gently over a low heat for 10 minutes.

5. Roughly chop the plantain and banana, drain the yucca, sweet potato, and yammi, and add to the coconut milk along with the cilantro and the thyme. Burst the scotch bonnet chillies in your fingers (watch your eyes) and add to the pot. Continue to stew over a low heat.

6. While all the ingredients are cooking, you need to get the fish ready. Traditional Ron Don is made with whatever fish comes in, but ideally you want a fish with tough meat that is not going to break up too easily. Gut, clean and scale all the fish and chop into three sections: head, middle and tail. Score each side of the fish with a large knife and then smother each piece in a dry mixture of chicken stock and black pepper. Make sure that the seasoning gets in all the cracks and holes.

7. Heat a good drizzle of cooking oil in a large frying pan. Crush the reserved garlic cloves and add to the hot oil. Fry for 5 minutes to flavour the oil, then remove and discard the garlic.

8. Now add all the fish pieces to the oil and fry on each side until golden and cooked through: about 4 minutes a side. Set aside on kitchen paper.

9. Lastly, clean the lobsters and chop into good chunks and add to the coconut milk along with the fried fish pieces and cook for a further 20 minutes. Serve in large bowls with a good sprinkle of cilantro, a dash of chilli sauce and freshly squeezed limes.

A huge thanks to Piney and his family and crew for all their help.

CHAPTER 8

cartagena to quito

THE HIGHS AND LOWS OF CYCLING IN COLOMBIA

All I want from life is to be in love, ride my bike and drink
good coffee.

Anon

They say there is a fine line between madness and genius, and
whichever marketing brain decided to use the word 'super' to
describe the freeze-dried ball of reconstituted noodles he was
trying to flog was clearly mad. For three days and three nights, the
eight-man crew of the aptly named *Vagabond Prince* had been
living on block after block of this dehydrated, rehydrated, nutri-
tion-free slop, a favourite of penny-pinching students and, apparently, Colombian boat captains, and the miniscule self-pumping
loo that serviced a continual stream of groaning shipmates looked
and smelt anything but 'super'.

Coming from a nation with a distinguished naval history, I had
hoped to relish my time under sail. I fancied myself singing sea
shanties and dancing a merry hornpipe under the yardarm. In
reality I wasn't coping so well. It was too hot to stay on deck. We
were unable to swim in the perfect blue Caribbean waters because
of a threat of sharks, whose silver fins occasionally flashed in our
wake. We were forbidden to shower, due to our captain's reluctance to fill up his fresh-water tank, and after only a short time at
sea I felt, looked and smelt like a salty dog. Spending my daytime

hours below deck, languishing in the cramped, fume-filled cabin, I tried everything not to think about my next bowl of noodles and began wondering whether taking on the infamous Darién Gap would have been preferable to my current situation.

The dirty, traffic-clogged Pan-American Highway, which allows you to drive, or even bicycle, from the wilds of Alaska to the tropical climbs of Central America, comes, as I have said, to an abrupt end in Panama City. Man can walk on the moon, build canals that cross countries and dig tunnels under seas, but to date the Darién Gap, which connects South America to the Central American isthmus, still awaits man's tarmac-treatment. Famed for its impregnable swamps, dense jungles, hostile bandits, drug-running locals and washed-out roads, it holds a mythical status among the travellers who congregate in Panama City looking for a passage into South America. The dog-eared travel guides that are exchanged freely between the unshaven, malodorous, sandal-wearing backpackers heading north and south simply advise you not to make the crossing, and thus rumours abound in the grubby youth hostels of Panama City as to the various different ways of negotiating the dead end.

'You could catch a boat across the Gulf of Urabá and then hike the Unguía–Paya route but you need a guide.'

'A day's walk and a dugout canoe will get you to Turbo, but all the immigration posts are closed.'

'I met a guy who made it across the great Atrato swamp by motorboat, but it was pretty sketchy.'

'You can fly direct to Quito.'

'You can try and hitch a ride on a sailing boat heading for Colombia.'

No jungles, no bandits, no swamps, no baggage handlers, no check-in, hoisting the main sail at sunset, six sheets to the wind on a southern tack. This all sounded too good to be true. So I decided to test my sea legs and set a course in the triumphant wake of Captain Morgan and Sir Francis Drake and sail for South America. But I needed a boat. I asked around the yacht clubs and called various numbers pinned to notice boards, but nothing was leaving Panama City for weeks.

In a backstreet cyber café I was emailing my parents with the news that I would be going against their wishes and cycling into Colombia, but still had to find a way of getting there, when I overheard a Colombian boat captain looking to make some quick cash by sailing some 'gringos' to Cartagena, Colombia. I confirmed my interest and he said I could have free passage if I could get at least five other customers to the port of Colón by the following evening. I spent the next 24 hours tirelessly trawling the hostels of Panama City selling this 'unique cruise', and I managed to press-gang an international crew of an Israeli, an Australian, an Argentinean, a Mancunian, a policeman's son from Portsmouth and two German hippies. Together we set sail for Colombia, but I quickly realised that life at sea was not as romantic as I had hoped.

ٚ

'Aquí, aquí,' I cried like a marooned sailor, gesturing at the two women paddling towards us in a thin dugout canoe, one of whom was holding aloft two plump lobsters as big as her arms. 'Aquí, aquí!' I continued, waving frantically in a noodle-induced hysteria, but the two dark-skinned women advancing on us didn't speak Spanish. Since sunrise on our fourth day at sea we had been navigating our way through the sandbanks, jagged reefs and pristine palm-covered islands of the San Blas archipelago, and this was our first sighting of their inhabitants. Strung out along the Caribbean coast of Panama from the Golfo de San Blas, almost all the way to the Colombian border, the San Blas Archipelago is made up of almost four hundred picture-perfect islands, of which only a few are populated by the fiercely independent Kuna Indians. Having resisted changes to their culture since the Spanish first arrived in the Americas over five hundred years ago, the indigenous Kuna have lived an almost unchanged existence on these small islands for millennia. They have their own language, their own laws and their own independent government, and watching the canoe cross the crystal-clear waters towards our immense white hull, I was transported to another age.

Coming alongside, the two slight women lay down their wooden paddles and began to trade. Their stern faces were decorated with golden nose rings and they were dressed in sarongs and simple rainbow-coloured blouses, emblazoned with the geometric designs of fish, birds and jungle animals. Their shins and forearms were tightly wrapped in bands of infinitesimal beads, and at their feet, in the hull of their crude dugout canoe, was a writhing mass of sea life as vibrant and colourful as their clothing.

Gleaming silver tarpon, lobsters with menacing claws tied with blades of palm, coral crabs, yellow-tailed snapper, square-headed jack with bulbous black eyes, flaccid octopus, wide-mouthed grouper. Like the famished crew of an old English galleon after months at sea, we hung over the side of our boat bartering with the native women for food. Our animated haggling intensified as the stubborn women held up their catch. Securing four large lobster, I raced below deck and put some water on the boil in our small galley. While the unfortunate creatures turned pink in the bubbling pot, I dived into the calm, cool waters, protected from the thundering waves of the Atlantic and the hungry sharks by reefs and the small palm-covered islands of golden sand that stretched towards the horizon.

Cracking legs and claws in my teeth, I sucked and slurped on the tender meat. Sweet fishy juices dribbled down my chin and on to my bare chest. Hacking the top of a ripe coconut I quenched my thirst on the cool clean water inside. I gazed through the pure, turquoise waters at the shoals of psychedelic fish that darted in and out of the forest of coral below me and away to the series of picturesque islands all around. I was eating freshly caught lobster in one of the last unspoilt corners of our planet. I was in paradise.

Taking another swim after lunch, I walked ashore on to one of the small islets, home to a handful of Kuna families. I peered at the primitive homes constructed from palm thatch; I admired the strength and patience of an old man patiently chipping away, with crude tools, at a felled palm trunk, which in time would become a means of transport and commerce, and I wondered what the blackened fish hanging over a smoking fire would taste like. There was no sanitation here, no running water, and other than the palm trees and coconuts, no land to cultivate. As we weighed anchor, waved goodbye to these proud people and set sail for Colombia, I was left wondering what paradise might look and taste like for the Kuna who inhabited these small islands ... and hoped it didn't involve Pot Noodles.

⚄

The unblemished islands of San Blas quickly faded into the horizon and back out at sea we returned to the doldrums. Fatigued from the constant roll of the ocean, the crew languished in various parts of the boat doing their best to ignore the heat and slow progress. We passengers played endless games of cards, grumbled about the food and the heat and shared our plans for our travels in South America.

A jolly bunch, we seemed to encompass every demographic of the free spirits that travel the gringo trail. Raviv, our hairy Israeli, fresh out of military service, was always sleeping; Rachael, our happy-go-lucky Australian, regaled us with her crazy antics; Paul, our shaven-headed, tattooed man from Manchester; Sebastian, our impossibly handsome Argentinean, who managed to look and smell immaculate at all times; Martin from Portsmouth was between jobs as an aid worker; the earnest couple from Germany paid for their nomadic lifestyle by selling an assortment of shabby jewellery and friendship bracelets made from feathers and shells. We had a first mate, a wiry black man who was forever pulling on ropes and tightening winches, and there was our captain Fabio, a competent man looking forward to getting home to his wife in Colombia. Overhead the mainsail flapped in what little breeze there was, while beneath us the tired engine spluttered and gurgled to push us forward. Under a blazing tropical sun we crawled impatiently towards Colombia. Quietly I longed for a storm, a squall, some wind. Anything to break the monotony of this never-ending voyage.

☙

I was languishing half asleep at the stern of the boat, a fishing line wound round my big toe, in the hope of catching anything that would taste better than noodles, when the boom swung on to our port side with a tremendous crash. The boat listed on to a starboard tack; the engine changed its mantra from a rhythmic splutter to an anguished roar. Our captain was looking intently into his binoculars.

The clatter and unnatural change in our course woke the crew from their various states of slumber. The binoculars were passed from person to person and a package, bobbing some way off our starboard bow, was pointed out. Our captain explained the situation and as we steadily approached our new target, I sat back in stunned and thoughtful silence.

As well as coffee and Shakira, Colombia is also renowned for another illustrious pick-me-up. But you don't take coals to Newcastle, and I had assumed we weren't in any danger of winding up with a double-dealing captain keen to make a quick buck. Only an idiot would take cocaine back into Colombia. What I had not accounted for was finding the stuff during our journey.

With its limitless number of islands, the route we were sailing into Colombia was a favourite for those trying to get 'the good stuff' out. Apparently it is not uncommon for those making runs to jettison their cargo to evade capture from the well-equipped, multinational naval force that polices these waters. This results in boxes with a colossal street-value bobbing innocently up and down on the ocean waves, and, according to our captain, a situation of finders-keepers applies to those lucky enough to come across one.

Our abrupt change in direction began to make sense. The captain explained that in the next group of islands there were congenial locals who would be quite happy to take the cargo off our hands in exchange for a significant amount of cash and, with a floating democracy in place, if the box contained something more than a few bags of Gold Blend we would take a vote. Sell the booty and split the cash, or leave the coke to the mercy of the ocean and the next lucky punters. Suddenly the show of hands of a gang of people I had only known for a matter of days was going to determine whether I continued my travels into South America on a state-of-the-art motorcycle or spent what remained of my youth behind bars in a Colombian hell-hole.

'Hecho en Colombia' read the sinister words stencilled on the tatty plastic sacking of the parcel floating next to us. Lifting the package dripping with water on to the deck, we anxiously investigated its contents. Nothing. Just a few strands of seaweed and damp bubble wrap. There would be no cash prize or festering in jail, but as we turned back on to our original tack, I began to wonder what kind of country I was about to enter.

After six nights at sea I longed to escape the claustrophobic conditions of our boat. As the orange glow of a city rose from the horizon, a feverish excitement overwhelmed the weary crew. We had arrived in South America and the port of Cartagena, an exquisitely preserved fortified colonial city, with a dark history of slavery and pirates. It was alive with energy, the perfect introduction to a new continent. The spirited tempo of salsa and vallenato resounded on every street. Handsome men in loose-fitting guayabera shirts drank cold beer in the balmy evening air, while beguiling women meandered in flowing white dresses that accentuated the rich tone of their olive skin. Striking pink and purple bougainvillea spilled over the wooden balconies of perfumed colonial plazas that reverberated with the tolling of church bells and the rattle of the horse-drawn carriages over cobbled streets.

Allegedly I had just set foot in one of the most dangerous countries on earth, but as far as I could tell, Colombia was bursting with life and positive energy. And, for the first time since leaving Mexico, it looked like my culinary fortunes were about to pick up. Food seemed to be everywhere and Colombians clearly loved to eat. Gone was the monotony of rice and beans. In Cartagena I breakfasted on a calorie-packed arepa de huevo, the signature dish of Colombia's northern coast. A thick maize pancake filled with an egg and seasoned mince, deep-fried and eaten on the hoof, washed down with glasses of sweet orange juice squeezed by happy vendors on every corner.

I walked the city's ancient battlements, built by slaves to protect their colonial masters from invading English pirates, where vivid hand-painted stalls sold bowls of refreshing ceviche. Clams, octopus, conch and shrimp, drenched in lime juice, were the perfect antidote to the midday heat. Voluptuous black women wrapped in colourful robes stood behind towers of watermelon and cocada, a sugary treat made of grated coconut and molten panela (unrefined sugar) flavoured with tropical fruit. After a week of eating and enjoying Cartagena, the despondent thoughts that plagued me in the later stages of Central America vanished. Cartagena and Colombia restored my energy and reinstated my enthusiasm for the road. Pulling myself away from her plentiful charms, I packed up my bike and rode into the sultry heat of Colombia's coastal lowlands.

⚄

The coastal roads and palm-lined beaches of Córdoba soon morphed into the lush, damp meadows of Antioquia, where fine-looking cows, the happiest I had seen in some time, chewed the cud and rested from the heat of the day in the shade of ancient trees. The throbbing drone of cicadas replaced the rhythmic crash of the surf, and as I pedalled further inland, the quiet roads began to undulate over striking green hills. The calm qualities of my new surroundings filled me with enthusiasm, and as the hills rose and the valleys deepened, the dark shades of the Andean foothills began to fill the horizon.

I camped on a grubby piece of wasteland next to a petrol station, where the presence of a dormant, but heavily armed, security guard had provided me with some assurance of my safety during the night. I woke at sunrise when the soothing, nocturnal murmur of insects and amphibians was replaced by the disturbing and familiar din of the road. Old-fashioned jeeps skidded in the dirt; swarms of motorcycles revved their high-pitched engines. This was more than simply a place to fill up on four-star, the petrol station was bus stop, taxi rank, trading post and bustling social meeting-point. Children with heavy baskets of ripe mangoes and slices of sticky pineapple passed fruit through the windows of buses to the passengers trapped inside; men pushed self-decorated wagons, serving gloriously strong and horribly sweet shots of coffee from dusty Thermoses, and, against the odds, the familiar smell of frying food succeeded in overcoming the acrid odour of fuel and combustion.

Keen to sniff out the source of these delightful aromas, I packed up my tent and wearily made my way towards two multi-coloured umbrellas, set up in the shade of a cluster of trees. A buxom black lady with a wide grin was hard at work. Her improvised kitchen was a temple to North Colombian street cuisine, and at her altar a noisy congregation of bus drivers, policemen, motorcyclists and truckers was grabbing at the food.

Buñuelos, perfectly fried spheres of cheesy dough, were piled into neat pyramids, while others bobbed up and down in a shallow vat of hissing oil. Carimañolas, deep-fried mashed yucca stuffed with minced beef, were stacked on dented metal trays like bullion in a bank vault, and towers of patacones sat next to mounds of golden arepas de huevo.

Plastic beakers of chilled fruit juice, guava, papaya, mango and maracuja (passion fruit), provided a fresh contrast to the otherwise oily flavours of the delicious deep-fried offerings. Reused bottles of home-made aji, a spicy salsa made with chillies and tangy tree tomatoes, were passed from customer to customer along with enthusiastic roadside banter, fuelled by a steady supply of strong Colombian coffee.

It was as I was taking a bite from a buñuelo that the unmistakable outline of another cycle tourist became recognisable on the crest of the hill. Running from the shade of the trees, shouting and waving my arms like a crazed groupie, crumbs of breakfast spewing from my mouth, I gestured towards him and towards my bicycle as if to say, 'Look, look, I'm one of your lot.' But it became very clear, very quickly that, as cycle tourists go, Torsten, a middle-aged German, and myself had come from very different moulds.

'Desayuno?' I suggested, handing Torsten a delightfully warm arepa wrapped in a grease-stained paper napkin. 'No,' he replied unequivocally, pulling a plastic sack of what appeared to be bird-seed and a bruised banana from the bag between his handlebars.

'Café?'

'No!' came another stern negative, and I watched his prominent Adam's apple bounce up and down as he emptied what remained of a bottle of fluorescent-pink energy drink into his mouth.

🚲

Cycle tourists are like dogs, and with our brief introduction over we began sniffing each other's bottoms. How much weight are you carrying? What pedals are you using? Caliper or disk brakes? Drop handlebars or flat? Slick tyres or knobbly ones? A derailleur or internal gear system? *Sniff, sniff.*

Torsten's bicycle was brilliantly clean. Every dirt-free compo-nent glistened in the sun as though it had just come out of the box. His minimal equipment was meticulously packed in four clean Ortlieb panniers. His entire setup was as spotless and streamlined as he was, and together Torsten and his bicycle were a testament to German efficiency. I was not. As he ran his questioning eyes over my untidy rig, I could hear the white-coated technicians in his mind tutting in baffled disbelief at the dirty, overloaded, scruffy excuse for a cyclist and bicycle that stood before him.

'Vas is das?' I heard them say as he took in my colourful collection of souvenir stickers, which must have added a few grams of extra weight. 'Vas is dis?' they proclaimed at the chunky plastic hamburger bell, leather dream catcher, rosary beads and the various other lucky charms and trinkets that hung from my handlebars, weighing me down further.

'And vi are you not varing zee Lycra. Nein nein nein, Zis is very inefficient.'

This silent ritual over with, Torsten unclipped his multi-buttoned digital cycle computer and thrust it towards my face. 'Alaska!' he barked proudly, displaying his total distance. A figure close to 12,000 miles. 'Six meses,' he then broadcast in Spanglish. I hung my head in shame. In six months Torsten had cycled the same distance it had taken me over a year to cover. And it showed. We could not have looked any more different. Short, overweight, unshaven and clad in baggy shorts and a crusty, sweat-stained T-shirt, I was the antithesis of the man who towered over me. All elbows and knees, his tall, gangly frame of bones and sinew was tightly packed in a figure-hugging fluorescent Lycra outfit that accentuated every one of his lumps and bumps in disturbing detail. An oversized helmet dwarfed his long, thin face. He gave the impression of a man ready to be fired from a cannon in a circus.

We were an odd couple, but with Torsten's tortured Spanglish and my small anthology of German picked up from old war films, we established that we were heading the same way and would ride on together. 'Schnell! Schnell!' I cried, climbing back into the saddle. Leaving behind a bemused crowd of breakfasting locals, who had witnessed this bizarre roadside union, we rode together into the foothills of the Andes and towards Colombia's second city. Medellín.

☙

We gently climbed, our surroundings changing almost with each turn of the pedals. The near stagnant muddy water that meandered in the rivers and streams began to increase its pace as it ran downhill. Going in the opposite direction, we began to slow down.

No longer sharing the road with laidback, washboard-chested coastal locals in straw hats and plastic sandals, I was now cycling past barrel-chested farmers in heavy boots, jeans and ponchos. Palm trees became thirsty plantain and papaya, their enormous translucent green leaves spread out around heavy bunches of fruit.

The stony streams by the roadside came to life with running water that raced and gurgled its way downhill, this ever-increasing flow feeding the moist leaves of monumental ferns that fanned out from the moss-covered cliffs that rose above me. The road began to twist and turn through continual switchbacks that hung, precariously, to the sides of the steep valleys. For months I had been cycling in an oppressive, tropical climate, dripping with perspiration and operating in a permanent state of fatigue. But now, climbing higher into the foothills of the Andes, the altitude forced the temperature down. My sweat damp T-shirt was cool as it clung to my body on short-lived downhill runs, and as I advanced uphill, the invigorating air filled my lungs.

For all my apparent inefficiency, Torsten and I moved forward at more or less the same pace. Each day we came together for lunch, but Torsten was not a 'foodie'. He harboured a strong distrust of local cuisine and insisted on surviving on a steady supply of biscuits, jam, birdseed and bananas. Sitting in the small family-run restaurants in the villages and towns along the way, stout vaqueros watched in silence across colourful tablecloths as Torsten carefully unfolded his spotless penknife, spread two biscuits with a flawlessly flat layer of jam, pressed each half together, wiped clean his blade, then slid this strange sandwich into his mouth. Opposite him I refuelled on generous plates of boiled cow's tongue smothered in tomato and onion sauce topped with a fried egg, and deep bowls of beef sancocho, a hearty Colombian stew loaded with meaty hunks of gristle and bone that I gnawed in my fingers. Of our opposing diets, mine was clearly the more indulgent, but if it was good enough for herding cattle on the steep slopes of the mountains, it was good enough for cycling up them.

Leapfrogging each other throughout the day, we reconvened in the evenings in pre-arranged towns and villages, and with the price of a room and a bed now halved, I took a break from my tent and wallowed in the relative luxury of the budget truck-driver dormitories and cheap guesthouses we settled on. Higher into the mountains the temperature dropped and at the end of each gruelling day cycling uphill I was always grateful for the heavy blankets and a soft mattress.

🚲

The town of Valdivia perched precariously on a pass between two bottomless valleys. In the accelerating darkness the twinkling lights of its houses and the tolling of its church bells gave it an almost imaginary aura. Since crossing the gushing, brown waters of Rio Cauca shortly after lunch, I had been cycling uphill for over thirty kilometres. I was ready to drop and the first sight of this small town could not have come too soon.

Torsten was waiting in front of the town's only guesthouse, a charmless, unfinished, concrete premises that doubled as a canteen. A soap opera blared from an old television, a handful of unappetising empanadas, deep-fried pastry pockets filled with potatoes and mince, waited to be rescued from a grubby hotplate, and Torsten was meticulously scrubbing each link of his chain with an old toothbrush. A couple of rosy-cheeked children followed his every move, and they couldn't believe their luck when an additional Aryan athlete pulled up on another overloaded bicycle.

Our room was compact, with a glassless window that provided a view across the dark mountains. But for the stale smell of its previous occupants and damp-stained walls, it was almost romantic. The walls that separated us from our neighbours didn't reach the ceiling, giving the impression of being in a long dormitory, and two flimsy single beds, piled with heavy, woollen blankets, almost completely filled the space. Pushing my most important possessions under the bed, I kicked off my shoes. The pungent reek of long months of cycling filled the room, and doing what I could for Anglo-German relations I placed them on the windowsill, peeled off my clothes and collapsed into bed.

🚲

'Up! Up! Thomas, *vamos*! *Vamos!*'

I opened my eyes and was greeted with the unsettling vision of a man in tight-fitting yellow and pink Lycra. It was a little after six in the morning. I pulled a heavy blanket over my head in protest. 'Das es verboten,' I quipped from inside my soft bunker, but Torsten was not amused. He wanted to get going, and pulling my aching frame out of bed I waddled down the cold, concrete corridor to the communal shower where a vast, hairy man was rubbing his genitals with soap.

'Pardon! Pardon!' After waiting in turn, I did my best to wash under the ice-cold water that trickled out of a rusty pipe, pretending to be a shower. 'Aaah, oooh, aaah.' For the reaction it elicited, the water might as well have been boiling hot, but I cleaned the bits that needed cleaning and back in our room I dried off with an old T-shirt, put on most of my clothes and opened the wooden shutter to a morning of dense fog and the sound of rain. My heart sank.

In over 10,000 miles of bicycle travel, I had had nothing stolen. But on a bitterly cold morning in the mountains of Colombia, someone had swiped the tatty, worn-out, fetid footwear that had been on my feet since New York. In a country that was meant to run amok with merciless guerrillas and cold-blooded drug barons, where kidnappings were, apparently, commonplace, somebody had run off with my shoes. Hardly an exciting story to recount to my grandchildren when they pestered me for Werther's Originals and adventurous tales from the road. Slowly I came to terms with my loss and the depressing reality that I would have to continue cycling into the Andes in my socks and the only other footwear I possessed. A pair of sandals.

Outside Torsten was ready to go, standing by his bicycle bulging in his finest Lycra. He looked down at my feet, and before he could take offence, that I was perhaps mocking his Germanic fashion sense, I explained my predicament and that I needed a coffee. Bitterly cold, my toes were already curling up in protest at the icy rain that had soused my socks, and I skipped around the puddles and into a bar that had just opened its doors.

'Dos cafés, por favor.'

The owner poured two cups of black coffee from an ornate stainless steel urn festooned with complicated levers, valves and gauges, on top of which perched a large bronze eagle. I took my first sip, a few rays of morning sun broke through the cloud and drizzle, and what had been a miserable morning began to improve. Torsten went to use the loo, I gulped the last of my cup and was ready to take on the day.

Boisterous laughter shattered the peace of the morning, and a gang of men stormed into the bar. Wrapped in traditional Antioquian ponchos and wearing characteristic black and cream woven cowboy hats, they clumsily sat down at the table next to me and bellowed at the barman for beer. Judging by their smell and behaviour, they had been up all night.

I was handed a beer. I politely declined. The offer was made again. I declined once more. The offer was not to be resisted. Hoping for a little peace, and thinking it might warm my toes, I accepted. A small bottle of Poker beer was placed in front of me.

'Colombia y paz!'

'Colombia y paz!'

I too raised my bottle and drank to Colombia and peace. The man beside me then pulled a thin test-tube from his trouser pocket. It was sealed with an orange bung, and in its rounded bottom lay a drift of white powder.

'Colombian diamonds,' the man said proudly, holding the tube within inches of my face while gently tapping it with his fingernail like a mad scientist. Removing the rubber bung with his teeth, he ejected a small mound of pure, white powder on to the back of his hand. Holding down one nostril with a finger and implementing a short powerful sniff via the other, the white powder vanished up his nose. He offered me the tube.

I politely declined.

'Take it,' he insisted. 'It's pure!'

I tried to explain that I was travelling by bike, and that cycling through the Andes and cocaine were not a good combination.

'Take it!'

The man's intoxicated demands became more pronounced. Taking hold of my shoulder he pushed me back into my seat. 'Take it!' he shouted, showering my face with beer and spit.

When I declined again, he bent his other hand behind his back. When it returned it was gripping a gleaming, silver revolver. The heavy weapon hit the table and I stared in disbelief at the barrel pointing towards my chest. 'Tocarlo!' he said quietly, and holding up my arm he tapped a substantial mound of white, crystalline powder on to the back of my hand, and at gunpoint I sniffed.

Rewarded for my efforts with a series of firm handshakes and forceful slaps on the back, I took a long pull on my beer, which helped to cleanse the unpleasant and bitter taste dripping in the back of my throat. My nose tingled in contact with the cool mountain air and the numbing sensation gently moved to my teeth and gums. My heart thumped in my chest. My cold toes began twitching in my sandals. I wanted to tell my new friends about where I was from, where I had been and where I was going. But soon bored by my broken Spanish ramblings they left me free to go, and I gestured to Torsten, who had witnessed this whole fiasco from the safety of the bar. 'Vamos! Vamos!' I reached an arm over Torsten's shoulder and we stepped out into the now bright sunshine. The valleys and mountains were breathtaking. Relishing the clean air that swelled in my chest, I pedalled out of town with unparalleled energy and enthusiasm on my way to Medellín.

🚲

I never saw Torsten again. We planned to meet for lunch but I think the early morning drink and drug abuse was the straw that broke the camel's back, and at the top of a long climb I lunched alone.

At a wooden shack of a home that doubled as a restaurant, a hand-painted sign leaning against its wall told me there was only one dish worth eating on the menu. Bandeja Paisa, and judging by the number of stocky vaqueros squeezed around its tables, they did it well. Considered by many, especially the proud people of the Paisa province, to be the national dish of Colombia, the bandeja Paisa isn't really a dish. Translated as 'tray of the Paisa', if rumours were to be believed this traditional feast was so riddled with fat and calories it made the full English breakfast look like a health plan. Considering the hedonistic path my day had taken, it seemed only right to put in an order.

The Paisa province of Colombia is also celebrated for its abundance of handsome women, and the young Paisita that walked out of the busy kitchen, buckling under the weight of my lunch, was impossibly beautiful. Figure-hugging jeans, tight white blouse, rich ebony hair, hazel skin, exotic eyes and in her arms a tantalising array of Colombian home cooking. A perfectly braised skirt steak, a stack of crispy chicharrón, a ceramic bowl of slow-stewed beans, a heap of steaming rice, two still-sizzling chorizo, a pair of grilled arepas glistening in molten butter, golden shallow-fried plantain and a perfectly fried egg. The only visible greenery on this hazardously fatty platter was half an avocado.

Inside this small wooden building the rowdy banter of the vaqueros merged with the chink and clink of plates being scraped clean. Outside the dull clunk of cattle bells mingled with the sound of the wind and, with every gust, the view from the window changed, as dense billows of cloud and mist swirled and spiralled through the valley and over the top of the craggy ridges. The numbness of my toes reminded me of the morning's events. I had no shoes. I had been forced to take drugs at gunpoint. I had cycled up a mountain in flip-flops. But here at the top I had enjoyed this remarkable Colombian tray of hearty local food, a testament to the hard-working people of the Paisas who filled the tables around me. In my wet socks, I raised my glass of milk and made a quiet toast.

Colombia y paz.

Leaving Medellín with a pair of new leather boots, the type favoured by Colombian coffee farmers, I cycled with warm toes into central Colombia, following a well-irrigated valley between Medellín and Manizales. The climate was warm and balmy and passion fruit and guava farms decorated the lower slopes in tidy stripes, while the higher slopes were blanketed in a dark green crop of Colombia's most prominent export: coffee. Manizales, perched high on a hill in the heart of coffee country, would, I hope, provide me with an insight into this wonderful commodity, but locals had been forewarning me for days about the steep climb into the city. It was still twenty miles away, and so in the late afternoon I began looking for a suitable place to camp.

Pulling into a small farmstead constructed of bamboo and corrugated metal on a little fruit farm, I asked if I could pitch my tent, in order to sleep and so attack the hill in the morning with a fresh pair of legs. In a manner typical of Colombian hospitality, I was greeted like an old friend and taken in to their home. After being given a welcome bowl of sweet coffee and a hearty plate of rice, beans and fried plantain, I was shown to a small area of concrete that was protected from the lightly falling rain by an overhanging tiled roof. I unrolled my camping mattress and hung up my mosquito net while the family's four inquisitive children watched and questioned my every move. Eventually their father, Milton, ordered them to bed, and after saying goodnight I curled up on the floor and was quickly asleep.

It was still dark when I opened my eyes. A few feet away, Maria, the young mother, was blowing into the previous night's fire, doing her best to catch a flame in the damp, early morning air. While doing so, she chatted energetically to one of her daughters, who was putting all her efforts into grinding handfuls of soaked maize that would become fresh arepas. I pushed myself up from the floor, and the scene in front of me swung around in a violent circle. As a flood of dizziness rushed into my head I fell back on to my mattress with a thud. Burning up and damp with sweat, I mustered enough energy for another attempt at being vertical, and began to gather my gear. I accepted a kind invitation for breakfast and, hunched over a bowl of chicharrón and beans, I mulled over my situation. I felt terrible, and was stuck on a fruit farm in the back country of Colombia some twenty miles downhill from the nearest town. I could take some paracetamol and drink plenty of water, then try to make it up the hill. If that failed, I could flag down a truck and get a ride, I thought.

Before I could put together anything resembling a decision, Maria had placed a testing hand on my forehead. She pronounced me to be very ill.

Maria was right, but I did what most men do in these situations and brazenly claimed everything was fine. I was only a few hours' ride from the next town, and my flawed plan was to get there, find some medicine and a place to stay until I was better. In a voice that contrasted sharply with the soft tone that had delivered my original diagnosis, Maria asserted that more cycling was not an option. Arguing was futile. I was ordered into bed.

I was sent to the children's room, which had three beds, and I was put in one of them. The walls were made from split bamboo and a rusty corrugated metal roof sat upon a zigzag of bamboo rafters that were thick with cobwebs. A network of crudely connected wires ran from beam to beam, culminating in a naked light bulb that hung in the centre of the room. The worn-out springs of the bed squeaked and twanged as I climbed on to the soft mattress and I gratefully closed my eyes and drifted to sleep.

I don't know how many hours I had been asleep, but when I woke the sheets underneath me were soaked with sweat. I was quivering with fever and I started to think more seriously about getting to a doctor. Replacing her hand on my forehead, Maria gave some orders to her two young sons, aged nine and seven, and within an hour they returned, dwarfed by large bundles of leaves and twigs, like commandos on a camouflage exercise.

Maria explained that these were herbs that could cure fever. I wondered whether I would eat, drink or even smoke the small, green leaves the boys were busy plucking from the branches. Back in matron-mode, Maria ordered me to my feet. The leaves of the herb, called mata ratón (mouse bush), then began to be laid on the bed. Before long a thick matting of foliage covered the mattress. Maria ordered me to strip and get back into bed. I did so reluctantly, while Maria's daughters sniggered and giggled. I climbed butt-naked on to the bed and my back arched abruptly as it came into contact with the cold leaves. I drifted back to sleep.

The next morning I was ordered out of bed again. I stood on the cold concrete floor and looked down at the leaf-covered mattress. The day before they had been lush, green and supple, but now they were yellowing, dry and brittle. Maria picked up a handful and crumbled them in her fingers. She declared that the leaves had extracted some of the fever from my body, but that there was still more to come out. The dried-out leaves were replaced with a fresh green batch and I was ordered back into bed.

🚲

For three days I drifted in and out of a confused sleep, haunted by dreams. The humid heat of the day was unbearable and I longed for the cool of the evening when the restless flies would finally give up and go elsewhere. As darkness fell, all manner of strange creatures congregated and danced around the bare lightbulb. I caught vanishing glimpses of the plump tails and tall shadows of the rats and mice that went to work, scratching and scurrying, behind the flimsy bamboo walls. I was given fresh passion fruit juice in the mornings, mashed plantain with cinnamon and panela at lunch time, and a hot blend of honey and herbs before bed. My leaves were changed daily and my fever gradually subsided. I was slowly nursed back to health.

With my strength recovered, and full of gratitude to Milton and Maria, I offered to pay for my keep. Milton would not hear of it so I offered, instead, to work for my keep. In the course of my stay I had learnt that Maria's family were tenant farmers on a small coffee holding in the hills above Risaralda, and that with harvest under way they would indeed be grateful for another pair of hands. Ten days' picking coffee would go some way to repay this wonderful family for taking me in and restoring me to health, and as a bonus I would get to understand more about one of the world's greatest commodities.

🚲

We rounded another tight hairpin in the dirt road that ribboned across the hillside, and the dead-weight of the large old lady sleeping next to me crushed me once more against the sharp edge of the wooden seat. The driver shifted down through his gears and the tired engine of the chiva bus grunted in complaint as we approached another seemingly impossible gradient. Colombians call these gaudy hand-painted buses chivas. A derogatory word, also given to girls who are too generous with their affections. Judging by the number of passengers squeezed on to her uncomfortable wooden benches and hanging from her roof and sides, this particular chiva more than lived up to her name. Completely overloaded with gun-bearing soldiers in military fatigues, farmers with fine straw hats, mothers and children and a cargo of plantain, sacks of coffee and fruit-filled baskets, she struggled around each tight curve of the dark green coffee-covered hillside as though it might be her last.

After three hours of stop-starting our way through small hamlets and coffee fincas, dropping off and collecting the various characters whose lives depended on this daily white-knuckle ride, we pulled into the small town of Risaralda. Heavy sacks of coffee beans and baskets of plantain were thrown from the roof, and passengers hurried to climb on and off. Realising I had lost all feeling in my left leg, and wishing I had stuck to my usual mode of transport, I made it on to the pavement where I crumbled in an undignified heap. In the late afternoon light the little town looked shabby. No sooner had my feet remembered they were attached to my legs than I was huddling up with eight others under the canvas roof of an old Jeep. Revving and bouncing our way up another weather-beaten track, we journeyed further into the hills. The light was fading. I peered through the open back of the Jeep, able to discern no more than ghostly shapes moving in and out of the dense mist on the hillside. My normally reliable sense of direction had abandoned me, but Milton knew exactly where we were. He gently tapped the driver on the shoulder and we skidded to a violent halt.

I climbed over the other tightly-packed passengers. After a long day on the road I was filled with the rewarding sense of arrival. Knowing a little by now of Colombian hospitality, I anticipated that I would soon be warming my hands around a steaming bowl of hot chocolate or warm coffee.

The glow from the Jeep's red tail-lights disappeared into the mist and the smell of burnt diesel evaporated in the damp evening air. I looked around for a house, a path, a light, something that resembled life and hot chocolate among the never-ending rows of coffee plants. Milton pointed a determined finger at the hillside, proudly identifying his finca.

I scanned the hillside for a sign of life.

'Allí, allí.'

I tried again. Running my eyes to the end of Milton's finger, and just beyond a dirt-stained fingernail, I saw what I think I was meant to be looking at. High up on the hillside a single light flickered against the dark green hillside.

I hardly had time to say a word before Milton set off at the kind of pace that could only be achieved after years of climbing these steep slopes. I was left puffing, panting and red-faced some way behind. Following paths or sometimes just tracks left by animals or water finding its way down the hillside, we made our way towards 'the light'. Milton waited for me with encouraging words at the top of each hill, only to set off again on my arrival, leaving me fighting for breath. Pushing past damp rows of coffee plants, stumbling up steep, muddy slopes, I grabbed at whatever I could to stay on my feet. My legs were caked in mud, I was soaked wet with perspiration and the water that hung in the damp air. We climbed for half an hour, an hour, two hours, until a chorus of barking dogs announced our arrival.

A single exposed light bulb cast long shadows over the scene that greeted me. Uneven layers of rusty metal roofs; a disorderly collection of wooden walkways; naive religious icons hung crookedly on the walls. A zigzag of bamboo beams, hats and machetes hanging where they could, and in the centre a group of exhausted-looking men, clad in worn-out jeans, filthy shirts and Wellington boots, sat around a wooden table. My presence was acknowledged with a brief inquisitive glance. I offered a hesitant 'buenas noches' but the collective attention of these hungry men had already returned to the steaming bowls of food they cradled in their laps. This would be home for the next ten days.

⛵

Thwack! Thwack! Thwack!

Disturbed from a series of dreams that had taken me a long way from the wooden floor, old foam mattress and dirty quilt that was reality, I was quickly reminded of where I was. I glanced at my watch: 5.13 a.m. and someone is chopping wood. However damp and malodorous my blanket, all I wanted to do was pull it back over my head, but the sound of footsteps, creaking floorboards and conversation indicated that the day had begun. Not wanting to make a bad first impression, I pulled on my wet boots, ran my hands through my hair and wandered into the chill morning air.

My mother once left a pig's head on the London Underground. A self-proclaimed bargain-hunter, when the butcher offered her the whole thing for fifty pence, she couldn't bear to leave it behind. The problem was, she did. Somewhere on the Circle Line between Tower Hill and South Kensington. No doubt it caused quite a stir at London Transport's lost property office, or an unusual afternoon for the brave police officer assigned to dealing with a 'suspicious package'. And it meant I never got to enjoy some of the piggy treats that can be made from the head of this noble beast. This was about to change, however, when I realised it wasn't the sound of chopping wood that had woken me from my slumber, but Fabio, Milton's father-in-law, hacking at a large pig's head with his machete.

'Buenos dias, Thomas,' he announced cheerfully while removing the second ear from the pale, bloody face that grinned at me from a small wooden table.

'Buenos dias, Fabio,' I said, transfixed by the crude dissection taking place in front of me.

With a second hairy ear removed, Fabio then began yanking and tugging at the pig's face, peeling it away whole from its skull. Playfully he held it in front of his own face while dancing a small jig, much to the delight of his shrieking grandchildren, who were rushing about looking for stray books and socks before their long walk to school.

A master of his machete, within only a few minutes of vigorous slicing, chopping and scooping, all that remained of this once magnificent animal was a blood-soaked skull. Three more powerful and well-placed *thwacks* came down on the pig's cranium. Pulling it apart with disturbing ease, he revealed a nest of shiny pink brains. Sliding two fingers deep into the cavity and giving a sharp yank, Fabio held aloft a perfectly formed pig's brain, dripping in scarlet blood and cerebral juices.

'Desayuno, Thomas!'

Reaching his fingers back into the cavity he then popped the eyes from their sockets and put them aside to be boiled in hot chocolate, apparently a great source of vitamins for Fabio's pregnant daughter, and lastly the strangely long, purple tongue was cut out. My early morning lesson in butchery was complete. The plastic bucket of head parts was sent to Fabio's wife, who was stoking the fire in her crude smoke-filled kitchen. The brains were chopped into rough chunks and seared in a heavy black skillet with a large sliced onion. A handful of eggs were broken in and scrambled. A generous heap of this rubbery mix of grey-matter and eggs was heaped on a bowlful of rice and handed out to the men along with grilled arepas and hot coffee.

'Buen provecho!' I offered, chewing tentatively on my first mouthful. My colleagues were already shovelling the stuff down. I got the impression that coffee picking was going to be hungry work. Feeling stronger for my pig's brain breakfast I accepted a large plastic bucket to tie round my waist and was armed with a rusty plastic-handled machete.

Chickens and ducks pecked about in the dirt and a stubborn cockerel filled the morning with its shrill call. I was given a brief explanation about which coffee beans to pick – the scarlet ones the size of rosehips; and which ones to leave – the unripe green ones. Working like a team of locusts we pushed systematically through the tall branches and dense foliage, moving from bush to bush and stripping them of fruit.

As the sun rose and burnt away the thick mist that had been hanging in the valley since the night before, the bewitching natural beauty of the landscape was unveiled. I could see for tens of miles, from the valley basin below to the mountains beyond. Patches of cloud cast shadows on the landscape. Streams of smoke twisted high into the windless sky, representing the other farmsteads where lunch was being prepared. A simple radio, hung round one worker's neck, filled the morning with the lively tempo of salsa, which combined with the gentle rat-tat-tat of coffee beans hitting the bases of our plastic buckets and the occasional chorus from the team as a favourite song was played. As the vibrant beat of another salsa track drifted across the hillside, I lost myself in the beauty of my surroundings and the simple process of picking coffee.

We returned to the farm for lunch. As I was a guest, Fabio's wife had saved me an ear as a treat, stewed whole in black beans with plenty of garlic. The others had to make do with crunchy slabs of chicharrón, made from the face skin, and they looked on with envy as I pulled at the large flap of skin and cartilage floating in my bowl. With its network of dark capillaries, it looked like a boiled offcut from an old leg. Feigning enthusiasm I sucked on the slimy flesh and then bit through the tough cartilage with a crunch. You can't make a silk purse from a sow's ear but it would be fair to say I made a pig's ear of my lunch.

After lunch the buckets of picked coffee beans were taken to an uncomplicated shed with a large wooden hopper. Fabio yanked a small engine to life, and a series of cogs removed the husks and flesh from the fruit, so only the valuable beans came through the other side. These were rinsed in water, and we carried them in heavy sacks on to the roofs of the farm buildings. The crude roofs made from corrugated iron were rolled back on a series of runners and the beans spread out on the flat concrete surface beneath to dry in the sun, making them lighter to transport to the co-operative pick-up point in the small village four kilometres away.

We then went back into the hills to pick, and as Fabio's children and grandchildren returned from school they all joined us, along with his wife. Three generations laughing, teasing and singing as they picked the crop that provided them with a livelihood.

For ten days I became part of this wonderful family, picking, washing, drying and cleaning the coffee that covered this fertile valley. Every morning I longed for the simple and delicious breakfast, prepared from scratch using fresh local ingredients found on the farm, and every evening as we walked back from the hills with the sacks of freshly picked beans slung on our shoulders, joking and laughing, I longed for the hearty supper that was always waiting. There was no machinery for the farming and no machinery for the cooking but the farm worked perfectly. Sipping on the bowls of coffee at the end of each meal during my time at Finca las Palmas, the beverage had never tasted so good.

From the city of Pereira I followed the wide river Cauca towards Cali. The river Cauca flowed through the broad and sunny landscape and in these warmer conditions coffee was replaced by the tall leaves of sugar cane that swung in the welcome breeze. I did my best to rest up in Cali for a few days but it proved impossible. The world capital of salsa, the whole place jumped to addictive sultry beats that pumped from every building and every street corner, and after a week I pulled myself away for fear of immoral ruin. Leaving Cali, the road south began to climb again and slowly I made my way to the city of Popayán. An important town during colonial times, due to its location between Quito and Cartagena, Popayán was a holding station for gold and riches pilfered from indigenous tribes. With the majority of the Spanish treasure passing through the city it became rich and opulent, and its white-washed colonial building and gold-encrusted churches were a testament to its once-powerful position. Following the colonial gold trail, the climbing began in earnest as the road carried me south of Popayán into the high Andes towards Quito and Ecuador. The road snaked and twisted between bottomless valleys. I was surrounded by the kind of natural splendour that makes you bite the back of your hand in disbelief, but after three days of climbing a punishing series of endless switchbacks, with little in the way of downhill reward, I was exhausted.

🚲

In other parts of the world children and teenagers entertain themselves at weekends by playing football, listening to music or chatting up the girl or boy next door. In the small villages that line the highways of southern Colombia, they have found another way to pass the time.

Take one old bicycle, preferably with functional brakes; pick a slow passing truck and establish a grip on the back; get pulled up the mountain for ten kilometres. Freewheel back down at break-neck speed. Repeat.

I was forever being passed by these pint-sized joyriders hanging to the back of trucks, overloaded with baying cattle, sloshing milk churns and sugarcane, only to see them reappear a little later in a blur of speed and colour. I decided I wanted in. Biding my time for a particularly sluggish eighteen-wheeler to struggle into a steep incline, I applied a short, sharp burst of power, came out of my seat and reached forward with a desperate hand, finding some purchase on a rusty corner.

What I had failed to realise before attaching myself to a twenty-ton truck with my arm, was that a fully loaded bicycle and well-fed cycle tourist weigh considerably more than a nine-year-old on a BMX. As the driver put his foot down my arm did its best to remove itself from my shoulder.

My timing was all wrong, I had grabbed at what I could, and instead of hanging from the back of the lorry I now found myself moving quickly up a mountain attached to its side, stuck between a massive spinning wheel on my left and a substantial cliff drop on my right. The driver turned into the apex of another hairpin, and what little tarmac I had to ride on began to vanish. It was decision time. Hang on and try your luck with the wheels, or let go and take the drop.

Dusting myself off some way down from the road, my trusty steed seemed miraculously unscathed, but I wasn't quite so durable. My left arm and shoulder were a stinging mess of cuts and grazes and my helmet, which had thankfully been on my head and not being used as a fruit basket, was a tangled mess of foam and plastic. Bag by bag I gathered up my kit from the stony slope I had tumbled down. I checked and double-checked that everything was in working order, and bruised and battered I continued into the mountains, arriving some hours later at a charmless petrol station-cum-restaurant-cum hotel. The surly owner wouldn't allow me to check into a room until four o'clock. Despondent, I leant my bike against the front of his restaurant and sat in the warm afternoon sun watching the passing traffic, metaphorically licking my wounds and eating ribbons of shredded green mango, doused in salt and lime, sold by a young boy making a killing.

Colombians know how to do business. Every coach that pulled in to refuel dumped a horde of hungry, tired passengers into the restaurant. I watched the mix of colourful characters, heading north and south, climb in and out of each bus. A smart coach with blacked-out windows and drawn curtains pulled in late in the afternoon and the usual locals filed out, rushing to be first in the loos and to get in the queue for coffee and food. Then followed two pretty blonde girls, tentatively emerging from the bus, clutching holdalls, digital cameras and guidebooks.

'Hello!' I piped up as they walked past.

The two girls explained they were on their way from Quito to Medellín. I explained I was cycling to Rio, from New York, and then went through some of my stock answers about punctures, miles-per-day and where I slept. 'How many hours is it to Ecuador?' I asked, trying to gauge how many days' ride I had to the border.

'Eight,' they replied in unison, 'and we have another fourteen to Medellín.'

'Wow, that's quite a ride!' I replied, aware of them eyeing my grazed arms, bruised swollen hands, blood-stained clothes and smashed helmet.

'So what's Colombia like? Is it safe?' they asked.

'It's absolutely wonderful!'

I woke the next morning at just before six. It was cold this high up and the way my body felt I might as well have been beaten up the day before. The cuts and grazes on my hands and arms didn't hesitate to remind me of the previous day's adventure. I contemplated a shower but the thought of standing under cold water was too much to bear. Slowly I packed up and forced my bike out of the door and down the dark corridor.

Back on the road at this early hour the towering landscape of mountains, valleys and steep cliff-faces seemed peaceful. Shafts of light from the rising sun, like spotlights in a theatre, picked out high passes, craggy ridges and thin lines of falling water. A half-hearted sequence of stretches added a little life to my tight legs. Apart from a failed hitch on the back of a truck, I had been riding an absurdly heavy bicycle uphill for five days, and the mountainous terrain in front of me promised more of the same. Looking at my digital speedometer , the previous day's downhill had been unsympathetic. I had only managed to add 32 miles to my grand total. Surely there was something better I could be doing with my time?

I continued sluggishly on an empty tank into the next small roadside hamlet, and on arrival I began the search for fuel. Spying an old lady selling cups of stagnant coffee and soapy hunks of white cheese wedged between what appeared to be lumps of soggy Yorkshire pudding, I joined the queue. Chatting with the truckers and bus drivers who had converged at this small makeshift kitchen for the same reasons I had, I enquired hopefully about the road ahead. To my question about how far it was to Ipiales, I received three different answers.

I asked how much of it was uphill. Each of the men inhaled through his teeth, and the varied answers that come back made me wish I hadn't asked. Disenchanted, I said my goodbyes, got under way and climbed over a high pass into the next valley. A distant river barrelled and twisted across its floor like a roller-coaster, and from my new vantage point I could see what the next few hours had in store: one, two, three, four, possibly five switchbacks. I did some sums. Seven perhaps eight kilometres of sweet descent, but on the other side the road mirrored itself in a gruelling ascent.

What goes down must come up, I muttered to myself, and, carefully picking a favourite album on my iPod, I pushed off. The morning sun was warm on my face. Surrounded by the breathtaking scenery, I picked up speed.

Go in low, come out high, I told myself as I banked into each swooping curve like a motorcyclist, holding the tight corners with the precision of a downhill ski champion. These moments make it all worthwhile. This is the dream. I'm coasting down a mountain on a bicycle in the Andes listening to the Rolling Stones!

Like a drug, the thrill of the descent pumped a powerful hit of adrenalin through my veins and I was euphoric, yelling at the top of my voice and grinning like a junkie.

But what goes up must come down, and the short-lived high was coming to an end. Carrying as much speed as I could into the fast approaching incline, gravity and momentum, which had just given me a few minutes of ecstatic pleasure, turned their back on me. I hurriedly shifted down through my gears, the weight of the bike and bags beginning to work against me.

Two hours later I was still climbing the same hill. Only four-teen kilometres had been added to the day. My eyes stung from the sweat that poured from my forehead; the small of my back throbbed in complaint at the weight of my load; my neck was tight from being perpetually hunched; my wrists were sore from contin-ual pressure, and my worn-out calves screamed at me to stop. Mentally I scrutinised every last item of my heavy load.

Do I really need a watercolour set?

Surely I can live without my torch?

How often do I use my bloody camping stove?

Another couple of hours crawled by, there was no shade, and the sun punished every metre of progress, forcing me to search anywhere for encouragement. A luxurious cool breeze; a patch of exquisite landscape; a thumbs-up from a truck driver; a slug of cold water; a favourite song. If my tattered map was to be trusted, the highway town of El Pedregal was now only a few miles away. Dog-tired and famished I began to envisage some of the gastronomic treats that might be waiting for me when I got there.

I was snapped out of a daydream about crispy empanadas drizzled with hot sauce, followed by a deep bowl of meaty sancocho, swimming with soft plantain, golden corn and cilantro, by a stern-looking soldier at a military checkpoint on the outskirts of town. Heavily armed troopers stood alert around armoured vehicles; bunkers, walled with sandbags and tented over with camouflage netting, concealed large, mounted machine guns. A sinister concrete building was set back from the road, painted in the shades of the surrounding countryside. I chatted cheerfully with the officer in charge, who checked my papers. He didn't think I should be on the road after dark. Informing me there was no guesthouse in El Pedregal, he offered me a piece of floor in his small barracks. Being surrounded by enough military hardware to storm a small nation didn't fill me with confidence, but not wanting to seem ungrateful I accepted.

The bright lights of the lorries rumbling to and from the border dazzled me as I walked the short distance into town with Carlos, the officer who had checked my papers. There was only one place serving food in town, but Carlos, after being told about my quest and love of food, assured me I would go to bed neither hungry nor disappointed. We took a table together in the concrete building where the usual men of the road were either engrossed in the television on the wall or the food in front of them. The almost glamorous middle-aged owner greeted Carlos warmly and after a little flirting he ordered our supper. A jug of fresh mango juice was placed on the table. I took a long swig from the cold metal cup and I never wanted it to end.

A golden, savoury cake of ground sweet corn, baked in a clay oven and filled with fresh white cheese and molten butter, was put down in front of me and I enquired what it was. 'Arepa de choclo,' answered Carlos proudly through a full mouth. I took a bite and it was sublime. The warm, sweet dough a perfect foil to the salty butter and local cheese.

The arepa was followed by a steaming bowl of sopa de mondongo, a robust stew made from slow-cooked cow's stomach and vegetables, garnished with plenty of cilantro and lime juice. After such an action-packed few days, its powerful, meaty flavours went to work on me like a magical, bovine medicine and nosily I slurped it up. In the simple open kitchen the patron patiently stirred a blackened metal cauldron big enough to boil a child in. Noticing the speed at which I devoured my first bowl, she offered me a second and I raised my bowl like Oliver Twist. Totally satisfied and basking in the wonderful feeling that only good, healthy, home-made food can provide after a hard day, I reflected on my new surroundings. Just a dusty little town on the highway in the Andes of Colombia, but after a day on a bicycle somewhere completely sacred.

After another two days of going uphill I arrived in Ipiales and the border with Ecuador. The air was cold and thin. Gasping for breath I said goodbye to a country I had fallen in love with and entered another. From the border, where the usual money changers, pickpockets and disgruntled border officials did everything to make life worse, I rode towards Quito. But in Ecuador it seemed as though someone had dimmed the lights and turned down the volume. Gone were the smiles and friendly cheers of encouragement from the roadside. Gone were the picturesque colonial farmsteads with their flower-covered porches. Here the homes were functional, unfinished concrete, spewing construction steel. It rained, it was cold and I wanted to turn around.

Sheltering from torrential rain in a dirty roadside hamlet just north of Quito, I surveyed my options for dinner. A few limp-limbed chickens did another turn in their mechanical rotisserie; a plate of worn-out humitas, a sweet tamale, waited for that unlucky customer to save them from another night under the heat lamp; a bored teenager with too much hair-gel prodded and probed a row of disturbingly red hotdog sausages. Not at all tempted by the usual suspects that made up the options in these small Ecuadorian towns, I began to wonder if my hunger could hold out until breakfast.

But hello! What's this?

At the end of the street, sheltering from the rain under a tatty umbrella, an old lady was fanning frantically at the coals of her small grill. I took a seat on the cold steps of the grocery store from which she served, and watched her work while a steady stream of customers pulled in from the rain.

I ordered a bowl of grilled chicken gizzards, served on a heap of sweetcorn and fried kernels of salted maize and it was immediately clear that she knew what she was doing. As the evening passed by the buses, trucks and pick-ups splashed through the rain-filled potholes of the main street. We didn't talk much, but that seemed normal here in Ecuador, but from what little was said, and my persistent interest in the secret of her giblets, it was obvious we enjoyed a common love of food, and it wasn't long before our conversation turned to Cuy. I expressed my dismay at having only found this traditional dish strung up like freshly run-over roadkill in front of the tourist restaurants en route from Otavalo to Quito, and my keenness to see how these rodents were prepared at home. I was invited for lunch the following day.

⚰

Cuy, conejillo de Indias – Indian rabbits, or guinea pigs as we know them in the pet shop – have been an important food source in Peru and Ecuador since pre-Inca times. Fifteen centuries later, they still remain an Andean delicacy, and on average Peruvians and Ecuadorians gobble down twenty-two million of these tasty rodents every year. Most Andean households keep cuy at home in the same way we might keep chickens. Considered a speciality, they are mostly saved for special occasions. Rather like a bottle of champagne or perhaps a box of Ferrero Rocher, a mating pair of guinea pigs are a typical house-warming gift for a newlywed couple. Playing an integral role in Andean religious and ceremonial practices, as well as providing dinner, cuy are also used in the traditional medicine of the region. A live cuy is rubbed over the body of someone sick. The cuy's squeaking indicates the diseased area of the human patient. The hapless beast is then split open to allow his internal organs to be examined, thus furthering the diagnosis of the human.

I was not sure if I wanted a mystic rodent to determine what was wrong with a niggling knee that had been pestering me for weeks, or the increasing numbness in my undercarriage, but I still arrived at 8 a.m. at the small house I had been given directions to the night before, ready to cook and eat my first guinea pig. Paula welcomed me into her home and directed me down a dark passage to the rear of her house, where an open concrete courtyard with the now familiar gas rings and stone washstand made up the basic kitchen.

A filthy monkey chained up in the corner shrieked and jumped on its chain as I arrived, and I began to wonder what else might be on the menu, but reading my concern Paula quickly assured me that he was only a pet, before pointing me in the direction of two makeshift cages filled with brown fur. Lunch.

Fifteen sweet-faced, wide-eyed, ginger-haired guinea pigs.

I feel strongly about animal rights but I have no problem in taking another animal's life for food. After months cycling through some of Latin America's poorest communities, I understood that animal welfare is a luxury only a few lucky countries can afford. However, when it was explained that Paula's husband was out of town and if I wanted to eat guinea pig I would have to do the dirty deed myself, I wondered if really wanted to go through with it.

Reaching my arm inside the cage, like a crane-and claw-game at a fairground, I felt about for my cuddly toy. The guinea pigs clambered over each other in a mad panic to escape. 'Cuy cuy,' they squeaked. I saw how they got their name. Unlucky guinea pig in hand, I offered a few words of thanks. Under Paula's instruction, I placed one hand around the animal's neck and as quickly as possible forced down hard with my other hand on to its nose.

'Cuuuuyeeeeek.' *Crunch!*

After a few death throes and panic-stricken wiggles the animal was dead. I had killed a guinea pig and its lifeless form hung limp in my murderous hands. Given no time to mourn the dead pet, my next job was to remove its hair. I dipped the corpse into a pot of boiling water, then plucked the soft ginger hair from every part of its body. Soon a very different kind of animal was lying on the table. Bright white, with skinny little legs and a rather plump midriff, was a mini pig. I began to see how this animal had earned its Western name. I cut it open, gutted and cleaned it under a cold tap, my initial inhibitions about murdering pets gone. Grinding a little fresh garlic and cumin, I rubbed the plump carcass inside and out, and my guinea pig was soon doing a turn with a handful of chickens, trussed up on the rotisserie grill of the restaurant over the road.

Within half an hour, my roasted cuy, smothered in a traditional peanut sauce, was ready to eat. It looked a little like a post-apocalyptic rat and I wasn't sure where to begin, but pulling a back leg away from the body I began chewing. The fine bones crunched in my teeth and I sucked and chewed on the meat, which was lean and tender, a little like rabbit but without the gamey undertones. The skin was deliciously crunchy and I peeled it off the animal's back like a mini pork scratching. Then I ripped off its head and sucked on the brains, apparently the best bit. Licking my lips and sucking every last bit of flesh off its tiny bones, I looked down at the miniature skeleton left on my plate. I had eaten my first guinea pig. Perhaps now I could go home?

It's better to be the pot than the lid.

Colombian proverb

Carimañolas: Meat-stuffed Fried Yucca

Makes 6 Carimañolas

1 kg yucca, peeled and cubed
50g butter
5 large eggs
150g plain flour
olive oil
1 onion, finely chopped
2 large jalapeño peppers, finely chopped
3 garlic cloves, finely chopped
1 teaspoon ground cumin
1/2 teaspoon dried thyme
1/4 teaspoon chilli powder
220g minced beef
4 teaspoons tomato paste
1 teaspoon sugar
vegetable oil, for deep frying
salt and freshly ground black pepper
to serve: fresh salsa or sour cream

A hearty breakfast favourite from the steaming hot Atlantic coast of Colombia, carimañolas are found at almost every street stall. Dipped in a little salsa or sour cream, they make a great energy-packed start to the day.

1. Put the yucca in a large saucepan with a pinch of salt and enough water to cover. Bring to the boil, then reduce the heat and simmer until tender but not breaking up. Drain and place in a large bowl with the butter. Mash with a potato masher.
2. Add 2 of the eggs, one at a time, stirring well until smooth.
3. Now add 1/4 of the flour and 2 teaspoons of salt, and stir well into a stiff dough. Leave to cool.
4. In a large frying pan, heat a little olive oil over a medium-high heat. Add the onions and peppers and cook until soft. Add the

garlic, cumin, thyme and chilli powder, and cook for another 30 seconds or so.

5. Now add the minced beef and cook until no longer pink. Spoon in the tomato paste, sugar, and a few pinches of salt and pepper to taste. Simmer, stirring, until thick, then remove from the heat and set aside.

6. Roll the cool yucca mixture into balls about twice the size of a golf ball. Using a finger or thumb, press a deep hole into the centre of each and put about 2 teaspoons of the filling inside. Gently work the yucca dough around until completely enclosed.

7. Now heat the vegetable oil in a deep pan to 165–170ºC.

8. In a bowl, beat the remaining 3 eggs with 3 tablespoons of water. In another bowl, place the remaining flour.

9. One at a time, dip the carimañolas in the flour, then the egg, covering all over and shaking to remove any excess. Add to the hot oil in batches and cook until golden brown: about 2 minutes. Remove with a spider or a slotted spoon and drain on kitchen paper until they've cooled a little.

10. Serve warm with some fresh salsa or sour cream for dipping.

Roast Guinea Pig

Serves 4

One pig per person
1 plump guinea pig
5 garlic cloves, peeled
2 teaspoons cumin seeds
1 teaspoon salt

The peanut sauce
150g butter
1 leek, sliced
150g peanuts
240ml single cream
salt and freshly ground black pepper
to serve: boiled potatoes

If you want to start cooking your pets, here is a recipe from the Andes of Ecuador.

1. First make the peanut sauce. Melt the butter in a saucepan over a low heat. Add the sliced leek and sweat until soft. In a liquidiser, blend the peanuts and cream until smooth, then add to the leeks. Heat through, stirring well. Season to taste with salt and pepper. Set aside while you prepare the guinea pig.

2. Take the guinea pig from its cage. Place one hand around its neck and force the palm of your other hand down on its nose until you hear a crunch. The crunch lets you know its jaw has broken into its brain.

3. Bring a large pot of water to the boil. When it starts to boil, turn off the heat and dip the guinea pig into the hot water. This will help the hair come away easily.

4. Now pluck your wet guinea pig, removing all the hair from the body, head and legs.

5. With a sharp knife, make a small incision halfway up the belly of the guinea pig. Place your fingers inside and with a firm tug remove all the guts and discard them. Wash out the body cavity under a cold tap.

6. Using a pestle and mortar, grind the garlic, cumin seeds and salt into a smooth paste. Smear this paste inside the body cavity of the guinea pig, in its mouth and over the skin.

7. Cook on a barbecue, turning every few minutes until the skin is golden brown and crispy, or roast in the oven for 25 minutes.

8. Serve with boiled potatoes and the peanut sauce.

CHAPTER 9

the amazon

MESSING ABOUT IN BOATS

> Believe me, my young friend; there is nothing, absolutely
> nothing, half so much worth doing as simply messing
> about in boats.
>
> *Ratty, The Wind in the Willows*

In 1540 Francisco de Orellana, under the orders of the Spanish
Crown, went out with a team of fearless conquistadors to explore
the lands east of Quito in search of rumoured cinnamon and gold.
A brave young man of thirty, he led his company of fifty men and
horses over the mountains and down into the tropical jungles of
what is now the Ecuadorian Amazon. Soon stumbling across the
navigable waters of the muddy Rio Napo, he decided to continue
by river and, after constructing a fleet of small boats with the help
of natives, ventured further downstream. Having to endure all the
usual hardships of sixteenth-century backpacking, skirmishes
with local people, starvation, cannibalism and rampant disease,
Francisco and only a handful of his men survived and followed the
river until reaching its mouth at the Atlantic Ocean, over eight
months later. Albeit accidentally, Francisco de Orellana had
become the first European to cross the continent by river, and in
his honour the great waterway he had navigated was named after
the fierce female warriors (which his brave team of conquistadors

later discovered, to their disappointment, were men with long hair) who had attacked him en route. Francisco de Orellana had discovered the Amazon.

Much to the relief of my tired legs and tender undercarriage, after reading about this ancient route across South America I hatched a new plan to get to Rio. Instead of continuing south along the mountainous Pacific coast through Peru, Bolivia, Chile and Argentina, I would now follow Francisco de Orellana's epic trail and head east across the continent by boat on the waters of the Rio Napo and the Amazon. Lago Agrio, Coca, Pantoja, Iquitos, Leticia, Tabatinga, Manaus and Belém. By all accounts the route was still passable and, with a good amount of patience and a pinch of good luck, I would arrive with bicycle intact on the northern coast of Brazil, in what I hoped would take considerably less time than it took Francisco de Orellana. Leaving Quito, I cycled uphill for three days and crossing the Andes I looked down across the peaks that stretched eastward into a hazy horizon. I raced downhill through tight verdant valleys where water fell down steep cliffs shrouded in mist, crashed over boulders, gushed in twisting streams and made its journey from the snow-capped peaks of the mountains into the Amazon and towards the Atlantic Ocean.

撶

Heavy guerrilla activity, regular kidnappings, cocaine trafficking and international arms dealing are just some of the attractions listed in the guidebooks that warn travellers not even to go within sniffing distance of Lago Agrio, a notoriously sketchy oil town deep in the jungle on the borders of Ecuador and Colombia. I hadn't planned on making a visit, but after three days of heavy, tropical rain had washed out the roads of my planned route, I found myself nervously navigating the rain-filled potholes of Lago Agrio's main street in search of a cheap and safe place to rest, before following what remained of the road deeper into the Ecuadorian jungle the next day.

Mercifully the guidebooks for this notorious neck of the woods are as reliable as road signs, and this apparent den of violence and vice was more than hospitable. I found a cheap and dirty guesthouse to leave my belongings in and after dining on a delicious meal of Lago Agrio crayfish, stewed in spicy coconut cream, I slept well before setting out in the pouring rain on what would be my last day on the bicycle for some time. Through small communities of palm-thatched huts on stilts I continued to ride alongside the strange rust-stained metal pipe that had been by my side since I crossed the Andes east of Quito. Snaking over the landscape, through rivers, forests, villages and schools, it had almost become invisible, a part of the scenery. Children played on it, politicians advertised on it and old ladies waited for the bus on it. But the original purpose of this steel serpent was to suck oil from the wells of Coca, aka Puerto Francisco de Orellana, where I hoped to find my first boat downstream and start my long river-journey to Brazil.

🚲

I stopped waving, lowered my arm and felt very, very alone. The small overloaded motorboat that had carried me for fourteen hours downstream from Coca was fast disappearing round a tight bend in the river. Thirty minutes earlier I had longed to escape its hemorrhoid-inducing wooden seats, cramped conditions and nauseating gasoline fumes, but now, as I stood alone on a muddy bank of the Rio Napo, deep in the Ecuadorian jungle, all I wanted was for it to come back.

A blond-haired man with a bicycle and a few dirty bits of luggage, I must have cast a strange and jarring figure to the small group of semi-naked, silent locals who gazed expressionlessly at me, no doubt wondering why I had turned up in their small jungle community. Naturally, I was wondering the same thing myself. My foul-smelling clothes were sodden with sweat, a team of mosquitoes was fast turning me into a slapping mass of frustration and I had no idea when or indeed how I would be able to get further downstream. I decided that standing on the riverbank feeling sorry for myself was unlikely to help my predicament. I needed to find a place to sleep. But eyeing up the ramshackle group of huts that stood between the tree line and the river, I wasn't too hopeful of landing a bed.

Slapping the side of my neck where a hungry mosquito had gone to work, I tentatively asked whether there was a guesthouse in the area. No response. I tried asking if there was anywhere to sleep. The same blank stares and embarrassing silence.

Eventually an older man sporting a wide smile and a silver digital camera on a string around his neck came forward from the crowd to my rescue. I followed him through the small village, the crowd, dressed in their baggy nylon shorts and dirty T-shirts, at a safe distance behind, until our bizarre convoy came to a standstill at what I was told was the Nuevo Rocafuerte community disco, a large wooden shed with a thatched roof. The doors were unbolted and after wheeling my bicycle into the darkness, I picked a spot, rolled out my excuse for a mattress and collapsed on the dance floor. I had been awake for hours and was weary after my first long day travelling on the river. I lay back and wallowed in a puddle of self-pity. I had made a terrible mistake.

A shard of late afternoon sun came through a crack in the doorway. Something above me caught just enough of the light to cast a magical galaxy of infinitesimal stars across the room. I looked up to see a huge silver mirror ball suspended from the ceiling. My journey downriver was not going to be easy, but if there were mirror balls in the jungle, I was sure I could survive.

The next Iquitos-bound cargo boat for three weeks was leaving in a matter of hours from the border with Peru at Pantoja. Rather than spend three weeks sleeping on the floor of the disco, I set out to find a boat, a pilot and a passage downstream, and eventually succeeded.

After two hours in the narrow canoe, listening to the monotonous throb of the motor as we pushed through the murky waters, we rounded a small island in the river and the palm-roofed shacks and camouflaged military tents of Pantoja came into view. Like an oversized piece of washed-up litter, a rusty, two-storey object listed heavily to one side on the riverbank.

'Es el barco para Iquitos,' announced our driver, pointing ahead before cutting the motor.

I wasn't sure what I was expecting to find, but the sorry excuse for a boat that waited for us on the muddy beach of the Rio Napo was not it. Old, decrepit, dirty, rust-stained, it was no more than a collection of steel panels badly riveted together, and the thought that it might be capable of moving off the beach, let alone floating, was beyond my imagination. Tattered and torn sun-bleached tarpaulins hung from the roof, the crew's oil-stained washing was drying on various lines strung up above the engine room, but painted in bright yellow and red on the front the optimistic name *Siempre Adelante* ('always onward') supplied me with some hope. Our captain may not have had a riverworthy boat, but he had a sense of humour.

With my passport stamped by a bored border official, I paid the toothless captain the equivalent of twelve pounds for my week-long cruise downstream. Bed and board included. My bicycle and bags were carried aboard by a gang of muddy, bare-chested deckhands, and as I swung almost comfortably in a small nylon hammock, the smells of cooking that had somehow managed to overcome the odour of unburnt gasoline were surprisingly promising. A hint of garlic, a little onion and perhaps some spices – encouragement enough for a hunger that had been brewing gently since a meagre breakfast of stale bread spread thinly with month-old fluorescent margarine. The clang of a metal cup being hit on the side of the boat signalled that dinner was served, and I eagerly grabbed my plastic plate and joined the handful of other passengers en route for the galley.

The first thing that hit me when I climbed carefully down the steep metal steps that led into the dark, humid underworld of the bottom deck was the intense heat and deep stench of machinery and animals. A small farm had been loaded aboard and amid the huge piles of plantains, cages of clucking chickens and ducks, the vibrating oil-stained mass of the engine rapped out its mechanical rhythm. *Kugga dugdunk, kugga dugdunk, kugga dugdunk.* Queuing as patiently as my patience allowed in these conditions, I finally arrived at the small service hatch above which was crudely painted 'La Cocina'. Inside this tiny, rust-infected cubicle, no bigger than an airplane toilet, a large man in a sweat-smeared grey tank top and filthy nylon shorts was bent over a large aluminium pot. Lifting the lid and releasing a thick cloud of steam, he slipped in his ladle and, with all the grace of builder mixing cement, dolloped a heap of grey slop on to my plate before thrusting it through the hatch.

'Buen provecho!' he offered with a black-toothed smile. I immediately recognised him and my formidable hunger vanished in an instant. I had seen him wrestling a mud-encrusted pig on to the boat as we arrived in Pantoja, and later elbow-deep in the engine. Our chef was seemingly a man of many talents, but personal hygiene was not one of them. There was more dirt on his fingers than fingernails, and as I stared on in disgust he pinched a boiled grey plantain with his fingers from a pot of murky water and added it to my plate. 'Gracias,' I replied, taking my plate from his filthy claws, quickly turning tail and heading for the comparative comfort of the upper deck for a well-needed lungful of fresh air.

Back on deck I was greeted by the sound of plates being scraped clean as the locals aboard wolfed down their lunch. Perhaps it tastes better than it looks, I thought, as I sat over my plate like a spoilt child refusing to eat his supper, tentatively turning my spoon through the swamp of broken fish bones, unidentified floating objects, black hair, overcooked rice and river water that sat in my lap.

It can't be that bad, the others are eating it.

River water is probably harmless once it's been boiled.

Come on, you've eaten worse than this.

Mentally prepared, I moved the first loaded spoon into my mouth. Not wanting to put my taste buds through any avoidable misery, I swallowed as fast I could before loading up another heaped spoonful. My body was having none of it. Clearly having more sense than its owner, it went into some kind of dietary autopilot and would not allow me to eat. I tried to put the spoon in my mouth, I wanted to put the spoon in my mouth, but my hand simply wouldn't obey the command. Eventually, giving in to basic instincts, I shamefully offered my bowl to another passenger, whose face lit up with gratitude, and, still hungry, skulked back to my hammock in disgrace, lightly amused by the irony that in setting out on a quest for the world's perfect meal I had almost certainly found its worst.

⚲

For a week the *Siempre Adelante* trudged down the Rio Napo towards its destination in Iquitos. Days and nights were spent watching the riverbank move gently past. The water carried the occasional felled tree or fishermen in impossibly thin dugout canoes, forced to paddle cautiously in our rolling wake. Every evening we were treated to flamboyant sunsets and at night a refreshing breeze blew through the boat, while the rumble of the engine mingled with the strange whoops and calls resonating from the forest. Flashes of lightning and rolling thunder preceded biblical rainstorms, which sent everyone aboard into a frenzy of hole plugging and protection from the water that poured, trickled and dripped through the roof, and blew in through the open sides of the boat, which the tatty tarpaulins failed to cover.

I was never bored. There was always someone or something to look at. Grabbing hours of sleep when I could, I existed in a relaxed flux between sleep and consciousness, this surreal routine broken only by our celebrated arrival in the small jungle communities whose livelihood relied on this twice monthly connection to the world beyond. Whole communities would line the riverbank to get a glimpse of us. Men grilled caiman and meaty-looking fish over well-fanned fires before hurling leaf-wrapped parcels of meat on board in exchange for a few soles, and children worked the hammocks carrying baskets of stringy but delicious boiled yucca root and weird and wonderful fruits, cupuaçu, pitomba and Brazil nuts.

Our arrival was a chance to trade and our crew, a scruffy team of men and boys, worked tirelessly for hours loading the boat with more and more cargo, which provided compulsive viewing for the passengers. Cages of poultry, piles of timber, squealing pigs, bunches of plantains were all carried aboard up flimsy gang-planks, to be sold downstream in the great markets of Iquitos. But it was the buffalo-loading shows that never failed to pull me from my hammock. Clearly terrified, our crew and some brave villagers would begin by attempting to lasso the hard-horned heads of these huge, irritable beasts. Failed efforts caused the buffalo to charge and turn, their dangerous bony heads searching for contact, forcing men and boys to hurl themselves into the muddy river for safety. With the head finally secured, ropes would be tied around the back ankles and then the front, finally bringing the beast to the ground. The mud-covered and exhausted men pulled hard on ropes, doing their best to ensure that the thrashing bundle of muscle on the riverbank didn't work loose and begin charging, kicking and bucking.

With the buffalo secure, the crew would then try to sedate the animal. With no fancy tranquillisers to choose from, the weapon of choice was a large polythene sack, which a courageous man had to slip over the buffalo's head. The animal's frantic gasps for breath sucked the plastic tight into its nostrils and mouth and slowly but surely the impressive heaving of its large chest subsided. Cruel, and at times hard to watch, this momentary asphyxiation gave the team their chance to catch their breath before pulling on ropes and pushing under the temporarily lifeless body. Each heavy beast was eventually hauled and pushed up the gangplanks and on to the lower deck; others fell into the river, men jumping in after them to remove the bag before they drowned. At each stop this battle of man and beast was completely enthralling, and the result would be about twelve docile and exhausted buffalo roped together on the lower deck with a herd of pigs, countless chickens, a number of noisy cockerels, several turkeys and stacks of wicker baskets loaded with duck. Our roof was piled high with bundles of bright green plantain and stacks of lumber. Around me, above me and below me, a vibrant, loud and smelly forest of hammocks, people and cargo made their way towards Iquitos.

⚬⚬

Shortly before dawn broke on our sixth morning on the Rio Napo, the red lights high on the radio masts of Iquitos could been seen blinking faintly on the dark horizon. Enjoying the quiet and cool breeze of the early hours on the roof, I watched the darkness melt into a new dawn and as we turned a bend in the river the sun spread across the calm waters of the mighty Amazon. Every passenger on the boat seemed to collect along the rust-infected railings to enjoy this long-anticipated glimpse of our gently approaching destination: barges weighed down with lumber, women washing clothes in the shallows, fishermen casting hand-nets, stilted wooden docks piled high with plantains and fish, cumbersome riverboats moving in and out loaded with cargo. I too was transfixed by the energy of this lively river port until a light tap on the shoulder distracted me.

The old lady who had been hanging in the hammock next to me for the last four days advised me to take good care of my stuff. 'Lots of thieves around,' she said. I thanked her for her concern, told her I would indeed be careful in town and returned my attention to the port.

'No, no, Thomas,' she said, insistently, pointing out the fleet of small canoes, loaded with men paddling frantically, which were drawing alongside. Before I knew what was happening, gangs of bare-chested men, flashing gold teeth and sporting home-made tattoos, were shinning up the sides of the boat and swinging in over the railings. We were being attacked by a ruthless gang of river pirates and, instead of doing my duty like an Englishman, I fled for my bags and bicycle while chaos erupted around me.

It turned out this motley crew were here to help. They made their living helping passengers ashore with their goods, and perhaps lifting the occasional digital camera from an unsuspecting gringo. They lived on tips and once we had pulled into port I was only too happy to part with a few soles to have Junior, a slightly too charming man wearing a dirty Tottenham Hotspurs football shirt, take my kit ashore. The port was tightly packed with other overloaded ships similar to ours.

Landing on what was no more than a beach, we were soon engulfed by a mass of swarming people. Like crabs feeding on a washed-up dead fish, men climbed all over the *Siempre Adelante*, stripping her of her cargo. Enormous bunches of plantains were thrown from the roof to children swimming in the water below, pigs were hurled over shoulders and raced, kicking and squealing, down flimsy gangplanks alongside enormous sacks of rice and huge blocks of ice. No cranes, no heavy machinery, just muscle, sweat and what looked like back-breaking hard work. It made compulsive viewing to witness a port working in a way that perhaps European ports had operated before the introduction of the crane and container.

Saying a sad goodbye to the *Siempre Adelante* and her crew, whose basic charms had won me over in the last week, I headed for Iquitos, where I would lick my wounds. Smelling similar to one of the other animals aboard ship, and with a level of personal hygiene now not dissimilar to the cook's, I was longing for a guesthouse where I could wash in water that didn't have the clarity of a muddy puddle, and to stretch out on a flat bed without worrying that a flatulent local had squeezed in beside me in the middle of the night. Apparently the hardest leg of my river journey was behind me, and in Iquitos I would relax.

⏚

The two fans that wobbled and spun from the cobweb-decorated ceiling provided little relief from the stifling midday heat, and as the young waitress placed a shot glass of cool murky liquid in front of me I didn't think twice before knocking it back.

I ordered a beer, my mouth alive with the citrus fishy twang of the shot of leche de pantera (panther milk). By all accounts it was a powerful aphrodisiac, but in this sultry heat it would take more than a few millilitres of fishy, chilli-infused lime juice to get me going. The oppressive heat and humidity of this jungle city, over 2,000 miles upstream from the Atlantic, attacked me like a fatiguing illness.

This small backstreet cevicheria was the only antidote I had found to the heat of Iquitos and every day for five days I had retired here at midday to eat, drink and read until the cool of the afternoon arrived to offer some respite. At the tightly packed tables around me, businessmen, secretaries, policemen and traders all had the same idea, taking an hour out of the day to enjoy heaped plates of the restaurant's signature dish, arguably the national dish of Peru, ceviche.

Patriotic Peruvians and imperious Chileans will both claim they are the sovereign heirs to this fish and citrus dish, traditionally made from the plentiful corvina (sea bass) of their Pacific coasts. But having eaten exquisite ceviche in every country south of the United States, I think I can say with some authority that this healthy, clean and refreshing dish has never tasted better than in the soaking heat of Iquitos in the heart of the Peruvian Amazon. The meaty flesh of the corvina may well be some 600 miles away on the other side of the high Andes, but in Iquitos they have their own fish, which took its name from a ferocious Indian warrior called Pirarucu.

According to Amazonian legend, Pirarucu spent his days terrorising the villages of the Amazon and taunting the gods, until finally, after pissing off the men upstairs, he was struck by a lightning bolt and his body thrown into the depths of the river. There he was transformed into a giant fish that now terrorises the waters. The pirarucu is one of the largest freshwater fish in the world. It can grow up to ten feet long and weighs in at around a healthy four-hundred pounds. Natives of the Amazon dry its large scales to use as jewellery, the long tongue is used as a grater and as sandpaper by carpenters, and its meat, with cod-like texture and flavour, is used in various local dishes, including ceviche.

At its most basic, ceviche is no more than a plate of raw fish marinated in lemon or lime juice. The marvellous citric acid found in the juice changes the molecular structure of the fish in a miraculous kind of short-term pickling. Add a little chopped cilantro, some finely diced red onion and some chopped chilli and your scientific experiment is now a culinary masterpiece, 'cooked' to perfection without the use of heat or fire. Healthy, quick to digest, refreshing, rammed with vitamins and easy to prepare, it would seem that ceviche and human digestion were made for each other.

Tender cuts of pirarucu, doused in lime and mixed through with red onion and chilli, arrived at my table on a heap of almost translucent slices of boiled sweet potato and chewy yucca. This lightly chilled plate of fresh local food was perfection. The lime juice was clean in my mouth, the fish didn't sit heavy in my stomach and the chillies drew a little fresh sweat, which dribbled cool from under my arms and down my back. The root vegetables added a subtle amount of starchy sustenance that meant I wouldn't go hungry, and with my plate clean, I felt clean. I had eaten just what my body needed. No cream, no lactose, no red meat, no rice, no black hairs, no gristle. After the horrific dishes that came from the galley of the *Siempre Adelante*, every heaped plate of pirarucu ceviche I enjoyed in Iquitos, washed down with bottles of ice-cold Iquitena beer, was a gift from the river gods. But after five nights in this jungle city feasting on ceviche, it was again time to move east. A cargo boat was heading for the border with Colombia. Back at the bustling port, I found the boat I was looking for, the *Victor Manuel*, and climbed aboard in search of a hammock space.

⍰

Huuuuuurght ... putt. Sheee, sheee.

Woken from a blissful mid-afternoon siesta I peered out from the nylon cocoon of my hammock and stared with disappointment at the large Peruvian lady who had invaded my personal space while I slept, and now swung next to me, far too close for comfort.

She conjured another bundle of phlegm into her mouth and spat it on the floor in the small gap between our hammocks.

Huuuuuuurght – putt.

An unshaven leg that hung over the edge of her hammock came to life, and the flip-flop-clad foot at the end of it rubbed her puddle of spittle into the metal deck as if to conceal the evidence.

Sheee, sheee.

I thought I had seen the worst of Amazon river travel, but as I lay back in my hammock doing my best to ignore the human cacophony that went on next to me, I knew it was going to be a very long ride downstream to Leticia and back into Colombia. As our horn blasted, darkness fell and the gangplanks were heaved aboard, I quietly longed to return to the lively city whose lights shone out of the darkness of the jungle, but instead I had another four nights of river travel to deal with.

I opened my eyes after a limited night's sleep to the sight of an array of hammocks hanging in every available space, their material stretched tight round the smooth contours of their occupants. Madonna's 'Material Girl' bleated from the ship's tannoy.

'Desayuno ... desayuno ... desayuno.' Clearly enjoying his dose of Madonna, a chirpy young man in a pretty apron and what looked like eye shadow worked the hammocks, offering the passengers their breakfast from a tray loaded with plastic cups and a sack of what could best be described as bread. I took my ration of mashed plantain, flavoured with cinnamon, sugar and river water, and the sadly familiar hard, doughnut-shaped object that disintegrated into a carcinogenic dust when I bit into it. In the humid climate of the Amazon, wheat is hard to come by and bread is therefore a luxury, and these objects that looked and tasted like they could survive a mission to Mars were the next best thing.

However, already satisfied that I had found the world's worst meal on my all-inclusive cruise from Ecuador, the food on the *Victor Manuel* had to be better, and with a fierce appetite I quietly looked forward to my lunch. It was, alas, another rice and river-water-based dish in which, if you had the patience to search, you might be unlucky enough to uncover the remains of some unidentified creature: a shard of bone, a nugget of gristle, a flap of skin, a long black hair ... But hunger provided my gravy and after having just about cleaned my bowl, I went below deck into the tiny cooking area to see where the treats on this vessel were coming from and to find out a little about the cooks on the Amazon.

'Hola, guapo,' the cook said in husky voice, in response to my greeting.

Nonplussed, I quickly scanned for a tell-tale sign of gender. Firm round breasts; big hairy manly hands; high heels and slender ankles; big Adam's apple.

The cook spoke again, asking me what I'd like in a frankly flirtatious manner.

Puzzled to be confronted by a man in a frilly apron and high heels while floating down the Amazon, I had completely forgotten why I had come to the kitchen in the first place. Dumbstruck, I muttered the first thing that came into my head. I asked him if I could take a photo of him.

'Claro, guapo. Momentito.' He called his partner over. 'Carlos, venga venga!'

Carlos appeared from behind the scenes in pair of old yellow Marigolds and an apron, but his muscular build made it clear who was wearing the trousers. 'Hola,' he said in a deep voice, releasing a large smile before pouting perfectly and leaning seductively against the door of the tiny kitchen. He placed one arm affectionately around the shoulders of his better half.

'Listo!' they both exclaimed in perfect unison, ready for their shot. I raised my camera and clicked.

'Otro, otro!' they both giggled, pulling more seductive poses for my camera.

From wanting to gather a little information about cooking on the river, I now found myself involved in a bizarre transsexual photo shoot, but once the camera stopped clicking we spent some time drinking coffee and chatting and I was able to find out more about the life of a cook on the riverboats of the Amazon. Carlos and Jamie had been together for a little over three years and had worked on six different boats. They explained that for the gay community of the upper Amazon, working as a cook aboard the numerous riverboats was a good way of life. Often not accepted in their communities, where machismo is considered the norm and work is hard to find, working on the boats gave them a chance to make a living, travel and be together.

Into the grubby, smelly and fume-filled world of these river cargo boats, Carlos and Jamie injected charm and optimism. To meet either one of them on their cheerful breakfast run was the perfect way to start the day on my otherwise tedious trip downstream towards Colombia. After four nights on the Amazon we arrived at the border and the shabby city of Leticia, from where I then had to cross the border into Brazil by road and find a space on a huge passenger ferry further downstream to Manaus.

After the relatively laidback affair of procuring passage in Ecuador and Peru, where money talked, in Brazil things were a little more serious. Men with menacing guns patrolled the port; passports and papers needed to be stamped at every turn and busy crew members dressed themselves in smart white uniforms. On board, the boat had showers, a designated eating area and a bar, which was at the centre of a large sun deck designed for people having a good time. Music played day and night. Bikini-clad girls danced under the falling water of deck showers, while handsome bronzed men in board-shorts vied for their affections. In the huge open lower deck of this ship, a vast and vibrant web of multi-coloured hammocks used every possible piece of metal railing. Hundreds of people were crammed aboard for our journey east to the Amazon's largest city, Manaus.

Nobody hung more than a foot apart in any direction. The mother and child going to stay with family; the soldier returning from leave; a pretty girl in her twenties looking for employment; and the man being sent downstream on a work project, making the most of his three-night cruise. When he wasn't sleeping off the booze in a sweaty stupor accompanied by seismic snoring, he was on the top deck doing his best to drown himself in more cheap beer. On our last night sleeping together, his body decided enough was enough. I watched, entertained, as he tried to remember where he was sleeping amongst the confusing network of coloured fabric, before doing his best to climb into his hammock, a task that is hard enough when sober and requires a definite technique. Every failed attempt ended in a bump on the floor. He finally stood up, frustrated and perplexed, staring at the hammock. His eyes rolled in his head, and after making an exaggerated swallowing action, three days of beer and riverboat cuisine spewed out of his mouth like a burst drain, accompanied by a terrifying retching noise that woke every resident of the hanging community around us. His body purged, he collapsed lifeless across his hammock, his head hanging over the side, gurgling what vomit remained like a blocked plughole. Not unfamiliar with the sufferings of alcohol-induced illness, I would, and indeed should, have shown a little more compassion towards the semi-conscious man next to me, but since my panniers had just been decorated with a multicoloured cocktail of beer and beef stew, I snapped.

'You little fuck!'

I jumped from my hammock, my bare feet making contact with the warm, slippery, lumpy mess lining the floor.

'Mother fucker!'

Lifting the man under his armpits, I heaved him to his feet. I dragged him to the railing, his legs wobbling like those of a newly born foal, held up his head via a clump of hair, and once his violent convulsions were limited to no more than a trickle of yellow bile, I let him go. He collapsed on the floor like a puppet cut from his strings. Managing with great difficulty to get him back into his damp, malodorous hammock, I poured some water over his face and climbed back into my own hammock as a quiet round of applause sounded from the community of hammocks around me. I lay awake, my nostrils full of the rancid smell of vomit. Unable to get back to sleep, I climbed the metal stairs to the upper deck to enjoy the cool night breeze. The coloured lights of other vessels passed in the night and, as the traffic increased, the glow of a

THE AMAZON

settlement appeared above the dark belt of the tree line. The sun rose over the Amazon and, turning into the dark waters of the Rio Negro, I witnessed the sight of a modern city rearing out of the jungle. We had arrived in Manaus.

☙

I'm not sure what Charles Goodyear was trying to cook when he accidentally spilt some natural rubber, sulphur and lead on to his stove top, but the consequence of this rumoured accident changed the Amazon for ever. Until that fateful day in his kitchen, natural rubber had limited uses, but Goodyear had stumbled across the process of vulcanisation, which enhanced this natural material. The substance made from the sap of the rubber tree was transformed into something that no longer perished in high or low temperatures. Goodyear's vulcanised rubber was durable, could withstand huge pressures and always returned to its original form after being stretched. The new industrial era couldn't get enough of the material. With the advent of the automobile and the invention of the pneumatic tyre in the late nineteenth century – which also comforted the tender-bottomed cyclists suffering on the hard-rimmed wheels of their 'bone shakers' – Goodyear's discovery ignited a rubber boom. Northern Brazil had the highest density of rubber trees in the world, and as demand soared for this new black gold, what were once ramshackle jungle outposts, such as Manaus, transformed almost overnight into sophisticated jungle metropolises.

By the end of the nineteenth century, Manaus had developed into the opulent heart of the rubber trade and one of the richest cities on earth. A thousand miles upstream from the Atlantic and surrounded by dense primary jungle, it boasted an electricity network before London, a telephone system before Rio de Janeiro and electric street cars while New Yorkers were still travelling the streets of Manhattan in horse-drawn carriages.

As demand for rubber grew, so did the personal wealth of the self-appointed 'rubber barons', but the new super-rich of Manaus were equally hasty in blowing their cash. The flaunting of wealth became a sport. The super-rich of Manaus were rumoured to light cigars with high-value bank notes and import the finest food and wine from Europe, some even quenching the thirst of the horses in their stables with buckets of chilled French champagne. Their wives and girlfriends were equally extravagant, ordering the finest European furnishing for their palatial mansions and, disgusted at washing their fine linen in the murky waters of the river that provided their wealth, sent their dirty laundry to Lisbon and Paris to be laundered. Indeed, Manaus was soon being dubbed the Paris of the Amazon, complete with its own imported market, a replica of Les Halles, a horseracing track and an opera house, the imposing Teatro Amazonas, imported almost entirely from Europe and shipped upriver to this new El Dorado.

The opulence of the rubber barons was exceeded only by their brutality and short-sightedness.

Rubber trees grew only in dense primary rainforest, and to ensure their colossal profits, the barons had to acquire and control vast tracts of impregnable jungle. These plantations needed protecting from rival barons and many built up private armies to defend their claims, gain new land and capture native labourers. Local Indians were enslaved and bred like cattle, and horrific brutality was employed to acquire and hold on to this labour force. As the Indians continued to die, demand and supply soared. The total destruction of the rainforest and its aboriginal inhabitants was only prevented by the sudden collapse of the Brazilian rubber market, caused by the Great Rubber Theft of 1876. An English planter, by the name of Henry Wickham, perhaps the world's first 'bio pirate', secretly collected 70,000 highly perishable Pará rubber tree seeds and, after successfully smuggling them back to England, planted them in the glass-roofed hothouses of Kew Gardens. They germinated successfully and were shipped to new plantations in Sri Lanka, India and Singapore. By the 1920s almost 95 per cent of the world's rubber came from British colonies in the east, and the golden age of Brazilian rubber had come to an end. Henry Wickham was knighted for his efforts, while Manaus was abandoned and left to decay back into the jungle.

༃

Today Manaus is booming again, nothing on the scale of its rubber days, but thanks to government free-trade incentives it has become a new centre for foreign investment in Brazil. It's a bustling city of two million people, where buses and motorcars jam up the busy streets that run between silver skyscrapers, office blocks, supermarkets and multiplex cinemas. Walking its lively streets I almost forgot I was a thousand miles upstream and surrounded by jungle – but the tourist-hunters don't let you forget it, and determined guides and lodge employees wait on the docks to offer you endless ideas for your 'authentic' jungle experience. Eat monkey; stay with an indigenous tribe; take some mind-bending drugs with a shaman; eat ants; catch and eat your own piranha.

Exhausted by the heat and hassle and an unsuccessful mission to find cheap digs, none of which came within my budget, I returned to the ship in the late afternoon to retrieve my bicycle. I climbed down into her fetid bowels, where the bright eyes and damp bodies of the men working to unload her cargo shone in the darkness. The air was heavy with humidity and the men's words echoed off the steel panels of the hull. My imagination ran wild with the horrors of slave ships and claustrophobia. I was shown to my bicycle, which was then tied to a rope and winched into what remained of the daylight. The captain, a broad-framed, middle-aged man who was always dressed in a spotless and tight-fitting white Naval uniform, took a keen interest and after a little conversation in my undeveloped Portuguese he invited me to stay onboard while I was in Manaus.

༃

For two days a team of men worked to unload the boat in a chain that ferried the cargo from the hull on to waiting trucks. Then, as if a controlling figure had flicked a switch, this well-oiled human machine slipped into reverse and the boat was reloaded for its journey back upstream. My time in Manaus had almost come to an end.

On my last day in the city I had pulled myself out of my hammock and hung over the railings, watching and listening to the port go through its motions. Beer bottles, rice, lumber, building equipment, ice. The boat filled up with cargo, the captain had finished his turnaround, and in the morning he would begin taking passengers for the journey back upstream. The empty deck I had enjoyed for two nights would again be overrun with people and hammocks and I would have to find a boat to take me downstream to Belém and the Atlantic Ocean. Joining me on the rail of the boat, the captain seemed happy with another profitable turnaround. He was the only member of crew who had the patience to listen to my early attempts at Portuguese, and we got on well. When he asked me to join him on a night out before he set sail, I was only too happy to accept. The captain's visit to Manaus had been a success. He wouldn't be back in the city for a few weeks and it was clear he wanted to celebrate on his last night. We started out at a small bar on the waterfront that was full of dockhands,.

'You like girls?' he asked me with wide eyes, while filling my glass and popping a salted brazil nut in his mouth. As he directed a chauvinistic hiss towards the curvaceous, semi-naked beauty serving our beer, my fears of being enticed back to his cabin subsided, only to be replaced with the realisation of what he was hatching for later that night. His level of desire seemed to increase with every beer he drank, and it was clear he was planning to go out with a bang.

Like all South America's cities, the massively uneven distribution of wealth means the majority of the population lives below the poverty line in sprawling makeshift slums. I'd cycled through many of these areas of extreme poverty on my way into almost every city south of San Diego, so I should have felt fine, but rumours I'd heard about Brazil's favelas scared me and, as the captain led me away from the well-lit and lively marina into the dark backstreets of Manaus, I became increasingly unnerved. The reassuring glow of the city's streetlights was gradually replaced by the more atmospheric glare of illicit bars spilling over with locals enjoying their Saturday night. I followed the captain closely as we made our way down a series of ever-narrowing, darkening streets and alleys and, from the inquisitive stares of the locals hanging about in the doorways of shops and eating at the small grills set up on the street, I became certain I was being taken into an area I shouldn't go to. Our dimly lit surroundings became more and more decrepit and what were established shops and bars soon became crudely built wooden shacks. The broken pavements and rain-filled potholes were replaced with uneven wooden alleyways that bridged the filthy swamp of litter and stale water beneath our feet. The stench of sewage was heavy in the humid air. Bright eyes and white teeth flashed in the shadows as fast-tempo Forró music jumped and resonated around this ramshackle collection of buildings on stilts connected by duckboards and gangplanks. At last we climbed a steep set of old stone steps. I glanced back over the patchwork of tin roofs and the twinkling lights of the favela we had just passed through, and looking ahead I saw that we had arrived in a district of run-down colonial buildings.

Patches of European ceramic tiles clung to what remained of the crumbling walls of once opulent homes and warehouses, small symbols of the area's long-lost affluent past. Women hung over the ornate twists and turns of rusty wrought-iron balconies, while other groups of girls stood on corners and in once grand doorways trying to attract the attentions of the intoxicated men who staggered past. This area of the city clearly specialized in the oldest of trades and the captain was a well-known face. Most men got out of his way, while others hassled him for work, and various women flocked to him trying to secure his business. In this apparently lawless corner of Manaus, here was a man who commanded respect and offered employment. This gave me some feeling of safety.

We arrived at the imposing steps of a tall, decaying colonial building, iron balconies overgrown with plants rising up its front wall. The captain exchanged a few words with a foul-looking man at the door and we were shown inside. The tall doorway led into a tiled courtyard, around which a wide staircase led up four or five floors towards an opening in the roof that exposed the night sky. Shouts and calls of pleasure and thumping music echoed off the walls.

Taking my shoulder, the captain led me up the stairs. On each crowded landing I caught brief glimpses of dimly lit sex through the doorways. On the third floor a large woman sat behind a metal desk, a scantily clad girl on each side of her, the look in their eyes dull and disinterested. Serving a rowdy line of men jockeying for her attention, the large woman made notes in a substantial ledger before taking the men's dirty banknotes. Then she handed out tickets and the men dispersed into the numerous rooms I had just passed.

Other sweat-drenched, drunken men clambered up and down the uneven wooden staircases as we made our way further upstairs into a long room that held an ocean of moving bodies, its decaying ceiling and walls still decorated with ornate plasterwork. In the centre of the room, on a high stage, naked girls gyrated and squatted to the music, while grubby hands reached up for a feel.

The captain shooed away a group of disgruntled men and we took their seats around a small table in front of a makeshift bar. A man with a small monkey on his shoulder placed an ice-cold bottle of beer and two glasses on our table. I raised a glass with the captain, who gave me a wry smile and a satisfied wink, and took stock of where I was. A run-down brothel-cum-strip club, in the slums of a huge city, in the heart of the biggest jungle on earth.

Reeking fishermen fresh from the river, oil-stained deckhands and mechanics, limbless drug-addled vagrants, merciless tattooed river pirates, well-dressed policemen and officials, petty thieves, greedy pimps, plus a boat captain and a cyclist. It was all too easy to categorise the intoxicated and lust-demented faces of the men in this sordid room.

Women soon joined us at our table. The captain groped and played with them, and it wasn't long before he needed a stronger fix. He left the room, I assumed to negotiate with the woman at the metal desk, leaving me at me the mercy of this mass of anonymous humanity.

A rancid man in a filthy T-shirt threw his arms around me, releasing a foul blast of alcoholic fumes into my face, while offering me a swig from the bottle he was clutching. I politely declined, but he carried on prodding my face with his bottle.

Other than a well-tanned girl in a cheap Marilyn Monroe wig rubbing herself up and down a pole, I was now the only blond in the place, and was attracting unwanted attention. The smell of stale alcohol, perspiration, men, women and cheap pleasure became too much. In the overwhelming humidity and airlessness, everyone and everything I touched seemed to be dripping wet. I needed to leave, but where could I go? I had no idea where I was and without my chaperone I didn't fancy my chances.

Panic forced me to my feet. I muscled my way through the huddles of men and women loitering on the stairs and made it to the door, where the relatively fresh air of the street outside was a luxury. I took a seat on the steps, did my best to look inconspicuous and waited.

A few doors down the road, a boy of no more than ten, frantically fanning the coals on an improvised grill with a piece of cardboard, caught my attention. I hadn't eaten for hours. I wandered down to see what was cooking. Five or six fish-shaped objects spat and crackled in an oily metal skillet. Each one had a row of white saw-blade teeth, their blackened, shrivelled skin and hollow eyes giving the impression that they had undergone some kind of atomic attack. The boy's eyes lit up at the sight of a potential customer. Gesturing at me with a small clenched fist and a wink, he told me it was piranha, 'bom afrodisíaco'.

I admired the young man's business acumen and put in an order. Waiting to be overcome by waves of uncontrollable desire I fiddled through the bony fish but was left with nothing more exciting than a set of sticky fingers. I kept going and ate three more piranhas before a spent captain staggered out of the brothel and at last we could return to the ship. I had eaten my first piranha and had certainly had an authentic jungle experience.

⚘

Clunk. Creeeeeeeak. Clunk.

The day didn't start well. I was woken from a poor attempt at sleep by the sound of crates of beer being loaded on to the ship at the ungodly hour of 5 a.m. I had enjoyed little more than one or two hours of sleep and the combination of beer, heat, mosquitoes, fog horns and hammock discomfort had left me suffering from what can best be described as a deep-core headache. Clumsily I clambered out of my hammock and as I straightened myself, my tired back let out a succession of small cracks of complaint at being put through weeks of crooked sleep. I have had enough of this, I thought to myself. Today I had to find a way to Belém at the mouth of the river. The sun began to cast a warm glow over the port as it was coming to life, but the thought of negotiating a 'good deal' amongst the ticket touts and dodgy captains that worked the docks filled me with little enthusiasm.

The *Rocha Neto* was a tall, three-layered, blue and white wooden vessel in the classic riverboat style, a vessel that would not look out of place on the Mississippi. It was a little rough at the edges, but had a certain old-fashioned charm. I managed to get a decent price for the two-night trip to Santarém, and as quickly as I could I bagged what I hoped would be a good hammock spot on the top deck. Not too near the bathrooms, thus avoiding the stench of stale urine; not too close to a light bulb, thus avoiding the night-time raids of bird-sized insects; and near enough to the front of the boat so as not to be kept awake by the mechanical jazz of the engine. I used my three weeks of honed hammock-slinging skill and picked myself what I thought was a prime piece of Amazon riverboat real estate.

More and more passengers drifted aboard as our official time of departure came and went. 'Max paseros – 151' informed a hand-painted sign on the wall ahead of me, but I had already counted well over that number on the upper deck alone, and still they were coming, slinging their hammocks wherever they could find a gap. As the boat gently rocked on the wake, my toes stroked the bottom of a plump Colombian lady hung almost directly above me, while underneath a cheerful young man from Suriname would have to enjoy an aerial view of my well-honed backside for three days. This boat was packed and idling on the busy dock in the sweltering midday heat of Brazil's hottest city. As the temperature rose, what had been a calm situation now teetered on the brink of chaos.

Stay calm, Tom, stay calm, I told myself, but my fuse felt dangerously short. Just as I reached boiling point we pulled away from the jetty with a chug of engines, and soon a cooling river breeze washed over the boat and calmed the situation.

The *Rocha Neto* was filthy and overcrowded but in its favour it had a couple of colourful young men with operational taste buds. Dinner was served within a few hours of leaving Manaus. Sitting with the other passengers along the edge of the lower deck, I enjoyed a very tasty beef stew accompanied by garlic rice on what had to be one of the best seats in the Amazon. Perched on a sack of rice, in a cool breeze, I ate my supper and watched as the warm orange sun spread across the water, creating silhouettes of the passing river traffic. It was a perfect Amazon sunset. Men in canoes tossed nets for fish, other passenger boats chugged past and swallows dived for insects on the surface. When I thought it couldn't get any better, two pink dolphins, a species only found at this point in the world, surfaced just feet away before disappearing in a collection of silver ripples.

᪣

As the Amazon gets wider and wider, it is easy to forget you are on the river. The towns that line the riverbanks soon become cities and efficient ports, and traditional canoes now share the waterways with mammoth oil tankers and large passenger ferries like the *Santarém*, the huge adventure-less vessel that would take me on the three-night cruise to Belém, and the end of my river trip. On this boat there were showers that didn't smell of urine, air-conditioned cabins, a bar area and even a cinema, but wanting to keep a watchful eye on my wheels I slung my hammock below deck in steerage and got cosy with the huddled masses. Passengers above me, people below me, the never-ending bump and grind, I had seen it, heard it and smelt it all before, but after almost a month of travelling on the river I was tired and longing to get back on my bicycle. Never seeming to sleep properly and never seeming to properly wake up, I carried on with the river routine. Sleep, eat and read. Sleep, eat and read. The same plate of rice and tough sinew stew. I seemed to have slipped into Amazon autopilot. On these big anodyne boats I missed the adventure of the *Siempre Adelante*.

Slumped over the top railings, enjoying the tranquillity of another Amazon morning before it was shattered by the loud samba on the dance deck, I sipped at a necessary cup of sweet coffee and watched the banks of the river close in on our ship as we entered the Tajapuru Narrows, which snake through the islands at the mouth of the Amazon. Further ahead, I noticed a flotilla of canoes. Five, six, seven, eight slender boats lined up along the river in what must have been a fishing ground. But instead of getting out of the way as our vast ship bore down on them, the figure at the back of the first canoe in the line-up began a determined paddle in our direction. Picking up speed with every strong stroke, he quickly covered the ground between us and, changing his paddle for what appeared to be a crude hook bent from a rod of construction steel, he stood up. As the canoe moved within metres of our port side, he lunged forward, throwing his hook in our direction. Finding purchase on one of the old tyres that protected the side of the ship, his rope, which now connected our huge vessel to his flimsy canoe, snapped tight. Taking the strain the man held on for all he was worth while his canoe jumped and jived on the wake that spilled from our stern. To get a better idea of how dangerous this manoeuvre is, try to imagine waterskiing behind a cross-channel ferry. Water filled his canoe, waves crashed over his boat and body, but pulling and pulling on the rope the brave man hauled himself to within touching distance of our side.

Leaping from his boat to ours, he hung on with one hand and hurriedly worked away with the other, tying a series of knots, which fastened his canoe to the ship. Now the incentive behind his daredevil antics became clear. Piled high in palm-woven baskets, that had miraculously managed to stay in the boat, were kilos of sweet-water shrimps and bundles of tropical fruit. More and more entrepreneurial heroes were closing in and soon each side of the ship was overrun. Some made it, some didn't. Hooks missed their targets, ropes slipped through wet hands and for one unlucky team of salesmen the wake effortlessly flipped their canoe and they and their cargo were tossed into the river. But before long ropes and hooks were slung along our sides, men were clambering aboard and a dozen or so canoes had been lashed to each side of the ship. For these men we were a floating business opportunity. This was take-away, Amazon style.

Kilos of fresh shrimp were passed to eager customers, money changed hands, women haggled and fruit was squeezed and tested. Palm hearts, bags of açaí, cupuaçu and cacao. They were delivering everything the jungle and the river had to offer. Within an hour of frenzied transactions it seemed every passenger on the ship was nibbling away at a bowl of fresh shrimp and the decks were scattered with discarded pink shrimp heads. It was an amazing thing to see. Treating myself to a bundle of fresh palm hearts, half a kilo of shrimp, a couple of cacao and a bundle of brazil nuts, I was a happy man as I picnicked in my hammock, waiting, with the rest of the passengers, for the skyscrapers of Belém to appear and my journey down the world's greatest river to come to an end.

Be brave. Take risks. Nothing can substitute experience.
Paulo Coelho

Amazon Ceviche

Serves 4
1 large yucca root, peeled and thickly sliced
1 large sweet potato, peeled and thickly sliced
800g fresh white fish fillet*
1 small red onion, thinly sliced
2 small chillies, chopped
1 bunch of fresh cilantro (coriander), chopped
juice of 10 limes
salt and freshly ground black pepper

1. Boil the yucca and sweet potato for 15 minutes until soft. Remove from the water and leave to cool.
2. With a sharp knife, chop the fish into small pieces and put into a large bowl. Add the onion, chilli, cilantro, a pinch of salt, a couple of grinds of black pepper, then pour in the lime juice, making sure all the fish is submerged. Leave in the fridge for 20 minutes.
3. Make sure to remove the stringy core of the yucca root, then arrange the slices of yucca and sweet potato on 4 plates.
4. Take the fish, which should now be white, from the fridge and stir with your fingers. Heap the marinated fish on top of the sliced sweet potato and yucca and serve chilled with a bottle of very cold beer.

* In Iquitos they use the abundant and meaty freshwater fish of the Amazon. You can use firm sea fish instead, such as flounder or sea bass.

Fried Piranha

Serves 4
4 medium-sized piranha
3 garlic cloves, peeled
oil for frying
50g flour
salt and freshly ground black pepper
to serve: 4 limes

1. Clean and scale the fish thoroughly and with a sharp knife make a series of diagonal cuts along both sides.
2. Using a pestle and mortar, crush the garlic and mix with a little salt and pepper. Rub this mixture into the cuts along the sides of the fish. Wrap the fish in a damp banana leaf (or a damp tea towel) and set aside for 30 minutes for the flavours to penetrate the flesh.
3. In a large frying pan, heat the oil to hot. In a deep plate, mix the flour with three pinches of salt and black pepper.
4. Take the fish, dab each side in the flour and place in the frying pan. Fry until golden brown underneath, then turn carefully and fry until golden brown on the other side.
5. Serve hot with a squeeze of fresh lime juice and eat with your fingers.

CHAPTER 10

brazil

WHERE THE NUTS COME FROM

> Nothing would be more tiresome than eating and drinking if God had not made them a pleasure as well as a necessity.
>
> *Voltaire*

Tall and tan and young and lovely, the girl from Belém walked by. Her flawless physique moving gracefully in plastic flip-flops that supported a pair of impossibly slender caramel legs, tatty denim hot-pants and round buttocks that rolled hypnotically in perfect union with the tightening muscles of her midriff and the glossy black hair that stroked her wide shoulders. Stopping briefly, this Amazonian beauty inhaled, pressed a finger on one of her nostrils and then noisily blasted a jet of mucus from her other nostril into the street. Repeating the process with the other side, she then wiped her nose with the inside of her arm, smashing the lustful thoughts racing through my eager little brain.

You can't do that, I muttered to myself as she floated elegantly by.

'Psssssssssst!'

Releasing the Brazilian equivalent of a builder's wolf-whistle, the man in the bike shop behind hissed loudly, and clearly enjoying the compliment a small smile split the girl's face before her captivating curves climbed the narrow pavement that ran under a row of crumbling colonial buildings and she disappeared for ever. I returned my attention to my bicycle and the man behind me went back to work. Lifting a heavy block of wood above his head, he brought it crashing down on my back wheel.

Thuddoink!

I winced. My buckled rim rang out in complaint. Suspending the wheel between his hands by its axel, he ordered me to give it a spin, carefully studying the rhythmic wobble that repeated itself on each revolution. Stopping the wheel, he lay it down on the floor.

Thuddoink! Thuddoink!

My five-week cruise down the Amazon had not been without problems. On the crossing from Ecuador to Peru, my steed had to endure the weight of an oil drum that had come untied below deck, which badly buckled the wheel. The bare-chested mechanic hitting my wheel with a block of wood in this dirty backstreet bike shop in Belém was my only hope. He applied another whack.

Thuddoink!

I had seen enough, and went in search of a coconut for breakfast.

From a dented polystyrene cool-box that sat on two plastic stools, a skeletal man casually took a coconut in one hand and with the other applied three firm and well-placed hacks with his long machete. Enough fibrous husk came away to reveal a little of the soft cranium-like shell hidden inside. After sliding a straw inside he handed it to me in exchange for a sheet of dirty Brazilian currency.

I took a long pull on the straw. It had been a frustrating morning negotiating the labyrinth of Belém's muggy backstreets in search of the city's only bike shop, but the chilled water that filled my mouth tasted wonderful and uncontaminated. Sucking and probing with my straw inside the shell, I tapped every last refreshing drop before handing the spent coconut back to the man. I made a karate-chop gesture with my hand and, replicating my action with his machete, his first swipe shaved away a scoop-shaped piece of husk, and his second split the nut in two. He handed me the two halves, and with my improvised scoop I scraped out the rubbery white flesh that lined the inside of the shell. Picking it up in my fingers, I dropped it into my mouth like a mother feeding a baby bird and its cool, slimy texture slid deliciously down my throat. I bought a bag of Brazil nuts from a man sitting in a doorway peeling them from their hairy shells, and wandered back to my bike.

At the Borracharia do Pele, my back wheel was now spinning smoothly in front of the mechanic's satisfied smile and not for the first time the expertise and resourcefulness of Latin America's bike shops left me impressed. Putting the wheel back in place, I replaced my worn-out brake-pads, paid my bill, and after taking some directions wobbled away, ringing my bell as I negotiated the cobbled streets towards the main road that would lead me to the highway and south for São Luis. After more than five weeks on the Amazon, without so much as turning a pedal, I was back in the saddle on the other side of South America, in a new country with a new language with new people with new habits. Welcome to Brazil.

撶

Life these days is full of lists written by so-called experts. They include 'The Twenty Best Sex Tips To Drive Your Partner Wild' and 'The Greatest Low-Carb Recipes', which might go some way to making you look like the emaciated, air-brushed specimens that adorn the front covers of glossy 'lifestyle magazines'. Another nonsensical chart that makes regular appearances on the pages of these publications, is of the 'Ten Things To Do Before You Die' variety.

But apart from persuading us that if we haven't thrown ourselves off a bridge with a piece of elastic tied to our ankles, or jumped out of an aeroplane, we haven't lived, all that these lists achieve, other than filling the coffers of travel agents, is to send armies of young gullible professionals jetting around the globe to be chased by bulls down the alleyways of some Mediterranean town, snowboard down mountains and attempt to have sex on aeroplanes. Another recurring item in these meaningless guides, which always appears next to a busty Brazilian in a tiny G-string adorned with jewels and feathers, is 'Do Carnival in Brazil'.

Starting on Shrove Tuesday, a day in England when we eat pancakes, in Brazil a five-day binge of music, food, alcohol and sex kicks off, before everyone embarks on forty long days of personal reflection and abstinence until Easter. With its name believed to derive from the Latin *carne vale*, 'O flesh, farewell!', many today choose to ignore the Lenten abstinence bit, but the five days of drinking, dancing, eating and 'whoopee' is taken very seriously, and revellers from all over the world flock to the Carnival hot spots of Rio de Janeiro and Salvador to get in on some of the action. Lucky enough to be cycling in Brazil in early February, I would get to tick 'Carnival' off my list, but due to some bad planning, a bout of galloping dysentery and some unfavourable headwinds, my plans for a pre-Lent Brazilian bender were going to be a little less glamorous. Instead of gulping down caipirinha and gyrating my rusty British hips on the beaches of Salvador, I found myself cycling on a monotonous highway that bisected the arid scrubland of the impoverished north-eastern Brazilian state of Pará, somewhere between Belém and São Luís.

Sharing this tiresome and seemingly never-ending road with an occasional truck, I pushed into a stubborn headwind, the tedium of the ride only broken by the radio mast of another forgettable dust-bowl community appearing on the horizon, with its broken-down vehicles, feral dogs and dilapidated gas stations, where pot-bellied truck drivers sat scratching their balls, sipping stale coffee and watching football. Nonetheless, after eight hours alone with nothing but my thoughts, they were a sight for sore eyes and an oasis where I could speak to someone, find some shade, fill up my water bottles and fuel a caffeine addiction. I never dreamed that I would spend my first carnival in such surroundings.

Cachoeira seemed no different to any of the other nondescript hamlets that came and went on this uninspiring leg of my journey.

Dusty strips of earth flanked the highway. Political slogans and the badly painted portraits of local politicians adorned the white-washed walls of single-storey homes. A few shops had their windows boarded up and an open-air bar with a pool table was, unusually, empty. A couple of raw-boned mongrels slinked over the road past a gang of turkey vultures that was ripping and tugging at the stiff corpse of an animal that hadn't looked both ways before crossing. Beyond a cluster of shady cashew trees – the town's only redeeming feature – was a small bridge that spanned a shallow river. Beyond that, filling the road and pouring into the sandy banks of the river, a dancing, hugging mass of Brazilians throbbed as one to the dull thud of axé music that thumped from a bed of speakers on the back of a truck. Hot, tired and despondent, this was the last thing I wanted to get involved in, but a bicycle bearing bags and flags proved to be poor cover. I was hailed at once with shouts of 'gringo' and invited over.

I was soon engulfed by the crowd and being interrogated by a gang of drunken rural men.

'Gringo, gringo!'

Clinging to my bicycle, I scanned the scene desperately for a way out.

'Americano, yes?' hollered a man in my ear, taking hold of my shoulder and spraying the side of my face with alcoholic gob.

'Inglês,' I responded.

'Ahh, Inglês. David Beckham. You stay with me!' he bawled back into my tender eardrum before wrapping me up in his clammy frame. With the competence of a riot policeman, Fernando led me through the masses to the other side, into a shantytown of criss-crossed backstreets that existed behind the façades flanking the highway. Cachoeira became suddenly much, much bigger. Mud-built and concrete homes stretched for blocks under a confusion of electrical wires that ran from each building.

Fernando's house was unfinished. Metal construction rods spewed from untidy brickwork and piles of sand and cement waited to be mixed, but he took me through his small construction site proudly explaining his grand plans until we arrived at a large sandy garden. Palms sprouted from the ground and a dense mango tree dropped small yellow fruit that buzzed with flies and filled the air with the smell of sweet decay. On a small veranda he showed me two metal hooks where I could sling my hammock and then threw me a towel. Together we walked beyond the garden to a section of river that ran through a verdant oasis of undergrowth. Clear water carved its way through the sand and, after unpeeling myself from my Lycra, I sank into one of the deeper pools and let the gentle current run over my naked body. Fernando sat next to me and while busily rubbing himself with soap he explained that tonight was the open party of Cachoeira's carnival and that there were going to be a lot of 'gatas'.

He winked before popping the soap from his hands towards me. I didn't know what 'gatas' were at this stage of the evening but I cleaned up all the same.

Back in the house, refreshed and in the jeans and T-shirt that I saved for nights like this, I was introduced to various cousins, nephews and nieces of Fernando's extended family. I was immediately given a bowl and ordered to help myself from the aluminium vats of rice, beans and a meaty stew being warmed on a wood fire that billowed smoke into the garden.

An elderly woman in a floral apron stood guard over her simple kitchen with a long wooden spoon, her frizzy grey hair framing the deep wrinkles of her brown face. She identified the meat as 'peba'.

I asked with polite curiosity, wondering what I was eating and already adding a second heaped spoonful to my bowl, what a peba was.

She elucidated that it was 'peba caipira'.

Turning a shard of bone in my teeth and pulling it from my mouth with my fingers, I tried again. What kind of animal was peba?

She confirmed that it was indeed an animal.

After only a few weeks in Brazil my Portuguese was still

extremely limited. Undaunted, I reeled off a few farmyard animals, in order to find out if it was one of those.

'Peba! Peba!'

We were getting nowhere. Chewing on the tender chunks of flesh that lurked within the rich stew flavoured with onion, cumin, paprika, tomatoes and green peppers, I let my taste buds try to unscramble what I had in my mouth. Perhaps it was mutton, but I hadn't seen a sheep since Colombia. It was far too gamey for pork but then perhaps it was goat, a young goat, or maybe rabbit.

Putting my best culinary detective skills to work I attempted to imitate a goat, but once the laughter had died down – by now the whole family was involved – I was faced with shaking heads and a collective announcement: 'No, é peba!'

Crossing sheep and goat off the list, and holding my hands above my head, I hopped on the spot, continuing this strange game of animal charades, but the shaking heads and giggles told me it wasn't rabbit I had in my mouth. I released a couple of loud snorts that any wild boar would be proud of, but the answer remained the same.

'No, é peba!'

I gave up. Whichever one of God's tasty creatures it was, peba would have to remain a mystery. I accepted an offer of more, and I was waiting for another ladle to be emptied into my bowl when I felt a light tug on my trousers. I looked down. One of Fernando's young nephews was staring up at me and, in the same way a magician lifts a rabbit from a hat, he proudly pulled from a plastic bucket a plump and disorientated armadillo.

'É peba, Thomas.'

⚙

Bloated on armadillo stew, I walked with Fernando's family to a broken concrete football pitch in the centre of this small community. A band was starting up and under an almost full moon and the orange glare of a few streetlights, the town began its carnival celebrations. Happily ensconced at plastic tables, surrounded by spent beer bottles, the majority of Cachoeira's men were already roaring drunk. Their wives and girlfriends companionably compared what little clothes they were wearing. Young couples' bodies moved as one in time to the band and children chased each other through the bustling mass of people throwing bags of flour at each other, while entrepreneurial old ladies fired up small stoves. Sharing a round of drinks with Fernando's family, I immersed myself in the carnival around me. I enjoyed the natural high that swelled throughout my system whenever I found myself in these unique situations. Every backbreaking hill, never-ending road, lonely hour, aching muscle, dry mouth, cracked lip all fused together to give me one perfect moment that made travel by bicycle so special. And then blackout.

The town was plunged into darkness, followed by a brief silence and an angry wave of jeering, hissing and booing that spread like a virus. Eyes flashed in the shadows, sweat-damp skin glistened in the moonlight and burning cigarette ends flew about like fire flies.

I asked Fernando's cousin, whose arms were draped over my shoulders, what was happening.

'É normal,' she returned into my ear, citing a decrepit and corrupt electrical company. Then she shrugged her tight shoulders and moved her arms to around my waist, saying the blackout could last anything from an hour to a few days.

Expecting to be swept up by a phalanx of outraged, machete-wielding farm hands on a march for the governor's house, I witnessed quite the opposite. Rows of candles suddenly flickered into flame, illuminating the faces of the food vendors who continued to work their blowing grills, preparing grilled chicken hearts. Car radios turned up their volume, and along with the gentle hum of a few petrol generators and the rumble of the occasional truck that passed through town pulling on its horn, the beat went on into the early hours until, seemingly one by one by one, every light in the town flickered back to life. A massive roar went up from the crowd and a new energy surged into the celebrations. The band started, and once again I was swallowed up in a rolling sea of people, while my hips tried to follow the fluent motion of Fernando's cousin's body. This small hamlet in northeast Brazil may not have had any floats or feathered dancers, but I felt blessed to have been given the opportunity to enjoy my first carnival in Brazil here. Cachoeira was a long way from Rio, but it ticked all the right boxes.

The well-pedalled path for those unhinged enough to spend two years on a bicycle in the Americas is the Pacific coast route from Alaska to Argentina, and that had indeed been my initial plan. But after 12,000 miles and nearly two years in the saddle, I found myself facing the wrong ocean. The Atlantic. My Amazonian short-cut had brought me to the other side of the continent, and ensured that my journey south to Rio was now a little shorter. But I had other reasons for coming to Brazil too. Sticking to the tried and tested Pacific coast route I would have to endure the lung-busting peaks of the Peruvian Andes, the salt-flats of Bolivia, and the solitude and cold of Chile's Pacific coast. But from what my map told me, in Brazil it was a relatively flat 3,000-mile route all the way to the cold caipirinha that waited for me on Ipanema beach. In Brazil it would be sun, sea and cycling all the way to Rio, and to use some jargon from my days in advertising it was a 'no brainer'.

But entering a new country by bicycle the plucky cycle tourist has to learn quickly the rules of the road, written and unwritten, and it soon became clear why so few people decide to take on Brazil on a bicycle. Not many people cycle tour in Brazil because Brazilians can't drive. Perhaps it's the fact that the majority of the population prance about in plastic flip-flops, which leave them unable to control the pedals, or perhaps it's a rogue gene, but putting a Brazilian behind the wheel of a motorised vehicle is not a good idea. Just look at the way they play football, have sex, wear bathing suits and dance, and then imagine that temperament at the controls of a speeding truck. They either go fast very quickly, or they slow down very quickly, and there is nothing in between.

Getting in a car with a Brazilian is a nerve-shredding experience. Sharing the road on a bicycle with dozens of these aspiring racing drivers is suicidal.

This doesn't mean to say there are no Brazilians on bikes. As with all other Latin countries, the bicycle is still the hardest-working vehicle of the hardest-working class, but I quickly learnt that the luxury of riding on the smooth black stuff was the privilege of truck drivers and those few lucky enough to own a car. With no hard shoulders to the roads, the downtrodden cyclist has to make do with the man-eating potholes, roadkill and litter by the side of the road, and God forbid that I should even try and treat myself to a little comfortable riding. I would be horned angrily a few seconds before an enormous juggernaut would fly within inches of my panniers, whipping up a turbulent vortex of dust and wind that left me no other choice than to retreat red-faced and swearing into the gutter where I apparently belonged.

With a life expectancy of no more than a few hours on these deadly highways, I left São Luis, needing to find another way south. Investing in a detailed Quatro Rodas map and consulting some cycling locals, I began to plan an alternative route south for Fortaleza. I was advised that to follow a series of dirt tracks and the beach, literally cycling along Brazil's famous coastline, would be my safest way south. All I had to do was keep an eye on the tide, avoid falling coconuts and keep the Atlantic on my left.

Riding the vast expanse of Brazil's northern beaches, I spent days on unending open stretches of flat pale sand. The shadows of clouds moved with the wind over the flat surface in front of me like dark spirits. I was alone on huge beaches where the pounding surf kicked up sheets of white mist, while ahead of me palm trees, sand and surf converged on an infinite horizon. I stopped to pluck coconuts from trees before sipping at the fresh water inside, I swam in the brackish water of rivers that meandered into the sea, I ate fresh fish and shrimp in small fishing villages. It was so peaceful, so clean and so breathtakingly beautiful. When the sand was firm and the going was easy, I was cycling in paradise.

Well, almost, because the two things that will wreck a bicycle faster than you can say WD40 are salt water and sand. Brazil's northern beaches may look like paradise in the postcards, but I quickly discovered they are a dry and harsh environment, with little to no shade, fierce coastal winds and confusing tides. After my first few days riding the beach, my bicycle wasn't the only one complaining. Together we made slow progress.

I was at the mercy of the tides which rushed in and out, cutting deep rivers and lagoons in the beach, swallowing my wheels and forcing me to get out of the saddle and push through dusty dunes. The sun and salt dried my face and split my lips. There was no fresh water to wash in and at times nothing but coconuts to eat during the day. I pushed forward, heaving my bike through clogging and heavy sands. Spits of sharp rock did their best to tear my feet and tyres, and when the wind picked up it blasted my face and stung my eyes. Delayed by the tide I would wait for hours on shadeless beaches for the water to return to the sea, allowing me to pass, only to find the sand too wet to support my load. But by traversing these small rivers and following the sand-filled tracks, which had proved a bridge too far for the greedy property developers and weekenders, I was able to find the hidden gems that have remained clean, intact and almost completely untouched by the outside world.

🚲

Neto II, Isla Chica, Nando, Grande Dios, Cisne Branco.
Reading the names through sun-scorched eyes, I began to cheer up. Since the previous morning I had been mostly pushing my bicycle through soft sand, trapped on one side by the sparse ridges of wind-sculpted sand dunes and on the other by the pounding waves of the Atlantic. Apart from a couple of slow-moving donkeys and a young man on a motorcycle who disappeared into the haze as fast as he came out of it, I had spent two days alone in this immense and hostile landscape. But the names I now read, proudly painted on the sides of the jangadas that rested on the beach, were a sign of life. Simple crafts of

pre-Colombian origin, used for fishing the coastal waters on Brazil's northeast coast for thousands of years, these crude rafts were made of logs and planks lashed and pegged together below a large mainsail. This beached flotilla meant that the jangadeiros who owned them must be close by, and leaning my weight into my handlebars I pushed away from the ocean and was overjoyed to see a few tiled buildings hidden amongst a cluster of palm trees that appeared in a gap between the dunes.

The only street of this small village was an uneven stretch of sand-covered stones and bricks flanked on either side by a line of small white-washed fisherman's homes. Fishing nets and sails, propped against walls to dry, gently flapped in the breeze and, other than a heavily pregnant dog with sagging nipples that was asleep in the shade, and a few caged birds, the place was deserted. Guessing the time at around three or three thirty, it was still too hot for any self-respecting Brazilian to leave the comfort of the hammock, but after the day I had had it was late enough for me to call it quits. I found a little shade under the branches of a cashew tree, took a last long pull of my warm water and waited.

The sound of scuffed footsteps first drew my attention to the gaunt figure of a man making his way along the sand-dusted cobblestones. All elbows and knees, he wore nothing more than ancient blue flip-flops and a shabby pair of red nylon shorts, which hung on his bony hips. The sun glanced off his taut shoulders, his long arms bulged with veins and his large hands swung by his sides.

'Boa tarde!' I offered politely from my position under the tree.

'Diga, irmão, tudo de bom?' said the cheerful weathered face that stopped in front of me.

I squinted back at him and confirmed that all was well with a clumsy thumbs-up. He came and squatted beside me under the tree and, rocking gently on his sandals, keenly examined my bicycle before ushering me to my feet and leading me up a small hill away from the village.

'Phiiiiiiiish!'

If there had been a door on the small breeze-block house, roofed with rusty tin, we would have knocked, but instead my cheerful guide clapped his hands before letting out a short hiss that announced our arrival to whoever was lurking within. Leaving my wheels outside, I entered. Inside it was dark and cool and my burnt eyes scrambled to adjust to the shady surroundings. A naked frizzy-haired child of perhaps one or two years pushed a broken truck across the dirty concrete floor, on to which a stringy man swinging in a hammock sporadically spat into a puddle of phlegm. In the other corner an old crone, efficiently sucking the flesh off a fish skeleton, spared me a glance before returning her attention to the zealous evangelical preacher in a shiny blue suit forcing his message through the interference on the small television. On top of the TV set sat a broken ceramic statue of St George trying to spear a feeble-looking dragon. His spear was missing.

'Graças Jesus,' said the old lady, through gums and fish bones, in response to the bawling minister.

The minister continued, to roars of approval from his congregation until the applause was interrupted by an oversized oily hulk, advertising some kind of newfangled bodybuilding contraption available to all evangelicals with only ten monthly payments of 50 Reals. The old woman's attention returned to her fish, and making the most of the commercial break, the man who had brought me to this house said a few words to his friend in the hammock, after which he shook my hand and escaped into the bright sunshine that cut a sharp angle through the doorway. The man in the hammock asked me if I needed somewhere to sleep, an offer I was grateful for. We introduced ourselves.

'Wilson.'

'Thomas.'

The minister was back, but the next break signalled the end of the televised service. The old woman got to her feet and shuffled into the only other room in the house and in one fluid movement

Wilson rolled from his hammock and slipped into his waiting flip-flops before walking into the sunshine.

Outside, the long shadows of coconut palms and single-storey buildings stretched over the cobblestones and without the intense heat of the middle of the day the small village had come alive. A girl raced past us on an improvised hobbyhorse made of a long stick and old plastic fishing reels. Two boys pulled two meaty crabs on leads made of string, taking their pets for a walk. Mothers and daughters sat in the afternoon shadows cast by their homes, patiently weaving intricate patterns in lace, while on the beach under simple palm shelters their husbands looped repairs in bundles of nylon netting. A man worked a large pair of scissors on the head of another sitting on a small stool. His tight black curls falling to the ground were quickly gathered up by the breeze.

Opening a heavy wooden door, Wilson entered what appeared to be some kind of fishermen's community building. Dated government posters explaining what size fish could be kept and which thrown back shared the walls with religious psalms painted on to crumbling plaster. On the floor, a group of six women sat on their haunches and read from a Bible. Wilson said I could sleep in here. Finding two metal hooks in the wall I put up my hammock, checked it was securely fastened and then sat on the cool concrete floor with my back against the wall. Its stony chill refreshed my tired legs and as I listened to the readings from the Bible, young children peered nervously through the door at the strange sunburnt man who had arrived from the beach on his bicycle.

Wilson's offer to eat with his family could not have been more welcome. I walked back to his home, clapped my hands and wandered in. The old woman was back in front of her television and was now transfixed by Brazil's other televised religion, the novellas, or soap operas, but Wilson was nowhere to be seen. I wandered through the house and came out on to a dusty clearing where Wilson was in a hammock under a wide-branched tree. His youngest child was asleep in his lap while his daughter sat on the ground next to her mother, Maria, watching as she weaved an intricate pattern in lace. Deposing his small, still sleeping child and taking a seat on a log, Wilson began to talk.

⚙

Wilson was forty-four. He had been a fisherman since he was twelve, and like his father before him he was now the head fisherman of this small community. He still used his father's jangada and for four days in every week he went out to sea with one other man to make his living and feed his family. He fished the coastal waters with a series of lines and small nets, often having to brave high winds and violent storms. After four days on the ocean, drinking coconut water and eating raw fish, he found his way back to this tiny village hidden on Brazil's vast coastline. He told me he would set sail again in two nights, but in the meantime he was home.

Kissing her husband affectionately on the forehead, Maria took her lace-work and two children back into the house, and when she returned she placed a warm deep bowl in my hands. It wafted sweet fishy smells into my nostrils. I sipped at this rich soup of mussels and coconut milk and, as dusk fell on the small fishing village, the first star of the night burst through the deepening blue sky and a fine breeze blew off the waves, brushing through the dense coconut palms. The falling sun brightened the edges of the thick clouds that rose above the earth to the west and quiet music and muted conversation echoed from the other homes in the village. Returning once more from her kitchen, Maria now held a plate stacked with hunks of fried golden fish. Shrivelled heads with sunken eyes, blackened tails with broken fins and tender bellies wrapped in tight crunchy skin.

Wilson said a short grace and then we began tearing with our fingers at the sticky meat, chewing on the crispy skin before dipping the tender flesh in farofa and sucking the skeletons clean. Wilson and his wife sucked at the heads and shared those I had discarded, and with nothing but a collection of bare bones left on the plate, Maria joined Wilson in his hammock, resting her head on his bare chest while he contentedly picked his teeth with a fishbone.

⚙

The next morning I swam in the ocean as the sun rose and watched a handful of men on the shore unroll sails and check their nets before dragging and pushing their jangadas to the water, leaving trails in the sand like nesting turtles do. Wilson came to find me with a mug of sweet coffee and a slab of sticky cocada, which his wife had given me. We tore in two the sweet cake of grated coconut boiled with sugar and ate it on the beach, watching the triangular sails of the village's jangadas cut through the white horses before vanishing into the clean line of the horizon. Wilson invited me to stay for another night. I could have stayed forever, but it was already hot and regretfully I began to reload my bicycle, surrounded by the village's children who pestered me with questions.

They asked about my bear bell, a souvenir from the Rocky mountains. Then they enquired about the pump, now removed from its place on the frame and being passed from hand to hand. Next they lighted on the small compass that hung from my handlebars. I began to explain its purpose but my young audience had already diverted their attentions to my far more interesting hamburger bell. All except for Wilson, who had taken the compass in his hands and was studying it with confused amazement.

After some time he asked if it needed batteries.

'No,' I replied and, picking up a coconut to act as the globe, I tried to explain the basics of magnetic polarity.

Wilson listened, but my geography lesson fell on deaf ears. He was more interested in my compass than my coconut. Turning it in his hands and shaking it, he marvelled as the needle slowly returned to point north. More and more excited by his discovery, he began to walk in small circles around the beach, and then up the hill towards his house. He led the way, looking down at the compass; I followed clutching my coconut. Exhausted fishermen were disturbed, friends were gathered and all marvelled at this small device I had for so long taken for granted.

Does it tell the time, asked one intrigued jangadeiro. Is it electronic, asked another, prompting me to restart my flawed coconut demonstration.

But I was as baffled as they were. Wilson had spent the majority of his life at sea on a basic wooden craft on which I wouldn't cross a shallow river, he had never failed to return to this small beach on this vast coastline and he had never seen a compass. With no choice but to leave my compass hanging proudly around Wilson's neck, I waved goodbye and continued my journey on firm sand south towards Fortaleza, looking back over my shoulder every so often, wondering whether I should go back for my compass and whether Wilson would be better off without it. But soon the palm trees of the village had vanished and by nightfall the orange glow of Fortaleza, one of Brazil's great coastal cities, was glowing on the horizon.

🚲

Squinting through sleepy eyes I peered across the mud at the old truck, its heavy bonnet slung forward on its hinges like the broken wing of a large beetle.

A man half immersed in the engine called to another man in the cab to turn over the engine. The huge vehicle choked and wheezed in complaint. I know nothing about engines but his truck was not healthy.

This failed roadside repair had been going on for hours, distracting me from sleep, but at sunrise I had had enough and, unpeeling myself from my wet hammock, I was pleased to find the night's rain had stopped though the sky was still solid with clouds that marched in off the sea. An uncomfortable night hanging amongst a cluster of trees next to a mechanic's workshop a few kilometres north of Recife had left me uninspired. On the other side of the road from where I slept, a heavy-set man pushing a cart of what looked like bamboo stopped in front of a gazebo thatched with palm and torn canvas, under which sat a rusty old press. He began nailing a piece of torn cardboard to one of the uprights.

CALDO DE CANA
1R

I crossed the road, avoiding the thickening traffic of old lorries bundled high with untidy stacks of long canes. The man was now pouring what appeared to be petrol from a dirty green plastic bottle into a small rusty tank on top of the engine. Leaving my bike on its kickstand, I tipped the rainwater from one of his plastic chairs and took a seat.

'Um caldo de cana, por favor.'

He yanked at a small rope and his little engine spluttered to life. He pushed a small lever, whereupon a large metal cog began slowly rotating. From a pile next to him he hacked at a thick length of cane with his machete before feeding the offcuts into the two heavy wooden rollers of his press. The cane was chewed into one end and from the other a murky green liquid dribbled from a small lip into a jug.

He cut the engine and poured some of the contents of the jug into a plastic beaker. The liquid looked like a stagnant puddle on a sunny day. Served in a dirty beaker by this wild-eyed and almost toothless man on the edge of a six-lane highway surrounded by pollution, litter and noise, this roadside refreshment could not have looked any more uninviting. But I took a long swig and found that it was sweet and refreshing. I emptied my cup and handed it to the man for a refill. This was the commodity that British colonists had called white gold. It was the engine behind the transatlantic slave trade, and it had shaped the social and political history of Brazil. Today, in a world of soaring oil prices and the desperate scramble for sustainable alternatives, it will continue to determine Brazil's future for years to come.

More sugar is produced in Brazil than anywhere else in the world, but sugarcane is not a native plant of South America. It came from Polynesia, introduced by the Portuguese into Brazil in the sixteenth century once Europe had developed a sweet tooth. Sugarcane, first planted here in 1516, was initially cultivated on a small scale in coastal plantations worked by local Indians. But once demand grew amongst Europe's expanding cities, sugar became big business. The Portuguese needed a vast and compliant workforce, and so they began to ship in slaves from their colonies in West Africa, where they had already established important trading outposts for ivory and spice. For the slave traders their new human cargo, shipped across the Atlantic in a horrendous voyage known as the 'middle passage', was merely an extension of a well-oiled commercial machine that was already in place and making Portugal one of the richest and most powerful nations in the world.

The 'middle passage' took anything up to six months. It became an important component of a trade triangle whereby slaves were shipped from Africa to work on 'New World' sugar plantations. Sugar was sent to Europe where it was exchanged for European goods, such as guns and steel, which were shipped to Africa and used to purchase more slaves. Such was the influence of sugar on the slave trade that by the time slavery was finally abolished in Brazil in 1888, over six million Africans had been removed from their homeland and shipped there to work the plantations. And today the commodity that shaped the history of Brazil will no doubt influence its future. Sugarcane, which can be processed to make ethanol, is once again big business in Brazil, making a few Brazilians incredibly rich while many others are forced to work for a pittance.

◪

'Oupa!'

'Ouooha!'

Bare-chested and in tatty shirts, some pushing robust bicycles, others in straw hats or sweat-drenched bandanas, tired men materialised one by one from the compact walls of sugarcane that grew by the side of the red earth track I had been following since sunrise.

'Ouooha.'

Greeting each other with deep voices, these hard-working men, plantation workers, had begun their journey home, emerging from the crops with hollow chests, taut physiques and bloodshot eyes, their feet coated in the rich russet earth from which grew the commodity they had been slashing and cutting, the crop that swept across the rolling hills of the landscape like a thick green carpet. I was cycling a fertile coastal strip, south of Recife, through some of Brazil's oldest sugar plantations, where the descendants of those Africans brought to Brazil are still working the land today.

'Ouooha.'

'Ouh!'

I rode in silence amongst these men, some on foot and others on sturdy bicycles with machetes and water bottles hanging from their handlebars. Apart from their simple greetings, the squeaks of their chains and the wind brushing the tops of the crops, there was no sound. The group made their journey home towards the bells that echoed across the sugarcane and mingled with the cool evening breeze.

'Ouooha.'

'Oopa!'

Five miles, ten miles, as the sun set our small group of riders grew. Our pace was steady and we were followed by a flock of small birds that hopped from the slender leaves of the sugarcane. The soft chime of a bell drew closer from an unseen local town where I assumed we were heading, and the intense temperature of the day was replaced by a soft climate and a cool wind that seemed to blow away my weariness and that of the men around me. The once sharp sunlight was now a soft glow that accentuated the innumerable green hues of the crops. On the horizon, the setting sun blazed at the edges of dense clouds.

The road carried us past twisting red tracks that led deeper into the crops towards ancient trees. We passed a football match being played on a dirt pitch cut away from the crops, where russet dust flew at the bare feet of the players as they challenged each other for possession of a tatty ball. A small crowd cheered and heckled the audacious tricks, well-placed passes and strong challenges of the men engaged in Brazil's national game. Joining them

I sat astride my bike leaning forward on my handlebars. A warm and comforting glow covered everything, enriching the colours around me and sending long shadows from the feet of the players. The crops rolled in the wind and the great trees throbbed and whistled with the night-call of cicadas.

I arrived in the small village as dusk fell and I could understand why it wasn't on the map. On the outskirts the homes were no more than recently put up, mud-built tenement houses with bent metallic roofs. Nearer the centre the buildings were older, more sturdy and painted in confident bright colours. A cobbled main street led to a crumbling and insubstantial baroque church surrounded by a few single-storey homes, between which dirt sidestreets ran into the green backdrop. As the cortador de cana returned from work, this small town, an island in an ocean of sugarcane, sprang into life. Chairs and benches were set out in front of homes, a typical Latin American extension of people's living rooms, and in the village's only bar, an open-sided shed, men in nylon shorts and sandals played their shots and waited round a small pool table. Three pretty girls with tight black curls and slender limbs rolled past me, all balanced on the same bicycle that was much too big for them, followed by two men in straw hats on horseback who tapped the sharp hips of their horses, urging them forward on the cobblestones. A small but well-voiced congregation sounded from the open doors of the church. In front of one house, tables were unfolded while pots and pans were laid out on a floral tablecloth. The menu of this part-time restaurant was permanently painted on the turquoise wall.

TEMOS
Tapioca
Cocada
Sucos
Pastel

With thick wings of fat swinging under her arms, a large black woman slowly ferried her kitchen on to the street. Pots, saucepans, gas rings and a heavy blue canister. Her young daughter helped her to organise her stand, unstacking plastic chairs, while her husband, a skinny man with a swollen belly, lay slumped in a wire rocking chair sipping cachaça from a dirt-misted glass.

'Boa noite!'

The man of the house offered little more than a nod of recognition but the big-armed woman, whose voluptuous and confident posture made her immediately appear comforting, ordered her daughter to get me a chair.

I was told I would have to wait a while for my supper, but this was Brazil and patiently I noted down the day's events in my diary while the women set about making pastel, a popular street food of these small towns and villages. I watched her work. She rolled out thin sheets of pastry into long rectangles, on to which she placed a handful of small maggot-like shrimps before folding each one over to form a envelope. Then she dipped her chubby fingers in milk and sealed the edges with a series of firm pinches.

By the time small bubbles were running up the sides of the oil-filled deep metal bowl and accumulating in a rolling boil, she had made over a dozen of these delicate shrimp-filled parcels. She slid each one into the piping-hot oil and each released a short hiss before vanishing into an oily foam. After a few minutes she fished each one out with a pair of tongs, leaving them to cool in neat rows in a dented metal tray.

Swollen like a plump pillow by the warm air inside, the golden pastry was blistered and crisp. Holding my pastel I nibbled away a corner, before squeezing out a fishy waft of steam. I dribbled in a little home-made molho de pimenta, a punchy Brazilian hot sauce, and began eating. The pastry was brittle on the outside while remaining soft and soggy on the inside, flavoured with the salty taste of the shrimp that waited at the bottom.

As the night drew on I asked the woman what was the secret of these perfect little parcels, the best I had tried in Brazil.

'Uma cachacinha,' she whispered, glancing at her husband who by this stage had drunk himself into a motionless heap, and it seemed only fair that the magic ingredient of this perfect Brazilian street snack came from the potent liquor, the national drink of Brazil, that was made from the sugarcane that surrounded the village. As I said goodnight, she advertised that she would be serving breakfast at sunrise, and after slinging my hammock and mosquito net under a wooden lean-to that protruded from the crumbling back wall of the church, I drifted to sleep already looking forward to my first meal of following day.

Tapioca was one of my favourite puddings as a child, and thinking about it today still conjures up happy childhood memories of teasing my sister with blown-out cheeks full of what I claimed was frogspawn, before squirting the slimy translucent beads through the gaps in my teeth, sending her running from the table and leaving her untouched bowl for me to enjoy. Few people eat tapioca in Britain any more. Perhaps its strange name, that sounds more like a venereal disease than a pudding, is too uncommercial for supermarket shelves, or maybe its slimy texture is too 'Eeeew, gross!' for Britain's increasingly squeamish children. Either way, what was once a staple of the Victorian kitchen, and a dinner lady's favourite, has now almost completely vanished, like so many other traditional British recipes.

But other than bringing back fond memories of something my sister decided to spit out rather than swallow, until I cycled into Brazil I knew little about the origins of tapioca, and had no idea it was made from the cassava or manioc root, a native plant of Brazil, which has been cultivated and processed in South America for nearly 5,000 years. A relative of the ubiquitous yucca plants that decorate dentists' waiting rooms and suburban gardens, cassava is easy to propagate. It grows well in low-nutrient soil and it can be harvested every two months, providing plenty of well-needed carbohydrate. European colonists soon discovered the virtues of this exotic crop, which could be prepared in large quantities and would keep dry for several years, making it an ideal food for the crew and cargo of slave ships. Once exported from Brazil, cassava spread throughout Africa, Asia and Europe, fast becoming and remaining a dependable food source for developing countries, as well a favourite nursery pudding in Britain.

A staple ingredient for the indigenous tribes of Brazil prior to colonisation, used in the preparation of porridges, cakes and breads, today cassava in its many different forms is still an integral ingredient of Brazilian cuisine. From every fisherman's home to the smartest restaurants in Rio, a plastic tub of farinha, a rough sawdust-like meal ground from roast cassava root, is spooned over beans, mixed into rice and blended with sauces to make every meal go that little bit further. The slender brown tubers of cassava are peeled of their rough skin before their white fibrous flesh is boiled and eaten in the same way we eat potatoes, or is added to stews. Strips of cassava root are deep-fried, sold by street vendors and eaten like chips, and starchy mashed cassava is used to thicken bobó de camarão, a heavy shrimp stew with its roots in the slave trade. Farofa de manteiga, a dish made from frying the farinha with butter, onion and parsley, is served as a condiment with almost every meal in Brazil, and the starch extracted from cassava roots is ground into a fine white flour that is used for baking pão de queijo, a puffy bread roll made with fresh cheese that is found in every bakery in Brazil, while the unground, chalk-white beads of starch become what we know as tapioca.

∞

Waking in my hammock behind the church, I found the village engulfed in a thick mist. Its buildings and trees were no more than shapes suspended in the steely fog. The air was damp and cold and my lower back complained loudly after another crooked night's sleep. I packed up my kit and returned to where I had left the woman the night before.

A gang of customers, wiry men clutching used plastic bottles of water and machetes, sipped at coffee and ate their breakfast while other men came in and out of the gloom, their arrival announced by the slap, slap of their plastic sandals on the soles of their feet.

The broad smile of the woman from the night before was more uplifting than any cup of coffee. I asked her for a tapioca.

Two well-loved blackened frying pans sat above the blue flames of her tabletop stove. She rubbed the surface of one with margarine, then sprinkled a handful of pure white tapioca beads into the pan, evenly covering the sleek black surface. The tapioca began to bond together as it came into contact with the heat. She asked if I'd like grated coconut. I would. She took a generous handful from a plastic washing-up bowl and dusted a layer over the tapioca. Cheese? Yes please. She pinched the corner off a block of fresh cheese wrapped in a blue plastic bag and crumbled it over the coconut in her thick black fingers, before folding one side of the congealed tapioca like an omelette. Molten cheese soon began to dribble from the edges and brown in the pan. My breakfast was ready. She scooped it into a paper napkin and handed it to me, and I took my first bite, the rubbery tapioca squeaking in my teeth as I chewed over the salty taste of the molten cheese mixed with the sweet meat of the coconut.

The woman then offered me a glass of fresh cashew juice, sweetened with panela, the natural extract of sugarcane. Sitting on the kerb with the sugarcane workers, I noticed muscle-bound, shirtless men drifting in and out of the grey mist with caged birds balanced on their broad shoulders.

'Are they for sale?' I asked the man sitting next to me.

Apparently surprised at my idiot question, he patiently explained that the men walked their birds so they sang more beautifully, then rose to his feet shaking his head before getting on his bicycle and disappearing into the fog himself. The other customers didn't talk much. They sipped their coffee and fruit juice and ate their tapioca until one by one they too returned into the mist, some on foot and some on bicycles. I finished my own breakfast and thanked the woman, and pedalled out of the village. The smoky mist that cloaked the landscape allowed me to smell the damp red earth that stuck to my tyres, and through the gloom I listened to the creaking and squeaking of the sugarcane workers drifting past me and back into the fields.

Of all Brazil's coastal cities, perhaps Salvador is her most historic. Built on the shores of the Baía de Todos os Santos, a vast natural harbour, ideal for protecting ships from fierce Atlantic storms and marauding English pirates, the city's fortunate geographical position in relation to the southern Atlantic Ocean ensured that it quickly became the most important trading post in the Americas. By 1650 a soaring demand for sugar in the coffee houses of Europe had made it one of the richest cities on the planet. But, like Bristol and Liverpool, its foundations were laid on the labour and lives of African slaves.

Three hundred years before I cycled along its fortified seafront, its harbour would have been filled with slave ships waiting to unload their human cargo. But it was pristine cruise ships that lay on their moorings in the Bahia de Conception now, unloading a cargo of tourists who come to Salvador to admire the colonial architecture, gold-filled churches and magnificent plazas of its historic centre, known as El Pelourinho (or 'pillory', a place for whipping slaves), built on the vast fortunes made from the slave trade.

But as well as providing enormous wealth and a seemingly inexhaustible work force, the Africans who survived the horrendous conditions of the 'middle passage' also introduced their own distinctive culture to Brazil, and nowhere can this be seen, heard and tasted more than in the state of Bahia, of which Salvador is the capital.

From the fluid forms of those practising capoeira in the street, an Angolan martial art developed by slaves to look like a dance so their masters didn't sense trouble, to the tribal drum beats and African rhythms within samba roda that thump and roll from every street bar, and the colourful clothing and religious practices of the mysterious Candomblé religion, in Bahia you cannot fail to feel the deep African influence that is at the beating heart of the state. But as well as holding on to their musical and religious traditions, which have allowed the cultural identity of those Africans who came to Brazil to survive and outlive the dark days of slavery, they also preserved their culinary identity, and when cycling in the state of Bahia you are never far from the unmistakable smell of frying dende oil, the quintessential ingredient of Bahian cuisine.

Extracted from the fruit of dende palms, which were imported from West Africa as a foodstuff for slaves, dende oil soon became a valuable commodity in its own right. During the industrial revolution it became popular as an industrial lubricant. Today, under its other name of palm oil, it is used in almost every product on our supermarket shelves, from detergent to crisps. But in Bahia it is predominantly used for cooking. Cycling south from Salvador I rode through the lush palm groves of the Costa de Dende, where Brazil's first dende palms were planted.

All along this lush section of coastline I rode between pristine beaches and plantations of palms whose sharp fronds hung over abundant clusters of bright orange fruit. Heavy-set men, their shoulders stained red with oil, harvested clusters of the fruit, which lay by the roadside waiting to be collected. I rode through small towns and villages where shop shelves were lined with glass bottles of deep red oil, glowing in the bright sunshine. In one rundown bike shop a man even suggested I oil my chain with this viscous lubricant, but as the principal ingredient of Bahian cuisine, it is the smell of frying dende oil that hangs in the air of every street corner at dusk that will always remind me Bahia.

A key ingredient in moqueca, a hearty fish stew made of tomatoes, pepper and fresh fish slow-cooked in dende oil and coconut milk and garnished with fresh cilantro, it is also used liberally in caruru and vatapá, which are both eaten with Bahia's signature roadside snack. Mexico may have its tacos, El Salvador its pupusas and the Americans their hamburgers, but in Bahia fast food comes in the form of acarajé, which, after two years of pedal-powered roadside research, I can reveal is the best way to fuel a cyclist's engine.

'Hotel Bon Jesus' in black paint on a turquoise wall told me I had found what was, by all accounts, the cheapest place to stay in the small harbour town of Valença, Bahia, capital of the Costa de Dende.

'Pisssssssh!' I hissed though the metal bars while clapping my hands. After a short wait I heard a jangle and the sound of footsteps belonging to a leather-faced old woman clutching a large bunch of keys.

'Boa noite, filho!' Her face cracking into a smile, she unlocked the metal gate, and after coming to an agreement that she had a room at ten Real, a little over two pounds, she led me down a cool corridor, past a line of wooden doors, each one locked with a crude latch and padlock.

Cell 15 had no windows. The walls were stained with damp mould and a faded picture of Leonardo da Vinci's *Last Supper* hung crookedly on the wall. The single bed had a broken-down foam mattress that looked like it housed more life-forms than a GCSE biology project, and with my bicycle inside there was little room for anything else. A fluorescent striplight barely attached to the ceiling flickered to life, giving me a better view of this room, and I wondered if Jesus would be happy to have his name endorsing such a flea pit. Paid up, I stripped out of my scuzzy clothes and a gang of hungry mosquitoes began whining with anticipation at the British feast.

I clapped my hands and was pleased to see a couple of bloody smudges, but I was fighting a losing battle. I pondered whether my talent for finding the most rundown accommodation in the Americas could somehow be exploited for future financial gain. *The Hungry Cyclist's Guide to the Worst Places to Stay in Brazil.*

Back in the corridor, a trail of wet footprints on the cool concrete led me to a much needed shower. The communal bathroom held no great surprises. A grubby lavatory-shower combination, it had all the usual charms of budget Brazilian accommodation: slimy floor, offensive smell and a seat-less toilet beside which sat a plastic basket full of recently soiled paper.

The shower was a pipe sticking out of the wall. I turned the industrial-looking lever and icy-cold water rushed over my tired and over-heated frame, washing away days of sweat and travel. Realising I had left my soap behind, I glanced at the soap dish in the hope that the last occupant had done the same thing. He had, and a shard of soap encrusted with pubes awaited me.

Ten minutes later, relatively clean and in comfortable clothes, I wandered past the owner, who was transfixed by a soap opera, and walked into a balmy evening to enjoy my favourite end-of-day pastime, the one that makes riding a bicycle in tropical heat worthwhile: strolling the streets of a small town in search of food. I crossed into the centre of Valença over an old bridge that ran above its heavy river walls, built of thick grey stone. Various-sized fishing vessels painted in red, green, blue and yellow bumped into each other on the tidal swell, while children dived from their decks into the water to play with a broken polystyrene box bobbing in the dark river water.

The heavy stone walls had once turned this river into a busy harbour, and the colonial warehouses were signs of the town's boom years, when boats would have journeyed upstream to the sugar, cacao and dende plantations of the interior, returning to fill the warehouses before the goods were shipped north to Salvador. But today those buildings that hadn't been left to decay were transformed into internet cafés and ice-cream parlours where youths lingered in designer clothes and hair gel, waiting for a chance to email friends and 'chat' online.

Tree-lined promenades ran along both sides of the Rio Una and their foliage chattered with bird life. Under the branches a number of kiosks sold beer and salgadinhos to men sitting at plastic tables and chairs. Some played dominoes, others stared at a football match on the television, one was having his shoes buffed by a young boy sitting on a wooden box. A young couple stared lovingly at each other, enjoying an early evening date, and a man with a basket of boiled peanuts on his shoulder worked each table like a bumblebee pollinating flowers. Judging by the spent shells that littered the cobblestones he had been busy. I counted the bells that rang across the tiled roofs of this small colonial town. Six, seven, eight ...

'Gooaaaaaaaaaaaaaaaal!'

The loud and elongated call screamed in synchrony from the televisions on the counter of each kiosk. Men looked up from their dominoes, the shoe shiner stopped shining and the man on the date turned away from his impossibly beautiful girlfriend. She began to study her nails.

Further down the promenade a voluptuous black woman sat behind a table jammed with aluminium pots and pans, her abundant form wrapped in immaculate folds of white material and her wide black face crowned in a loosely tied white turban. The unmistakable smell of dende oil was drawn into my nose and to the back of my throat, and I knew immediately what she was selling. Behind her two women sitting on upturned buckets chattered while popping black-eyed peas from their pods, while another thumped a huge pestle into a wooden mortar, mashing the peas, onion and seasoning into a smooth paste. But there was no doubt who the boss of this operation was, and I placed my order for an acarajé with the woman wrapped in white.

In a deep metal bowl behind her, a cluster of golden spheres bobbed up and down in hot dende oil like frying tennis balls. Taking each acarajé out with a long metal spoon, she let it cool in a metal tray. The fried paste of mashed black-eyed peas looked rather like a large falafel. She then split each one in half with a large knife. None of her lids matched their pots but she knew what was inside each one, and like a drummer she moved from pot to pot with her wooden spoon, scooping the ingredients from inside.

'Molho de pimenta?'

I said yes and she seemed surprised, before spreading a little potent red sauce on either side of my acarajé. Next came a heaped spoonful of vatapá made from bread, shrimp, coconut milk, dende oil and ground cashew nuts, mashed into a thick, creamy paste, which was followed by a spoon of caruru, a spicy stew made with fresh shrimp, nuts, quiabo (okra), onions, dende oil and peppers.

As I perched on a small plastic stool, doing my best to eat my acarajé without spilling it into my lap, the river turned black and sleek under the clear night sky, reflecting the activity of the towns-people going about their evening.

The crust of the acarajé was crispy and flavoured with the bitter taste of the dende oil that had also given it a deep golden colour, but inside the mashed black-eyed peas were soft and tender and had absorbed the moisture of the vatapá and caruru that oozed from the sides and fell into my lap. The dende oil in the vatapá and the caruru was rich and heavy, and while its bitterness mingled with the piquant flavours in my mouth, its saturated fat hung in my stomach, leaving me full and content.

This perfect combination of recipes has remained intact for hundreds of years, and has allowed the Africans, removed from their homelands, separated from their families, holed up in the hull of a rancid ship and put to work in the horrifying conditions of the sugar plantations, to hold on to their cultural identity. For although we prepare and consume food for sustenance, nutrition, comfort and nostalgia, ultimately what we eat defines who we are, to ourselves and to those around us, and watching the women preparing the acarajé for the customers lining up at their stand, I was witnessing the influence of food at its most potent. As I pottered back to my room, I wondered what kind of culinary iden-tity we held on to in England.

🚲

I was sad to leave Bahia. Its profound Afro-Brazilian culture, laid-back attitudes and perfect beaches had won me over. As I headed south for Vitória, Brazil seemed to change. With every mile I rode the country became more efficient, more organised. My blond hair and blue eyes no longer attracted the amorous stares and wondering looks of local women. The roads became smooth and well kept. Food and drink became more expensive. There were more cars on the roads and houses became more robust. Grand, gated villas with aggressive barbed wire and security cameras replaced welcoming fishermen's houses, and resorts and harbours were built over once idyllic fishing villages, turning them into empty ghost towns of holiday homes only busy at weekends and public holidays. Forced away from the beach, I now rode along roads that were smooth and busy with speeding Europeans. The further south I rode, the more western Brazil became, as if to warn me what would greet me on my return to England, now only weeks away. And then I saw it.

Rio de Janeiro 703 km

What for over two years had been no more than an answer given when people asked where I was heading, was now a real and measured distance. I could work out how long it would take to ride there. A place I had imagined for over two years was now only two inches away on my map, and appearing at regular intervals on the green and white signposts by the roadside.

Seven hundred and fifty-two days after landing in New York, I found myself standing in a pair of worn-out red flip-flops on the dusty pavement of a small highway town 60 kilometres north of Rio. Night had fallen, but as I looked south a lessening of the darkness and a hazy dome of orange light reminded me how close I was to my destination. The next day I would arrive in Rio de Janeiro and my journey would end. But for the time being my attentions were more short-sighted, focused on crossing four busy lanes of traffic. Tempting me over this torrent of cars, trucks, buses and motorcycles were some small bars and the camps of street vendors. But having come this far relatively unscathed, I had to show prudence. Those of you who have tried will know that attempting to do anything at speed while wearing flip-flops is destined to end in painful, toe-stubbing disaster. Take into account that the whole population of Brazil is getting around on a pair of these colourful bits of plastic and you have some idea about the pace of life in this part of the world.

Waaaaeeeern!

Beeeeeeeeeep!

Prancing like a young lamb I made a clumsy dash to the other side, just avoiding the chrome bumper of an oncoming truck, and leapt up the kerb into the safety of a small roadside drinking den. On the bar a few tired salgadinhos waited to be rescued from behind the grimy window of an old hotplate, and perched on stools, staring blankly at a television, a handful of truck drivers appeared to be in the same predicament. One of Brazil's terrible soap operas was coming to an end and its addictive theme tune, which sadly I knew by heart, filled the bar.

I asked above the din for a beer in my best Portuguese, but there was little response.

The second attempt just about hit its target and the uninterested barmaid, lurking behind the scenes, pulled herself unenthusiastically out of her chair and came to my aid.

After I repeated my request for a third time, she opened a chest freezer with her fat arms and dug out a dusty garrafa of beer and a small glass, which seemed to have been a jam jar in a previous life. She thumped both unceremoniously on to the bar in front of me, and popped the top off the beer with an opener tied to a long string. I found a small plastic table as far away from the television as possible, and after letting the bubbles settle I gulped down my first magical cup of ice-cold beer. Second and third cups followed closely.

As the barmaid replenished my beer for the fourth time, with impeccable Brazilian urgency I took the opportunity to potter to the food stands that were feeding the night's passing trade: a young couple enjoying some time out of the house; a doctor picking up a snack on his way home from work and a team of pyjama-clad children en route to karate. Taking my place in the informal queue, surrounded by the welcome smells of grilling meat and frying oil, I eyed up what treats awaited me on my last night on the road. There wasn't much on offer but what there was looked good and I was soon back with my beer clutching a brace of bamboo skewers, one with grilled calf's heart, the other with beef covered in farofa, and an oily paper-bag stuffed full with deep-fried chips of cassava root. The food was fresh, but nothing special, and my surroundings would hardly qualify as being glamorous, but after another long, hot and exhausting day in the saddle I could not have been happier.

The town I had stopped in had no redeeming features. It had no historical centre, no ruined temple or gold-filled church. It had no crashing waterfalls or perfect beach. In fact, there was no reason at all why I should have been there, but perhaps that was what made it so special, and once again I had my bicycle to thank for allowing me access to this completely authentic Brazilian town, enjoying this less-than-perfect, but magical, roadside meal. The same bicycle that had led me out of New York over two years before and north towards the Great Lakes; that had carried me slowly through the vast plains of the Midwest and over the snow-covered passes of the Rocky mountains; that had endured the wind and rain of the Pacific coast of the United States and the dry heat of Mexico's deserts; that had journeyed with me through the hardships of Central America, and into South America and the coffee-covered hills of Colombia; the bicycle that had climbed with me over the Andes and descended into the running waters of the Amazon; that carried me along the beaches of northern Brazil, and that had led me to this small town just short of Rio de Janeiro. The bicycle, the remarkable invention that allowed me to travel slowly and quietly wherever I wished. A machine so clean and efficient it used only the energy I was willing to exert, and a means of transport that had totally exposed me to the climate, culture, people and terrain of the countries I visited. It provided me with the highest of highs and the lowest of lows; moments of devastating loneliness and moments of perfect solitude. It had allowed me to be overcome by the invincible rush of adrenalin and the overwhelming power of exhaustion. It had left me at the mercy of coincidence and then imprisoned me in the slow progress of the task ahead. It had introduced me to a world of new friends and carried me to a world of new places, where I believed I had encountered the real flavours of the Americas.

Food was my fuel. By travelling by bicycle I was burning wonderful amounts of calories every hour and, unless I replaced them, I was going nowhere. Breakfast, lunch and dinner were my only significant appointments, and having to stop at least three times a day to refuel I could not help but be exposed to the real flavours, smells, ingredients and people of the culinary cultures I rode into. I was never trapped by the limitations of soulless tourist restaurants with 'foreigner-friendly' versions of local dishes. I ate where the people of the country were eating. Markets, homes, the street, the beach, rivers, campfires, trees and truck stops.

I never had any interest in sitting alone at a table in a tourist restaurant while some jumped-up manager wondered why a malodorous Lycra-clad Englishman was putting off his other customers. I wanted to demolish countless slices of New York street pizza after a hectic day cycling in Manhattan. I wanted to perch at the counter of a diner in America's Midwest, eating home-made pie served by a surly waitress old enough to be my grandmother. I had dreamed of grilling steaks with a cowboy under a blanket of stars in the plains of Montana and of eating moose burgers lovingly prepared in the calloused hands of a Canadian lumberjack. I fantasised about fishing Dungeness crab from the icy waters of the north Pacific before tearing them apart with my bare hands, and pulling nets with a Mexican fishing crew. I needed to listen to the sounds of mariachi mixed with the chopping of tripe at a smoky taco stand in southern Mexico, and I wanted to burn my tongue on piping-hot pupusas with my little brother in the backstreets of San Salvador. I wanted to wake up to a breakfast of black coffee and pig's brain in the misty hills of Colombia and I wanted an old lady to teach me how to butcher a guinea pig in the Andes of Ecuador. I longed to sink my teeth into piranha outside a brothel on the banks of the Amazon, and I longed to have my nostrils filled with the powerful smell of frying dende oil in Brazil. I wanted the real thing, I wanted to find the perfect meal in the Americas, and thanks to my bicycle I was able to find it, time and time again.

🚲

Other than the mouldy mattresses, filthy bathrooms and flatulent truck drivers, the Brazilian breakfast, or café de manhá as it is more romantically known, is another perk of parting with a little cash to stay in the safety of a pousada or guesthouse, but it remains something of a lottery. If lady luck is looking down on you, you are woken by the smell of freshly brewed coffee to find the little old lady who offered you shelter from the storm busy arranging her home-made jams while her perfectly formed daughter bounces back from the local bakery in her hot pants, cradling a bundle of freshly baked bread. However, if your budget determines that you have to frequent the lower-end flea pits of the Brazilian highway, the leather-faced hag who reluctantly took you in the night before will point you towards a dusty Thermos of foul-tasting coffee, a pile of stale hotdog buns and a tub of fluorescent margarine that looks older than you are. Sadly it was the latter café de manhá that got me on my way on 6 June, my final day on the road.

I wish I could tell you that my arrival in Rio de Janeiro was a stress-free and enjoyable affair, but as I have learnt from cycling into London, New York, Vancouver, Los Angeles, Mexico City and Quito, cycling into any of our planet's great metropolises is an exhausting and nerve-shredding experience. Cycling into Rio de Janeiro was no different. Peaceful tree-lined back roads became noisy, traffic-choked, multi-lined highways. Green hillsides morphed into an ugly shambles of industry, commerce and mass accommodation. Industrial wastelands were followed by soulless warehouses, filthy tyre shops and garish gas stations. Graffiti-covered bridges criss-crossed above me emitting their dull thunder, while intimidating concrete barriers and vivid green traffic signs channelled the ever-growing river of traffic. Lines of overloaded trucks charged forward puffing heavy fumes into the air, while rushing buses jostled for positions that barely existed. Hyperactive motorcycles weaved their way through this chaotic mess, and as a humble cyclist I was left to make do with what was left of the narrow, litter-strewn shoulder. My lungs and mouth filled with foul-tasting air and my wet skin became coated in the dusty filth of exhaust. My ears burst with the unnatural din of engines, gearboxes and combustion, and whatever calm and peaceful thoughts I was enjoying hours before were soon overrun by outbursts of frustration and the bouts of aggression that were needed in order to compete in this endless race to the death. Battling through the rundown suburbs of Rio de Janeiro, my mood sank. This was not how it was meant to be. Where were the breath-taking views of mountains flowing into the sea, the beaches, the Corcovado's open arms, the Pau Azucar and the Dois Irmãos? Tired and dispirited I limped through the suburbs, the financial centre, the port, past the airport and ferry terminal and then, emerging from the long shadows of some skyscrapers, I came to a sudden halt that forced a shiny Speedo-clad rollerblader to stumble and swerve past me, releasing a chorus of Portuguese expletives.

'Pardon, pardon,' I hollered apologetically, but his Speedo-wrapped bottom had already vanished into the current of people that now rushed around me. Standing astride my bicycle, amidst the joggers, walkers, runners and street vendors, I looked in complete wonder at the view in front of me. The Dois Irmaos rose out of the city, the steady and timeless forms of these mountains dwarfing the beach of Ipanema that stretched in a smooth arc, the ocean, the sand, the road, the buildings, the crowds, all following the crescent of this famous seafront. I had seen it countless times before, in films, magazines and postcards, and I had painted it in my mind every day since I left New York, but to see it now was different. Propping up my bicycle on the sea wall I climbed down on to the beach, covered in a mass of bronzed bodies, bathing suits and bare skin. In a daze I searched for a space, then, kicking off my flip-flops, I collapsed in the warm sand. I wanted to take in everything, to remember it all. The smell, the sounds, the light, the people; the garish paper kites that fluttered effortlessly high above crowds; the surfers who crashed through the waves that pounded the beach; the distinctive calls of the vendors selling everything from hammocks to hot dogs.

Late in the day the sun gently continued its journey westward and soon it slipped behind the skyline of the city. The towering buildings that lined the beach cast their long shadows across the sand, a signal to the gathered Cariocas that their cherished beach time was nearly up.

'Piiiiiiiiiisht.'

I grabbed the attention of a passing man advertising what I was looking for.

A damp and refreshing chill now hung over the beach, and underneath the dark forms of the Dois Irmãos, the flickering lights of the Rocinha favela twinkled through the misty dusk, tumbling down the steep mountainsides like loose diamonds. Bright-coloured deckchairs were put away and beach umbrellas folded up like closing flowers. Surfers skipped out of the sea, untying the cords that connected them to their boards. The beach began to empty and my drink arrived. I took a long pull on the plastic straw. My caipirinha was magnificently strong, the powerful sugarcane liquor rushing through my system, leaving a trail of relaxed warmth as it evicted the stresses of the day.

I called to a man carrying a portable grill made from an old paint tin. He skipped through the sand towards me, happy to have found another customer this late in the day. Squatting on his heels in the deep sand next to me, he blew into his grill to revive the coals before holding a stick of fresh cheese above the heat. Delicately sprinkling it with chilli and herbs he turned it over the heat, and just as it began to blister and brown he handed me the stick. I took a bite and it was sublime.

'Travelling by bike?' asked the vendor, eyeing the bicycle leaning against the wall behind me.

'Yes,' I said, conversing quite comfortably in Portuguese by now.

'Where have you cycled from?'

'New York.'

'And where are you cycling to?'

'Here,' I replied.

Another vendor, carrying an enormous sack of Globo biscuits, spied that I had money to spend and came bounding my way. Globo biscuits, made of cassava flour, are a typical Rio beach snack and served nowhere else in the world. I had been hearing about them since the Amazon, and now was my chance to try one. I gave the man two Real. Unwrapping a paper bag, I pulled out what looked like a Styrofoam doughnut. Perhaps on any other beach in the world they would have tasted like expanded polystyrene doughnuts, but here on Ipanema, in Rio de Janeiro, at the end of the road, they were salty and delicious and the perfect foil to the sweetness of the caipirinha that gurgled in my glass as I sucked up the lime and cachaça at the bottom. I had come a long way for this moment, and, enjoying the little meal, sitting anonymously next to my bicycle in this magical place, I quietly enjoyed the end of my journey.

It is by riding a bicycle that you learn the contours of a country best, since you have to sweat up the hills and coast down them. Thus you remember them as they actually are, while in a motor car only a high hill impresses you, and you have no such accurate remembrance of country you have driven through as you gain by riding a bicycle.

Ernest Hemingway

Peba Caipira: Armadillo Stew

Serves 6

1 whole armadillo, shelled, boned and gutted and cut into
*   chunks*
juice of 4 limes
oil for frying
1 large onion, chopped
4 garlic cloves, chopped
1 pinch ground cumin
1 small chilli, chopped
6 tomatoes, peeled, seeded and chopped
1 fresh thyme sprig
500ml chicken stock
400ml coconut milk
salt and freshly ground black pepper
to serve: rice and chopped parsley

1. Marinate the armadillo meat in lime juice with a few pinches of salt for a couple of hours.

2. In a little oil in a large pan, sweat the onion until translucent. Add the garlic, cumin and chilli and continue to cook over gentle heat.

3. Add the armadillo to the pan and turn the meat so each piece starts to brown. Pour in the remaining lime juice. Season with salt and pepper.

4. Now add the chopped tomatoes and thyme and turn through the meat. Pour in the stock and allow it to come to a steady, gentle boil.

5. Once the contents of the pan are simmering away, pour in the coconut milk, lower the heat, cover the pot and cook for 1 hour, until the armadillo is tender and you have a rich meaty stew.

6. Serve with rice and a big pinch of chopped parsley.

Caruru

Serves 4

2 garlic cloves, peeled
1 large knuckle of ginger, peeled and chopped
150g cashew nuts
150g peanuts (unsalted)
large handful of fresh cilantro (coriander), roughly chopped
1kg okra
1 onion, finely chopped
2 green peppers, seeded and chopped
120ml dende oil (red palm oil)
250g smoked shrimp. Fresh shrimp (prawns) will do, peeled and
    washed
salt and freshly ground black pepper

1. Put the garlic, ginger, cashew nuts, peanuts and cilantro into a liquidiser or food processor and whiz to a smooth paste.
2. Chop the okra into small pieces.
3. In a large pan, soften the onion and peppers in a little of the dende oil over a gentle heat.
4. Add the contents of the liquidiser to the pan with the remaining dende oil and stir well.
5. Add the okra to the pan with 500ml water. Cover and stew on a gentle heat for 10 minutes.
6. Lift the cover and add the shrimp. Stir the contents of the pan well, season to taste, replace the cover and continue to cook for a further 10 minutes.

GLOSSARY

açaí – energy-packed Brazilian fruit that is normally served as a deep purple smoothie-style drink or as an ice cream. The small fruits grow on tall açaí palms in north-eastern region of Brazil.

acarajé – delicious bean fritters, traditionally served as a street food, stuffed with vatapa and carur in Bahia, Brazil.

achiote – a russet-coloured seed native to Latin America that is harvested from the annatto shrub. Ground to a powder it provides a sweet and peppery flavour.

adobe – a kind of clay used as a building material, typically in the form of sun-dried bricks.

agua de coco – the sweet refreshing water found inside a ripe coconut. Not to be confused with coconut milk, 'leche de coco', which is made from grated coconut flesh.

aji – a spicy Colombian salsa made from chillies, cilantro, onion and tree tomato.

arepa – a thick corn pancake eaten in Colombia and often topped with molten butter and fresh cheese.

arepa de choclo – a small cake/bread made from roughly ground sweetcorn. Served with molten butter and a slab of fresh white cheese.

arepa de huevo – a maize cake filled with an egg and deep fried. Typical North Colombian street food.

atole – a thick, warming drink made with maize that is often sweetened with ground cinnamon and brown sugar. Mexico.

axé – popular Afro-Brazilian music popular in the north east of Brazil.

bahiana – a term used for the women of Bahia, Brazil.

bajo – a traditional Nicaraguan dish made of plantain, banana, yucca and meat wrapped in banana leaves and slow-cooked in a pit oven.

bandeja paisa – a cholesterol feast consisting of chicharron, fried eggs, beans, steak, arepa, chorizo, beans and avocado.

banditos – a term used in central and Latin America for bandits, robbers and highwaymen.

barbacoa – a Mexican form of cooking where a sheep is slow-cooked in a hole dug in the ground covered with maguey leaves.

bobo de cameron – a Brazilian chowder made from shrimp and mashed cassava.

borracharia – a Brazilian bike shop. No more than a few spanners, but plenty of expertise.

bunello – deep-fried dough balls, often flavoured with cheese that are eaten with coffee in Colombia. Very popular at Christmas.

butte – a hill with steep sides and a flat top.

cachaça – Brazilian sugarcane liquor, the key ingredient in a caipirinha.

café de manhá – *breakfast. Brazil.*

caipirinha – a lethal cocktail made with cachaca, crushed ice and fresh fruit. The national drink of Brazil.

caldo de cana – the juice of sugarcane. Served chilled on the road side in Bahia, Brazil.

Candomblé – an African-originated Afro-Brazilian religion.

capoeira – martial art and dance form originating from Brazilian slaves.

carimañolas – meat-stuffed fried yucca balls.

carne asada – grilled meat. Slices of grilled steak diced and served with tortillas in a beef taco.

carne de dios – meat of the gods.

carne de sol – sun-dried beef, popular in the north eastern states of Brazil.

carnitas – chunks of braised or roasted pork

caruru – a Brazilian food made from okra, onion, shrimp, palm oil and cashew nuts. Often served inside *acaraje* as a street food. See recipe.

cassava – the starchy tuberous root of a tropical tree, used as food in tropical countries but requiring careful preparation to remove traces of poison from the flesh. Also known as *manioca, aipim.*

ceviche – a South American dish of marinated raw fish or seafood, typically garnished with cilantro, red onion and chilli.

charreada – a Mexican rodeo.

chateaubriand – a small cut of beef extravagantly cut from the centre of the tenderloin.

chicha – a potent pre-Colombian central American beverage, usually made from fermented maize or fruit such as pineapple.

chicharron – a piece of fried pork crackling.

chilli arbol (t) (tree chilli) – A narrow and curved chilli that is fiercely hot.

chinook salmon – the largest species of Pacific salmon. Often called king salmon.

chipotle chillie – a smoked jalapeño chilli.

chiva – a very colourful and uncomfortable local bus in Colombia. Also a derogatory term for a woman who is generous with her affections.

cilantro – coriander.

cocada – a sweet made from grated coconut and sugar often flavoured with fruit juice.

coq au vin (t) cock in wine – a casserole of chicken cooked in plenty of red wine.

Corcovado – the open-armed Christ the Redeemer statue in Rio de Janeiro.

cortador de cana (t) cutter of cane – a term used for the sugarcane workers in Brazil. Incredibly hard-working and poorly paid.

crème brûlée (t) burnt cream – a classic French pudding made of custard topped with burnt caramel. Sometimes flavoured with fruit and lavender.

crêpe suzette – a thin dessert pancake doused with a brandy/ Grand Marnier and citrus sauce that is set alight when served.

croque madame – a form of French fast-food, consisting of a hot grilled cheese-and-ham sandwich topped with a fried egg. A croque-monsieur has no egg on top.

cupuaçu – a fruit and member of the chocolate family the size of a cantaloupe that is eaten throughout Brazil. Renowned for its creamy, exotic taste it is used to make juice and ice cream.

cuyi – a guinea pig

derailleur – the mechanism on a bicycle that moves the chain out and up, allowing it to shift to different cogs when changing gear.

desayuno – breakfast

Dois Irmãos (t) The two brothers – famous twin mountains that tower above Ipanema beach in Rio de Janeiro.

dream catcher – a small hoop containing a thread lattice, decorated with feathers and beads, believed to give its owner good dreams. Originally made by American Indians.

Ducks – the Eugene Ducks, university football team of Eugene, Oregon.

Dungeness crab – an edible crab that inhabits the Pacific coast of the Americas from Alaska to lower California.

Époisses – a pungent cheese originating from the village of Époisses in Burgundy, France.

essence – petrol

favela – a Brazilian shantytown or slum.

finca – a small farm.

fleischkuechle – a seasoned ground-beef patty wrapped in a dough pocket and deep fried.

foie gras (t) fat liver – the liver from a goose or duck fattened by force feeding. Due to its rich, smooth and delicate qualities it is an expensive French delicacy.

formule – a set menu in France. Changing daily and always a cheap option.

Forró – folk music particularly popular in the north east of Brazil.

futomaki – a thick sushi roll wrapped in nori.

gangbang – an instance of violence, especially a shooting, involving members of a criminal gang. Not to be confused with the other meaning of gangbang.

gata – a slang term for girls in Brazil.

gordita – a thick maize tortilla split open and filled with tasty ingredients such as stewed meats and cheese.

guava – an edible tropical fruit with a pale pink, juicy flesh. Often used to make fresh fruit juice and jam.

guayabera – a traditional men's shirt worn in Latin America.

gusanos de maguey – a large moth larva that makes its home in the leaves of maguey cactus. A delicacy in southern Mexico and often seen at the bottom of tequila bottles.

home fries – sautéed sliced potatoes served at breakfast in American diners.

hominy – coarsely ground corn used to make pizole.

honshu – a Native American name for soap berries.

huipil – a traditional blouse of southern Mexico and the highlands of Guatemala.

Indian taco/bannock bread – a fried bread found throughout the United States made from a wheat dough deep-fried in oil or animal fat. Often served topped with beans, ground beef and grated cheese. They are also enjoyed with sweet toppings such as maple syrup, honey and sugar.

Itamae – a sushi chef.

jangada – a simple boat used by the fishermen of north east Brazil. Its design is believed to originate from pre-Colombian times.

jangadeiro – a fisherman who goes to work on a jaganda.

Jägermeister – a potent German digestif made from herbs and spices, A favoured tipple of American students.

Kuna – the indigenous people of the San Blass Archipelago between Panama and Colombia.

links – sausages, i.e sausage links.

loon – a large diving water-bird with a pointed bill, black plumage and a haunting call.

maguey – a plant, a sweet liquid gathers in the heart of the plant which can be fermented to produce the drink pulque whoch may then be distilled to produce mezial.

manoomin – wild rice.

maracuja – passion fruit.

mariachi – denoting a type of traditional Mexican folk music, typically performed by a small group of strolling musicians dressed in native costume.

menudo – a spicy Mexican soup made from tripe.

mezcal – a punchy Mexican spirit made from fermenting the sap of the agave plant.

milt – the semen of a male fish.

molho de pimenta – Brazilian hot sauce, popular in the state of Bahia.

molita de panzita – a rich offal stew similar to menudo made from a sheep's lengthy intestine.

New York strip steak – the tender cut of beef procured from the thickest part of a Porterhouse.

nigiri-zushi – a bed of sushi rice topped with raw fish.

nori – an edible seaweed often used in sushi.

Ojibwa – a North American Indian people native to the region around the Great Lakes.

ongos – mushrooms.

Pacifico – one of Mexico's best beers. Usually found in the north west of the country.

Paisa – a region of north west Colombia consisting of the local departments of Risaralda, Antiquia Caldas and Quinido. Famed for its good food, beautiful women and coffee.

Paisita – a woman or girl from the Paisa region of Colombia. By all accounts the most beautiful people in Colombia.

palapa – a Mexican beach hut.

panela – raw extract of sugarcane. Cane juice is boiled, evaporating the water to leave a pure and unrefined cane sugar.

panza de carnero – sheeps' stomach stew.

patacones – disks of fried plantain.

pasilla chillie – a small black chilli used in the cuisine of Oaxaca.

pastel – a pastry pocket filled with ingredients such as cheese, beef and shrimp. Deep fried and served as a quick street snack throughout Brazil.

Pau Azucar – the Sugarloaf rock formation that dominates the skyline and bay of Rio de Janeiro.

peba – an armadillo.

persimmon – a fruit that resembles a tomato with sweet flesh.

pico de gallo (t) roosters beak – a Mexican salsa made of chopped tomatoes, chilli and onion, dressed with cilantro and lime juice.

pigeon peas – a popular pulse grown in tropical climates and used in Puerto Rican Rice.

piñata – a brightly decorated figure of an animal, usually made of papier mâché, containing toys and sweets, that is hung in the air before blindfolded children smash the figure to scatter contents as part of the celebration of a birthday.

pirarucu – a giant prehistoric fish of the Amazonian rivers.

plantain – a member of the banana family containing high levels of starch. Harvested green, they are widely used as a cooked vegetable in the tropics. See *patacones* and *ron don*.

plat du jour – plate of the day. A daily special served in French restaurants and often made with leftovers.

poblano chile – a large green chilli pepper used in chilli rellano.

pomme dauphinoise – a baked dish of sliced potatoes with cream, milk, garlic and cheese.

pop shirt – a typical shirt worn by cowboys, rodeo riders, ranch hands and plenty of others in the Midwest. The buttons are made from poppers.

pousada – a small guesthouse. Brazil.

poutine – a French-Canadian concoction comprised of chips/french fries smothered with gravy and cheese curds.

pozolé – a Mexican pork and hominy stew often garnished with chillies and cilantro.

pulque – a Mexican alcoholic drink made from fermenting the sap of the maguey.

pupusa – the national dish of El Salvador. A maize pancake always served with curtido (see recipe).

quesadilla – a tortilla filled with cheese and heated.

rancheros – a person who farms or works on a ranch, especially in the south-western United States and Mexico.

redd – a trough in a riverbed made by a salmon when spawning.

reggaetón – a form of urban music popular with the youth in Latin America.

Rocky Mountain oysters – bull's testicles, often referred to as prairie oysters.

ron don – a traditional fisherman's stew from the Caribbean coast of Costa Rica. Derived from 'run down'.

sancocho – a traditional soup or stew of Colombia made with either beef, fish, pork or chicken.

sangre de tigre (t) tiger's blood – the fishy, citrus liquid in ceviche that is believed to be an aphrodisiac.

sangre de canero – a rich stew made from sheep's blood.

saskatoon – a shrub native to North America from Alaska that produces a small purple fruit, not to be confused with a blueberry.

Siempre Adalante (t) always onwards – the name of the boat that carried me on the Rio Napo from Ecuador to Iquitos, Peru.

snowbird – a term used for grey-haired Americans and Canadians that leave the northern States in winter for warmer climes.

sockeye salmon – a species of Pacific salmon. Also called red salmon because of the red colour males turn when spawning.

Soles – the currency of Peru.

sopes – little maize patties topped with a choice of fillings such as ground beef, cheese, salsa, cabbage and guacamole.

station wagon – a car with a longer body than usual, with an extra door at the rear for easy loading.

taco – a Mexican dish consisting of a fried tortilla, typically folded, filled with various mixtures, such as seasoned meat, beans, lettuce and tomatoes.

tall stack/short stack pancakes – a stack of pancakes served in most American diners. You get more in a tall stack than a short one.

tamales – a Mexican dish of seasoned meat wrapped in corn dough and steamed or boiled in corn husks.

tete de veau (t) calf's head – a traditional French dish consisting of boiled veal cheeks often wrapped around tongue and sometimes served with brain on the side.

tostadas – a deep-fried tortilla often topped with a seasoned mixture of beans, ground meat and vegetables.

tripitas – fried tripe served in tacos.

tripa – tripe.

tweaked-up – high (see *tweaker*).

tweaker (slang) – a person addicted to methamphetamines/crystal meth.

uramaki – similar to *futomaki* but without the nori.

vallenato – a popular form of folk music in the north of Colombia.

vaqueros – a Spanish term for a cowboy or cattle driver.

vatapá – a Brazilian dish made from bread, shrimp, coconut milk and palm oil mashed into a creamy paste. Often served inside *acaraje*.

yammi – a type of yam grown in the Caribbean and used in stews such as *ron don*.

Acknowledgements

This book only exists because of the kindness, hard work and dedication of many people. Of all those who were so friendly, kind and generous, I would like particularly to thank:

Elly James at HHB for her patience and tireless support; my mother for reading each chapter as it came and making sure I started the next one; Lucie Jordan and Claire Kingston at HarperCollins for their enthusiasm and for making this book a reality; Neil Gower for putting my words into pictures; Mari Roberts for her input, honesty, and exemplary editing; Katherine Patrick at HarperCollins for her tireless press work; the good people at Balham Library for taking me in while I writing; the late Maggie Noach; all my sponsors; Harry and Ed; Isla; Charlie Pyper for giving up on me; Jim Bob for taking an interest; St Hallum Murray – patron saint of cycle tourists; Oli 'my best geek friend'; Clarice; Sam Goulden at Macmillan; Nathanial Izzgey for his Flash magic; Drew; The General; The RockMan for his enduring spirit; Guns; Browning Hypnosis; the Lubows for their kindness, crab salad and chips; the Twelve tribes of Israel, Ithaca; Chuck at Sheldrake Point Winery; all at the Sagamok Anishnawbeck Pow-wow; Roger Rabbit's Diner for the perfect French toast; Starfire & Nick for a great weekend; Pat & Ralph Ledyit for breakfast; the late, great Paul Furey and all the people of Frazee; my Badlands Mom; Roger & Rev. Marilyn De Veer; Jason de Shaw 'You Got Cowboy'; Vance Anderson; Matt Newbold and Family; Chuck's Seafood Grotto; Nancy, Michael, Paul, Erik and Emily Wendlebow; John and Jenny Mitchell; Paula & Christoph Bowdrey; the Quennells for the turkey and pizzas; Chris and Michelle from King Salmon for that burger; Ken; Dakota; the Arnesons and everyone in their garage; Mo (just one more hour!);

Bill and Wendy; Bill de Clarion, an extraordinary force; the mighty Amir Rockman and his wonderful family; Armin Allen; Rob and Jill, for dinner, Amir's birthday and a perfect example; David and Gabi in Mexico City; Paullina Castro; Torsten; Elsa Holte for picking a good hammock; Piney for his wise words and good food; Henry Lopez and his family in Santa Rosa de Cabal, Colombia; Fabio Blandon and family for their unlimited kindness; Milton & Marihuana and all at Finca Las Palmas; Kendra and Jordan; the people of Nuevo Roca Fuerte; Gabi, Carlos and Mel at Canto Ecologico.org; Marcus and family, Brazil; Fernando and Denise in Salvador; Tia, Paula and To Yuan; Nicolas Commelto; Will Alllen and family; Emi and Elly; Toby and Mia.

During my journey I was raising money for Macmillan Cancer Support, who exist to help improve the lives of people living with cancer. I would like to thank everyone at Macmillan for their support and all those who sponsored me.

Finally, I would like to thank the many hundreds of unnamed strangers and friends who offered me kindness, warmth and food along the way. You put me up, put up with me, cheered me on, showed me the way, showered me, clothed me, shared your time, your homes, your smiles and your food. Without you this journey would not have been possible. You taught me that the world is a wonderful place and I am forever in your debt. The kindness you showed me is immeasurable and impossible for me to return. I can only strive to reciprocate it.

Wherever you are Thank you, Gracias & Obrigado.

Change the world. Bike to Work.

www.thehungrycyclist.co.uk